# The Land Reform Deception

# The Land Reform Deception

*Political Opportunism
in Zimbabwe's Land Seizure Era*

CHARLES LAURIE

WITH

FOREWORD BY STEPHEN CHAN

OXFORD
UNIVERSITY PRESS

# OXFORD
UNIVERSITY PRESS

Oxford University Press is a department of the University of Oxford. It furthers
the University's objective of excellence in research, scholarship, and education
by publishing worldwide.

Oxford   New York
Auckland   Cape Town   Dar es Salaam   Hong Kong   Karachi
Kuala Lumpur   Madrid   Melbourne   Mexico City   Nairobi
New Delhi   Shanghai   Taipei   Toronto

With offices in
Argentina   Austria   Brazil   Chile   Czech Republic   France   Greece
Guatemala   Hungary   Italy   Japan   Poland   Portugal   Singapore
South Korea   Switzerland   Thailand   Turkey   Ukraine   Vietnam

Oxford is a registered trade mark of Oxford University Press
in the UK and certain other countries.

Published in the United States of America by Oxford University Press
198 Madison Avenue, New York, NY 10016, United States of America.

© Oxford University Press 2016

First issued as an Oxford University Press paperback, 2017

Library of Congress Cataloging-in-Publication Data

Names: Laurie, Alexander Charles, 1974- | Chan, Stephen, 1949-
Title: The land reform deception : political opportunism in Zimbabwe's land
   seizure era / Charles Laurie, with Preface by Stephen Chan.
Description: New York : Oxford University Press, 2016. |
   Includes bibliographical references and index.
Identifiers: LCCN 2015031320
ISBN 978-0-19-939829-4 (hardcover : alk. paper); 978-0-19-068052-7 (paperback : alk. paper)
Subjects: LCSH: Land reform—Zimbabwe. | Land tenure—Zimbabwe. | Agriculture
   and state—Zimbabwe. | Fast Track Land Reform Programme (Zimbabwe) |
   Zimbabwe—Economic conditions—21st century. | Zimbabwe—Politics and
   government—21st century.
Classification: LCC HD1333.Z55 L38 2016 | DDC 333.316891—dc23
LC record available at http://lccn.loc.gov/2015031320

# CONTENTS

# FOREWORD

The British reaction to the Zimbabwean farm seizures in 2000 was hysterical. This is not to say it was wrong. However, it obliterated all room for negotiation. It also set into train a sanctions policy that, by itself, did no more than target leading members of the Mugabe regime; but, with the disinvestment that followed, caused tangible harm to the Zimbabwean economy and compounded the financial meltdown the seizures set into train. It also established assumptions that have dominated scholarship: that the farm seizures were planned policy; that they were planned at the highest levels in Zimbabwe; that Mugabe's Zimbabwe African National Union–Patriotic Front (ZANU-PF) party was united behind the seizures; and that the seizures followed a uniform pattern. None of these assumptions may be true. Very little of the scholarship that followed sought to ask questions of those who participated in the seizures or who were affected by them, so the assumption was that all were treated in a common violent manner and no local negotiations or variations occurred.

There have been conspicuous exceptions. Jocelyn Alexander traced the antecedents to the seizures of 2000 and the following years. There was always a tension surrounding landownership.[a] Blair Rutherford described a highly differentiated white farming community, so that there was no such thing as a uniform "white farmer" on his "white farm."[b] Ian Scoones, perhaps from too narrow a base, indicated that much seized land was made productive under

---

a. Jocelyn, Alexander, "'Squatters,' Veterans and the State in Zimbabwe", in *Zimbabwe's Unfinished Business: Rethinking Land, State and Nation in the Context of Crisis*, ed. Amanda Hammar, Brian, Raftopoulos, andStig, Nelson (Harare: Weaver, 2003); Jocelyn Alexander, *The Unsettled Land: State-Making and the Politics of Land in Zimbabwe, 1893–2003* (Oxford: James Currey, 2006).

b. Blair Rutherford, *Working on the Margins: Black Workers, White Farmers in Postcolonial Zimbabwe* (London: Zed Books, 2001).

new ownership and that the nationalization of land was not a complete failure.[c] However, the abiding received impression is one of seizure, violence, and failure, and this has been reinforced by elegant writing on the part of those who had farms seized and had to leave.

None of this is to downplay the very great violence used, the economic calamity engendered, and the cornerstone the policy of seizure established in the thuggery that melded with government policy in Zimbabwe. What has always been needed, in spite of this, has been a careful examination of the detail of seizure, its great contradictions and even its nuances. Charles Laurie's book provides these things. It will become a major contribution to a reworking of Zimbabwean narratives. Carl Watts's forthcoming work, based on huge archival work, on the internal workings of the Rhodesian declaration of independence and the international response should mean a new Rhodesian history.[d] Charles Laurie's should introduce a new, more complex Zimbabwean history.

The sheer scale of the investigation in Laurie's book is amazing. The ambition involved is magnificent but could easily have led to failure. Trying to do too much has often led to the completion of too little. However, Laurie's accomplished list of interviewees, and his scaling and charting of the seizures and violence, have set a new standard in what can be done in proper investigation. Generalizations on Zimbabwe will be much harder now.

One of the very real contributions of the book is the argument that Mugabe had never intended the farm invasions to be extensive. He had been embarking on a dramatic piece of theater for the benefit of the British, and with the perhaps desperate hope of forcing negotiations over a British contribution to the cost of land nationalization. I have myself suggested this was the case,[e] but Laurie is the first to provide evidence.

I wish to commend this book. As someone involved with Zimbabwe since the independence elections of 1980, I have become, I hope, knowledgeable about the vexatious politics of the country. I can say that no earlier book has provided so detailed a contribution to knowledge of Zimbabwe.

Stephen Chan
School of Oriental and African Studies

c. Ian Scoones, Nelson Marongwe, Blasio Mavedzenge, Jacob Mahenehene, Felix Murimbarimba, and Chrispen Sukume, *Zimbabwe's Land Reform: Myth and Realities* (Woodbridge, UK: James Currey, 2010).

d. Carl Watts, *Rhodesia's Unilateral Declaration of Independence: An International History* (Houndmills: Palgrave Macmillan, 2013).

e. Stephen Chan, *Robert Mugabe: A Life of Power and Violence* (Ann Arbor: University of Michigan Press, 2003), chapter 9.

# PREFACE

I was born in Zimbabwe and raised on a farm in Mashonaland Central, not far from Harare. I grew up immersed in farming life. It was wonderful to be raised with an awareness of farming concerns, from decisions of what crops to grow, to whether we would have good rains the next season. While it was a wonderful childhood and I was privileged to experience it, life was not easy for my father and the workers on his farm. Farming is not for the faint-hearted. It is an occupation replete with risk—anything from drought and insect problems to falling commodity prices can lead to disaster.

As a teenager I moved to the United States but always kept Zimbabwe at the forefront of my mind. Some people emigrate and become immersed in their new culture, adapting seamlessly. I was a Zimbabwean living in California no matter how many years I spent away from the country.

In mid-2005 I had an opportunity to undertake a doctorate at Oxford University. By this stage, the farm seizures had of course been going on for several years, and I felt the time was right to thoroughly examine what factors were really driving the violence that was engulfing my country. I think the timing of my study and my unusual personal experience of having grown up in both Zimbabwe and the United States offered me some key advantages for this kind of research.

First, given that the farm seizures had already begun, I had the benefit of being able to look back on events over several years. The early period of the seizures, which had been marked by enormous confusion and uncertainty, had passed. Patterns had begun to emerge by 2005. However, enormous gaps and unexplained questions remained in the key literature. There was also considerable variation in public opinion on the reasons for the farm takeovers.

Given my personal background, I had a strong starting point. I could understand the various pressures faced by farm workers and farmers. On top of that, I understood the basic considerations and historical pressures related to land-ownership and agriculture. At the same time, having been exposed to new ideas and perspectives in the United States and later in the United Kingdom, I did not find myself overly blinded by my early experiences in Zimbabwe. I did not see myself as "a farmer," nor did I feel the need to uphold a certain set of values held by the farming community. I had personal awareness of Zimbabwean farming, but I was also able to bring critical objectivity—within reasonable limits—as a result of having lived outside Zimbabwe for quite some time. Thus, I had the benefit of looking from the outside in, while knowing the basics of what the inside was all about.

As I set about designing my doctoral research project, I quickly saw that so much of what occurred during the land seizure era appeared to be contradictory. This was particularly the case when one considered the Zimbabwean government's explanation of events.

For example, if the farm seizures were really about righting the wrong of colonial landownership patterns, why did they take place 20 years after independence? If the farm seizures were meant to redistribute land, then why wasn't more land given to farm workers and other members of the rural community who had the requisite skills to farm the land? Surely members of the state security apparatus would not automatically make successful farmers. Also, if the farm takeovers were meant to redistribute land, then why were equipment and machinery stripped from farms and sold, when the farm could have been taken over in an orderly fashion and operated under new ownership as an ongoing commercial enterprise? The land redistribution agenda espoused by ZANU-PF did not make sense to me.

I also thought that the farm seizures were unnecessarily violent. Workers were essentially unarmed, and while farmers possessed firearms, there were obvious limits on how they could be used; indeed, I had heard farmers say that they knew that discharging a firearm in the midst of a farm invasion could bring about a fatal response from the state. Why then was there so much violence—including torture and demonstrable cruelty such as the maiming of livestock—when workers and farmers posed little physical threat? Accounts in the news media and early research projects, such as those conducted by the Zimbabwe Human Rights NGO Forum, indicated that much of the conflict was centered in the three Mashonaland provinces—but these areas had historically been a bedrock of ZANU-PF support. Why, then, was there so much conflict there?

I decided that I would use my doctorate to investigate these puzzling questions. This way I might get to the bottom of basic motivations and dispense with the political explanations that had muddied the waters.

I believed from the outset that it was important to gain perspectives from all the major stakeholders. I strongly believed that my research should not be "all about white farmers" or a piece that was solely intended to undermine

ZANU-PF's version of events. I wanted the research to be grounded in substantive data and from that data—whatever the conclusions—I would aim to shed light on the unanswered questions about the takeovers. Thus, if the data supported ZANU-PF's version of events then those would have been the conclusions I published.

I initially intended to compile two major data sets to underpin the doctorate. The first was mapping data, on which I had a head start due to the excellent (and brave) work of the Zimbabwe Human Rights NGO Forum. With some additional work on the Forum's data, I was able to use this information as a secondary data source to produce violence maps that allowed a longitudinal assessment of the geographical distribution of violence countrywide.

I had planned to complete about 60 interviews of farm workers, farmers, and government stakeholders. There were major concerns within the Department of Sociology at Oxford, who had been very supportive of my research from the outset, that I would be physically harmed during fieldwork, or that harm would come to respondents. We decided to carry out a pilot set of interviews to see how accessible I found the data. I completed nearly 60 interviews during the first fieldwork trip, but this also showed that I needed to gain the perspectives of a lot more people to shed adequate light on the research questions. Ultimately, I personally interviewed 111 people in total; all interviews were held face to face, except with one respondent whom I interviewed over the telephone because she lived in Australia and one in South Africa who was only available after I had returned to the United Kingdom.

On examining the enormous amount of data from the mapping data set and the interviews, my departmental assessors and I agreed that a further quantitative data set would be useful in providing a bedrock of statistical information for the research. This survey added a crucial third perspective that triangulated the data and allowed accounts from the other two data sets to be corroborated. Thus, only later in the doctorate did I undertake a major survey of commercial farmers, ultimately in 24 countries worldwide since so many had left Zimbabwe. It was infeasible to do a survey of farm workers, as I detail in appendix A, since this population was practically inaccessible using an online or postal method because of their lack of Internet access and fixed postal addresses. This population was also considerably more at risk than farmers, since most remained within Zimbabwe, and I was concerned that the mere receipt of an unsolicited questionnaire might bring harm to respondents.

The result of the collection of three data sets meant I had an enormous amount of information to analyze. Indeed, for my final examination one of these assessors said that I had enough data for three doctorates. What it also meant, however, was that I had a lot of information available to shed light on my research questions.

While any research study will inevitably involve compromises, the conditions within which this research was conducted were challenging. Certainly, conventionally "scientific" approaches involving lab-based social experiments or large-scale population surveys were not realistic options in the Zimbabwean context. However, the mixed methods research underpinning this book is unique in the literature on this topic for its breadth and depth. It includes method triangulation through in-depth qualitative interviews conducted across three different stakeholder populations alongside quantitative survey and mapping data. All of these data have been painstakingly collected, analyzed following the highest standards of rigor, and verified by leading social scientists at Oxford University. I earnestly hope that readers agree that the findings published here in *The Land Reform Deception* have done justice to the research topic.

# ACKNOWLEDGMENTS

Writing this book has encompassed one of the most stimulating, challenging, and rewarding periods of my life, and I am very grateful to all those who played a part in it.

I want to thank all the contributors from around the world who participated in this research. You took great risks to have your views included in the research for this book. I truly hope that the book brings clarity to the events you witnessed and experienced.

I am very grateful to my mum for her enormous contribution and tireless input to my doctorate at Oxford, which serves as the basis for this work. Likewise, my dad and family have never wavered in their support for my research efforts. What better way to finish a doctorate than by meeting your future wife in the process, and a fellow African at that. Robyn has patiently listened to me talk about my research just about every day since we met in 2009, proving that love knows no bounds.

Nic Cheeseman was an outstanding supervisor. He provided warm encouragement and excellent advice throughout, but particularly during more challenging periods. I am deeply grateful to him. Colin Mills, Heather Hamill, Federico Varese, Michael Biggs, Diego Gambetta, and Gavin Williams have all provided important feedback and insights. I am also grateful for the support of Professor Stephen Chan, who has shown great personal enthusiasm for my research and commitment to helping bring this book to publication.

Eric Jensen has been a steadfast and much-appreciated friend and colleague since we were at Cambridge University together. I am hugely appreciative of his enormous support. Sizwe Phakathi, Jonah Rimer, Nick Sabin, Rich McKay, and Allison Plunkett have been wonderful friends to me during this research.

Green Templeton College has been my home for several years. I want to thank the fellows and staff, particularly Colin Bundy and Chris Sauer, who have been a source of tremendous support.

Angela Chnapko shared my vision for this book. I am grateful to her and to all the editors and staff at Oxford University Press for bringing it to fruition.

The anonymous reviewers for this manuscript have made numerous insightful comments. I am very grateful for their time and input, which collectively have served to strengthen this book.

This research would not have been possible without the generous financial contributions from the Harry Frank Guggenheim Foundation, the Overseas Research Student award scheme, Green Templeton College, the University of Oxford's Department of Sociology, and the Anthony Storr Fund.

# FIGURES

# TABLES

# ABBREVIATIONS AND ACRONYMS

| | |
|---|---|
| Agritex | Department of Agricultural Technical and Extension Services |
| CA | Communal Area |
| CFU | Commercial Farmers Union |
| CID | Criminal Investigation Division |
| CIO | Central Intelligence Organisation |
| DA | District Administrator |
| JAG | Justice for Agriculture |
| MDC | Movement for Democratic Change |
| ZANLA | Zimbabwe National Liberation Army (military wing of ZANU) |
| ZANU-PF | Zimbabwe African National Union (Patriotic Front) |
| ZAPU | Zimbabwe African People's Union |
| ZIPRA | Zimbabwe People's Revolutionary Army (military wing of ZAPU) |
| ZNA | Zimbabwe National Army |
| ZNLWVA | Zimbabwe National Liberation War Veterans Association |
| ZRP | Zimbabwe Republic Police |

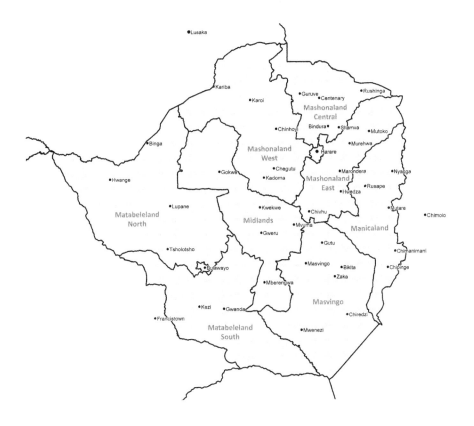

# Liberation War and Gukurahundi Timeline

This timeline provides an overview of key events in the 1961 to 1987 period, with a focus on conflict associated with the nationalist organisation ZANU (later 'ZANU-PF').

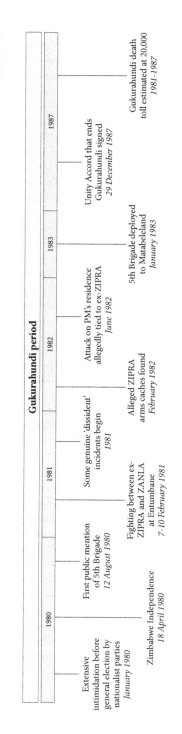

# Land Seizure Era Timeline

This timeline provides a visual representation of the key events during the 1997 to 2008 period. The timeline begins prior to the land seizure era with the war veteran payouts in 1997, which contributed to the first large-scale farm seizures in February 2000. Large-scale, violent and permanent farm seizures began soon after the February 2000 constitutional referendum. Historically, farm settlers had been removed by police but after 2000 the police and other state security services actively assisted the invasion of commercial farms. The end period of the land seizure era, as defined in this book, is March 2008, when most farm seizures had already taken place and violence had shifted almost exclusively to suppressing the opposition Movement for Democratic Change (MDC) party in urban areas.

| Phase I | Pre-Referendum Period (approximately January 1997 – February 2000). ZANU-PF in-fighting, rise of the war veterans, and rise of the MDC. |
|---|---|
| Phase II | Initial Farm Invasions (approximately February 2000 – June 2000). Politicisation of farm workers and land occupation. |
| Phase III | Land Redistribution (approximately June 2000 – May 2005). More formalised creation of farm invader groups, politicisation of workers, removal of farmers, land redistribution. |
| Phase IV | Post Commercial Farming Era (approximately May 2005 – March 2008). Majority of farms already seized, land and agri-property redistributed. Farm violence continues where remaining farmers resist. |

War veteran payouts
*September 1997*

'Black Friday'
*14 November 1997*

Constitutional referendum
*12-13 February 2000*
**Large-scale farm invasions begin**

Parliamentary election
*24-25 June 2000*

Presidential election
*9-11 March 2002*

**Monthly farm violence peaks at 1,673 incidents**
*March 2002*

Parliamentary election
*31 March 2005*

Farmland nationalised
*12 September 2005*

Operation Murambatsvina begins
*19 May 2005*

Presidential election
*29 March 2008*

**Inflation peaks at 89.7 sextillion $(10^{21})$ percent**
*November 2008*

| 1997-1999 | 2000 | 2001 | 2002 | 2003 | 2004 | 2005 | 2006 | 2007 | 2008 |
|---|---|---|---|---|---|---|---|---|---|

Phase I | Phase II | Phase III | | | | Phase IV

*Note:* Violence data for this timeline come from the survey and mapping project completed for this book.

# Land Seizure Era Violence and Farmer Eviction Timeline

This timeline shows when some acts of extreme violence were carried out against farmers, and demonstrates basic relationships between peaks in the level of violence and farmers being evicted.

**Key timeline events:**

- War veteran payouts — September 1997
- 'Black Friday' — 14 November 1997
- Referendum — 12–13 February 2000
- Organised extortion by invaders of farmers begins — approximately April 2000
- Parliamentary election — 24–25 June 2000
- Most violent month of land seizure era – 1,673 incidents — March 2002
- Presidential election — 9–11 March 2002
- Parliamentary election — 31 March 2005
- Operation Murambatsvina begins — 19 May 2005
- Farmland nationalised — 12 September 2005
- Inflation peaks at 89.7 sextillion ($10^{23}$) percent — November 2008
- Presidential election — 29 March 2008

| | 1997-1999 | 2000 | 2001 | 2002 | 2003 | 2004 | 2005 | 2006 | 2007 | 2008 |
|---|---|---|---|---|---|---|---|---|---|---|
| **Farmers who experienced violence for the first time** | ~ | 46.6% | 25.3% | 19.6% | 3.6% | 2.3% | 0.8% | 1.5% | 0.3% | 0.0% |
| **Farmers evicted** | ~ | 5.3% | 10.4% | 51.2% | 14.7% | 7.5% | 4.8% | 3.1% | 2.4% | 0.5% |
| **Incidents** | ~ | 1,346 | 3,783 | 3,869 | 3,460 | 1,713 | 710 | 2,672 | 3,382 | 556 |
| | Phase I | Phase II | Phase III | | | | Phase IV | | | |

**Farmer Murders:**

- Farmer Murder — David Stevens — 15 April 2000
- Farmer Murder — Martin Olds — 18 April 2000
- Farmer Murder — John Weeks — 14 May 2000
- Farmer Murder — Allan Dunn — 7 May 2000
- Farmer Murder — Tony Oates — 31 May 2000
- Farmer Murder — Willem Botha — 23 July 2000
- Farmer Murder — Henry Elsworth — 12 December 2000
- Farmer Murder — Gloria Olds — 4 March 2001
- Farmer Murder — Robert Cobbet — 6 August 2001
- Farmer Murder — Terry Ford — 18 March 2002
- Farmer Murder — Charles Anderson — 2 June 2002
- Farmer Murder — Don Stuart — 27 November 2005

*Note: Statistics are unavailable for years 1997-1999. Analysis for this research begins in January 2000. All data for this timeline come from the survey and mapping project completed for this book.*

| | |
|---|---|
| **Farmers who experienced violence for the first time** | Year survey respondents first experienced an incident of violence or intimidation. |
| **Farmers evicted** | Year survey respondents were finally evicted from their farm. |
| **Incidents** | Total acts of violence and intimidation from the mapping data set. |
| **Phase I** | Pre-Referendum Period (approximately January 1997 – February 2000). ZANU-PF in-fighting, rise of the war veterans, and rise of the MDC. |
| **Phase II** | Initial Farm Invasions (approximately February 2000 – June 2000). Politicisation of farm workers and land occupation. |
| **Phase III** | Land Redistribution (approximately June 2000 – May 2005). More formalised creation of farm invader groups, politicisation of workers, removal of farmers, land redistribution. |
| **Phase IV** | Post Commercial Farming Era (approximately May 2005 – March 2008). Majority of farms already seized, land and agri-property redistributed. Farm violence continues where remaining farmers resist. |

# The Land Reform Deception

# 1

# Overview of the Land Seizure Era

In February 2000, farm invaders operating with the tacit approval of Zimbabwe's ruling Zimbabwe African National Union–Patriotic Front (ZANU-PF) party began to violently seize control of the country's commercial farms. Over the following eight years, these invaders targeted both farmers and farm workers in a campaign of violence that largely transferred control of the country's commercial farms to ZANU-PF supporters and beneficiaries. This period, which I have termed the "land seizure era," witnessed the most politically, socially, and economically transformative developments since Zimbabwe's independence in 1980.[1]

Initially, these farm invaders were "war veterans" who had fought against the white minority Rhodesian government during the 1970s Liberation War.[2] With the assistance of state security forces, which the ZANU-PF government controlled, these war veterans moved onto commercial farms across Zimbabwe with little interference from, and often the direct support of, law enforcement officials.[3] By late 2002, 90% of farms—comprising 10 million hectares—had been seized without compensation to their title-holding owners.[4] Farmers and most farm workers were evicted in the process. By 2009 less than 400 of the estimated 4,300 commercial farmers who had been present in Zimbabwe in 2000 remained on their land.[5]

The seizure of commercial farms had disastrous consequences for Zimbabwe's agricultural industry. Since independence in 1980, agriculture had been the backbone of the nation's economy. The country was regarded as an "African agricultural success story," with commercial agriculture accounting for 75% of national agricultural production in 1995.[6] The agriculture industry continued to grow each year from 1996 until farm seizures began in 2000, with 2002 showing a 22.7% decrease.[7] By 2007, agricultural production had fallen to just 42% of 1998 levels.[8] Zimbabwe went from exporting crops prior to the land seizure era to being the "most food aid dependent country in the world," with between 65% and 80% of the population relying on aid in 2009.[9]

Farm seizures also had serious implications for the livelihoods of hundreds of thousands of farm workers. Prior to the land seizure era, commercial agriculture was the "largest formal sector employer in the country and made significant contributions to national income and export earnings."[10] In 1995 commercial farms employed 334,000 farm workers, 26.9% of the national workforce. Yet by 2007 just 25,000 workers, 3.1% of the workforce, were employed on commercial farms.[11]

Unsurprisingly, the chaos generated by farm seizures had a ruinous effect on Zimbabwe's macroeconomic performance. Inflation, already severe in 2000 when the land seizure era began, dramatically worsened as a result of violent farm takeovers.[12] By November 2008, inflation was uncontrollable, reaching 89.7 sextillion ($10^{21}$) percent, the second highest recorded rate in world history.[13] In 2000 Zimbabwe's GDP growth rate was –3.1%, compared to Botswana, Mozambique, Zambia, and Namibia, which averaged 2.6%. By 2008 Zimbabwe's growth rate had plummeted to –17.7%, compared to 5.0% for all of these countries.[14]

## LAND REFORM IN ZIMBABWE: A BRIEF OVERVIEW

Since the invasions of commercial farms ultimately resulted in land being transferred almost entirely from white commercial farmers to black ZANU-PF supporters, the land seizure era is considered by some researchers to be the culmination of a land redistribution effort that began long before independence in 1980.[15] Sam Moyo; Ian Scoones et al.; Mahmood Mamdani; Prosper Matondi; and Joseph Hanlon, Jeanette Manjengwa, and Teresa Smart all see the land seizure era as being one phase in a long-standing land reform process.[16] Similarly, Lionel Cliffe et al. identify the Fast Track Land Reform Programme, adopted by the government in July 2000, as being the next stage in a long series of postindependence land reform programs.[17] Meanwhile, Sam Moyo and Paris Yeros largely developed the notion that the occupation of farms was part of an organized land occupation movement led by war veterans.[18] There is no doubt that war veterans played a significant role in leading the first farm seizures in early 2000. However, evidence in this book shows that these events were spontaneous with little or no preplanning, as compared to the more organized and state-led occupations that emerged later in the land seizure era.[19]

This book argues that the land seizure era was never intended to be a genuine and authentic large-scale land redistribution program. While the seizure of commercial farms and associated farm assets did ultimately lead to land redistribution, this was a byproduct, a sideshow, for the primary objective of the ZANU-PF-dominated government was to retain political power.

The ruling party found itself fundamentally threatened politically by the Movement for Democratic Change (MDC) in 2000. In response, it turned to the historically emotive issue of land reform in order to manipulate the political environment to retain power. Without these pressures, the large-scale redistribution of commercial farms would not have begun in 2000. Indeed, according to Matondi, "Since 2000, the radical land reform programme had become a theatre of contests, policy attention and government interests, especially in the farming areas themselves."[20] Matondi is entirely correct, but the real coup de théâtre was ZANU-PF's decision to portray limited initial occupations, intended to suppress the MDC, as a genuine large-scale land reform program.

Nevertheless, through unintended pathways, the seizure of commercial farms led the government to devise new land reform policies and concoct an ex post facto land reform program. Once land seizures had begun and started to slip out of control soon after the referendum in February 2000, the government needed to co-opt the takeovers, regain control of events on the farms, and formulate a politically acceptable framing of events. This initial reframing of events was the hastily devised "Fast Track Land Reform Programme" (FTLRP), launched on July 15, 2000, which gave the false impression that the farm seizures were part of an overarching government land program that began at independence in 1980.

The issue of land redistribution long preceded the 2000 farm seizures; the white domination of the country's commercial farms had been a major popular grievance for decades and was a key factor in sparking the Liberation War that lasted from 1964 to 1979. At independence, nationalist veterans of the Liberation War had expected land allocations from the country's new leader, Robert Mugabe. However, Mugabe faced a dilemma in that, at independence, white farmers produced 90% of the country's maize and cotton, while commercial agriculture accounted for one-third of formal wage employment, earned 40% of the country's foreign exchange, and supplied the manufacturing sector with 40% of its inputs.[21] It was not feasible for him to introduce reforms that could disrupt the sector.

Nonetheless, substantial land reform did take place in the 1980s with farms purchased on a "willing buyer, willing seller" basis, largely from landowners who decided to leave Zimbabwe during or immediately after the Liberation War. By 1987, "40,000 households had been resettled on two million hectares," according to Bill Kinsey.[22] Robin Palmer reports that by June 1989 52,000 families—416,000 people—had been resettled.[23] Resettlement continued through the early 1990s. Cliffe et al. explain that 23% of formerly white-owned land was transferred to black farmers between 1980 and 1996.[24] This compares favorably with Kenya, where only 15% was transferred by 1996, and with South Africa, where after 17 years of land reform, just 6.9% of white-owned land was transferred, against a target of 30%.[25]

The problem for the government was that it in the euphoria of the early post independence period it had set the nearly impossible target of resettling 162,000 households by the end of 1984.[26] The government needed to contend with ensuring that the economically vital commercial farming sector, which was dominated by white farmers, remained productive and that it had sufficient funds to pay for the costs associated with buying land under the "willing buyer, willing seller" program. This meant that despite a very major resettlement accomplishment, the program was tinged with failure.

By the 1990s the land reform efforts had seriously floundered. Charges of corruption and cronyism in land allocation surfaced in the 1980s, and the Zimbabwean government accused British and American donors of reneging on promises to provide funds for land purchases. For these and other reasons that are beyond the scope of this book, land redistribution slowed dramatically into the 1990s but remained a prominent and vitriolic feature of ZANU-PF's political rhetoric.

## The Road to Compulsory Farm Seizures

With the expiration of the Lancaster House agreement in 1990, compulsory land acquisition measures were passed in 1992 under the Land Acquisition Act.[27] However, these measures were instigated alongside the willing buyer, willing seller model. The combination of these two approaches resulted in nearly all attempts at compulsory acquisition being legally contested in court and almost no land was acquired for land reform until 1997.[28]

By 1996 a £44 million grant provided by the British government for land reform programs had largely been spent and the program had expired. Conditions on how this grant and any future funds could be used had been bitterly disputed. British representatives alleged that, since independence, aid had been subject to corruption and they demanded future programs be more stringently managed and earmarked to specific objectives in order to improve delivery outcomes. The Zimbabwe government disputed these allegations and viewed "strings" tied to aid programs as the meddling of a foreign government in Zimbabwe's domestic affairs.

The most acerbic issue was the extent that the British government, as the former colonial power, held a responsibility to fund land redistribution programs in order to address historic landownership imbalances. In 1997 the new British Labour government began shifting its aid programs toward poverty alleviation, and as part of this shift, the secretary of state for international development, Clare Short, indicated in a now infamous written letter that the British government held "no special responsibility to meet the costs of land purchase in Zimbabwe."[29] While her statement indicated ongoing support for development programs in Zimbabwe, it broke the specific linkages of British responsibility to colonial-era land disputes.

In November 1997 the Zimbabwe government issued a notice identifying 1,471 farms for compulsory acquisition. Then in September 1998 a donors' conference was held in order to establish the legal process for future land acquisition, identify stakeholders, and determine the extent that donors would provide funds to pay for land reform. Relations further soured at the conference, with the Zimbabwe government accusing donors of reneging on promised donations and of seeking to uphold the rights of its white former colonial subjects. Nonetheless, despite the intensifying polarization of views on the land reform question by 1999, 35 farms were purchased for redistribution that year.

The issue of land reform once again returned to the top of the political agenda in late 1999, when members of ZANU-PF sought legislation allowing for the legalized, compulsory seizure of commercial farms without compensation to the owner. This provision was largely supported by senior government officials, most of whom were ZANU-PF members, war veterans (who saw themselves as primary beneficiaries), and some people living in communal areas (community owned rural land)—although data from respondents presented in later sections show that the extent of this support was overestimated. The provision was strongly opposed by the MDC, the opposition party formed in September 1999. Drawing its support from the urban black population, white farmers, and black farm workers, the MDC campaigned for land reform but rejected compulsory seizures in favor of market-driven land redistribution.[30] The MDC was also supported, in principle, by some Western powers, including "European states, international donors and financial institutions and the western media."[31] Indeed, as Zvakanyorwa Wilbert Sadomba notes, the actual and perceived involvement of international groups in defending Western and (predominantly white) commercial farmer interests—against the Zimbabwe state—was a "turning point" that substantially escalated the political invective between ZANU-PF and the MDC. Accordingly, lines were drawn between the incumbent ZANU-PF espousing nationalist claims and the newly emergent MDC seeking progressive, nonracial policies.

On February 12–13, 2000, a constitutional referendum was held to decide, among other changes, the issue of compulsory seizures of commercial farms with no compensation to the farm owners. In a shock result for ZANU-PF, which had not suffered a political loss since independence, the MDC-led "no" campaign achieved a stunning victory in the referendum. Given that the MDC had been formed just six months earlier, the referendum result was a major political challenge for the ruling party.

The government initially responded calmly to the result, with Mugabe making a conciliatory speech in which he promised to accept the will of the people.[32] However, some war veterans soon began moving onto farms.[33] While war veterans initially spearheaded the seizures, they were joined by state security agents, youths, the rural unemployed, and in some cases traditional leaders.[34] With the direct collaboration of the government, these groups—called "farm invaders" in this book—began seizing farms across the country with virtually no opposition from law enforcement agencies.[35]

Farm invaders had two primary and often conflated objectives: seizing farmland and suppressing the MDC (figure 1.1).[36] A former senior officer in the Zimbabwe National Army, Steven Sebungwe, explained that evicting the farmer meant it was possible to get rid of the farm workers. This would disrupt the MDC's farm worker voting base, as well as making a farm, and all its assets, available to the invaders.[37]

These objectives were accomplished by violently attacking farm workers and farmers.[38] Farm workers were targeted because they made up a large part of the MDC's voting base, while farmers were targeted, in part, because they owned the farms and many were known to financially support the MDC.

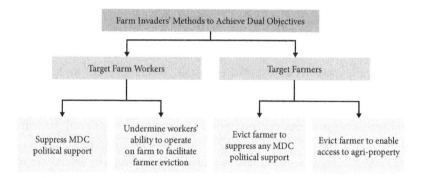

**Figure 1.1** Flowchart of Invaders' Dual Objectives

Especially after the referendum loss, ZANU-PF's rhetoric on land invasions became charged and combative. Farm seizures were described as the "Third Chimurenga" war; the first and second *chimurenga* wars were both waged against colonial governments, and this term therefore invoked strong histori- cal and racial justifications for the violent seizures. In speeches Mugabe "stressed his liberation war credentials, spoke of enemies, sell outs, traitors and war."[39]

The ruling party also began ramping up rhetoric about "patriotic history"— defined by Norma Kriger as a "brand of official nationalism [that] celebrates the military dimensions of the liberation war and sidelines nonviolent political struggles."[40] The emphasis on "patriotic history" sought to define ZANU-PF as the sole legitimate actor in Zimbabwean politics by carefully crafting the ruling party's interpretation of the nationalist struggle. This legitimized its role as a decision-maker, and its supporters as the rightful beneficiaries of the government's social and war service programs, key jobs and a range of social benefits.

Likewise, "patriotic history" sought to delegitimize the political voice of those who opposed ZANU-PF. MDC supporters, white farmers, and Western governments were framed not only as opponents of ZANU-PF, but as enemies of the nation. These groups were cast as being in cooperation with each other to undermine nationalist gains made by the ruling party. Thus, the increas- ingly shrill political arena was polarized between government supporters and their opponents, with little room left for moderates or for compromise.

## EXTENT OF COMMERCIAL FARM VIOLENCE

This combative talk inherent in "patriotic history" during the run-up to the land seizure era would ultimately go beyond mere political rhetoric. Numer- ous NGO and Western media reports have documented how political violence was widespread, intense, and often punitive during farm seizures.[41] While the government did not originally intend to allow such an extensive wave of land seizures, virtually all the farm takeovers in the early February to June 2000 period were at least influenced by the Central Intelligence Organisation (CIO, the state secret service), with the exception of a small number of "spontane- ous" farm invasions by war veterans right after the referendum result in Feb- ruary 2000. Soon after about June 2000, the CIO presence became greater and more formalized and the police and military also became more actively in- volved in facilitating farm seizures.[42] Without the moderating force of a pro- fessional and law-abiding state security apparatus, farm invaders could operate with near impunity. While the utility of employing violent measures for coer- cion may seem obvious, and indeed examples of such methods are common around the world, it is not clear in existing literature why such prolific violence by extensive state security resources, especially the military, was used against essentially an unarmed population.[43]

To understand this issue, it is necessary to look at the nature of the ruling party. ZANU-PF has a long history of relying upon violence to suppress political opposition. Ranger, Jocelyn Alexander et al., Kriger, and David Lan all recount instances of villagers, purported "sellouts," and farm workers being targeted by Zimbabwe African National Liberation Army (ZANLA) guerrillas—ZANU's military wing—during the Liberation War in the 1960s and 1970s.[44] ZANU's internal power struggles during the Liberation War were also marked by violence. For example, senior ZANU official Josiah Tongogara—an internal rival of Mugabe—was almost certainly assassinated, in the view of Daniel Compagnon, just six days after the signing of the Lancaster House agreement in 1979 that ended the war.[45]

Opposition to ZANU's leadership soon after independence was also dealt with by force. By 1980, according to Alexander, "The ZANU leadership had been pushed to adopt a more radical ideology as a consequence of wartime challenges from the left, challenges that were brutally suppressed and which had left an authoritarian political structure in their wake."[46] In the early 1980s, during what has become known as *Gukurahundi*, ethnic and political opposition to the ethnically Shona-dominated ZANU government was violently suppressed. Accounts of massacres and torture have been documented extensively by the Catholic Commission for Justice and Peace, demonstrating a legacy of brutal crackdown of political opponents that took the lives of an estimated 20,000 people in Gukurahundi.[47]

Nor has the use of violence been limited to rural areas. In 2005 the Zimbabwean government began an operation purportedly to clear slum dwellers on the outskirts of Harare. Some 700,000 people were affected. Known as Operation Murambatsvina, the raid had as its real purpose the suppression of political opposition in the urban poor.[48]

These episodes demonstrate how ZANU-PF is culturally attuned to react with force to any real or perceived threat. It is therefore unsurprising that ZANU-PF responded with violence to the supposed threat from the MDC among Zimbabwe's farm workers and farmers. Indeed, the scale of violence against farm workers and farmers between 2000 and 2008 was enormous, as farm invaders sought to suppress MDC support on farms and seize land and agri-property.[a] During the land seizure era, workers were targeted both in

---

a. "Agri-property" is defined in this book as movable farm assets such as farm implements, livestock, chemicals, and fertilizer, and equipment such as pumping and irrigation supplies.

higher numbers—unsurprisingly given that there were far more workers than farmers—and more aggressively. The accounts collected for this book show that there was a systematic effort by farm invaders to destroy workers' homes and personal property.[49]

A large number of workers were murdered, and there were many instances of torture, such as the whipping of victims with sticks wrapped in barbed wire and with bicycle chains.[b] Accounts from the Zimbabwe Human Rights NGO Forum ("Forum") and the farmer advocacy group Justice for Agriculture (JAG) detail beatings widely administered by farm invaders and sometimes by law enforcement officials.[50] There were also numerous cases of politically motivated rape of farm workers and their family members.[51] Since farm workers tended to be relatively poor, they could not easily replace lost assets or rely on financial resources to afford them much physical safety, compounding the extent that they were victimized.

The poverty of farm workers, as well as the fact that many were perceived to be migrants from neighboring countries and thus considered undeserving of the benefits emanating from land reform, meant that they remained particularly vulnerable throughout the land seizure era. There is extensive literature on the conditions faced by farm workers and on their relationships with their employers and with the state.[52] As later chapters will detail, workers tended to be almost totally financially dependent on their farmer employers, and most lacked any financial reserves or alternative forms of employment. This meant that workers tended to support the continued operations of their farmer employers and thus also of the MDC, which tended to uphold commercial farmer interests. Accordingly, farm invaders targeted workers widely and with very extensive violence in order to suppress their purported support for the MDC and in order to undermine their willingness to aid farmers in continuing farming operations.

A key consequence of the land seizure era was the loss of employment (see figure 1.2) and displacement of between 200,000 and 400,000 farm workers.[53] Considering that most workers had dependents to feed and house, and that upon their eviction (or that of the farmer employer) they would also have lost their livelihoods, we can begin to understand the scale of loss they experienced.

---

b. Farmers often had detailed knowledge of violence against workers because in many cases they provided either direct medical assistance or transport to local clinics for professional medical care. For instance, an anonymous survey respondent detailed that "senior workers were whipped with barbed wire in front of the whole compound at a *pungwe*." Therefore, this research relies on farm workers and farmer accounts to present a broad perspective on farm violence.

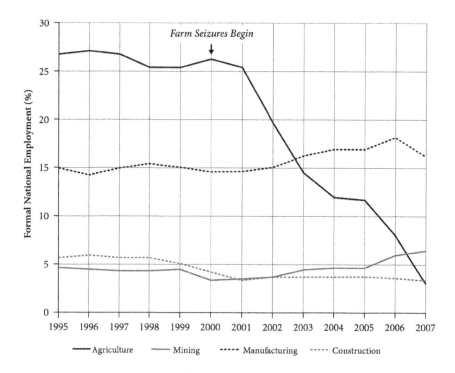

**Figure 1.2** Formal National Employment by Industry
NOTE: Robertson estimated 2006 and 2007 figures.
SOURCE: Robertson, General Zimbabwe Statistics

Workers tended to gain comparatively little from any redistributed farm-land. Moreover, their employment on mostly white-owned farmers made them untrustworthy in the eyes of many farm invaders. While their skills meant it would have been logical for farm workers to take control of redistributed land, their position meant they were competitors to farm invaders, who sought to undermine their claims.[54] Indeed, according to Moyo et al. workers consti-tuted just 8.1% of land beneficiaries.[55]

As with workers, farmers experienced severe physical violence and emo-tional distress. Indeed, the large-scale survey of commercial farmers under-taken for this book showed that, of the surveyed respondents, 31.8% experienced assault, 3.2% torture, and 9.4% attempted murder.[56] Twelve commercial farm-ers were murdered during the land seizure era. Forms of intimidation against farmers were also extremely widespread, with 88.1% of respondents indicating that they were subjected to threats, 68.6% that they experienced property damage or theft, and 21.8% that they suffered abduction or unlawful arrest. Indeed, data from the Forum record at least 21,491 acts of violence and intimidation against farmers, workers, and people in urban areas between 2000 and 2008.[57]

Yet some researchers claim that violence was not pervasive. For example, according to Sadomba:

> Land occupations were far from being chaotic; they were orderly, principled, with a few violent clashes of mainly minor assaults. Interviews with many white commercial farmers, a white lawyer who represented farmers and farm workers, not to mention the occupiers themselves, show this.[58]

Instead Sadomba blames the unrest on farms on "criminal elements."[59] It is true that some farm invasions were more orderly than others. However, there are so many major and egregious documented examples of violence being employed that Sadomba's claim lacks credibility. The argument that violence was not extensive relies on narrow definitions, such as that used by Sadomba. Such claims are politically motivated and provide no serious supporting evidence.

## WAS THERE GENUINE DEMAND FOR LAND?

The land issue has been central to ZANU-PF's political agenda since its founding in the 1970s. The party used the slogan "Land is the Economy, the Economy is Land" in the 2000 election campaign and "Our land, Our sovereignty" in 2008. ZANU-PF has highlighted grievances over land for so long it is hard not to assume that it was indeed the core objective of the farm takeovers. Mugabe's speeches after 2000 were replete with references not only to a purported widespread and long-standing desire for land but to a fundamental connection between landownership and the nationalist struggle. The president claimed in the 2001 publication *Inside the Third Chimurenga* that "the land is being delivered to its rightful owners, the Zimbabwean people," and insisted that there were only a "small number of our people who are not enthused about farming."[60]

The assumption that land formed the core of grievances during the colonial period is taken for granted in much of the current literature. Ben Cousins and Ian Scoones assign it a central role in saying that it "fuelled" support for the liberation struggle, which is certainly true.[61] The importance of the issue is also discussed by Alexander, Lan, Ranger, and Kriger.[62] Alexander and McGregor state that "ZANU-PF was right in identifying a widespread desire for more land in the communal areas."[63] Sam Moyo especially identifies that there was broad demand for land in communal areas, and McGregor notes how ZANU-PF exploited "popular grievances over land."[64] Christian Mucheke, a legal officer in the President's Office, also cited a major demand for land: "We should not undermine the need for land distribution at that time. It was very necessary."[65]

Yet casting doubt on this presumption, a Gallup national opinion survey of 1,900 voters conducted in 2000 found that only 9% of respondents believed land reform was the most important issue facing the nation.[66] Compagnon highlights a study conducted in 1995 and endorsed by the Zimbabwean government, which found that only 2% of communal area peasants sought land.[67] Instead, these individuals wanted help with existing farm projects and in gaining access to formal employment.[68]

Numerous respondents, from police to CIO, stated in interviews that many people were not explicitly or solely demanding land. Edison Bubye, of the Zimbabwe Republic Police (ZRP) said, "We want employment. All this, this is nonsense. No wonder people voted against the constitution because . . . at that particular time, people were not even bothered about land."[69] Wilfred Mhanda, a former commander in the Liberation War, noted that "our national liberation struggle was driven by political, economic, social and cultural demands and not by land, as has been alleged. Land redistribution was just one of the key economic demands and not the purpose of our struggle."[70] Thompson Mupfure, a former guerrilla in the Liberation War and senior government official, offered similar views. He emphasized that guerrillas went to war in the 1960s and 1970s so that the benefits of the country could be shared equitably:

> We did not want independence to destroy [the economy]. We did not want independence so that we can become poor, no. People wanted independence so that they can enjoy the fruits of being treated equally like everyone else, whether you want access to education, you want access to jobs, so that when you are doing the same job [as] a white man, whether you are a journalist or an academic, whether you are black or white, it does not matter.[71]

As Mupfure states, guerrillas fought for many reasons, but predominantly for voting rights and a nonracial society. Land was only part of the story in achieving this goal, but it did gain prominence as the war progressed, particularly when the population in rural communities swelled by nearly 50% between 1969 and 1976.[72] While there is no doubt that many people genuinely wanted land, improved livelihoods, better jobs, and service provision were often the primary desire for the majority of people.[73]

Yet for war veterans who had been raised on the land issue and who had not gained substantially in the postindependence period, the subject of land remained vital. Land was a fundamental promise of the Liberation War, the benefit they had been waiting for since 1980. Land had always been a key issue for ZANU-PF, but when war veterans found a way to assert themselves, primarily through the charismatic Chenjerai Hunzvi beginning in the mid-1990s, their demand for land re-emerged as *the* dominant issue in the party. Even if they accounted for only a small percentage of the population, the war veterans possessed major political influence, had connections throughout the government and state security apparatus, and occupied a prestigious social position due to their wartime service. Land may not have been a prominent issue for much of the population, but it became the crucial issue linking key stakeholders. ZANU-PF's defeat in the 2000 referendum showed that the party would struggle to retain power without the support of these stakeholders, especially the war veterans, who therefore had to be placated through land redistribution.

The most likely explanation for disagreements among researchers and stakeholders in Zimbabwe over the demand for land is that land stands as a proxy for a range of socioeconomic needs; gaining access to land can be connected to better employment prospects as well as improved wages and greater social support from the government. Land functioned as a "catch-all" term for a range of demands that were harder to articulate, but the vast majority of rural Zimbabweans would prefer better jobs over land when given a direct choice between the two, as later chapters will show.

## SOCIAL AND ECONOMIC OUTCOMES OF THE LAND SEIZURE ERA

Given the government's record of extolling the virtues of land redistribution, it might be assumed that the seizure of farms resulted in substantial social and economic gains for the country.[74] After all, the takeover of farms was a fulfillment of nationalist objectives espoused long before independence. It seems reasonable to believe that the redistribution of these vast and productive assets from ostensibly "wealthy" farmers to the greater population, who could then in turn use the resources to be productive, would result in major social and economic gains.[75]

However, the farm takeovers instead resulted in a social and economic catastrophe for Zimbabwe. The takeovers exacerbated the economic crisis triggered in 1997 by the unbudgeted payout to war veterans in the form of pensions (see chapter 2), with disastrous effects on employment, inflation, and social services.

In an environment of violence, instability, and uncertainty over personal and property rights, production and investment on commercial farms inevitably

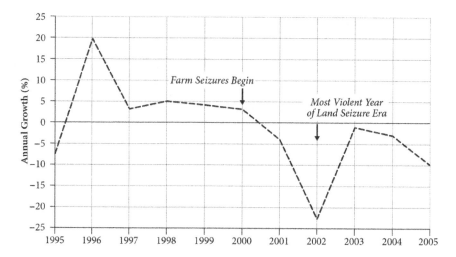

**Figure 1.3** Annual Growth of Agriculture Industry
NOTE: Annual growth rate for agricultural value added based on constant local currency.
SOURCE: World Bank, "Zimbabwe Statistics."

decreased (see figure 1.3). With employees unable to work, farmers faced extensive practical problems in continuing operations. Unemployment reached 60% in 2002 and 95% in 2009—the highest in the world.[76]

Furthermore, life expectancy dramatically decreased during the land seizure era. By 2003, Zimbabwe's healthy life expectancy was the lowest in the world at just 34 years for men and 33 for women, with life expectancy at birth falling by 28% for men and 35% for women between 1990 and 2008.[77,78] While the HIV/AIDS epidemic was the leading cause of this decline, breakdowns in social services and medical care, reduced earnings, and insufficient access to food—directly brought about by the land seizure era—were also major factors.[79]

Inflation accelerated after 2000 as farm invasions severely undermined the economy.[80] Figure 1.4 shows inflation rates from 1995 to 2003, demonstrating a steep increase after farm seizures began in 2000. By 2008, inflation had reached an astonishing 89.7 sextillion percent.[81] As inflation increased, the Reserve Bank resorted to striking zeroes from the currency. For instance, on a given date ZWD$10,000.00 would become ZWD$10.00 with corresponding new banknotes issued. Despite these drastic steps, the Reserve Bank still ended up issuing a ZWD$100 trillion banknote in response to uncontrollable inflation. Ultimately, however, Zimbabwe was forced to abandon its own currency in February 2009 in favor of the US dollar.[82]

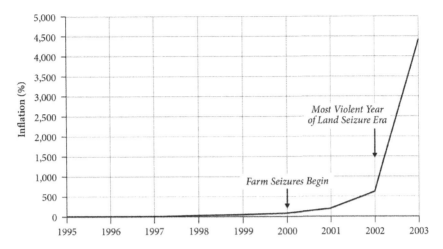

**Figure 1.4** Inflation: 1995–2003
NOTE: Figures reflect end-of-period consumer prices. Index: 2000 = 100. Post-2003 figures were too high for clear representation on this figure.
SOURCE: International Monetary Fund, "World Economic Outlook Database: Zimbabwe."

Zimbabwe's economic collapse came at a time when the rest of the region was recording strong growth. Figure 1.5 provides GDP for Zimbabwe and four neighboring countries.[83] All of these countries except Zimbabwe saw relatively strong increases in GDP for the 2000 to 2008 period, but Zimbabwe fell from having the second largest GDP in the region (behind South Africa) in 1990, to the lowest in 2009.

The United Nations Development Programme's Human Development Index (HDI), examining economic, health, life expectancy, and literacy levels, ranked Zimbabwe the lowest of 169 countries for 2010, and was one of only three countries whose HDI in 2010 was lower than in 1970.[84]

Not all researchers accept this bleak conclusion about the seizure of land. Hanlon, Manjengwa, and Smart, for example, present more positive findings on the impact of land reform.[85] Similarly, Scoones et al. claim that "there have been important successes which must be taken into account if a more complete picture is to be offered . . . the story is not simply one of collapse and catastrophe; it is much more nuanced and complex, with successes as well as failures." They reject as "myths" the widespread belief that land reform was a failure, benefiting largely the "cronies" of Mugabe.[86] Their research also disputes the idea that beneficiaries of the farm seizures were unable to invest in the land, condemning the rural economy to collapse and the population to food insecurity.[87]

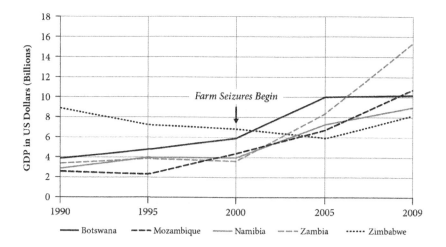

**Figure 1.5** GDP for Southern African Countries
NOTE: South Africa is not included because the relatively large size of the economy renders detailed differentiation of included economies difficult to depict graphically.
SOURCE: World Bank; Zimbabwe 2009 GDP data from the International Monetary Fund, "World Economic Outlook Database."

Scoones et al. are correct that it is important to understand the nuances of the agricultural economy after the farm seizures. Between 2000 and 2010 some 170,000 households were resettled.[88] Indeed, Scoones et al. show that the agrarian structure in their sample population changed substantially after the land was reallocated and often for the better in the cases of the actual beneficiaries. Landownership changed hands, additional land was cleared, and new farmers were introduced. Importantly for the researchers, they also show that the production of some commodities increased after 2000. They show how farming evolved, what kinds of investments new farmers made, and how they decided on commodity production. All of this provides a real contribution to the scholarship on how farming has changed since the take-over of commercial farms began in 2000. Moreover, their research provides a more differentiated picture than Hanlon, Manjengwa, and Smart, who, with highly debatable evidence, paint an implausible picture of agricultural successes.[89]

When considering the achievements of resettlement, it is important to know who the beneficiaries are and how they are faring.[90] Scoones et al. have over-reached in claiming that their evidence disproves the "myths" surrounding the land seizure era. These researchers examined a relatively small sample in a remote part of Masvingo province, and then—using what in some instances is a debatable interpretation of their data—they make representations for all of Zimbabwe. The researchers admit that their area of study is quite different climatologically, geographically, socially, and politically from the most intensively farmed—and vigorously contested—farming areas in Zimbabwe, the three Mashonaland provinces. It is therefore difficult if not impossible to make generalizations based on their data.[91]

However, the macro-level indicators that reveal Zimbabwe's economic collapse give a clearer indication of the negative overall impact during land seizures era. These figures cannot be ignored—they show that ZANU-PF's rhetoric on the benefits of land redistribution and national-level claims by researchers such as Scoones et al. are unsubstantiated. Far from delivering the promised economic and social benefits, the land seizures led to a catastrophic collapse in the economy.

## OBJECTIVES OF THIS BOOK

This book aims to shed light on what motivated the Zimbabwean state to target the country's highly productive, dominant, and economically important agriculture industry. The study explores how the land seizure era began by identifying the key political, social, and economic forces that influenced ZANU-PF's ability and determination to retain political power. It also explores the extent to which Mugabe supported the farm seizures, to what extent they were planned in advance, and whether they spiraled out of control.

The drivers of land grievances began during the colonial era but became even more prominent after 1997, when war veterans demands began escalating. This book examines the period from February 2000, the start of the large-scale farm seizures, until the March 2008 presidential election. By this time most farm seizures had taken place, and the focus for ZANU-PF had moved to suppressing the MDC in urban areas. However, this book predominantly focuses on the 2000 to 2005 period in order to understand the mechanisms driving and enabling the proliferation of large-scale farm seizures. During this time the vast majority of commercial farms were seized, and virtually all farmers and workers experienced some kind of coercion.[92]

Ultimately, this book explores whether the large-scale seizure of commercial farms was motivated by the political objective of preserving ZANU-PF's hold on power, and the extent to which the seizures were authentic and fundamentally a land redistribution exercise to address the injustices of colonial land-ownership structures. If the seizure of commercial farms was a genuine attempt at land redistribution, why did they take place 20 years after independence?

Why was land apparently unused after it had been taken over, and why did so many individuals with little farming experience gain land? Moreover, why were so many farms stripped of vital agri-property, severely undermining or rendering inoperable what were established, fully stocked and equipped commercial operations?

Chapter 2 provides a detailed background of events preceding the land seizure era. It details how ZANU-PF found itself facing a rebellion from the war veterans in the late 1990s as the national economy foundered, and, as a result, the party began making ever greater promises about land redistribution to appease this group. It shows that the government was aware of how important the agricultural industry was to the nation's economy and were cautious about disrupting it. It also explains how the dramatic rise of the MDC forced the government into taking drastic action to preserve its power. The chapter casts doubt on the claims that there was widespread desire for land among the general populace as the country entered the new millennium.

Chapter 3 explores why the government targeted the country's dominant agriculture industry. It outlines the buildup to the planned seizure of commercial farms and, crucially, outlines the extent of farm seizure planning undertaken by the government during the referendum period in early 2000. The chapter details how the original scope of planned farm seizures soon gave way to uncontrolled, large-scale farm takeovers, and then explores how the government sought to regain the initiative by reframing the takeovers ex post facto as being part of a land reform program.

Chapter 4 looks into the strategies deployed by war veterans as they moved onto farms. The chapter notes that many of the farm invaders' tactics were adapted from the Liberation War. It examines how invader groups were originally kept under the relatively disciplined control of war veterans; but as more claimants began to compete for the land, violence became more intense and invaders became less willing to bypass farms where the farmers had enjoyed good relations with the local community. The chapter also explores how farmers responded to the invasions following the collapse of the rule of law in the countryside and the indifference or active hostility of the police.

Chapter 5 assesses the first of two key objectives of farm invaders: suppressing the MDC by targeting farm workers and farmers. It examines where ZANU-PF concentrated violence and why, ironically, the party appeared to use higher levels of violence in provinces where the party had the most political support. Moreover, the chapter explores how ZANU-PF relied upon coercion to suppress the MDC and ultimately retain political power, and how these objectives were tied to the geographical location of MDC supporters. Evidence also shows why such extensive violence was used against largely unarmed workers and farmers when less violent methods would likely have been sufficient to take control of farms.

Chapter 6 explores the second key objective of farm invaders: the takeover of land and the seizure of agri-property. It details the extent to which farm invaders were motivated by the aim of seizing land or by capturing valuable and easily salable agri-property, such as farm equipment and crops. This question is fundamentally important because it frames the actions of ZANU-PF and its agents as either correcting a historical injustice of landownership inequity—albeit a contested one—or engaging in common theft. The validity of ZANU-PF's land redistribution program hinges on correcting colonially inspired land injustice, but even the ruling party provides no justification for the seizure of personal assets. The chapter also explores the typology of invaders in order to understand who they were and how their relative levels of power influenced the quantity and quality of assets they could seize. Finally, the chapter assesses how invaders located land and agri-property and the role of violence in seizure of these assets.

Chapter 7 evaluates the initial consequence of farm invaders moving on farms. The proliferation of short-term extortion schemes by invaders seeking money, land, and agri-property from farmers pointed to the breakdown in farm security. It also highlights farm invaders' rapid awareness of opportunities for personal gain after breakdowns in the willingness of security officials to enforce property rights. Evidence shows how extortion rackets emerged, who was targeted, and why they became so widespread. This chapter also analyzes why longer-term protection schemes were, by contrast, very rare. The chapter details the components necessary for long-term protection schemes to emerge, gives examples of how they operated, and explains why they tended to be unstable and short-lived.

Chapter 8 examines the methods used to evict farmers and seize their assets. It shows how chronic and acute vulnerability affected farmers' decision-making about whether to remain on their farms and how to cope with security risks that threatened their safety and that of their workers and farm assets. Data show how different types of threats undermined farmers' ability to operate their farms as a viable commercial business. Accounts also underscore that coercion tended to be experienced differently by farmers and workers because of the varying objectives of farm invaders.

Chapter 9 assesses the consequences of the land seizures for commercial agriculture. Data show the impact of breakdowns in property rights on agricultural production. This is followed by an in-depth discussion about the impact of the collapse of the agricultural sector on the national economy. The discussion also examines research that points to increases in production and a stabilization of the sector after the farm seizures, to understand what these findings mean and how they correlate with data put forward in this research.

# ZANU-PF's Land Redistribution Gamble

In the 1990s, Zimbabwe's ruling ZANU-PF party faced two key issues that would ultimately lead to widespread land seizures: the decline of the national economy and the party's diminishing popularity. Indeed, while it was the widespread seizure of commercial farms starting in early 2000 that triggered the collapse of the economy and the onset of hyperinflation, the economy was already in decline well before 2000.

Inflation and unemployment were increasing by the late 1990s. The land issue was becoming particularly emotive and important for some war veterans, given its connections to the Liberation War and because it was one asset that retained value as the economy weakened. At the same time, land was also a bedrock issue for ZANU-PF and featured prominently in its political messages.[1] Many impoverished war veterans who struggled to find employment began to blame ZANU-PF for failing to deliver on promises of land redistribution: the more ZANU-PF espoused a land agenda, the more poignantly it appeared to be failing to deliver on the issue. Thus, a rift formed between war veterans and ZANU-PF over land and other benefits. The problem for the ruling party was that it relied on war veteran support because, as key actors in the Liberation War, war veterans possessed enormous social influence. Furthermore, they had historically been committed—and violent—participants in ZANU-PF's electioneering.[2] For a nationalist party, losing the support of the soldiers who fought in the war and who functioned as coercive agents during election campaigns was politically disastrous.

At the same time, Mugabe was unable to simply seize farms and redistribute land to appease war veteran demands. Farms were central to the national economy as a critical source of employment, tax revenue, food, and exportable commodities. Furthermore, Mugabe did not possess the legal authority to seize this land without compensation to the owners. As a result, Mugabe found himself caught between appeasing both restive and impoverished war veterans, whose demands for land were politically too salient to ignore, and colonially descended and relatively wealthy farmers who provided critical commodities and functioned at the heart of the nation's economy.

## US AND BRITISH INVOLVEMENT

There was also a major international dimension to the polarization of the political landscape during 1997 and 1998. Mugabe and ZANU-PF had sought to attribute the slow pace of land reform to both the British and American governments reneging on commitments to fund land redistribution.[3] However, the British and American governments pointed to millions of dollars in aid given to support land reform in the 1980s—and to the extensive fraud and corruption that accompanied the program.[4]

The debate over the extent to which—if at all—the British government in particular had "reneged" on land reform commitments is exceptionally contested. The root of the disagreements lies in the informal commitments made during the 1979 Lancaster House conference, how they were interpreted, and how they were later manipulated by both the Zimbabwean and British representatives.[5]

In 2009 the United Kingdom's Africa All Party Parliamentary Group (AAPPG) undertook an evaluation of the commitments made at Lancaster House. The body received submissions from the UK and Zimbabwean governments as well as individuals who played a key role at Lancaster House. The AAPPG recognized that for the nationalists land reform was a key demand, and they noted that the Patriotic Front lobbied extensively for assistance with land redistribution efforts.[6] The Zimbabwean government's submission to the enquiry also makes no mention of specific financial figures.[7]

While no specific sums were agreed at Lancaster House, the AAPPG report shows the Patriotic Front harbored *expectations* that the British and American governments would support land redistribution. According to the AAPPG: "What they had received was assurances from the British and American governments that funds would be committed to assist with land reform. . . . Land resettlement could only occur through the willing buyer–willing seller scheme, which Britain had pledged to support."[8] But how did the commitment to "assist" with land reform translate into numbers?

Since 1980, the British government claims to have given Zimbabwe £47 million for land reform (the Zimbabwean government says it received £36.5 million; differences in accounting explain the discrepancy).[9] The Patriotic Front envisaged much higher numbers. The so-called Kissinger fund from the United States would have seen Zimbabwe receive US$1.5 billion. However, this fund was part of a relatively long-standing effort to provide a pool of money to facilitate an end to the Rhodesian independence crisis, and figures had been discussed during the earlier Ford administration, not the more recent Carter presidency. The Lancaster House agreement was made during the Carter administration, and no mention of funding anywhere near the US$1.5 billion level was ever agreed. The AAPPG report notes that Nkomo and Mugabe specifically asked about the Kissinger fund money and stated that "it is possible that the huge scale that Kissinger envisaged influenced not just the Patriotic Front's expectations, but also Britain's."[10] The Patriotic Front likely agreed to the Lancaster House terms with the understanding that the support for land reform would be at Kissinger fund levels.

There is some validity to ZANU-PF's claims in the 1990s and 2000s that British "assurances" over funding for land reform were not honored. Clearly, no precise figures were specified, and there were differences in interpretation of what amounts would ultimately be given by the UK. At the same time, evidence also suggests that the substantial sums that were donated for land reform were skimmed by corrupt officials, and much of the land purchased for popular redistribution efforts was taken instead by senior officials in the government.

For example, Peter Msasa, a military intelligence agent, recounted what became of some farms purchased using funds from the British government: "Instead of resettling . . . [ordinary land claimants] they [government officials] were taking those farms. That's how ministers got the farms, instead of giving [farms to] the people."[11] According to Msasa it was these corrupt practices that led to a rift between the Zimbabwean government and the British over continued support for land redistribution: "I am sure that's where the problems [for] the British and the government started, when the British said, 'No, you were supposed to resettle the people, and you are taking those farms.' So that is when the British stopped paying." Another military intelligence agent, Daniel Inkankezi, made a similar claim: "The land issue, while there were slight progress because the British government was sponsoring that, everybody else knows, right. The government was not honest in dealing with the poor people, all right, because the ministers were grabbing all the farms and all that to themselves during that period [the 1980s]."[12]

It is certain that the British sought an exit from what could have been a very long-term aid commitment that would have involved some of its funding being siphoned off by ZANU-PF beneficiaries. These governments and organizations had become very reluctant to commit major funds to a government that was seen as corrupt. This was especially the case given that demands for accountability in aid funding were escalating during the 1990s.

However, the ruling party also deflected responsibility by attributing perceived failures in the land redistribution program to the British. Indeed, ZANU-PF has a long and well-worn history of attributing a range of political and economic failures to the former colonial power.[13] As demands from the war veterans for land and greater benefits heated up, the ZANU-PF government knew it lacked the funds to pay for an expanded land program. It was therefore logical for the ruling party to point an accusing finger outward to the British, Americans, and other Western aid agencies. The political row of over funding was further fueled by Western governments' insistence that conditions be applied to funding and that no farmland (i.e., commercial farms) be seized without compensation.

By 1998, worsening relations between the British and Zimbabwe governments saw ZANU-PF actively accusing the former colonial power of meddling in the country's domestic affairs and favoring white farmers. Indeed, British political interests did seem to be particularly aroused when the welfare of its former white subjects was threatened, but then again the preservation of property rights was increasingly a global concern. When ZANU-PF then faced major political opposition in 1999, and the British appeared to support at least the principles of the Movement for Democratic Change's (MDC's) land policy, ZANU-PF was able to easily frame its new political opponents as a league of puppets operating at the behest of the British colonizers and white farmers.[14]

## A POTENT POLITICAL CHALLENGER EMERGES IN THE MDC

The emergence of a political alternative in the form of the rival MDC party in 1999 meant that these growing frictions became critically important. The MDC threatened ZANU-PF's political control at a time when the ruling party was aware of its falling popularity. The MDC also appeared to threaten war veteran interests because the party advocated market-driven land reform rather than outright seizure of farmland without compensation to farmers. Accordingly, while the MDC presented a political threat to the ruling party, it also brought an opportunity for ZANU-PF to use the land issue to regain war veteran support by defining a common interest. However, the critical importance of agriculture to the economy meant that by using land as a political tool,

ZANU-PF was also risking potentially severe economic problems if it lost control over the issue in the process. The key event determining whether land could be seized without compensation to the farmers was the constitutional referendum of 12–13 February 2000. It was the result of this referendum, in which voters opposed the government's agenda, that marked the beginning of the land seizure era.

## Who Were the War Veterans?

A "war veteran" is ostensibly any individual who served in the Zimbabwe People's Revolutionary Army (ZIPRA) or ZANLA armed forces during the Liberation War. The term is extraordinarily contested in sociopolitical circles, however, which had consequences both before and after the land seizures commenced. Even the origin of the term points to iterations of contest and debate. As Kriger explains, former guerrillas from the Liberation War had been called "ex-combatants," but the term had become stigmatized in society due to the rampant corruption of some individuals. With the passage of the War Veterans Act of 1992 "it was hoped [the term 'war veteran'] would provide new respect to the ex-guerrillas."[15]

The term "war veteran" is contested in large part because of the difficulty in defining wartime service. The obvious image of a war veteran is of an armed guerrilla who fought against the Rhodesian state. However, how does one classify youths and sometimes children, called *mujibas* during the war, who played roles as lookouts and messengers and undertook a host of other explicitly non-combatant but important tasks? What about female civilians in rural villages who provided food, shelter, and information to guerrillas? How would one class political detainees or those who received military training but never saw active service? Also, would nationalist political leaders who never saw combat but played political and diplomatic roles be considered "war veterans"?

Even among veterans who had undoubtedly served in the war there was disagreement over who could genuinely use the term, and there existed a concomitant pecking order among the claimants. Kriger highlights how the fault lines between "military veterans" and "political veterans" underscored a debate been "true" versus "fake" veterans:

> Military veterans often glorified their arms training and violent overthrow of the colonial regime and disparaged political resisters for having failed to defeat colonialism. Veteran politicians valorised their role as political educators, organisers, guerrilla recruiters and political leaders of the liberation movements; they frequently taunted ex-combatants about their youth, political inexperience, lack of education and use of violence.[16]

There was often considerable mistrust between military and political veterans, highlighting these cleavages. Some military veterans believed that political leaders had been traitors to their cause during the Liberation War.[17] The former viewed the latter as having had an easier time in the war and believed that, for self-serving reasons, they had abandoned the core principles of the struggle after independence, one of which was the transfer of wealth (including land) from the white minority to the black majority.

Tensions over the definition and identity of war veterans also influenced ZANU-PF's policy agenda in the 1990s, because the senior party members tended to favor a constructed narrative about the Liberation War that largely focused on land policy objectives and the centrality of violence to achieving the party's aims. This meant there was little room for progressive measures to emerge within the party's doctrine. It also resulted in fault lines forming between many veterans and the ruling party. By the mid-1990s some veterans blamed the party for admitting members for political reasons who, according to Kriger, "had been hostile to the liberation war or who had made insignificant contributions to independence."[18] Given that ZANU-PF very much depended on the support of war veterans, the need for the party to remain preoccupied with addressing the legacies of the Liberation War is clear.

While the term "war veteran" has been disputed for decades, what Brian Raftopoulos called the "ideology of sacrifice" remained the pervading attitude among genuine war veterans and served to unite their demands for recognition from the state.[19] This meant that, because of their wartime service and suffering, war veterans felt entitled to certain benefits from the state, the scope of which included demobilization pay, preferential job access, disability benefits, pensions, and in 1997, a lump-sum payment.[20] With so much to gain, there was obviously an effort by individuals who participated on the fringe of the Liberation War—or not at all—to seek inclusion. Corruption and political manipulation in the award of government jobs and benefits had become widespread by the mid-1990s.

As a result, the Chidyausiku Commission was established in 1997 to investigate alleged corruption in the management of the War Victims Compensation Fund, which, in theory, was intended to provide former Liberation War combatants with compensation if they had been injured. In practice, the administering of the fund had been "grossly inefficient and corrupt," with the fund soon "looted by the former fighters, primarily service chiefs, senior army commanders and civil servants."[21] Such individuals were able to falsely claim levels of disability of over 100% or more despite having no injuries. Doctors such as Chenjerai "Hitler" Hunzvi attested to the false claims in order to personally benefit. While the Chidyausiku Commission found numerous instances of corruption, most senior officials were never successfully prosecuted, and indeed Hunzvi became leader of the Zimbabwe National Liberation War Veterans Association in 1997, although he remained dogged by charges of embezzling funds.

This corruption enraged rank-and-file war veterans who felt cheated out of their benefits. Worsening the problem, the broadening of the term "war veteran" meant that more people received benefits, which then reduced the overall availability of benefits to those who had actually served in the war. The notion of wartime service was also watered down in the process, creating friction among those who had actually been armed fighters and took repeated risks during the war. Moreover, the involvement of the ZANU-PF elite in the siphoning of funds worked to alienate many war veterans from the party's proclaimed nationalist mission, heightening grievances with the party.

## Mobilized War Veterans: The Need to Reward Core Constituents

In the 1990s, there was growing dissatisfaction among many war veterans over the perception that relatively few had gained sufficient economic benefits under ZANU-PF rule for their Liberation War service. In order to reward some war veterans with civil servant positions—but particularly to try to mend political ties with the war veteran constituency—ZANU-PF increasingly promoted ZANLA war veterans and those with Liberation War credentials within the party and in the civil service.

War veterans increasingly enjoyed key positions in state institutions, particularly in the state security sector. According to Edison Bubye, a member of the Zimbabwe Republic Police, "The entire police hierarchy [during] my time in the 1990s was dominated by the freedom fighters.... From the top brass down, it is all ex-freedom fighters."[22] Ronald Jongwe was a member of the army and also reported large numbers of war veterans in the military: "They [war veterans] are all over the army and in the army right from the top, most of them. I think three-quarters of the army is them and even three-quarters of the police."[23]

The advantage of using patronage to reward war veterans was that it could potentially keep this influential constituency loyal and beholden to ZANU-PF. The disadvantage was that if these constituents became dissatisfied, ZANU-PF would face insurrection from within its own state security and government services. Jongwe emphasized this potential problem in saying that because war veterans populated the senior ranks of the military, and indeed large numbers of middle ranks as well, they exerted a tremendous potential threat if they decided to oppose Mugabe and ZANU-PF. The regime, therefore, had to "listen to these people."[24]

Bubye was even stronger in identifying the potential power war veterans had over Mugabe:

> Mugabe had so much fear of the war veterans because these were people who were fighters themselves who would say, "Right, we'll go back to the war and fight against you." . . . So Mugabe had so much fear of these people. These are the people who could make Mugabe shake. These were [the only people who could] challenge Mugabe.[25]

A second problem was that war veterans typically had a stronger allegiance to fellow veterans than to ZANU-PF, a claim also supported by Kriger, who noted ambivalence between many war veterans and the ruling party.[26] Thus, the government had to remain wary about their loyalties. Hastings Lundi, a senior CIO agent, gave an example of how the CIO, as with other branches of state security, operated as an "old-boys network," hiring and protecting fellow war veterans and in some cases their families.[27] In explaining how he was recruited, Lundi identified both the prevalence of war veterans in the state security forces and most importantly the active awareness of fellow war veterans and their historical Liberation War service. Speaking hypothetically, he stated:

> You are in because your father fought the war . . . or you are in because your daddy died some time back and then they want to look after you. . . . Most of the guys who are there, it's your war vet friends, or maybe my father fought the war, or my father probably is like a senior government guy, or my uncle he gets me in.

Regardless of whether war veterans were unemployed or held political positions or jobs in state security or the civil service, they were bound by their shared Liberation War ties, as Lundi demonstrates. Bubye elaborated on these ties: "What you should remember as well is that the war veterans, whatever their affiliations, is that they were just going as one, as 'war veterans.' They were the same people." Jongwe explained further: "What affects one who is in the police as a war veteran will affect one who is a war veteran in the army."[28] This bond was not simply social but manifested in political action, especially in seeking economic compensation for Liberation War service. As a result, this network, which occupied many key professional positions throughout the heart of the Zimbabwean government, was able to influence policy to support the interests of war veterans.

### GROWING POVERTY OF WAR VETERANS

Given both the important historical role of war veterans in combating the Rhodesian colonial government, their current employment in key offices throughout the government, and their active network binding fellow veterans from a multitude of professions together, Mugabe needed their active and loyal political support. The relationship between ZANU-PF and war veterans had never been entirely free from tensions and had gradually deteriorated as war veterans began demanding greater concessions from the government for their wartime service. These demands came about because many war veterans who were not employed in government were experiencing increasing economic hardship as the economy began to face a growing crisis. By 1997 war veterans had begun openly defying the ruling party and Mugabe in public—a taboo that had occurred only rarely since independence.[29] In one of the earliest and most infamous incidents, Mugabe was openly heckled and booed by war veterans at the symbolically significant Heroes Day celebration in August 1997. The flummoxed president was forced to cut his speech short, a deep humiliation inflicted by his erstwhile supporters in front of a national audience.

Discontent among increasingly impoverished war veterans was exacerbated in the 1990s by ZANU-PF's tendency to promote the historical and emotive land issue in an effort to enlist their political support. Over time this mobilization strategy had the unintended consequence of actually highlighting ZANU-PF's inability to deliver widespread land redistribution even after holding power continuously since 1980. It also starkly highlighted the ruling party's threadbare and ineffective policy platform. Christian Mucheke, legal officer in the President's Office, described growing discontent among war veterans: "[Mugabe] was not trusted by the war veterans. . . . They were not amused for two reasons. The first reason was we wanted land, and we still have no land. Two, we have no economical power. The strength is in the land."[30]

In 1997 Chenjerai "Hitler" Hunzvi rose from relative obscurity to lead the resurgent Zimbabwe National Liberation War Veterans Association (ZNLWVA), a major organization representing about 200,000 people.[31] The ZNLWVA

> represents war veterans of varied objective class origins, some employed and others not, some with key positions in the state, the security apparatus, and the private sector, some based in the countryside. . . . They tend to be identified mainly with the visible elite of bureaucrats, political leaders, and businessmen, but in fact the majority is part of the rural and urban poor.[32]

The breadth and varied membership of the ZNLWVA was to play a central role in later developments during the land seizure era, because it meant that group's leadership could influence individuals in a wide variety of critical government positions. When the ZNLWVA, under Hunzvi's leadership, began demanding—"with increasing ferocity"—pensions and land in 1997, with the land issue in particular "now couched in the more popular discourses of nationalism and liberation," Mugabe and ZANU-PF faced a problem of bifurcated loyalties from deep within the state power base.[33] As Kriger notes,

> In the 1990s the intense rivalries within ZANU PF over recognition for unpaid of [sic] national service had to do with ideas of justice but also competition for power, resources and dominance in national history. Political and military veterans competed with each other for recognition of their distinctive and allegedly superior contributions and denigrated the contributions of the rapacious leadership.[34]

Hunzvi was able to highlight the disparity between a minority of war veterans who had personally benefited by obtaining lucrative government positions, and the majority who remained poor. It was this ability to rouse sympathy by highlighting genuine inequities and by exposing ZANU-PF's failure to deliver on core nationalist ideals that allowed the war veterans, although relatively few in number, to mobilize broad rural support.[35] According to Stephen Chan in his 2003 biography on Mugabe, with the power of this mobilization behind him, Hunzvi felt empowered to take on the president, claiming that "Mugabe would be a traitor to them [war veterans] and their cause."[36] Sadomba stated that war veterans threatened to "disown" Mugabe as "patron of their association."[37] Such an attack struck at the core of Mugabe's and ZANU-PF's identity.

The strategy also served the war veteran leadership. By ratcheting up pressure on Mugabe, they could garner more support from their membership. Senior military intelligence agent Daniel Inkankezi said, "In fact the war veteran leadership at that time, all of them were supposed to be in court for one reason or the other, for one crime or the other because they had all embezzled monies."[38] Thus by focusing negative scrutiny on Mugabe and ZANU-PF, the war veteran leadership was able to deflect attention away from their own misdeeds while consolidating support among their membership.

Given the socialist ethos of the Liberation War, the fact that some war veterans faced far worse fates than others was a particular cause of anger. Hunzvi seized on these disparities among war veterans as a rallying call and used the ZNLWVA network to deeply undermine the validity of ZANU-PF rhetoric. While ZANU-PF was extolling the nationalist and socialist virtues of the war in its various political campaigns in the late 1990s, the veterans themselves were gradually rebelling against the government and using this same nationalist and socialist ideology to highlight their poverty far more authentically.[39] These war veterans posed a real threat to ZANU-PF, which was increasingly

seen as having betrayed the Liberation War ethos: "They [war veterans] threatened, 'We'll go back and fight. We'll fight. We'll go back and drive you [senior
ZANU-PF officials] out of your government. We're the people who put you
there [in power].'"[40]

In September 1997, the government capitulated. War veterans were each
paid an unbudgeted lump sum of ZWD$50,000 (US$2,778), plus monthly pension payments of ZWD$2,000 (US$111).[41] Kriger notes that many benefits were
"retroactively provided in statutory instruments promulgated in terms of the
War Veterans Act."[42] However, the motivation for the payments is contested.
Sadomba argues that the payment was for backdated unpaid demobilization.[43]
According to Hammar and Raftopoulos, however, it was the fear of "losing
their [war veteran] support or the prospect of a violent challenge from them"
that led Mugabe to concede to war veteran demands in the form of greater financial support from the government.[44]

There is no doubt that the government found itself compelled to make the
concessions to the war veterans. In doing so it had to find a valid historical
justification—the "unpaid demobilization"—in order to save face, but this was
merely window dressing. In having to make the payments, the government
then sought to achieve greater influence and strengthen ties with war veterans.
However, as subsequent chapters will show, this effort was only partially
successful.

The total number of recipients is unclear, but there were an estimated 50,780
veterans at the end of the Liberation War in 1980.[45] A very large number would
have still been alive in 1997 and eligible for the payout. Angus Selby notes that
"the gratuity alone exceeded total expenditure on land since Independence."[46]
The enormous payout led to the Zimbabwe dollar falling in value against the
US dollar by 71.5% on what became known as "Black Friday."[47] The veterans
were overjoyed, emboldened, and now committed to ZANU-PF through self-
interest. The problem, however, was that many war veterans quickly spent
their lump-sum allocations, and skyrocketing inflation rates rapidly diminished the purchasing power of the monthly allocations. Indeed, national inflation, ironically triggered in large part by the war veteran payments, reached
28.0% in 1997, 41.1% in 1998 and 64.4% in 1999.[48] Soon war veterans found
themselves again sinking deeper into poverty as the national economy
declined.

In November 1997 the government published a list of 1,471 farms to be com-
pulsorily purchased and redistributed. At the same time, Mugabe was becoming more aggressive, stating that mass appropriation of land would be
concluded by 1998. These steps were announced by the government in an
effort to quell the "shrill" land reform discourse occurring by late 1997.[49] Still,
few direct measures were taken to provide land to war veterans. Indeed, after

a delisting process and numerous legal challenges, about 640 of the 1,471 farms had been delisted by the government in 1998.[50]

War veterans' discontent was heightened by Zimbabwe's participation in the war in the Democratic Republic of Congo (DRC), beginning in 1998. The United Nations estimated the cost of deploying 10,000 troops was US$3 million per month.[51] According to Kriger, "In six months, the government spent more money on the DRC military venture than it had spent on land purchases since 1980."[52] Such vast spending on a foreign war raised questions about the government's priorities. Moreover, charges of corruption soon surrounded senior government officials, who allegedly benefited personally from access to minerals in the DRC.[53]

In this context, the poverty faced by war veterans became a key political issue toward the end of the 1990s. Petros Mzingwane, a war veteran, said that after facing extensive dangers during the war, veterans were demobilized with only a ZWD$300 lump sum and forced to return to rural areas to "live in that same hut, to see the colonizer still enjoying [privileges], and him [the war veteran] two, three, four, five, ten years later—he's seeing himself worse off than the time when he was in Mozambique or Zambia [in the war]."[54] He elaborated:

> The ex-combatant is married. He has children. Some of the children are not going to school. His wife is not properly dressed. His mother is sick. Some of his relatives are dying of AIDS or other diseases, and you can see that this person is starving. This person is undernourished.

Mzingwane stated that war veterans were left "waiting for land, sitting in town rotting, building anger." These feelings of betrayal by a nationalist government that had promised to improve their lives in return for their wartime service made war veterans ripe for rebellion. Mzingwane framed the crisis this way:

> He's [war veteran] a soldier without a gun. . . . And this is a person who has been very patient for many years and you [the government] don't answer his grievance and he [war veteran] is repeatedly telling you, "Can you solve this problem [of poverty]?"[55]

Mzingwane emphasized that when it came to land, the war veteran grievances were not so much fundamentally opposed to white farmers on racial grounds (although there is no doubt many war veterans resented the perceived privileges of this group) as targeted at the government for failing to live up to promises of greater equality made during the Liberation War and after independence.

These complaints were hard to ignore and even harder to dispute, and they quickly reached sympathetic ex-combatants employed in various government offices, and particularly in the state security sector. Denton Masumu, a political affairs officer in the Liberation War, explained that Mugabe was caught in a bind when soon after Black Friday in 1997 even "the army general [Solomon Mujuru] himself said to Mugabe, 'I am afraid you cannot send me to go and discipline the war veterans. No, I think their cause is right.'"[56] According to Lundi, it was in this way that Hunzvi exposed Mugabe's weaknesses by highlighting and fomenting war veteran discontent that undermined the government from within.[57]

Mugabe had few options. Bubye explained:

Mugabe at that time was having problems with these people [war veterans] because having given the money [in the 1997 payouts], which was not enough, they went back and said, "Look here, we want something, you understand? We are not satisfied. We can't be living as destitute in this country. We've got no jobs. We've got no money." And Mugabe, having exhausted all his coffers, didn't know what to do with these people.[58]

With the economy deteriorating rapidly, Mugabe had few resources available to him to placate war veterans in the late 1990s. As Alex Siwaze, a politically moderate veteran of the Liberation War, pointed out, Mugabe had to then "pick the land [as] a political gimmick. He had not any other trump card to use in order to remain in power."[59] In this way the issue of farmland ownership became the key focal point of political dispute prior to the land seizure era.

### THE TIPPING POINT

War veterans believed that the wealth of farmers—starkly apparent by their relatively large, productive farms and equipment such as tractors and irrigation—was directly connected to their landownership, a perception that fostered growing bitterness as the economy weakened. The more the economy declined, the more the war veterans demanded tangible land assets that would hold value against the devaluing Zimbabwean dollar.[60]

These arguments resonated with other war veterans, and ZANU-PF politicians were quick to seize the issue and foment it further with promises to rectify wealth imbalances in exchange for political support.[61] By the late 1990s ZANU-PF's rhetoric on farm ownership focused on the "fairness" of land distribution. The productivity of the agriculture industry, the interests of the economy, and the legal property rights of farmers were rarely mentioned. For example, according to farm worker Richardson Banongwe, "These people [ZANU-PF] said the white farmers had taken the land during the armed struggle. And they said now it's our turn. We want our land. We fought for our land."[62] This simplification served to cast farmers as wrongdoers and to redirect war veteran discontent away from ZANU-PF.

Thompson Mupfure, a veteran of the Liberation War and senior politician, explained that Mugabe was adept at identifying concerns and then fomenting them to his political advantage.[63] In Mupfure's view,

> You always have anxiety amongst the lower classes, the people who see rich people with everything. I mean they have good houses, good cars, children go to the good schools, they have property—the property class, and I'm not talking about race here. I'm still talking about class distinctions here, that the lower classes are always envious. They envy, and that you can't stop.

According to Mupfure, Mugabe understood this feeling with poorer war veterans and found an opportunity to "incite" them over the land issue. By instilling in war veterans a sense of being deprived of land, Mugabe was in effect encouraging radical demands that ZANU-PF would then move to satisfy, thereby cementing the ties between the ruling party and their key constituents.

This strategy rapidly escalated tensions between the ruling party and commercial farmers. Sam Moyo claimed that "ZANU (PF) leaders were calling for a speedy reclamation of land from the 'whites.'"[64] Ketani Makabusi, a farm manager, stated that after independence in the early 1980s there was a prevailing attitude of "Let's move forward. There wasn't really . . . animosity from black guys towards white guys. Let's all get on with our business, but there was an acknowledgment that something has to be done about the redistribution of land, but let's work up something amicably."[65] Makabusi said that both he and his extended family lived in rural areas, and they did not believe that land demands were as widespread or strong in the 1990s as ZANU-PF's rhetoric at the time suggested. So while the land issue was recognized by blacks and whites, it remained one of many priorities. He added that even "a lot of commercial farmers themselves acknowledge something has to be done about this land issue." What changed the tone of the land issue, however, was both its intensifying politicization in the late 1990s as ZANU-PF increasingly highlighted the issue to placate war veteran demands and the growing media coverage of the land debate: "The media, the publicity, and how it took place—literally hatred was imparted into the people, I believe, by the media . . . by propaganda, but it was blown out of proportion."[66]

ZANU-PF's "propaganda" campaign occurred in the news media but also directly with members of the state security services. Agnes Sengwe, a member of the army, said that in the late 1990s the military officers widely promised "land for all by year 2000."[67] Bubye said that talk was also "hotting up" among the police about being given land.[68] Likewise, Samuel Limpopo, a police officer, remembered that "every speech of his [Mugabe's] was about land."[69] Limpopo believed that Mugabe's strategy was to avoid explicitly ordering war veterans to seize land, but to intensify expectations that land redistribution would occur. He could then stoke outrage that hidden political forces, in the form of the political opposition, were denying war veterans their just benefits.

Meanwhile, squatting on farms—the practice of temporarily occupying land without formal claims—which had occurred at various times since independence, was becoming somewhat more common in the late 1990s, with about 30 farms occupied in 1997.[70] At this stage, prior to 2000, squatting still tended to occur only occasionally, was driven by efforts to reclaim "ancestral" homelands and was uncoordinated, and occupations were not generally coercive or political in nature.[71] Most important of all, while the government would sometimes support demonstrations on farms prior to 2000, the government still actively protected farmers' property rights, and the police or other government officials would soon remove any squatters. Hammar, who studied land-squatting disputes in late 1997 near Gokwe in northeast Zimbabwe, recounts one instance where newly arrived settlers were given disputed lands, only to later be evicted by the rural district councils.[72] This was far removed from the large-scale farm seizures that were to come.

### Emergence of the MDC

Facing this growing crisis from angry war veterans in 1999, the government proposed several changes to the constitution. These were largely intended to entrench ZANU-PF's power and to allow the government to seize farmland without compensation.

To assess levels of support for noncompensatory farm takeovers among black rural farmers, ZANU-PF's largest constituency, Lundi was tasked with going to "literally every village" in one province over a four- to five-month period to seek the views of the rural black population.[73] He emphasized that the study was a genuine effort by the government to understand the viewpoints of rural villagers: "I think they really went out to genuinely find out what people were thinking." Far from supporting land redistribution, Lundi found, most villagers instead were demanding improvements to the economy. In one Mashonaland province, Lundi heard "nothing about compulsory acquisition of farms."[74] When asked about compulsory land redistribution, some villagers said that they "want our [white farmer] neighbor to remain there because he is helping us a lot." Lundi commented that "not all people really spoke in terms of 'grab the farms, I want to be a farmer.' The people were saying,

'I don't want to be a farmer. . . . I'd rather go and work in town.'" He noted that there was no "overriding theme in terms of landownership or seizing commercial farms." According to Lundi, villagers stated that they wanted greater employment opportunities in general, not the seizure of commercial farms. Bubye, a member of the Zimbabwe Republic Police, made similar claims: "Zimbabwean people, what they're after, is they're after employment, housing, AIDS drugs. . . . A better economy, that's what Zimbabweans are after. The ordinary Zimbabwean people, and not everyone wants a piece of land."[75]

Lundi elaborated on the relationships that in some cases existed between commercial and communal farmers:

> I think some farmers had very good relations with their neighbors in the countryside. Actually some of them actually fought on behalf of the farmers to say, "Don't go there [and seize the farm.] He's our mate. He helps us. He gives us his tractors to plow our fields. We go to him for extension services."[a]

Lundi explained that in some areas, rural farmers had no intention of taking over commercial farms: "You will find sometimes maybe unholy alliances between white farmers and communal farmers who was [sic] supposedly the land-hungry guys who were supposed to invade the arrested white farmer's land." While Lundi's statement would not hold for all rural communities, they certainly raise doubts about ZANU-PF's professed belief that rural small-scale farmers were clamoring to dispossess commercial farmers. Lundi's testimony also supports claims made by many farmers interviewed for this book, who believed they had relatively good relationships with local community members. For example, an anonymous farmer survey respondent stated, "I and my father had a history of helping local township people with land tillage."

Compagnon reached similar conclusions, noting that in one study conducted in 1995 and endorsed by the Zimbabwean government, only 2% of communal area peasants wanted land. They instead sought help from existing farming schemes and access to formal employment.[76]

---

a. Lundi's unique access to senior officials and personal involvement in many events during the land seizure era provide key insights in this research. Given that Lundi references specific conversations, some of his accounts cannot be directly corroborated. However, his specific claims are evaluated against the entire testimony provided in his interview. As with all respondents, Lundi's interview was assessed for veracity against the 110 other interviews conducted for this book. There is no evidence to suggest that his account was untruthful or exaggerated. Moreover, his claims fit logically with other testimony, particularly by other state security officials and senior ZANU-PF officials. They also fit a chain of causality supported by the body of evidence gathered for this research and by substantial existing literature. See appendix A for an expanded discussion of data collection.

These findings worsened the government's predicament. In the first place, ZANU-PF had continually used the purported widespread demand for land as a key component of its political platform.[77] Evidence from their own investigators that the demand was much weaker than publicly claimed highlighted the extent to which the party's political message had lost relevance for large sectors of the population. It also meant that if the government did want to seize land without compensation in order to placate the war veterans, there was not going to be as much public support as had previously been presumed. Lundi recounted heated debates in meetings to discuss changes to the constitution.[78] He reported that when Patrick Chinamasa, who became minister of justice after the land seizure era began, stated that the public wanted compulsory acquisition of farms, there was an "uproar" from attendees. Despite this opposition, and despite the fact that ZANU-PF's own fact-finding mission to rural, noncommercial farming areas had found that there was not a widespread demand for land, the compulsory acquisition clause was included in the referendum anyway:

> The government then . . . possibly misrepresented people's views in terms [of compulsory acquisition]. . . . They [ordinary Zimbabwean people] didn't really want the compulsory acquisition of farms. It was only four [of 10] provinces that wanted the compulsory acquisition of farms. But then that clause was inserted in the constitution, which was then put to the referendum.[79]

These revelations oppose the assertions of Alexander and McGregor, who state that "ZANU-PF was right in identifying a widespread desire for more land in the communal areas."[80] McGregor noted that ZANU-PF exploited "popular grievances over land."[81] Sam Moyo also identified a widespread demand for land in communal areas.[82] While there is no doubt that land was needed and demanded by the rural population in some areas, Lundi's, Bubye's, and Compagnon's evidence suggests that the demand for land may have been less widespread than these accounts claim, and may have in fact been largely confined to a vocal and self-interested war veteran subsector and a smaller population in communal areas.

While these debates were continuing, a powerful political opposition group had emerged. Morgan Tsvangirai had been the president of the National Constitutional Assembly (NCA), an organization formed to promote inclusiveness and accountability in constitution-building. In this role, he "built on mounting popular criticism of the government—of the state of the economy, the effects of structural adjustment and corruption."[83] In September 1999, Tsvangirai founded the Movement for Democratic Change (MDC). Lundi explained that "all the political parties in the past, they flopped because there was no money for them."[84] The MDC was different. ZANU-PF "underestimated the MDC," according to Lundi, and especially its financial resources, which government supporters claimed came from Sweden, the British Department for International Development (DFID), and US Agency for International Development (USAID), among other sources.[85] Mugabe framed this alleged financial support as an effort by the "international community" to induce "regime change" in favor of the MDC.[86]

Since the MDC opposed compulsory farm seizure without compensation, commercial farmers were another source of financial support for the new party.[87] Jabulani Sibanda, ZANU-PF provincial chairman, war veteran, and leader of ZNLWVA, stated that ties between the MDC and farmers were well known:

> It became obvious at that particular time [in early 2000] that our white community—our white Zimbabweans—had grouped on the side of MDC more than any other political party. . . . It became obvious that now the MDC, it's a white-sponsored political party. And automatically this compelled most the of War Veteran's Association to resist it, regardless of some things they [MDC] could have said that were good. But it was opposed.[88]

Battle lines were now being drawn. The MDC and their urban, farm worker, and farmer supporters were on one side, and ZANU-PF, with war veteran and rural supporters, was on the other. ZANU-PF framed the confrontation militaristically, conjuring images of the liberation struggle to appeal to war veterans.[89] Loyalties were also defined racially, with "urban and educated middle-class blacks criticized [by ZANU-PF] for behaving 'like whites' and 'forgetting where they came from,'" while rural areas, where ZANU-PF held extensive support, were framed as the moral heartland of the nationalist cause.[90] In contrast, the MDC supported purchasing commercial farms for redistribution on the open market.[91] This approach resonated with voters, such as farmers and farm workers whose livelihoods would be preserved, and with urbanites that benefited from a stable economy and were less likely to be seeking rural land.

To counter the growing MDC threat, Mugabe claimed that the opposition was "led by whites" and by the British government.[92] This claim of British financial support for the opposition has been confirmed by several intelligence sources consulted in research for this book, but details of the involvement have not been made clear.[93] Mugabe stated, "We are aware that the British Government are working closely with the opposition MDC and other hostile so-called civil groups to trigger urban unrest, in the hope that a ZANU (PF) Government will capitulate or fall in violent circumstances."[94] This claim of British involvement in Zimbabwe's internal affairs was reiterated by ZNLWVA leader

Jabulani Sibanda, who stated that "once it is a government that is sponsoring a party in our country, we will feel that when that party comes into place, it will be a puppet government. We would rather have our own government that is failing until we get a government that will represent our people."[95]

Mugabe also linked the MDC with white farmers in order to further conflate the MDC with the colonial era.[96] Sam Moyo, who sought to justify the seizure of white farms, implies that white farmers provided strong financial support to the MDC.[97] After independence but prior to the land seizure era, the political participation of white farmers had been negligible. However, when ZANU-PF began to promise the seizure of farms without compensation in 1998, farmers' land rights were threatened more fundamentally than at any point since independence. This galvanized some farmers into political action. With the MDC, farmers found a party that was neither hostile to their land rights, nor prejudiced against their racial group, and thus a mutual alliance was formed.

To further undermine the MDC threat and shore up support from their core war veteran constituency—especially war veterans in the security services—ZANU-PF disseminated rumors that, by resisting large-scale land redistribution, the MDC and its white farmer allies were targeting war veteran financial interests. Ronald Jongwe, a member of the army, described how in early 2000 news spread through the military that war veteran pensions would be stopped if the MDC gained power: "He [Tsvangirai] will stop everything," soldiers were told by ZANU-PF representatives.[98] In response, "The war veterans [were] saying, 'No, we will not allow this thing. We are invading [the farms].'" Jongwe stated that "this came out in the [news] paper that this is what this opposition is planning. It is to chase away every soldier, every existing soldier, every existing police, and they are going to bring their own. So would you vote for, or would you let such a government in? And they [soldiers] said no, that would be foolish to. It was a big no." Moreover, Jongwe explained that "behind the scenes" Mugabe was telling war veterans and military officials, "You guys—don't sit on your laurels [of victory in the Liberation War]. You must get up. The opposition is coming—strong." By propagating fears that an MDC takeover would result in war veterans losing their pensions and their hopes of future land grants, ZANU-PF began realigning its interests with the powerful war veteran constituency.

### FARMER SUPPORT FOR THE MDC

Mugabe's efforts to undermine farmers by provoking outrage among war veterans over farmers' alleged connections with the MDC were not merely political posturing. Mugabe was genuinely angered by the connection between white farmers and the new MDC opposition party. In one incident television footage of an MDC political rally in Bindura (Mashonaland Central) was filmed and broadcast on state television. In this rally white farmers were infamously shown writing checks for the MDC. ZANU-PF seized upon these inflammatory images as evidence that farmers lacked gratitude to ZANU-PF for recognizing their landownership rights after the Liberation War. Indeed, this footage was identified numerous times during interviews of government agents, farm workers, and farmers conducted for this research as being a key moment in which white farmers' political rejection of ZANU-PF was made overtly public, bringing severe negative repercussions.[99] According to farmer George Harding it "infuriated the government," and the government "really bought a big stick down on us for that. I mean we paid. We paid a severe price for that."[100] Moreover, ZANU-PF used the images as evidence of a close political connection between white farmers and the MDC, thereby racializing the issue in order to discredit the MDC.

Tendi put it succinctly in saying that ZANU-PF "held the view that whites could not legitimately engage in politics."[101] Jabulani Sibanda, a war veteran, stated that for many war veterans, seeing whites clustering around an opposition party suspected of receiving British support "activated within the people the spirit of nationalism."[102] This led many to overlook ZANU-PF's failures in government and the dire state of the economy: "It was as if a greater enemy had come." Sibanda believed that, despite corruption in the ruling party, "at the end of the day people will defend that which is wrong if something worse is threatening." Inkankezi described farmer support of the MDC as "a huge, huge blunder they will live to regret. They made a huge blunder. They were pumping money to Tsvangirai like I don't know, writing checks and checks and checks. . . . Even if they were supporting MDC, there was a better way of doing it than start writing checks like that [and openly opposing ZANU-PF]."[103]

Farm worker respondents agreed that white farmers made a serious miscalculation by openly supporting the MDC.[104] Farm foreman Thomas Rackomechi commented, "What should have been done is that the white people should not have been seen on the forefront. They should have done this [give support] on [sic] a hidden way."[105] James Mwengi, another farm foreman, concurred that the problem came not so much from whites supporting the MDC, as from the public, financial nature of this support.[106] He said that "the friction came in between the whites and the blacks when Morgan [Tsvangirai] had a rally in Banket. . . . It was more white people issuing checks, issuing cash to Morgan." This public support attracted disproportionately high attention. The symbolic effect of even small numbers of white farmers confronting ZANU-PF and the war veterans helped to frame the political narrative.[107] ZANU-PF used the state media to emphasize the public financial support of farmers for the MDC and to suggest that this could lead to a return to colonial-era power structures. This had a rallying effect on the war veterans because, as Rackomechi put it, farmers should "leave the black people to their own politics. The minute they [MDC] got involved with the white people, that's when the problems started."[108]

John Nkomo, vice president of Zimbabwe, ZANU-PF national chairman, and Minister for Lands, Land Reform and Resettlement, stated that problems with land seizures began in 1999: "It was because, what I describe as greed, on the part of the farmers to feel that they could sponsor an alternative political party actually openly."[109] Nkomo added that it was an "affront" because since independence, ZANU-PF had "proceeded on the basis of a policy of reconciliation, and . . . over almost 20 years we had proceeded very cautiously, quietly . . . waited, negotiated" so as to preserve an amicable relationship with farmers, only to then have farmers actively support an opposition party when their interests were threatened. Nkomo said, "It was painful on the part of some of us who went to Lancaster House or were attending all those conferences, to come back with a constitution that was totally racist in that it had entrenched clauses protecting the rights of those we regarded as a minority, but also entrenching the representation of the minority in parliament," and then have this same minority back an opposition party.

Senior CIO agent Lundi stated that CIO officials had written "intelligence reports" about farmers in "every district" well before the February 2000 referendum, so the farmers' political affiliation was known to the government. Lundi stated that he used to go to rural country clubs where farmers congregated for social events on weekends to survey their attitudes.[110] Such a venue was ideal because country clubs were where farmers relaxed, enjoyed themselves, and socialized, an environment where CIO agents such as Lundi could easily gain a deeper understanding of their attitudes. As farmers consumed alcohol during social events, they would become more expressive about political issues while talking with each other. Similarly, Lundi reported that MDC leader Morgan Tsvangirai visited various country clubs where white farmers congregated. Lundi noted that while Tsvangirai had previously been a trade union secretary general seeking better working conditions and higher pay for workers, "suddenly he was now like a darling . . . this transformation." It was clear that white farmers were closely allied with the opposition.[111]

Evidence suggests that financial support from farmers to the MDC was substantial. Nkomo claimed that at an MDC rally in Gweru each farmer "was supposed to part with some ZWD$500,000 [approximately US$9,600] or whatever in support of the formation of the MDC."[112] By funding the party, the farmers hoped to gain sufficient political support to prevent their farms being seized.

It is important to also note that many farmers did not provide donations.[113] Felix Umchabezi, a veteran of the Liberation War, stated that "most" farmers did not support the opposition, "but those who supported the MDC were the most important financiers of that organization because they had the financial resources.... They were vital."[114]

Farmers' financial support for the opposition also directly conjured up connections, rivalries, and historic grievances associated with the nationalist struggle and the Liberation War for ZANU-PF politicians. Daniel Inkankezi, a senior official in military intelligence and veteran of the Liberation War, echoed these views.[115] He explained that acrimonious views toward the commercial farming community were already held by some senior ZANU-PF officials who believed that many farmers had helped bankroll Ian Smith's white minority government and the overall Rhodesian war effort during the 1970s Liberation War. Inkankezi stated, "Mugabe has said it clearly, 'I gave you hand of reconciliation. We did not even taken [sic] one of you to court for all the atrocities [allegedly committed by Rhodesian forces in the Liberation War] and everything you have done [during the war].'" Speaking from Mugabe's perspective, Inkankezi explained that after the war, Mugabe had said to farmers, in effect, "Let's live together."[116] Their open financial support of the opposition was a dismissal of Mugabe's and ZANU-PF's perceived tolerance and mercy after independence: "Now they are biting the hand that feeds them." Inkankezi added, "Of course, some ministers also felt offended because . . . they are the older generation. Not only that, 90% of all the ministers in ZANU [PF] have been jailed for political activities before [Zimbabwe's independence], so it's like reviving old wounds." Inkankezi emphasized that the financial support for the MDC provided by some farmers convinced many ZANU-PF officials that "they [farmers] are still the same people that they were yesterday [during the Rhodesian era]."

According to senior CIO operative Lundi, Mugabe was outraged by this open dissent by farmers, did a "somersault," and quickly changed his attitude about protecting farmers:[117]

So Mugabe then started coming around [in support of some land seizures as opposed to protecting farmer land interests as had been done since independence] and saying: "If you [farmers] are doing this [openly supporting the opposition], why don't you talk to me if you felt maybe the way things I didn't really do to your satisfaction? I didn't make this compulsory acquisition thing in 1992 to likely forcibly force you off your farms . . . so why are you suddenly spiting me."[118]

According to Lundi, Mugabe stated that he had a "legal instrument" to seize the farms, and that the government could have "resorted" to using legal powers to seize the farms in the past, but he had instead protected farmer interests. Christian Mucheke, a legal officer in the President's Office, concurred in saying that "when the commercial farmers had now shown their support of the opposition, it infuriated the president and the party."[119] Lundi explained: "In Mugabe's book it's now about betrayal. And I think maybe it's the way he rose to power. It's 'you [white farmers] don't have to challenge, stand up to me [by siding with the opposition]. I've had people standing up to me and then I've had to dispense of them.' So in a sense it was, 'Who are you [white farmers] in the scheme of things? We [ZANU-PF] can take over the farms [to demonstrate power].'"[120] Researchers such as Rutherford concur, stating: "The open embrace of the opposition by white farmers is seen by many in ZANU (PF) as a fundamental disloyalty, a renunciation of the gift of reconciliation given by Mugabe himself."[121]

Mugabe's apparent surprise and outrage at farmers' political mobilization may appear to be at odds with earlier evidence showing that ZANU-PF was ratcheting up pressure on farmers in order to appease the demands by some war veterans for land. What would Mugabe expect farmers to do? Historically ZANU-PF had used commercial farmers as a foil, and indeed numerous farmer respondents commented that they had routinely felt targeted by the ruling party since independence.[122] Tendi's explanation that in ZANU-PF's view whites could not legitimately engage in politics can be taken a step further: whites could be the target of ZANU-PF's rhetoric and policies, but they had no right to fight back politically; they especially had no right to publically confront the ruling party.[123] This was because of ZANU-PF's sufferance to them after independence and due to the unfair colonial legacy that still benefited this comparatively tiny percentage of the national population.

War veterans also tended to perceive white support of the opposition as an act of treachery after the government's postindependence efforts at reconciliation. For example, farm manager Ketani Makabusi said that one war veteran on the farm where he worked told him, "We extended the hand of reconciliation [to farmers] and now they are stabbing us in the back."[124] Thomas Rackomechi, a farm foreman, noted that "some of these poor people [war veterans] are the ones who saw a lot of war. . . . They still have that bush [wartime] thinking . . . [that] a white man is a bad man."[125] For them, whites openly asserting political rights was unacceptable, especially when, in the eyes of some war veterans, they should have been humbly and quietly accepting ZANU-PF leadership out of gratitude for being allowed to keep their farms after independence.

The belief that white farmers provided a bastion of support for the political opposition—and therefore represented a genuine threat to ZANU-PF—is only partially accurate. In fact, a survey undertaken for this book indicates that active farmer support for the MDC was less widespread and more ambivalent than many accounts imply.[126] When survey respondents were asked which party they *privately* supported, only 51.7% of farmers chose the MDC, whereas 47.6% classified themselves as neutral, and 0.7% supported ZANU-PF.[127]

Respondents in the farmer survey were also asked about their *public* political affiliation. Just 27.5% of farmers claimed to have publicly supported the MDC, with only 16.2% considering themselves "active opposition supporters." Interestingly, 3.5% of respondents claimed to publicly support ZANU-PF. The fact that more farmers supported ZANU-PF publically than privately suggests that some farmers adopted the strategy of seeking protection by masquerading as ZANU-PF supporters. However, the majority of farmers, 69.0%, stated they were *publicly neutral*.[128] The survey results indicate that many farmers privately supported the MDC but remained neutral in public to avoid the consequences of being seen to confront the government. However, the government did not trust farmers to remain neutral in private. Armed with intelligence reports suggesting that support for the opposition was widespread on white farms, ZANU-PF continued to suspect that "neutral" farmers were bankrolling the MDC and therefore posing a substantive threat to ruling party interests.

### ZANU-PF THREATENS FARMERS AND UNDERMINES THE MDC

In the face of the MDC threat, senior government officials conceived a plan to intimidate farmers into cutting off financial support for the opposition. In November 1999, limited farm invasions were carried out in Svosve, near Marondera, ostensibly by discontented villagers demanding land. In reality, the "invasion" was planned and undertaken by the CIO using Second Brigade soldiers, police officers from Marondera, and at least three war veterans.[129] Lundi explained that "it was never government policy to say we were going to [invade farms]," but staging invasions could be used to "scare them [farmers] to say we can do this [ZANU-PF can invade farms]" if they continued to financially support the MDC.[130] These "farm invasions" were undertaken with the direct agreement of Justice Minister Emmerson Mnangagwa and the support of senior CIO officials who "felt maybe we needed it after the whites came out to support the MDC. They [government officials] said we needed to . . . just put some pressure on them [farmers] so they can withdraw from their support of the MDC."[131] However, Lundi emphasized that the staged invasions were "meant to be controlled," again suggesting that there was no planning for larger-scale farm invasions, or indeed farm seizures. He explained: "We were just thinking we could intimidate them [farmers] because they came out in Chitungwiza for the launch of the MDC." At this stage, ZANU-PF only wanted to threaten farmers by creating temporary disruptions on farms.

Counterintuitively, Mugabe had not given his consent to this plan, and in fact, according to Lundi, "in the initial scheme of things [staged invasions], he [Mugabe] was not involved."[132] After the invasion, CIO officials were urgently summoned to Harare for a meeting with the president. "He [Mugabe] was angry, saying, 'What is happening there [at Svosve]? . . . We don't want that.'" According to Lundi, Mugabe was angry with the plan and strongly opposed it:

> He [Mugabe] didn't approve it. He didn't think it was a good idea, the [staged] invasions. He said obviously at the moment we are grappling with the fallout of that "Black Friday," when the dollar crashed after the war veterans' [payout]. Since then the economy was kind of teetering. . . . The dollar I think had [now] recovered slightly. . . . So [he] said he didn't want any more distractions, something which was going to jeopardize his chances of getting more money from the IMF to settle the economic recovery.[133]

Lundi stated that Mugabe thought the staged invasions would send the wrong message to international donors. "That was the argument he emphasized. Obviously, if we are going to have any resettlement, we still want to have them compliant [with the law]. . . . You can't just have people walking in and, you know, literally just disturbing production . . . in November. You know it is the peak season for growing crops."[134] At that stage Mugabe had genuine concern that unrest on commercial farms would damage the economy.

According to Lundi, Mugabe ordered the "invaders" off the farms, an easy task for the CIO to undertake since the "invaders" were ZANU-PF officials and members of the state security services anyway. In order to give coherence to the operation and maximize the political value of the situation for ZANU-PF, Lundi stated that they arranged for Vice President Muzenda to attend a hastily arranged "rally in Svosve." At this rally Muzenda called for the "invaders" to "move out of the farms" because the government wanted to handle the land issue "properly."[135]

Indeed, Cliffe et al. identified sporadic farm invasions that began in 1998, noting that they were "often reined in by the ZANU-PF government."[136] This response was frustrating for war veterans and provoked the ire of radicals. Sadomba argued that "the state reaction to the 1998 land occupations was draconian. The Zimbabwe Republic Police (ZRP), the Central Intelligence Organisation (CIO) and the white-dominated judiciary attacked the land revolutionary actors by torching their shelters, scattering them in nearby mountains and bushes and finally arresting and slamming them with all sorts of judicial punishments."[137]

Lundi's account gives a rare insider view of Mugabe's attitude toward farm invasions and the economy in the period before the land seizure era. Despite his rhetoric condemning farmers and supporting war veterans, Mugabe understood the financial consequences of uncontrolled farm invasions and sought to limit and control them. These accounts suggest that he was actually attempting to maintain order and convey stability to international donors in order to obtain funds, and was not seeking widespread, extralegal takeovers. This claim that, at this early stage (before the February 2000 referendum), Mugabe was not intending to seize farms is further substantiated by interviews with Peter Msasa, a military intelligence agent, and Edward Chidembo, a senior member of the Zimbabwe Republic Police, both of whom had insider knowledge of events.[138]

Mugabe's problem was that despite efforts to uphold financial stability and guarantee ZANU-PF's political longevity, he had fomented a nearly uncontrollable political situation with the war veterans. By fueling war veteran discontent over land, Mugabe opened the door to demands that ZANU-PF simply could not meet. Blaming white farmers and the international community for the inaction on land redistribution was efficacious when state security could restrain war veterans from unilaterally seizing land. However, after nearly two decades of the government "dragging their feet," according to Petros Mzingwane, and with state security now heavily populated with war veterans sympathetic to destitute ex-combatants, Mugabe was on the brink of losing control.[139]

Mzingwane explained:

> The war vets have started the fire [of active discontent]. The *povos* [poor people] have joined it. So the government got overwhelmed, but at the same time in the same government there are also the war vets who have got the same sentiments as the guys who are outside. . . . They have got the same grievance, although the one who is still employed is better off than this one who is not employed. So the one who is unemployed, he tells the other, he says, "Listen, you are putting on a suit and I am putting on tattered clothes. . . . That is my sweat, so either you join in or we start quarrelling. . . ." The government got overwhelmed. They were just enveloped by the situation.

The emergence of the MDC was the catalyst that tipped the volatile situation into active, immediate demands for land. The party's opposition to land redistribution meant that, if it defeated ZANU-PF in the constitutional referendum, war veterans would risk losing their opportunity for land.

## The Constitutional Referendum: February 2000

In an effort to gain greater powers, including the legal right to seize white-owned commercial farms without compensation to the farmer, the government held a referendum on February 12–13, 2000 to amend the constitution on. Yet when the votes were tallied, the sensational news filtered through that Zimbabweans had rejected the proposed changes by a margin of 54.7% to 45.3%. This effectively marked ZANU-PF's first election defeat since 1980— and this to a no campaign led by an opposition party formed only five months earlier.[140]

Tendi has described how the ZANU-PF saw the result as a "worrying victory for the MDC."[141] This was an understatement. Daniel Inkankezi, a senior official in military intelligence in the Zimbabwe National Army, stated that ZANU-PF "panicked" at the result.[142] Msasa said it was "a very, very, big shock. They didn't expect that."[143] The situation remained "tense," and some ZANU-PF leaders believed that the British had manipulated the referendum result.[144] Inkankezi explained that "they never thought that would happen . . . it was an embarrassment for them . . . they didn't take it lightly."[145] Stephen Chan stated that it was at this point that "ZANU-PF entered a period of paranoia."[146]

While rank-and-file ZANU-PF members, and probably some senior officials, were shocked by the referendum result, other high-ranking leaders had known in advance that an MDC victory was possible. According to senior CIO agent Hastings Lundi, in the week running up to the referendum intelligence officials had signaled the growing strength of the MDC.[147] It was for this reason that ZANU-PF had ramped up its campaigning.

Given ZANU-PF's long hold on power, the referendum defeat not only confirmed the existence of a viable political threat to the ruling party, but also represented a considerable rebuff to its political agenda. Mugabe had expended extensive political capital on the referendum and had been defeated by a very newly formed party. Thoughts swiftly turned to the upcoming parliamentary polls, and according to Lundi "There was a real sense of trepidation that they [ZANU-PF] were going to lose the [parliamentary] election."[148] If ZANU-PF lost the parliamentary election in June 2000, senior members would be ousted and could face prosecution for crimes committed since independence, particularly during *Gukurahundi* in the 1980s. According to Limpopo, ZANU-PF leaders "killed a lot of people from the south—Matabeleland," and as a result,

> They were afraid if they would . . . lose. Losing the election [in June 2000], I think they would all be in prison now, so they didn't want that to happen, because those people they've got a lot to answer, which is why they don't want to leave. They want to die there [in positions of power] so that they won't be charged.[149]

Steven Sebungwe, a senior army officer, named senior leaders such as Mugabe, Perence Shiri (commander of the Air Force of Zimbabwe), Constantine Chiwenga (commander of the Zimbabwe National Army), and Paradzai Zimondi (head of the Zimbabwe Prison Service) as individuals with notorious back-grounds in *Gukurahundi* who had reason to fear prosecution.[150] Sebungwe stated that these individuals "closed ranks," since each one feared that "once Mugabe leaves power [i.e., in the 2002 presidential election], there is a chance he might be arrested, and he is very much fearful of that."

ZANU-PF had operated in a manner where criminal activity was an accept-able way for individuals and the party to achieve their personal and political goals. Sebungwe stated that "if you are near the president, you can do anything in the country. Break the law. Do anything. You are never arrested."[151] This meant that senior officials were bound together by the awareness of each oth-er's criminal activities, so senior officials only had something to lose and could face prosecution if they failed to comply with the party's political objectives: "Everyone in the ZANU-PF government is guilty. They all have their own cases to answer to. So how it works is that once you step outside the line, then they will say, '[Police] Commissioner Chihuri, open that docket and then you will be arrested.'"[152] This system had its own internal logic but rested upon the ZANU-PF leadership controlling the state security apparatus to determine party policy and enforce compliance. With the prospect of Mugabe and ZANU-PF losing power, senior members of the party risked being held to ac-count for their criminality.

The prospect of prosecution was a critical consideration for the party lead-ership. Senior officials were particularly vulnerable to prosecution because, unlike Mugabe who received immunity as head of state, they could be charged in both domestic and foreign courts.[153] A cable from the US Embassy in Harare, sent in September 2000, stated: "Senior ZANU-PF leaders greatly feared losing power, as they had done much worse things than most observers suspected, and were not willing to spend time in prison."[154] The cable suggested that an offer of "complete amnesty" for ZANU-PF officials and the MDC agreeing to drop its demands for a "Truth and Reconciliation committee" would be neces-sary to avoid further bloodshed and bring about a mediated solution. The MDC even began floating a deal to offer a preemptive amnesty to senior ZANU-PF military leaders in the belief that this would help to prevent vio-lence in the run-up to the June 2000 elections.[155] The September 2000 leaked cable revealed that retired general Solomon Mujuru—former commander of the army and a highly respected nationalist figure—was seeking to pursue an amnesty deal and sent an emissary to negotiate with the MDC, reportedly without Mugabe's knowledge: "Mujuru urged the MDC to agree to a complete amnesty for current and past GOZ [government of Zimbabwe] officials and ZANU-PF leaders."[156] In the cable a US government official added: "Mujuru's offer could be a sign of increasing desperation among ZANU-PF stalwarts, who see their loss of power as inevitable and want to ensure their immunity from prosecution for past misdeeds."[157] With its senior leaders fundamentally threatened by the prospect of the MDC eventually taking power, ZANU-PF decided that the best strategy was to strengthen and consolidate a one-party state, with Mugabe as president for life.[158]

Soon after the referendum result, Mugabe made a conciliatory speech where he vowed to respect the will of the voters.[159] In private, however, he realized the scope of the disaster and the scale of the personal rebuff dealt to him. Mugabe was in a vulnerable position, having expended enormous personal and political capital over the land issue and the new constitution, only to be dealt an electoral defeat by a new opposition party. Lundi reported that soon after Mugabe's conciliatory speech, he "went into hiding. . . . He just retreated away from the scene until when the damage was done and until they lost [the referendum] and things imploded." At this point senior ZANU-PF officials said, "'Okay, we'll rig the elections because we will lose this if the MDC comes into power.'"[160] However, while senior officials were rapidly planning measures to safeguard their interests, Mugabe apparently had other plans. Lundi said that Mugabe "really thought he was going to lose power, and in his book I think he was prepared to go [to leave power]. . . . He was really sort of [saying], 'They're [MDC] going to win again in June.' So in his book, it was, 'If I play it the right way [have a legitimate, nonrigged election], I'll lose.'"

Lundi was clear in his testimony that Mugabe was ready to "concede defeat." However, other senior ZANU-PF officials did not want Mugabe to be voted out or to leave office voluntarily: "There were some others in ZANU-PF who said, 'You aren't going anywhere. If you go, then I will have to answer for the things that you did, that I did in your name.'" These "four or five men" who were insisting that Mugabe remain in office felt, according to Lundi, that "if this guy [Mugabe] goes, I did some very terrible things in his name. . . . He was sending me [to do these illegal acts], so why should you [Mugabe] cut a deal and walk away and then I'm the one who was going to suffer?" Lundi also insisted that Mugabe wanted to retire, but senior ZANU-PF officials were saying to him, "You can't go, you die in that chair [in office]."

As a result, Mugabe's power declined after the referendum loss. Beginning within the internal power structures of ZANU-PF, the once all-powerful Mugabe began to lose authority to the most senior ZANU-PF officials, particularly those heading the state security services. This loss of control occurred gradually and was not necessarily obvious to the public. However, according to the testimony presented in this chapter, there is little doubt that ZANU-PF's humiliating defeat in the February 2000 referendum dealt a severe blow to Mugabe's standing within his party. Senior officials began to consolidate their own power, even to the point of exerting a strong, and according to Lundi, controlling influence over Mugabe.

The great threat to ZANU-PF "ignited a series of political interventions by the ruling party."[161] The first objective was to suppress the MDC, and the second was to seize farms for redistribution to appease the war veterans. Sadomba notes that "the state, as an actor, intensified occupations and targeted critical white commercial farmers to break the backbone of the MDC."[162] ZANU-PF believed that white farmers' support for the MDC was a key reason for the defeat in the referendum. It was also convinced that the influence of white farmers was crucial in persuading farm workers to defect to the MDC.[163] Ketani Makabusi, a farm manager, explained that when the referendum results were announced, there was "a very big change" in ZANU-PF's behavior: "The general remark was you [workers] have let us [ZANU-PF] down."[164] Mwengi described ZANU-PF's rationale for wanting to attack the farmers so as to undermine the support of the workers for the MDC: "They [ZANU-PF] wanted to . . . destroy the farms because the workers are the ones who will start to see, 'Ah this is good [promised MDC reforms], this is not good [ZANU-PF status-quo].'"[165] According to farm foreman Richard Chipembere, "They [ZANU-PF] wanted to actually crush down on the farming community so that we did not vote for the opposition. . . . They [ZANU-PF] feared that if they didn't actually kill workers and so forth, they were actually going to vote definitely for the opposition and make the opposition win. That was the main reason [for targeting workers]."[166]

Cliffe et al. arrived at similar findings: "Giving the go-ahead to farm occupations and to the use of violence in acquiring land in 2000 was probably seen by ZANU-PF as a means of mobilising rural support and punishing its political foes, the white farmers, 'their' workers and other supporters of the MDC."[167] Rutherford noted that the alliance between farmers and workers was immediately targeted by the state:

> When it was defeated [in the February 2000 referendum], the ZANU (PF) spokespeople and the state media began to blame "the whites," although they comprise less than one percent of the national population. But it was not only their votes for which they were criticized, but also along the lines of their interior frontier. White farmers were singled out for putatively forcing their employees to vote "no" against their wishes. Indeed, the first farm invasions that occurred a few days after the defeat of the constitution were declared to be punishments of white farmers for voting "no."[168]

ZANU-PF also believed internal disputes between war veterans and the ZANU-PF leadership had cost the party support, and contributed to the referendum defeat. Lundi stated that "when he [Mugabe] lost the elections [the February 2000 referendum], the war vets were then saying, 'You lost without our support. You need our support to win the coming elections.'"[169] Msasa, who worked in military intelligence, concurred, saying that after the emergence of the MDC and the referendum defeat, ZANU-PF realized it could not defend its position without the war veterans alongside.[170] The motivation behind the first farm seizures, therefore, was to bind ZANU-PF and the war veterans in an alliance that would seize land and suppress the MDC.

War veterans realized that their hopes of taking land were now fundamentally threatened because the MDC opposed land seizures. Nicholas Panhane, a war veteran and provincial leader for ZANU-PF, stated that "when we [war veterans] went to war, we are not fighting for these people [senior ZANU-PF leaders]. We're not fighting for them. We are fighting for the majority."[171] With the MDC referendum victory, "We realized that, now the MDC is come, we realized now the land is going, ZANU-PF is going, and once ZANU-PF is gone, we are no longer going to talk about the land." For Panhane and the war veterans he represented, the situation was simple. War veterans had fought for land during the Liberation War, and with the MDC emerging as a likely victor in the June 2000 parliamentary election, that key objective was slipping away. The result was a return to Liberation War–style militancy: "Those people [war veterans] have the history of the war. And we said, 'No, no, no . . . there is an issue [land redistribution] that has not been addressed. [The] MDC cannot come into power unless that issue has been addressed. Let's go back to it . . . let's get into the land.' We forcibly got ourselves into the land and Mugabe supported us."[172]

Meanwhile, the government's increasingly militant rhetoric was further polarizing the political environment. To cement the party's support among war veterans, Zimbabweans were divided into two fundamentally opposed categories. War veterans and ZANU-PF supporters were of course defined as "patriots." By contrast, the "sell-out" opposition—which came to include anyone who disagreed with the ZANU-PF government—was, according to Anne Hellum and Bill Derman, classed as "Rhodesians," "black collaborators," and British sympathizers.[173]

Indeed, this valorizing of ZANU-PF's mission began in earnest and soon became a well-honed message. By 2001, Mugabe was framing ZANU-PF's objectives in noble and militarized language: "All of us know only too well, our Party is under unrelenting attack. Our crime is that we have dared to begin correcting the land imbalances that affected our people for too long, this in the face of the heavy odds stacked against us. Because of this principled stand on our land."[174] He had also increasingly stoked racial tensions against the white farming community, tying their interests indelibly to the MDC in order to present a clearly defined threat for the war veteran-ZANU-PF alliance to counter.

The land question became the central issue in Zimbabwean politics after the referendum, because it was the only issue that ZANU-PF could use to rally support and cling to power. Thompson Mupfure, a veteran of the Liberation War and senior politician, explained that Jonathan Moyo, who became minister of information, was told by an international advisor to "identify an emotive issue and an issue which is close to the hearts of the people."[175] This issue would then serve as a rallying point for popular discontent, and serve to justify drastic—and illegal—methods of solving the problem. The issue selected by ZANU-PF was of course land.

Insofar as ZANU-PF's ties to war veterans were concerned, the reliance on the issue was obvious. According to Sadomba:

> Tactically, he [Mugabe] decided to "hijack" the land movement in a bid to use its cultural capital against the MDC and particularly against white commercial farmers. He started to work towards what many thought was a genuine alliance with the land movement, particularly the war veterans who led it, from around February 2000.[176]

Msasa summed up ZANU-PF's evolving thinking from his perspective in military intelligence.[177] He explained that the "MDC was becoming too hot for them." The ruling party knew it was losing the support of the war veterans, in terms of both their voting power and their willingness to suppress opposition political parties: "The slogan during the war, it was 'fighting for the soil.' . . . So they [ZANU-PF] realized, 'We didn't give these people [war veterans] land. So now MDC is here, so now it is taking our people [supporters].'" Msasa said that the obvious solution for ZANU-PF was to hand out land in order to demonstrate to war veterans that the ruling party was once again attuned to their demands: "Let's invade a few farms and allocate some to the people [war veterans] there so that they will realize it and say, 'Oh, that land, so now things are changing [i.e., ZANU-PF is allocating land after all].'"

According to Kriger, "From 2000 the ruling party legitimated treating privately owned land as if it were a public resource to which patriots were entitled, because land had been the objective of the liberation war."[178] Land was also a readily available and plentiful resource that could be seized and redistributed to entrench ZANU-PF's power. Mupfure explains: "They put their finger on a sensitive issue that then presented itself in the realm of the national liberation mold, to say that this is what we fought for—land is all that we fought for."[179]

It is important to remember that legislation already existed to allow the government to undertake land reform. However, the 1992 Land Acquisition Act did not provide for uncompensated seizures and did not permit war veterans to seize land without going through a legal process. The legislation was therefore useless to the government. ZANU-PF needed to take decisive action. The party had no real interest in making a genuine effort for land reform, but rather needed to exploit the issue to earn much-needed political capital.

The government could no longer rely on legal avenues to preserve its position, and instead resorted to intense political violence to suppress MDC support and gain access to some farms. The September 2000 cable from the US Embassy in Harare establishes how violence was of direct utility for ZANU-PF when confronted with political opposition.[180] In 2000 an emissary from General Solomon Mujuru "informed the MDC of the GOZ's [government of Zimbabwe's] intention to provoke violent confrontations nationwide as a pretext for cracking down on the opposition party and its supporters." The cable further stated that "160 Central Intelligence Organization (CIO) operatives had already been sent to key points throughout the country to carry out this plan. When people poured into the streets in protest, the army would shoot whomever it had to shoot."

The existence of such a plan is supported by Mupfure:

ZANU-PF, you know, continued to bombard them with propaganda that this opposition that has emerged is in fact sponsored by the same people who had taken your land away. So if you do not crush this opposition? Intimidate them, beat them up, kill them, you stand to lose the very thing that you fought for, and that is why a lot of my comrades then just went wild, went out on the killing sprees you know, killing people, killing stock, killing horses, killing dogs, killing cats, burning houses, occupying houses, and so forth. I mean the carnage.[181]

Similarly, Tendi argues that ZANU-PF's behavior underwent a drastic change after the referendum. He explains that ZANU-PF's prereferendum politicking "was an immediate forerunner to the unprecedented intolerance and exclusion characteristic of Patriotic [ZANU-PF] History after the February 2000 referendum."[182] Threats of violence had become a reality, and the land seizure era had begun.

## CONCLUSION

ZANU-PF found itself facing a rebellion from its core war veteran constituents in the late 1990s, and as a result, the party began making ever greater promises about land redistribution to appease this group. These promises were especially appealing to war veterans as the economy began to decline, since land was an asset that held its value and provided opportunities for war veterans to grow food and build homes.

While Mugabe and some senior ZANU-PF officials were offering political bait to war veterans by promising farm takeovers, the evidence shows that they were very much aware of the importance of the agricultural industry to the nation's economy and were cautious about disrupting it. Mugabe also feared negative repercussions from the international donor community. This is not to suggest that Mugabe had any loyalty to farmers politically or personally. However, there is no evidence that he intended universal, extralegal seizure of farms prior to the February 2000 referendum. In fact, Mugabe initially appears to have tried to protect farmers, such as by opposing initial demonstration on farms in November 1999. Mugabe's awareness of the importance of the commercial farming sector is one likely explanation why more extensive land reform had not taken place in Zimbabwe after independence. Only when ZANU-PF suffered a shock defeat in February 2000 was authorization given to move onto commercial farms.

This chapter also calls into question the assumption held by various authors that there was a widespread desire for land redistribution.[183] In fact, ZANU-PF's own internal assessment revealed that gaining access to land was a low priority for most rural voters. While some war veterans certainly did demand land, and many of these individuals were vocal and well connected, many others did not. Only when the government ceased to enforce property rights did demand for land and agri-property increase.

Meanwhile, despite ZANU-PF's claims to the contrary, most white farmers were aware of the negative consequences of opposing the ruling party and did not publicly support the MDC in large numbers.[184] This conclusion is somewhat unexpected, given that ZANU-PF had historically scapegoated commercial farmers, and that the MDC's platform largely favored the interests of farmers. However, the relatively small number of farmers who did publicly support the MDC was sufficient to allow the ruling party to frame all farmers as traitors who were intent on retaining the colonial privilege of landownership. Moreover, the private financial support by farmers of the MDC also resulted in substantial funding for the opposition even if this support was not manifested publicly. This finding further demonstrates that ZANU-PF did not consider white farmers to be legitimate political actors. Their involvement in politics, however small, allowed the government to radicalize war veterans and delegitimize farmers' political and property rights.

By focusing almost exclusively on the land debate, the government could deflect attention away from a raft of domestic problems, including the collapsing economy. The focus on land enabled ZANU-PF to make the farm seizures a nationalist issue and invoke the legacy of the Liberation War; the party was then able to portray violence against whites and political opponents as not only justified, but valid. Invoking the Liberation War also meant that the rule of law could be bypassed. The farm invasions were given a militaristic title—the "Third Chimurenga" war—as ZANU-PF moved the country to a quasi-war footing, where extraordinary measures could be justified. Supporters of Mugabe would present the "Third Chimurenga" as a mission for state survival and a struggle against colonialism. The reality was that the land seizures were undertaken as a quest for political survival, which masqueraded as a war against a colonialism that was already long dead.

Although ZANU-PF had now decided that its route to survival lay through conflict with commercial farmers, much was still uncertain about the form that the land seizures would take. The next chapter shows that the pace of take-overs would rapidly surpass the government's original intentions, forcing the ruling party to grope desperately in search of an overarching land policy that would allow it to regain the initiative.

# Mugabe Targets Agriculture

*Land Reform or Political Gimmick?*

After its defeat in the February 2000 referendum, ZANU-PF turned to farm seizures as a means of consolidating its support among war veterans against the threat of the MDC.[1] Existing literature provides almost no insight, however, into the specific events and mechanisms of *how* large-scale takeovers began after the referendum result. This has led to two widely held misconceptions. There are those who believe that the farm seizures were always intended as a means of redistributing land in order to address inequality in ownership. There are also some individuals who believe that the government had planned the farm seizures from the outset and was always in control of the takeovers.

This chapter sheds light on why the government targeted the agricultural industry, despite Mugabe and ZANU-PF recognizing the importance of agriculture to the economic fortunes of the country. It explains the government's basic objectives in the immediate aftermath of the referendum result, how the government responded to the political pressures and challenges it faced at the time, and how the land occupations spiraled out of control. Ultimately, this chapter challenges the fundamental misunderstandings about the crucial first stages of the land seizure era.

Early events in the farm seizure era unfolded rapidly, and the discussion in this chapter traces these first few months. See appendix C for a detailed flowchart of key events.

1. **November 1999**: Demonstrations on farms by purported war veterans continue. These are sanctioned by the government but are limited in scope and are intended to be a short-term measure to intimidate farmers into ending their alleged support for the opposition MDC.
2. **February 2000 (referendum period)**: Secret planning for small-scale but permanent farm invasions occurs just prior to ZANU-PF's defeat in the referendum on February 12–13 only when government officials realize that a loss is likely.
3. **February–March 2000**: After ZANU-PF's referendum defeat, some war veterans independently move onto farms, and in some cases those already demonstrating on farms take steps to seize them, but virtually all takeovers are controlled or influenced by the CIO. The limited farm seizure plan is put in motion. Conflicting messages from Mugabe and Minister of Home Affairs Dumiso Dabengwa contribute to the growing scale of takeovers.
4. **March–June 2000**: The scope of farm seizures rapidly escalates. State security officials and political leaders who should be controlling takeovers are actively participating in them, increasing the number of farms targeted and levels of violence. Small-scale seizures approved by government are becoming conflated with escalating demonstrations on farms, blurring the distinction between authorized and uncontrolled seizures.
5. **June 2000**: The period leading up to the June 2000 parliamentary elections sees a further spiraling in violence.
6. **June–July 2000**: Government loses control over farm seizures.
7. **July–August 2000**: Government moves to co-opt farm seizures.

## PLANNING FOR FARM INVASIONS

Undoubtedly some war veterans had nationalist motivations in seeking to seize white-owned farms, but, with few exceptions, they were not operating completely independently of the government's political objectives or those of the state security services. This has been widely recognized in the existing literature. Sam Moyo describes the early land seizures as "a controlled and orchestrated countrywide land occupation movement," and Selby agrees that they were "coordinated."[2] There is no doubt that the state and war veterans were in close contact, but the extent, timing, and objectives of this early planning and coordination have never been established. The evidence presented in this chapter—drawn from interviews with high-level officials and policymakers—shows that there was considerable confusion within the government over the farm takeovers. In fact, the seizures were not part of a preplanned effort to undertake large-scale redistribution in order to address inequalities in access to land. On the contrary, the government's decision to allow farm takeovers in the first months of 2000 was purely a reaction to the emerging political threat posed by the MDC.

The Minister of Home Affairs, Dumiso Dabengwa, played a central role in government decision-making when the farm invasions began and was a key participant in conversations with Mugabe about the direction the process would take. In an interview for this book, Dabengwa made it clear that the land seizures were rapidly conceived and not preplanned. The seizures, according to Dabengwa, were "not an organized government approach for taking over the farms. It was something that was spontaneous," that is, conceived after the shock loss to the MDC in the referendum.[3] Dabengwa added that, for Mugabe, large-scale farm invasions were "not his solution to the land issue."

Leading personnel in the security forces were equally aware that the government's decision-making was shrouded in confusion. Edward Chidembo, a senior member of the Zimbabwe Republic Police, was privy to many top-level meetings and explains what motivated the coordination between the government and war veterans: "I was in a provincial land reform committee myself and I saw what was happening. There was nothing planned about that. It was all confusion."[4] He described the seizures as a "political gimmick" and argued that the policy of seizing land "was planned in the sense that it was a political tool. It was not planned in the sense of improving agriculture or dealing with the [landownership] inequalities." Chidembo also elaborated on how the political motivations came about: "It was actually planned as a political tool to . . . get votes because suddenly there was the MDC treading on their [ZANU-PF's] movement, so it was a way of dealing with the political threat to Robert Mugabe."

Senior CIO agent Hastings Lundi corroborates this claim, stating bluntly, "No, it wasn't planned"—initial seizures were hurriedly prepared, and plans were never long-standing.[5] Peter Msasa, a military intelligence agent, and Daniel Inkankezi, a senior official in military intelligence, also stated that the farm seizures were not planned in advance as part of a land redistribution program.[6]

The government had repeatedly promised a major land redistribution effort. However, these accounts from senior politicians and state security insiders show that takeovers at the beginning of the land seizure era, starting in February 2000, were a response to a political threat and thus conceived to deal with that threat, not to solve the problems of inequity in landownership.

## ZANU-PF Reacts to Political Crisis

According to Inkankezi, if Mugabe had been asked why the farm seizures had been undertaken, he would have said, "'[My] back was by the wall. I didn't want to do this, but I did it.' . . . It is not questionable that . . . [it] was not the best of all things to do."[7] With the takeovers emerging as a "panic measure" and without any real planning or structure, the very risky strategy of seizing commercial farms fell into place.[8]

The political threat to ZANU-PF posed by the MDC, and the response in the form of farm seizures, became evident just before the referendum results were announced. War veterans had been demonstrating on farms since 1999, but these public, government-sanctioned events were never intended to be permanent. Lundi explained, "When we were about to lose the referendum [i.e., early February 2000], that was when they set it in motion. . . . That week, towards the referendum, we were having frantic meetings [to coordinate a response to the imminent MDC victory]."[9] Once the referendum loss became more likely, the CIO hastily began to plan and coordinate small-scale—but permanent—farm seizures. Lundi stated that senior ZANU-PF officials believed this would send a two-pronged message. First, "Farmers, if you keep on doing what you are doing [supporting the MDC], we are going to do more than this [undertake large-scale land seizures]." Second, Lundi stated that war veterans needed to be reminded that "we [ZANU-PF] haven't forgotten about you," meaning that the party was responding to their demands for land.

Even so, at this point few senior ZANU-PF officials appear to have been contemplating the possibility of allowing widespread land seizures. Indeed, the claim that the government was initially intent merely on intimidating white farmers over their real or imagined support for the MDC by undertaking small-scale seizures is supported by accounts from senior intelligence officials. For example, when speaking about the large-scale and uncontrolled farm seizures, Inkankezi made it clear that the government had no intention of allowing the large-scale takeover of land; the small-scale seizures planned in February 2000 were intended only to intimidate farmers.[10] He explained: "They [the government] thought they would threaten the farmers into submission [by invading some farms] because . . . after the referendum the government panicked a lot." However, he added: "I don't honestly think the government wanted to invade the farms" in any large-scale manner.

The government hastily crafted an initial plan in February 2000 when it became clear that ZANU-PF would lose the referendum. This plan envisaged the seizure of *five farms per district* across the country and was put into action right after the referendum defeat (this preceded the Fast Track Land Reform Programme, which was a more formalized process adopted by the government

in July 2000).[11] According to Lundi, this would allow the government to desig-
nate appropriate farms on which people in congested areas could resettle.
Properties that had previously been identified in a notice published in a newspaper, a process known as "gazetting," were candidates for seizure, but not all
gazetted properties would be seized. Seized properties would then be used for
the purposes of resettlement in order to reduce congestion in communal
areas.[12] This would fit in with Mugabe's altruistic rhetoric on providing land
for the common person, most notably impoverished war veterans.[13]

It appears obvious, in retrospect, that even a limited attack on the commercial farming industry represented a reckless gamble with the lifeblood of Zimbabwe's economy and food supply. Yet in understanding the government's
actions, it is important to realize that some officials believed at the time that
farming was a relatively simple profession, and that the redistribution of farm
ownership would therefore not necessarily provoke a major crisis. The government also assumed that farms were developed and fully stocked with equipment, meaning prospective farm invaders would essentially just need to
undertake turnkey operations. According to Msasa: "They [government] think
farming is easy. Farming is easy . . . because usually everything will be there at
the farm, tractors and everything [needed to operate the farm]."[14] Similarly,
Agnes Sengwe, a member of the army, said that the prevailing belief in government was that "whites, they don't farm. It's us the blacks who farm, so we can
do it."[15] Sengwe clarified that the government believed white farmers simply
owned the farm, but the black managers and laborers possessed the real expertise: "They [the government] thought it was easy. They just take over and then
things will start [by themselves]."

Christian Mucheke, a legal officer in the President's Office, corroborated
these claims, indicating that Mugabe also believed that black people held the
farming expertise: "He [Mugabe] was assured that, to start with, the farms are
being [tilled], planted, plowed, worked on by black people, and therefore if
they run it, they could do it better because what is happening here is the farmer
simply gives instructions. The manager is black. The worker is black."[16]
Mucheke said that this seemingly logical understanding of who truly possessed agricultural knowledge was extremely persuasive: "That thinking de-
ceived a lot, including the president. And they [senior government officials]
believed it [seizures] would work." If farm redistribution was controlled and
apparent knowledge resources were preserved, there seemed to be a logical
and smooth path placing farm ownership in the hands of ZANU-PF's
supporters.

Nevertheless, Mugabe had initially been opposed to farm seizures, as demonstrated by his putting a stop to the "staged" Svosve invasions that had been
carried out without his authorization in 1999. However, some small, sporadic

demonstrations had continued, and there is no doubt that, after the shock of realizing that his hold over the country was seriously threatened, he consented to the five-farms-per-district plan detailed by Lundi. Indeed, Lundi explained that senior ZANU-PF officials, such as Emmerson Mnangagwa (then the minister of justice and legal affairs) and Patrick Chinamasa (the attorney general), "had worked on him" to convince the president to support the farm seizures.[17]

The real purpose of the five-farms-per-district seizure strategy was to threaten farmers into withdrawing funding from the MDC because they implied that large-scale seizures would occur if this support continued. It was believed within the ruling party that this was vital to preventing a defeat in the June 2000 parliamentary elections. According to Lundi, the farm seizures were intended as "a message" to warn farmers to stop funding the MDC. Msasa stated that the government "just wanted to say [to farmers, farm workers, and other MDC supporters], 'Okay, since you said no [in the referendum], this is what we can do.' But they thought they would just do it [seize farms] temporarily, just to scare them."[18] Edison Bubye, a ZRP officer, concurred, saying also that giving war veterans land allowed them to "channel their energy" away from targeting the government, and that "it was the only way to satisfy these people and use them at the same time."[19]

Some war veterans were acting independently of this government scheme when they initially moved to seize farms in February and March 2000; others were operating at the behest of government ministers who were looking to strengthen their support base in the face of a major MDC threat in the upcoming June 2000 elections. However, according to both Msasa and Mucheke, war veterans and their associated groups moving onto farms were almost always guided and had direct input from intelligence agents.[20] Even in the earliest phases in February and March 2000, when some war veterans were "spontaneously" moving onto farms, Msasa said that the CIO would at least have known about the events in virtually all cases. The CIO also sought to influence the farm invaders; the invasions did not just happen purely in isolation from the intelligence services. Msasa explained: "After being advised by the CIO, if they [war veterans] want to invade, then they must do it this way [according to CIO directives], not just to go anyway."[21]

War veterans in most cases were immediately monitored by the CIO if they intended to invade a farm. Msasa added that even if the war veterans believed they were acting somewhat independently, the CIO was always behind such events, even as a basic organizing force or in an effort to "balance" what war veterans were seeking to undertake or to ensure that the invasions were "better organized."[22] When asked why war veterans would listen to intelligence agents, Msasa noted: "They [war veterans] are afraid of military people. They are also afraid of CIO." Thus, Msasa stated that the CIO always channeled and sought to shape war veterans' activities, even during the immediate aftermath of the referendum result.

During the early phases of the farm takeovers from February to June 2000, when the government was attempting to implement the five-farms-per-district plan, the state security services became overstretched as they sought to engage with the rapidly unfolding events. At first, the government could only implement its plan by sending supporters onto farms—or, more commonly, by co-opting war veterans who were already intent on doing so; and the war veterans already engaged in existing farm demonstrations were obvious candidates. Even if the CIO retained a strong influence over the first seizures carried out in the early months, the security forces were not well prepared for the task of directing and controlling the rapidly growing mass of land claimants. This would be a key factor in the government's temporary loss of control in the middle of 2000.

Meanwhile, there were multiple reasons why the government had to conceal its initial support for even a limited farm seizure program. When farm invasions began in February 2000 there was no legal basis for the government to seize land or to enable war veterans to do so. Farm invasions were a clear violation of farmers' property rights under Zimbabwean law. For this reason, the police often protected farmers' property rights during the early farm seizures, especially from February to about June 2000, when the government's attitude toward the takeovers was shrouded in confusion.[23]

To conceal government involvement in orchestrating the five-farms-per-district seizures, a "quick meeting was called," according to Mucheke, where "they chose war veterans [to lead farm invasions] who were not in the top ranking of the War Veterans Association to make it [farm invasions] appear like an ad hoc, a spontaneous, unguided action."[24] Indeed, Bubye noted, "You put war vets in front [of the farm invasion group], even if you look at it on TV."[25] Mucheke elaborated:

> It [the early planning for farm seizures] was virtually the baby of the CIO. They planned it. We had meetings. It was fully planned, but in order to get some international respect it was allowed to appear as if it was done spontaneously. It was allowed to appear as if it was some people, disgruntled people, who have done it.[26]

This strategy of allowing war veterans—rather than, for example, the military—to actually undertake the seizures, would, theoretically, shield the government from blame. Officials could simply claim that the farm invasions were part of a popular uprising and not state sanctioned. Mucheke stated that this subterfuge was also intended to guard against international criticism, by providing a "legitimate case before the United Nations and say, 'Look here, it was not us. It was our people.'" Indeed, members of the intelligence community interviewed for this book were very clear that, although the CIO could not necessarily control every situation, it had some involvement in almost every major event during the land seizure era. Accordingly, Mucheke said, the plan for the farm invasions "was treated as highly . . . secret, and because it was very private and confidential, classified information, you could not have it documented."

In reality, the government did contribute logistical support; the International Crisis Group has noted that vehicles were made available for farm invaders, a claim also supported by Alexander and McGregor as well as by accounts from both farmers and farm invaders.[27] However, in the early phase of the farm takeovers, this support was never intended to be for large-scale seizures, only the limited five-farms-per-district plan. According to government thinking at the time, the provision of some land would satisfy those war veterans who demanded it, would serve as a warning to farmers to stop supporting the MDC, and would mean that the government would not have to confront the objectives of the vital war veteran constituency. While the actions would violate Zimbabwean law, as long as the role of government in supporting the takeovers was kept secret, the seizures could be blamed on civil unrest arising from public demand for land.

Indeed, Msasa stressed that seizures were secretly organized so they would appear to have begun "independently."[28] Likewise, Mucheke affirmed the importance of actions appearing spontaneous: "To give this thing credence it was supposed to appear as if the people, the people have spoken, the people have wanted this, the people have acted. They don't want it to appear as if the government has made people act."[29] Chenjerai Hunzvi, a well-known ZANU-PF supporter, was thus deliberately not chosen to lead the five-farms-per-district seizures for "fear of attack from the international world" (although he had led initial demonstrations that occurred prior to the referendum, which were publicly sanctioned by government but were not originally intended to lead to permanent takeovers of farms).[30] Instead, Joseph Chinotimba was selected because at that stage he was dedicated to ZANU-PF but was not well known outside the party.

The government also had a ready supply of less senior war veterans to lead farm invasion groups. Thompson Mupfure, a former guerrilla in the Liberation War and senior government official, said that by 1999 the CIO knew which veterans showed sufficient "loyalty" to carry out government operations: "I think that the CIO meticulously went on an identification process [by 1999] that will show them those that were really motivated to commit crime because they were getting people to do crime, and so they then would have gone for the criminal element."[31] He continued: "They went for a diehard criminal who will do anything at the request of the government, and so when you look at the elements that committed crimes from 2000 up to now you realize that these are ordinary criminals ZANU-PF was using."[32]

In order to give the impression of spontaneity, Mucheke explained, the initial seizures planned by the CIO between about February and June 2000—as opposed to the small number of genuinely spontaneous events undertaken by war veterans during the same period—were designed to appear plausibly chaotic:

> The first time, it [farm invasions] appeared, as I said, very spontaneous. It appeared very unorganized. But the reality, if you remember that, you will see that in its disorganization, as it was made to appear like, it really occupied a lot of air space on the national television with no condemnation of it at all. So that means in that aspect of it the government had an interest in what was happening. Actually it was supporting it.[33]

While events may have been designed to appear spontaneous, the government was also clearly seeking to control and limit the takeovers, while still meeting the key objective of intimidating supporters of the MDC and placating some war veterans.

While only five farms per district were to be seized, a broader presence on farms was planned to warn farmers against supporting the opposition; these were a continuation of the existing demonstrations. However, the actual seizure of additional farms was specifically prohibited by government leaders so as not to undermine the farming industry any more than was necessary. Inkankezi stressed that during the demonstrations "[the idea to intimidate the farmers] was made clear. Don't disrupt anything [on the farms] but go and show presence there, that this is our land. So people went in there for almost a month or so without doing anything [i.e., committing violence or seizing additional farms]."[34] He added, "If you talk to the people who invaded the farms, there is not even a single one who thought it could go the way it went because they were told you are going to go there, camp there for one week or two weeks."

Joyce Mukwa, a farm clerk, indicated that initial radio broadcasts from senior officials made it clear that demonstrations were temporary: "When they started to invade farmers, they [the farm invaders] were told to go and sleep there—not cut a tree, not remove anything from the farm until such a time they are given the place where to stay. . . . They were sent there temporarily."[35] Farm mechanic Chenjerai Mapufuli also heard about the takeovers through

informal networks and was told the demonstrations were temporary and seizures would be limited.[36] Andrew Morfu, a horticulture manager, said, "According to his [Mugabe's] statement, he said he wanted to take a few farms and
then left [sic] some other farms."[37] Dairy manager Philip Mahobohobo concurred: "They said that first time, they said they are going to get [a] few and
leave the other white people."[38]

While the government in general was actively co-opting the war veterans,
senior officials remained worried by the likelihood of negative reactions from
international donors. According to Mucheke, government officials were especially concerned that the International Monetary Fund, the United Kingdom,
and the United States in particular would withdraw funding if the government
actively endorsed extralegal takeovers.[39] Mucheke also said that he had personal knowledge of Mugabe being advised that the farm takeovers were illegal.
Legality, however, was a secondary consideration to basic political survival for
Mugabe and ZANU-PF.

## ESCALATION TO UNCONTROLLED FARM SEIZURES

The demonstrations carried out by groups of war veterans since November
1999 had been initiated to demand land redistribution by occupying, but not
seizing, parts of a few commercial farms. These demonstrations, separate from
the five-farms-per-district plan that was meant to appear as a populist movement, were sanctioned by Minister of Home Affairs Dumiso Dabengwa and
were intended to be "symbolic," temporary occupations.[40] The purpose of
these public demonstrations was to intimidate farmers into ending their support for the MDC, but also to highlight government support for war veterans.
Thompson Mupfure explained that Mugabe sought to "divert the attention of
these people [war veterans] instead of focusing on the failure of government to
create employment, to expand the economy, to grow the economy, to make
service available."[41]

Even in the politically contentious period at the end of 1999, when the land
redistribution debate became heated and antifarmer rhetoric intensified,
senior government officials were concerned that demonstrations on farms
would cause problems with commercial agriculture. Indeed, many in the Cabinet were unaware why farm "demonstrations" were even occurring. Dabengwa assured the Cabinet: "We said it [demonstrations] must be peaceful and
that where the war veterans disrupted the operations of the farmers, the police
would act and get them out of there."[42] A report published by the International
Crisis Group affirms Dabengwa's claims that he sought an end to the demonstrations on the grounds that farm "occupations endangered farmers and
workers and obstructed farming."[43]

Despite the initial emphasis on maintaining the orderliness of these demonstrations, events on farms began to deteriorate in mid-February when the government lost the referendum. The defeat convinced war veterans that their interests were threatened by the MDC's growing power. Soon the war veterans' leader, Chenjerai Hunzvi, was having trouble controlling his most radical members, who were demonstrating on farms. As Dabengwa related: "He [Hunzvi] came to me and said, 'We think we can now pull out because we now have elements who are beginning to be disruptive at the farms, and yet this is not what the intention was. We are prepared to withdraw. We think we should withdraw before more problems come up.'" The extent to which Hunzvi was losing control within one to two weeks of the referendum defeat is worth emphasizing. According to Dabengwa, he observed

> three cell phones [of Hunzvi's], each one of them ringing telling him about problems that were taking place on the other farms. And he said, "I can't control some of these characters [war veterans] anymore. Some of them were becoming completely unruly, and I think the best thing is let's call for a withdrawal, and it must come from you, because it is you, Minister, who gave us the authority to demonstrate."[44]

By February 24, 2000—less than two weeks after the referendum—agitation on farms was already becoming serious, testing the police force's ability to maintain control. Dabengwa stated that "the police commissioner . . . [said] his police were being stretched out because they were getting many calls both from the farmers and from the war veterans and they had to go in between all the time to try and avoid any violence taking place." The situation required an unequivocal intervention from Mugabe on whether the war veterans had the right to continue demonstrating. Dabengwa said,

> I went to Cabinet and went to whisper to the president that the war veterans had come to see me and they had expressed their intention to withdraw because they were beginning to have problems in controlling some of the elements who were beginning to cause problems.

According to Dabengwa, Mugabe replied:

> I think that's right [that war veterans should withdraw]. But please emphasize in your [press] statement also that because we now have the Acquisition Act, the acquisition law incorporated in our constitution, . . . we can now acquire any farm we want to. There is no need for the war veterans to continue with their demonstration or occupation of those farms.[45]

Dabengwa left the Cabinet meeting thinking the decision to withdraw the demonstrators had been approved by Mugabe directly. In fact, the situation was about to become even more confused. Just prior to the Cabinet meeting Mugabe had been meeting with diplomats and the press. When asked what his reaction would be if somebody suggested that the war veterans should withdraw from the farms, Mugabe had said, "I think the demonstration has been very meaningful and as far as I'm concerned, I think maybe let them go on for another little while."[46] Dabengwa said that Mugabe believed that "there are still some pockets of stubborn farmers, so I think they can stay a little while." Not knowing that Mugabe had given the statement earlier that day, Dabengwa then called for the war veterans to withdraw—as Mugabe had agreed he should do—but he was now publicly contradicting the president.[47] The result was immediate confusion for all concerned.

That evening, the night of February 24, 2000, Dabengwa was telephoned by the commissioner for police, who asked why he had made a different statement to the president. To clarify the orders, the police commissioner spoke to Mugabe the next day. Mugabe reiterated that war veterans should take orders from Dabengwa.[48] Thus, in public Mugabe was saying that war veterans should remain on farms to protest (though not to permanently occupy), yet behind the scenes was saying that the war veterans should follow Dabengwa's orders and withdraw from the farms.

With evident disarray in senior ranks, war veteran demonstrators chose to follow Mugabe's public instructions and remain on the farms. Mugabe was in effect allowing war veterans to ignore the rule of law and to disobey police instructions to withdraw from the farms. Dabengwa believed that Mugabe's contradictory statement was a result of the president being put under pressure from some senior officials who sought to pursue war veteran interests. It is also apparent that Mugabe's inner circle had fallen into uncertainty and confusion as the president and other senior figures pondered their fate after the MDC's surprise victory. Perhaps most important of all, the government also began implementing its secret five-farms-per-district seizure plan right after the referendum. So while some officials were looking to reign in the high-profile war veteran demonstrations and restore order on farms, other officials were allowing some war veterans to begin small-scale farm seizures; the conflicting pressures of the government's secret and public objectives explain the apparently contradictory decision-making by senior officials.

The sidelining of law enforcement immediately became clear after Mugabe signaled that war veteran demonstrations could continue. Dabengwa was told by the Zimbabwe Republic Police commissioner, "There is no way I can do it [remove war veterans]. They are already crazy. They are already saying the president has allowed them to stay, so no one can tell them to get out when the

president has said they can stay."[49] The consequence for Dabengwa was a critical loss of authority.[50] The same was true for the police force in general.

With Mugabe's apparent blessing, war veterans quickly began to assert their
power, and the distinction between public, controlled, temporary demonstrations and the secret five-farms-per-district plan that would permanently seize
farms became blurred. According to Dabengwa, "They [war veterans] then
went on the rampage" and moved onto farms where they had previously been
prevented from demonstrating.[51] Mugabe had only authorized the war veterans to continue to *protest* on a few farms and had not given them permission
to *occupy* them.[52] However, there was effectively no one to stop them moving
onto other farms, because war veterans populated all branches of state security, especially in senior positions. This confusion, in conjunction with the five-
farms-per-district seizure plan, resulted in controlled, limited, and authorized
farm demonstrations giving way to violent, unlimited, and unauthorized farm
seizures.

## LARGE-SCALE FARM SEIZURES BEGIN

With the prospect of war veterans gaining land threatened by the unexpected
emergence of the MDC, and confusion in the government about whether war
veterans could continue to demonstrate on the farms or whether some farms
would be permanently seized, a tipping point had been reached. Within two
weeks of the February referendum loss, war veteran demonstrations ended
and large-scale farm invasions began.

Beginning in the Masvingo area soon after the referendum, some war veterans, along with other rural civilians, particularly the rural unemployed, began
taking over farms; in most, but not all, cases this occurred at least with the
knowledge of the CIO.[53] Petros Mzingwane, a war veteran who seized farmland,
described the invasions as a "reflex," an "eruption," an "instantaneous response"
by angry war veterans who perceived the referendum defeat and the growth of
the MDC's power as a sign of Western neocolonial interference: "It is very simple.
The British have come back and they want to take us over, recolonize. . . . Everybody stand up with knobkerries [clubs], with spears, anything—anything they
pick, because you [whites, British, MDC] have put them in that mental state."[54]
Mzingwane elaborated: "What they [war veterans] went through during the
war, so they are now seeing the same monster coming back [Western, colonial
influences]. . . . Now you don't have an AK-47. And you must fight back."

The decision to move onto farms also underscored an extreme frustration
among some war veterans and the rural poor over the inability or unwilling-
ness of the government to help improve rural livelihoods. The desire for land
by some people, particularly influential war veterans, reflected a genuine

longing for tangible improvements to their living conditions. The emphasis on land as a route to prosperity was also emblematic of their lack of faith that the government could or would provide strengthened social services.

Prosper Matondi explained that "officials in government ministries came from a background that emphasized orderliness and adherence to laws and procedures."[55] Yet in the eyes of many of the rural poor, this approach had failed to improve rural livelihoods in any meaningful way. As a result, war veterans began to insist on radical—and extralegal—changes:

> Existing laws and "standards" were meant to preserve the status quo and therefore did not facilitate their entry into commercial farms; they were seen as part of the colonial mentality that accepted that large farms make better economic sense than small farms, and "procedures" were regarded as "technical bureaucracy" to delay the resettlement programme.[56]

The decision to move onto farms, therefore, did not just represent a backlash against the supposed neocolonialist plot being undertaken by the MDC and its Western backers. It also reflected a loss of faith in ZANU-PF and the Zimbabwean government's domestic policies. The farm invasions underscored the willingness to resort to extralegal measures to achieve socioeconomic transformation. When coupled with nationalist justifications, these impulses quickly became uncontrollable.

## Escalation of Farm Invasions

Lundi explained that after the referendum Mugabe had retreated from the political scene. Largely because he had received a stinging rebuff from voters, he felt personally vulnerable and was seen by the senior ZANU-PF leadership as having been partially responsible for the defeat.[57] As the president re-engaged in public life in the period approaching the June 24–25, 2000, parliamentary election, he had little choice but to support the farm invasions in an attempt to rally voters for the ruling party (see chapter 5 for a discussion of the elections). Indeed, by this stage Mugabe was no longer merely allowing farms to be occupied, but was openly endorsing the seizure of land. Mupfure believed that, as the elections approached, Mugabe and ZANU-PF had decided that placating war veterans was the only route to political survival: "They [ZANU-PF] now say, 'Here is a chance. Go and invade land, loot, eat crops, fruits. Whatever you find take, loot, sell equipment, sell the produce . . .' and that kept the war veteran lot busy on the farms."[58] War veteran leader Alex Siwaze concurs, pointing out that farm seizures were "actually meant to make sure that these people will vote for none other than this sinking ship of ZANU-PF."[59]

June 2000 is therefore the critical point of departure when invasions vastly increased in scope. Realizing that the support of war veterans and the rural poor was vital to the outcome of the elections, and because the farm seizures were probably in all practical terms unstoppable by that point anyway, Mugabe fully committed his support to the farm invasions. Once the president more visibly and consistently came out in support of the takeovers, it meant that permission to participate was essentially granted to anyone. Law enforcement agencies were put in an even more impossible position, and a vast new supply of potential farm invaders began demanding land and agri-property.

With demand for farms increasing and all limits on seizures being ignored, the pace of invasions rapidly escalated. Accordingly, by about June 2000, farm invaders began targeting all farmers, regardless of whether the farms were gazetted or not and regardless of the scope of the five-farms-per-district plan.[60] Instead of five farms per district, yielding approximately 295 farms in total, all 4,300 commercial farms in Zimbabwe were now potentially available. According to Lundi, who had direct access to many senior ZANU-PF officials, some said, "'I'll be jobless [after the June 2000 election]. I might as well make hay whilst the sun shines.' Others [said,] 'Okay, even if they [MDC] come in, I've already made my money [by seizing farms].'"[61] According to Lundi, these individuals were prepared to take the risk of moving onto farms and thereby rapidly gaining wealth that would sustain them if ZANU-PF lost power: "They say in June, 'I won't be here, but by then I will have sent all the flowers to the Netherlands [from a seized farm] to get the money. I can still go and live comfortably anywhere. I've got the mansion.'" The belief among land claimants that their window of opportunity to seize land was closing rapidly created a sense of urgency and encouraged the circumvention of laws that would have ordinarily protected the rights of workers and farmers.

This was particularly the case as farm invaders realized the enormous financial opportunities that might be open to them if they could seize a farm. Lundi recounted that when the land seizures began in February 2000, crops such as tobacco and maize were quite far along in their growing cycle and had started to mature.[62] For farm invaders, the prospect of selling an entire lucrative crop was enticing: "In February the crops are almost ripening. Someone could just suddenly, without putting any labor, [harvest them and] he will be a millionaire." This potential for enormous financial gain gradually became apparent over the course of 2000; indeed it was the fundamental reason the original limited scope of farm seizures was soon ignored by farm invaders on the ground: "Then people said, 'Just forget the old man [ignore Mugabe's directives of limited seizures]. I'll go and seize that farm.'"[63] Lundi's account highlights how much credibility Mugabe had lost after the referendum and how by ratcheting up political invective and demands for land in the late

1990s—which initially avoided open support for land seizures—he had created an uncontrollable situation. This attitude quickly spread among other
farm invaders, who soon competed with each other for the same farms: "Actually people used to go round fighting amongst themselves, saying, 'This is my
farm, this is my farm,' because they will see the potential loot that they can
get."[64] The losers of these contests then simply moved onto another farm and
tried again, thereby expanding the scope of the takeovers.

## FARM SEIZURE FREE-FOR-ALL

Farm invaders who had personal firsthand knowledge of internal ZANU-PF
decision-making are emphatic that the government had completely lost control over the pace and extent of the seizures by about July 2000. Lundi, who
stated that farm seizures had become a "free-for-all," explained that they had
initially been planned and coordinated from the President's Office but then
went out of control: "Far from being controlled, far from being planned, it was
just like a scramble. Mugabe lost control of it and there was also just the criminal element within ZANU-PF anyway [pursuing further farm seizures for
personal gain]."[65] Lundi stated: "The government lost control because then
there were some serious power struggles in ZANU-PF. And the war veterans . . . there were people who were hiding behind the war veterans [i.e., using
them to seize farms]." He also believed that Mugabe lost control of the war
veterans' movement: "There were really some opportunistic guys." These veterans were making the most of the chance to seize farms, which were essentially undefended once police stopped enforcing the rule of law.

   In virtually all cases the CIO knew of war veteran movements and sought to
influence them; this would become more true over time as the CIO's capability
evolved to the point where the group—along with military intelligence (itself a
branch of the CIO)—essentially controlled all farm invasions, at least in terms
of deciding which farms were to be seized and by whom. However, in mid-
2000 the CIO—as with ZANU-PF—was a highly factionalized organization.
Its activities were influenced by the deeply rooted ties among war veterans in
various branches of government and the state security services. Different factions operated at the behest of key individuals such as Mugabe, Mnangagwa,
and General Solomon Mujuru. Although each faction always claimed to be
acting in the general interests of ZANU-PF, the tendency for CIO officials to
support particular land claimants clearly played a role in the spiral toward a
farm seizure free-for-all.[66]

   The growing number of land claimants, many of whom were well connected politically, massively contributed to the growing land free-for-all. War
veterans were obviously prominent and politically influential beneficiaries of

farms in the immediate aftermath of the referendum defeat. This meant, however, that individuals who were not considered war veterans could not easily participate in the lucrative seizure of farms. The simplest solution for prospective land occupiers who had not served in the Liberation War was therefore to expand the definition of "war veteran." Chenjerai Mapufuli, a farm mechanic, told how some farm invaders claimed that while they were not "holding a gun [in] the bush [during the Liberation War]," they were "fighting here at home" by preparing food for the guerrillas or serving as informants.[67] Another method was to move to a different area where war veteran status could not easily be authenticated. Farm foreman Tendayi Garamapudzi explained: "Let's take an instance like me. Everyone knows I am not a war veteran. If I go to different place—that's when I can be 'a war veteran.'"[68] Thus, broadening the category of beneficiary increased the number of claimants drastically.

Prior to the land seizure era, the label of "war veteran" had important socioeconomic implications (see chapter 2), and with the takeover of commercial farms this was even more apparent. Those entitled to call themselves "war veteran" could claim a de facto "right" to lucrative farmland and the opportunity to potentially gain from seized agri-property. By redefining the terms and stretching definitions, more and more people could participate in the farm takeovers. Even youths born in the 1980s could claim to have war veteran status (albeit a much weaker one) by virtue of "fighting" in the Third Chimurenga war, as the farm invasions came to be known.[69] This suited ZANU-PF because it allowed the party to build—at no real cost—what was effectively an army of supporters. Kriger explains how:

> Patriots included not only the liberation war veterans who spearheaded the land occupations but also the youth militia whom the ruling party began to mobilise in late 2001 ahead of the presidential election. The ruling party referred to these youths as "war veterans" in recognition of their contribution to what it labelled the "Third Chimurenga"—the fight for the land. ZANU PF thus linked its violence after 2000 to earlier episodes of violent resistance—the First Chimurenga in the late 19th century and the Second Chimurenga, the liberation war. Emphasising a shared history of racism, colonialism and imperialism, the ruling party also appealed to pan-African sentiment.[70]

The designation also meant that farm invaders could use the same war veteran label to achieve their personal objectives of seizing land and agri-property.

The obvious problem of allowing so many people to call themselves "war veterans" is that it watered down the status of the title and meant that the pool of legitimate actors and beneficiaries massively increased—rapidly fueling farm takeovers. There were more people "eligible" to participate, which meant that there was a great clamor among land claimants to get in quickly and claim resources before others could do so.[71]

## War Veteran Networks Fuel Farm Invasions

The most important driver behind the acceleration of farm seizures was demand from genuine and purported war veterans *within* the government. In particular, those meant to be controlling the process—members of the state security apparatus—were setting aside their professional obligations in order to personally gain from farm takeovers. This was occurring because ZANU-PF had brought the land issue to a head with its self-serving rhetoric, but then found it had created enormous demands and expectations that were far greater than those it had intended to fulfill. War veterans now sought immediate action to finally achieve one of the aims they had fought for decades earlier—the transfer of the country's farmland to black ownership.

What made the issue so serious for Mugabe was that war veterans populated all branches of his government. This had the effect of creating a supranetwork of wartime comrades in the core of government that began to operate independently of both ZANU-PF control and the boundaries of ordinary governance in seeking to escalate the land seizures. Wartime comrades sought to help each other achieve the unrealized nationalist goal of redistributing commercial farms, despite the caution of the ruling party's hierarchy over disruption to the commercial farming sector and the violation of legal norms.

Senior member of the Zimbabwe Republic Police Jackson Sanyati explained the power of this war veteran network and how it connected veterans in all branches of government, private industry, and even those unemployed in communal areas.[72] Fundamentally, these war veterans shared a strong common bond: "They [war veterans] can then understand each other better than me because for myself I'm not a war vet, I'm just an ordinary person. . . . If I try to talk to them [war veterans], they say, 'No, you are a Rhodesian, an ex-Rhodesian. You are an ex-Smith police officer. How can you talk to me? I don't understand you.'" Sanyati emphasized that the war veteran cause superseded the legal claims of farmers and workers and inspired claims of a more fundamental right:

They [war veterans] were saying, "We are taking land because it is our land. These people [farmers and workers] they don't have the right to stay here. . . ." From the beginning what they [war veterans] are trying to say is very simple here, what they are saying is "This is our land." No matter even they don't recognize law if it comes to terms of land. "We know this is your farm, but you are on our land, this Zimbabwean land. If you are now on this land issue, we don't recognize the law."

The activation of this supra war veteran network caused a serious problem for Mugabe. What really made the situation uncontrollable for him and ZANU-PF, however, was that there were a large number of war veterans in state security and senior government positions: the very individuals who were supposed to be controlling and limiting the farm seizures were the ones allow-ing it to happen. Msasa explained:

> It went out of control now. They say everyone wanted a farm, especially the army commanders. . . . The three big army commanders, air force commander and whatever, they all had farms. But then the other briga-dier generals, brigadiers, colonels, lieutenant colonels, you see, then they took advantage of that, and the police again, they did the same. So, you see, those commissioners, superintendents, they went in as well. So from there everyone goes in [and seizes a farm]. . . . Yes, it was out of control.[73]

Msasa added: "Remember, those people who were taking those farms are those people who implement the policies of the government, you see. So it's quite difficult now because if you are the person who should say, 'No, we shouldn't do that,' and yet you are going to grab one farm, you can't grab and then say to someone, 'You don't take that farm.' So it just can go out of control." Senior army officer Steven Sebungwe concurred: "It was out of control. . . . Everyone wants a farm. It is ministers who start grabbing those farms now for them-selves. That is where everything went wrong."[74]

Bubye emphasized that "if they didn't have war vets in the commanding positions, like in the police force, they could have stopped it. In a sense, they could have stopped it maybe after a few farms."[75] Sanyati noted, "The police were sidelined. They [senior officials] were saying, 'No ways, just give them [the invaders] the go-ahead [to seize farms]. . . .' We [police] had no powers to stop those people."[76] Bubye was more emphatic: "No wonder they can't stop them, because you can't send another war veteran to say go and kill them, go and stop them. They're speaking the same language [of a shared Liberation War history]."[77] A cable from the US Embassy in April 2000 corroborated these accounts in stating that Mugabe was "keenly aware of the immediate dangers" of farm invasions, but that he "feared the consequences of any police or army effort to forcibly remove the war veterans who had occupied the com-mercial farms."[78]

Given that many of the war veterans involved in the seizures were in state security positions and so were well versed in employing violence, and especially in view of the farm seizures being framed in militaristic terms, violence emerged as an immediate and central component of the takeovers. Again, the war veteran links served as a key driver by providing common ground between those who had relied on violence in the Liberation War. Sanyati described how some veterans had little hesitation in using force to attain the goals:

> That is [why] you can see that force was being applied now where the farmers were being beaten, because they're trying to resist. If you [farmer] try to think too much and if you're trying to reason up in a legal direction, in the legal line, you'll be in for it.[79]

The extent of the disorder that prevailed as the conventional boundaries of governance and law ceased to apply was exemplified by an account given by a farmer, James Adams, who explained events on his neighbor's farm: "They [the farmer] brought the vice president down and everybody else, and they [the vice president and other officials] said, 'No, no, this was not allowed. It can't be.' But it never changed because once people did things, then nobody will do anything to change it."[80] Similarly, rancher Brian Wheeler was about to be evicted by farm invaders only to receive a phone call from the minister of tourism, Francis Nhema. Nhema reportedly told Wheeler, "You're part of the tourist industry. You guys [Wheeler] must stay there. Don't, don't leave there. Whatever happens, don't leave."[81] According to Wheeler, Nhema then tried to force the invaders to leave, but ultimately failed. Wheeler stated that in response, the invaders became very aggressive: "The guys on the ground were going ape outside, shooting at us with catapults and throwing rocks. . . . They came to murder us. They'd actually come to kill us."

Such accounts exemplify how the war veteran network enabled disparate individuals employed in the civil service, state security branches, or private business, and in some cases those who were not employed at all, to link together through a nationalist ethos to achieve their common goal of seizing farms. These individuals, who now believed they had Mugabe's direct approval, routinely defied even the most senior government officials who sought some kind of moderation; any calls to respect the law were increasingly seen as being at odds with the rampant nationalism now overtaking the country. Obviously this nationalism provided fodder for a host of opportunists seeking to justify their criminal acts, further fueling demand for land and limiting the ability of law enforcement agencies to reign in farm seizures.

## No Turning Back on Farm Seizures

As the seizures began to far exceed their initial planned scope, Mugabe was in a bind. He could not easily order government officials to remove war veterans when he had allowed war veterans to "protest" on farms in the first place and then endorsed the seizures during the election campaign—especially when his officials were now seizing farms for themselves. Morfu noted how: "If he says, 'No, guys, stop doing this,' they will say, 'No . . . you give us the power to do this [in the first place], and now you are saying we don't have to do this?'"[82]

This was not simply a political conundrum. If Mugabe ordered the invaders off the farms, only to be disobeyed, his lack of control would become obvious; he had to be cautious to avoid a showdown that would expose the weakness of his position. From the perspective of farm foreman Telmore Nyakasanga, Mugabe's predicament was clear: "He [Mugabe] said, 'Just go [onto the farms] and do this and that [to achieve ZANU-PF's objectives].' Now to tell them, to say, 'Hey, my people, come back.' They're out. Just like lions, you know, you have to shoot them one by one [in order to stop them]."[83] Meanwhile, Sanyati noted, "If you wanted to control them, he [Mugabe] was going [to have] to use the force, his forces, the army, the police to stop them. It is very easy, but as I'm saying, police were sidelined. . . . We had no powers to stop those people."[84]

Senior officials actually became fearful of losing political support if they opposed seizures that were demanded by so many other influential figures. Conversely, participation in seizures served as a demonstration of party loyalty at a time when suspicion about political affiliation was rampant. Lundi stated that not participating raised questions of loyalty, which in turn drove more people to join the seizures.[85] Dabengwa agreed: "There wasn't much control. I think the minister of lands [Kumbirai Kangai] feared he would become unpopular if he did anything.[a] So, more or less, government decided to [turn] a blind eye to what was happening and leave things to develop as they were."[86]

A final indication of the extent that government had lost control of farm seizures comes from the International Crisis Group, which noted that in April 2000 the World Bank and the United Kingdom "had offered increased financial assistance in an effort to prevent seizures."[87] Given that Mugabe had historically blamed the lack of progress on land reform on a paucity of donor funds, particularly from the British, the decision of the donors to make funds available in April 2000 suggests there was an opportunity for genuine land reform to occur on a "willing buyer, willing seller" basis. Even with these funds

a. Kumbirai Kangai was Zimbabwe's land and agriculture minister until Mugabe reshuffled his cabinet in July 2000.

available, the government's decision not stop the seizures indicates, at some level, it *could* not stop them and had to condone the actions of the farm invaders or risk exposing its lack of control.

It is clear, therefore, from the accounts of numerous people who had personal knowledge of ZANU-PF's internal decision-making, that the government swiftly lost control of the farm seizures. This is a crucial point. The government framed the land seizures as an effort to redress the injustices of the colonial era, but the accounts of the farm invaders themselves clearly show that in fact the seizures were a political "gimmick" intended to preserve ZANU-PF's hold on power that went out of control. There is no doubt that some individuals were undertaking farm seizures for nationalist reasons, but the limited farm takeovers planned by the government were politically contrived to entrench ZANU-PF's power. Indeed, as late as April 2000, offers of donor funding presented the government with the chance to undertake a genuine land reform program. ZANU-PF spurred this last opportunity for peaceful change in favor of a more populist agenda. The acceleration of farm seizures and the widening scope of takeovers beyond the five-farms-per-district plan had little to do with redistribution of wealth from white farmers to the landless and needy. Indeed, the government lost control of takeovers because its officials saw an opportunity to enrich themselves by seizing farmers' property.

## GOVERNMENT CO-OPTS THE SEIZURES

By July 2000, with rampant farm invaders marauding across the countryside, violently seizing land and agri-property, the government turned its attention to the need to regain control. They did so not by reversing the illegal farm takeovers, but instead by establishing a legal framework to legitimize the seizures. In other words, the government sought to place the illegal land grabs within the framework of an official land redistribution policy that would allow Mugabe to operate within a legal basis. Co-opting the land invasions enabled the government to regain control by reigning in radical farm invaders, and by deploying state resources to suppress the MDC.[88] This involved using the resources and organizational capacity of a variety of state institutions, as Inkankezi explained: "When things really escalated and they were getting worse from the government's point of view, they wanted to try and put some organization on to the confusion. So that organization, obviously army is part of it, the police is part of it because those are people in the government."[89]

A first step was to form committees to regularize land seizures and provide bureaucratic processes to regulate the takeovers. District lands committees, which performed the primary role of allocating land, usually comprised the ZANU-PF chairperson, the Zimbabwe National Liberation War Veterans

Association (ZNLWVA) district chairperson, the head of the Department of Lands, the head of Agritex, the District Administrator Security Sector representative, and the customary chief's representative.[90]

According to Chidembo, who personally participated in a district lands committee, all such committees included representatives of the CIO, police, army, war veterans, and the provincial administrator—highlighting the central role of the state security services.[91] Chidembo stated that, at first, some members of the district lands committees, particularly the provincial administrators, genuinely believed that the land redistribution decisions undertaken by the committee would help to alleviate the real land inequity problems that existed in Zimbabwe. However, Chidembo reported that these administrators started to resign, owing to the fact that the committees quickly became mired in corruption: "And this is why you now have, anybody who decides . . . a minister decides to occupy a farm or a war veteran or a member of the army decides to occupy a farm and they have it because you know the whole thing just collapsed." Indeed, according to Timothy Ngavi, an accountant for the Grain Marketing Board (GMB)—which provided the agricultural inputs such as seed and fertilizer—reported that the allocation of resources by these committees was "political" and highly corrupt.[92] He said that in one instance when corruption was discovered, the offending individuals were fired by GMB officials, only to regain their positions shortly afterward.

The government also sought to erect a legal framework over the farm seizures in order to "legalize occupations *post fact*."[93] The first step was the Accelerated Land Reform and Resettlement Implementation Plan (also known as the "Fast Track Land Reform Programme"—FTLRP) announced in July 2000, which aimed to seize more than 3,000 farms.[94] Only with the implementation of the FTLRP could the seizure of farms begin to be presented as land reform program. Even then, the FTLRP was without any doubt a partisan and politically motivated reaction to the unintended large-scale farm takeovers; it was not in itself a genuine land reform program. However, it would soon become the main legal instrument for redistributing land, simply because farm invasions could not be reversed. Ultimately the transfer of vast quantities of land was implemented under the FTLRP. Indeed, Lionel Cliffe et al. identify the FTLRP as being the next stage in a long series of postindependence land reform programs.[95]

The FTLRP was a major departure from the initial five-farm-per-district scheme that would have yielded only 295 farms. The plan reflected the scale of the farm seizures that had already occurred, as well as the government's inability to control events. The government's own Utete report—the findings of a committee set up by Mugabe in May 2003 to examine the implementation and impact of land redistribution—stated that the implementation of the scheme was impeded by "administrative difficulties encountered by an over-stretched bureaucratic apparatus suddenly called upon to implement a complex pro-gramme in great haste."[96]

To further legalize the farm invasions, Mugabe issued a pardon in October 2000 to "those involved in political violence from the beginning of January to the end of July that year, covering both the Constitutional Referendum and the General Election."[97] In this way, the government could override legal obstacles to its agenda and appear to be supporting the invaders. The International Crisis Group aptly noted that "all these efforts were designed to camouflage the illegitimacy of the invasions while serving as a direct assault on the MDC's supporters."[98]

This effort to co-opt the seizures was inherently an effort to regularize and legalize what was a free-for-all of farm takeovers. It was also fundamentally a partisan move to entrench ZANU-PF support as the new landownership framework evolved. The district lands committees were highly partisan, and MDC-supporting land claimants were very rarely accepted. Indeed, farmers surveyed for this book indicated that 97% of those leading final farm takeovers were ruling party members. This claim is supported by Alexander, who identified instances where politicians stated that only ZANU-PF members would benefit from "Fast Track" land.[99]

## Justifying the Seizure of Farms: The "Land Redistribution Programme"

ZANU-PF's primary motive for allowing the initial seizures, and then co-opting the more radical movement that erupted in early 2000, had been to salvage its political power. As senior government official Thompson Mupfure put it, "This strategy [farm invasions] was never meant to address the land issue. It was a strategy to address a political issue."[100]

Soon after the referendum defeat, the police officer Edison Bubye recalled, Mugabe began "campaigning, should I say propagandizing people, to say, 'Look here, this is now a war. It's the British—they want to recolonize our country.'"[101] Inkankezi argued that the government's emphasis on addressing colonial-era wrongdoing was "just politics."[102] He noted that "they are only trying to drum it up [land expectations]. I think to start with, the idea was not to take the farms, but when it got out of hand, so that they don't lose face, they had to put some organization to it and try to make it as if it has been something on the drawing cards." Likewise, Lundi scoffed when asked whether the government really intended to undertake real land reform: "No, it wasn't a genuine desire to really say it was like 'land reform.' No, [land reform] was just a name."[103]

The farm seizures represented "political expediency which went terribly, terribly wrong," according to Lundi, who added that "'land reform' is a misnomer. To me it was like a faulty grabbing exercise which really, really went terribly, terribly, terribly wrong."[104] He added:

Individuals in government who considered the idea . . . they didn't think [about] the scope it assumed. I think it was beyond their wildest, wildest dreams. Their thought was it was just going to be something controlled, something maybe that they can use to . . . just knock some, whether it was some sense into the white guys' heads, I don't know. . . . But never in their wildest dreams did they ever think it was going to assume those proportions it did.

All the government could do was co-opt the seizures and frame them in the most politically expedient manner possible.

In Matondi's research into the "disorderliness" of the land reform program, he states that "the reforms were deemed 'fast track' without there being a sound economic or political reason why they had to be 'fast' as opposed to being carried out at a normal rate."[105] He also questions why there were no mechanisms for self-correction as the government's land program was implemented. Indeed, Matondi quoted a government official who summarized the fast track land reform as "do and ask later."[106] The reason that the FTLRP framework was concocted so hastily is that the government never intended or planned for large-scale land redistribution. Only when events moved beyond its control did the government conceive a scheme to capture the farm seizures within a legal framework. As Mupfure put it, "I think the strategy was not very much polished even from the beginning. You start on the invasions and then you keep polishing it."[107] It is because there was no existing plan for farm seizures that a structure had to evolve over time as pressures from government stakeholders and farm invaders evolved.

Ultimately the effort to co-opt the farm seizures was successful, insofar as it enabled the government to reign in independent farm invaders and allow the takeovers to occur within a newly defined legal framework. As its strategy evolved after the first, chaotic months of the farm seizures, ZANU-PF was increasingly able to entrench its control, secure the political support of war veterans, and suppress the fortunes of the rival MDC. Yet this came at a price. As the rule of law collapsed, Zimbabwe came to be regarded as a pariah state, where the government had gambled the welfare of its people in order to preserve its power.

## CONCLUSION

Evidence presented in this chapter sheds light on the question of what motivated the Zimbabwean state to attack the nation's economically critical agriculture industry. Prior to the February 2000 referendum, the government had not intended to target the agriculture industry. Government officials recognized the importance of the commercial farming sector to the economy and they knew that large-scale occupations would affect international donor funding. When threatened with political defeat in the referendum by the MDC, however, the government rapidly formulated a plan to undertake limited occupations of five farms per district. This, it was hoped, would warn farmers to end financial support for the MDC, alleviate war veterans' land demands, and provide some land to decongest communal areas. The government did not, at this stage, intend for the land seizures to turn violent.

Yet once limited seizures began, the initial limited scope was ignored because war veterans found that valuable farms and associated agri-property were relatively easy to seize. This was exacerbated by senior state security officials who were sympathetic to the war veteran cause and were not willing to enforce the law on farms. Indeed, individuals in the state security services and government began seizing farms for themselves. Thus, those meant to be restraining the seizures were in fact participating in them. The result was greater demand for farms. Mugabe and the government had little choice but to embrace the wave of uncontrolled seizures that followed, rather than reveal their inability to control them.

Some commentators, such as Sam Moyo, Paris Yeros, and Hanlon, Manjengwa, and Smart, believe the land seizures were a genuine effort to achieve land reform.[108] Evidence from this chapter shows that, on the contrary, the land reform aspect was purely a political "gimmick" intended to disguise the underlying political objectives that had little to do with addressing inequity in landownership. ZANU-PF had only one overriding motivation in triggering, and then co-opting, the land seizures—to maintain its grip on power.

# 4

## Strategy behind Farm Seizures

The previous chapter explained how ZANU-PF was compelled to support the rollout of a much more expansive campaign of land seizures than it had initially intended during 2000. But how were the seizures to be achieved? This chapter examines the strategies farm invaders used to seize farms. It provides detail on the methods deployed in evicting farmers, assesses how farms were selected for invasion, and analyzes the effect of changes to the composition of farm invader groups as the seizures escalated.

Just as the seizures themselves escalated far beyond their initial planned scope, this chapter shows how farm seizures turned into violent, uncontrolled events as a result of increasing competition for limited resources among farm invader groups. Finally, this chapter details how farmers were forced to make desperate concessions in the face of increasing pressure being placed on them to leave their farms and in the absence of the rule of law.

### HISTORICAL PATTERNS ROOTED IN THE LIBERATION WAR

Many of the strategies use by farm invaders during the land seizure era were, at their core, methods borrowed from the guerrilla movement in the Liberation War. This is no surprise given that in the early stages of the farm seizures, war veterans led most of the initial invasion groups.

Between 1969 and 1972, ZANU and its military wing, ZANLA, used a Maoist strategy of peasant "education" and mobilization, by which the war could be "given to the people," according to David Lan.[1] Indeed, Josiah Tungamirai, ZANLA's second in command, explained that the group's strategy was based on "mass political mobilization."[2] In Ranger's view, ZANU's heavy reliance on politicization and "education" meant it sought not only to mobilize the peasants, but to politically radicalize the population.[3]

In order to achieve this mass mobilization during the Liberation War, ZANU employed strategies that relied heavily on coercion and infiltration of civilian lives. A key initial step was to establish formal and informal village committees made up of elected officials or ZANLA appointees. The committee structure enabled guerrillas to infiltrate and embed themselves by "swimming among the people like fishes," in Ranger's words.[4] This way, nationalists could cultivate the impression that radicalism was popular within the villagers' own social networks, and guerrillas could lead by example, allowing villagers' sentiments to be established and enabling appropriate methods for ensuring compliance to be devised.

To achieve civilian compliance, ZANLA also relied heavily on political education meetings; these were known as *pungwes* during the Liberation War. *Pungwes* were intended to define and instill loyalty to the guerrilla cause. Attendance was compulsory and meetings sometimes lasted for days. Violence was a cornerstone of the process—reluctant participants faced physical assault, and suspected traitors were usually executed.[5] Civilians generally remembered *pungwes* with great fear, according to Kriger.[6]

*Pungwes* allowed ZANLA to determine civilians' loyalty, a vital component for any guerrilla movement, but an obligation especially demanded by ZANLA. Those who did not support the guerrilla effort, along with those who were so much as suspected of assisting the Rhodesian state in the smallest way, were accused of "selling out" to the whites. "'Sellouts' were usually killed or beaten publicly," according to Kriger.[7] Welshman Mabhena, a veteran of the war, governor of Matabeleland North, and senior ZANU-PF official who had extensive access to the ruling party's inner-circle planning, explained that coercion of civilians was effective in ensuring that they cooperated in delivering logistical support: "The guerrillas had gone out killing people. Anybody whom they thought was a 'sellout' would be killed—never spared. And that was set in the minds of the people."[8]

Evidence of selling out did not have to be substantial. According to Alexander, McGregor, and Ranger, "People's stories of sellout accusations emphasise the arbitrariness of killings based on a mere hunch or divination."[9] According to Lan and Kriger, commercial farm workers were highly vulnerable to accusations of "helping whites."[10] Ranger has shown that chiefs and headmen were attacked for cooperating with the government, as were government workers, rural councilors, agricultural advisors, rural elites employed by the government, and storekeepers. Christians were occasionally targeted for adhering to a "foreign" religion.[11] Informers for the Rhodesian army would be killed without hesitation.

Many of these same strategies were implemented in the land seizure era, as Chavunduka and Bromley have also noted. Indeed, ZANU-PF made a concerted effort to ensure that civilians complied with its political objectives.[12] The party again used *pungwes* and similar events to politicize rural communities. Demonstrative violence was utilized against civilians who were perceived to be opposed to the farm seizures, especially senior village officials and respected community members. Indeed, purported "sellouts" faced draconian punishments including beating, torture, and even murder.

The claim that the government's strategies during the land seizure era were borrowed from the Liberation War was frequently made during interviews for this book. For example, Peter Msasa, a Zimbabwean army military intelligence official, explained:

They used to use the same tactics [used in the land seizure era] during the war. During the war they would go to a village. They introduce themselves and then they will start saying, "Sellouts, we don't want sellouts." And then they will try one or two just to look who is a sellout, so that he will be killed in front of the people in an example.[13]

Msasa explained that, during the farm invasions, the population was already aware of mobilization strategies used during the Liberation War. Therefore, when farm invaders began making threats and asking for "sellouts," there was a preconditioned response of fear. In most instances, this would bring about almost immediate compliance.

## HOW FARMS WERE SELECTED FOR INVASION

In the initial stages of the land seizure era, prior to June 2000 during the five-farms-per-district plan, farms were selected primarily based on the farmer's political affiliation and on the farmer's treatment of farm workers (see chapter 5 for an in-depth discussion).

Edward Chidembo, senior member of the Zimbabwe Republic Police, explained that the district lands committees—which played a major role in deciding what farms to target after the government co-opted the land seizures in mid-2000—had wanted a more nuanced approach, where "good" farmers, who contributed to their communities, were distinguished from "bad" farmers, who had poor labor relations and were said to hold racist views.[14]

A first step in some farm invasions was for invaders to gather background information on the farmer. Horticulture manager Andrew Morfu and farm foreman Telmore Nyakasanga reported that farm invaders sought information on whether the farmer was involved with the MDC, had treated his workers fairly, whether he had a history of abusing farm laborers, and if labor relations with the farmer were generally positive.[15] Agents also wanted to know whether the farmer had a history of racism, or had had a prominent role in the Rhodesian military or government.

However, in almost all cases the level of support for the MDC was the key factor in determining which farms were to be seized in the early stages of the seizures. Any other considerations were at best secondary. According to Chidembo:

> I think the local land committees would have wanted to use that [more nuanced] criteria, but I think the directives . . . often contradicted that kind of criteria. . . . The directive usually came from higher up, was based on political reasons. . . . This program was a political program right from the beginning. It was never an agricultural program or a program to address inequalities and so on. It was a way for Mugabe to survive politically.

While some farmers who did display racist views and treated farm laborers poorly were targeted accordingly, other farmers were wrongly accused of such violations by farm invaders who wanted to seize their property. Morfu identified that there were no checks to determine whether negative reports were true. Thus, this method of selecting farms was easily abused, and negative information was often falsely presented, either by individual workers with personal grievances, or by farm invaders who wanted the farm for themselves. Farm invaders found that it was relatively easy to pay others to make allegations against a farmer, or to cooperate with other groups of invaders to make claims on each other's behalf. Indeed, Morfu said that farm invaders would contrive grievances:

> They [farm invaders] couldn't find the bad information about the boss whom I was working with. They couldn't find the information. The boss was good. He gave credit [loans to his workers]. He did everything. And our compound [the worker village] was also quite fine. It was a better compound than the people who are living here in town [Harare]. . . . So they couldn't find those [sic] bad information.

According to Morfu, in such cases the invaders would go to the district land committee (the institution tasked with overseeing land allocations)—or to an influential ZANU-PF official—and complain: "I am a black person. I need a farm. I need this farm. That white person must go because whether it's been a good thing or a bad thing, I must have this farm. So you must send that farmer a Section 8 [eviction order].[a] So they get a court order."

Similarly, mechanic Beton Mopane stated that "some of the war veterans, they were going to the head officers and lying—lying—talking bad things about the other farmers who were left on the farms."[16] He stated that farm invaders would often implicate the farmer as being a key supporter of the opposition: "They will say that he's the main guy who's causing problems here, so you mustn't live next to him, so he must go."

Morfu stated that in many cases the Section 8 eviction orders were forgeries.[17] Nevertheless, if the farmer went to the district administrator or other local officials, he would be told the matter was "political" and they could not intervene. Morfu said that the farm invaders would ultimately be successful even if the farmer thought he could secure additional legal remedy: "They'll just take it [the farm]. You [farmer] now take it to court or wherever you want to take it; it doesn't make any difference because it's just coming here from the top [senior ZANU-PF officials ordering compliance with farm takeovers]." A history of support for ZANU-PF could provide a small level of protection for the farmer, but only during the early months of the land seizure era, before farm seizures started to slide out of control and become more violent. Very few white farmers felt genuine affinity toward the ruling party (see chapter 2), though some gave support to ZANU-PF in an effort to maintain goodwill with local party officials. For example, Lundi reported that before weekend events, such as the visit of the provincial governor, farm invaders would seek "freebies" from local farmers: "They will give you lots of meat to take away" for the event.[18] Thompson Mupfure, a former guerrilla in the Liberation War and senior government official, remembered that he found a farmer giving cattle to Moven Mahachi, the minister of defense, while other farmers gave donations of money to ZANU-PF conferences, donated tractors to till the fields of local black farmers, and provided their skills and expertise to help local farmers.[19] This kind of support was recorded and provided nominal protection for the farmer during the early phases of the land seizures. War veteran leader Alex Siwaze emphasized that historically ZANU-PF officials had sought cooperation from farmers because it enabled them to gain access to valuable agricultural commodities.[20] However,

---

a. A Section 8 is an order of compulsory acquisition by the government. The document gives the farm owner 45 days to end farming activities and a further 45 days to vacate the farm homestead. A Section 5 is a preliminary notice of the government's intention to acquire a farm. This notice must be "gazetted" by being published for two consecutive weeks in an official newspaper. Anyone receiving a Section 5 notice can then receive a Section 8.

as more and more farm invaders began to seek farms, these kinds of historical efforts by farmers were quickly ignored.

Confrontations with farmers then became inevitable. In the early stages of the land seizure era, the level of violence on a farm depended on the personal attributes of the farm invader, such as whether he was a particularly aggressive person, the reputation of the farmer within the local black community, and the extent of the farmer's support for the MDC.[21] However, other attributes were soon also major considerations. Farms deemed to be more valuable—those containing better-quality land and more agri-property (movable farm assets such as farm implements)—also contributed to more violence. Additionally, the farmer survey shows that the government's role in encouraging invasions led to greater levels of conflict. Respondents were asked whether there were tipping points that specifically led to political violence and intimidation; that is, specific incidents that precipitated an upsurge in violence or intimidation. Among respondents, 51.4% claimed that government statements encouraging land and property seizures directly led to an upsurge in violence that they, or those they knew, experienced.

The extent to which these factors combined to produce violence varied considerably. The personal discretion of those leading each farm invasion was always crucial. If this individual thought the farmer was *mabhunu*—racist— and the farm invader was strongly opposed to such beliefs and was able and willing to use violence, then the farm was likely to be taken over violently. However, in some cases the farmer was *mabhunu* but also had a strong reputation for being a violent man himself. As such, he may have been perceived as presenting too formidable a target and would be bypassed by farm invaders seeking an "easier" farm to seize. For example, Elizabeth Shore, the spouse of a farmer, stated that one farmer in her area in Mashonaland Central was a notorious racist: "I can tell you there is the odd farmer in our area who is a complete horror story, and yet they [farm invaders] wouldn't try it [eviction] on him because they were probably scared of him. He is physically very large, not known to communicate well with the workers. . . . And they just let him be."[22]

Thus, the personal tendencies of the seizing invaders, the reputation of the farmer for poor treatment of labor and racist beliefs, the quality of land and volume of agri-property, and the farmer's level of association with the MDC were all fundamental considerations for how violently the farm would be seized. Yet the ultimate determinant was the personal discretion of the individual leading the seizure; how much he wanted the farm and what methods he could rely on to seize control.

Bubye explained that the war veteran groups would sing *chimurenga* war songs as they approached a farm to rally invaders by giving the seizures a nationalist ethos and validity, and to intimidate the farmer and workers.[23] The farmer would usually make a claim to the group about his landownership based on purchasing the farm on the market, to which the war veteran group would respond with nationalist rhetoric: "No, no, no, no. We're not having that. We are taking our land. Who are you? We are the war vets—we fought for this." If a farmer forcefully resisted to the extent that the invaders deemed the takeover too difficult, the war veteran group moved to an easier target, as Mopane explained: "Those people [farm invaders], they are just going and see if that man [the farmer] is brave enough or not. If he's brave enough, then they don't come again tomorrow. If he's scared, then they'll keep on coming until you [the farmer] leave that farm."[24] Thus, initially, farms were seized when possible and bypassed when the farmer successfully resisted.

Nevertheless, resistance usually brought only temporary respite until farm invaders gathered additional resources to allow them to take control. Beton Mopane, a farm mechanic, explained: "It was ending up by being a big violence on the farm [if the farmer resisted], with a group of people trying to fight the farm workers and the farmer."[25] An account from farmer Gerry Garner supports this claim that the more farmers resisted, the more pressure was placed to evict them.[26] Garner stated that initially a member of the state security approached him by threatening his children: "There were individuals [in state security] who came to me and said, 'We know where your kids go to school. We'll sort that out. We'll make you get off your farm. . . . They thought we'd just pack our bags and run. Mugabe said he'd chase us to the borders. I honestly believe they thought we'd pack our bags and run." However, many farmers resisted, and particularly after about June 2000 state security worked closely with farm invaders to escalate the conflict until they relented: "At every single invasion the police would confer with the war vet leaders. They would take the war vet leader aside and they'd chat to them. Initially they [police] had very, very good control. When, when they realized that we weren't actually going to move off the farms, then they allowed it to get more and more grubby [violent]." When asked why coercion escalated, Garner said, "I believe it's because we challenged them head on." This claim, that the more farmers resisted, the more pressure was deployed to remove them, was widely asserted in interviews.

## COMPOSITION OF A FARM INVASION GROUP

The composition and general behavior of farm invasion groups can be roughly differentiated by whether they came into being prior to the elections in June 2000, or whether they emerged once farm seizures slipped out of control after this period. However, there was considerable variation in these groups. As discussed in chapters 2 and 3, the clamor to be counted as a "war veteran" helped to drive the escalation of the seizures, and there is no doubt that farm invaders tended to become more aggressive as time went on. Farm manager Ketani Makabusi explained that "there was a time when we were permitted to [continue to] farm [pre-June 2000] and when there was like a scramble for land."[27]

In the early stages of farm invasions, prior to June 2000, farm invader groups were comprised of war veteran leaders plus youths, who were "street boys who had nothing to do at the time," and members of the rural unemployed.[28] Farmers tended to sum up the composition of farm invasion groups more succinctly, with one anonymous survey respondent stating: "It was more of a gang of thugs," highlighting from the farmers' perspective how the arrival of a war veteran group brought unrest and coercion. Sadomba states that "the organisation of the land movement did not have a conventional hierarchical formation, having been rooted in the structures, ethos and practices of guerrilla strategies and tactics and in the local traditional agro-religious formations."[29] War veterans directly employed in the military or government were not personally involved in farm takeovers in the early stage, because their employment meant that their time was occupied.[30] Moreover, in the early phase only limited takeovers were planned, so there was no need for employed war veterans to be involved.

Farm invasion groups tended to be large in the early stages, and then again as a final push was made to take control. As the leader of a farmer security group for a district in Mashonaland Central, Arthur Breckinridge, noted: "This is a numbers game. Never ever have I seen one, two or three of these fellows pitch up on a commercial farm and say, 'Right, we're taking it.' There's always a whole truckload of them."[31] Indeed, not all groups were large, since powerful land claimants typically provided other means of signaling their strength, such as travelling in military vehicles with armed supporters. Nevertheless, numerous survey respondents reported farm invasion groups numbering 100 or even in excess of 200 people.[32]

There were several types of farm invasion group leaders. In the early phases of farm takeovers, from February to June 2000, where invasions groups tended to be more ad hoc and loosely controlled, the leader was almost always a genuine, unemployed war veteran; police officer Edison Bubye in fact stated that farm invasion groups were "all led by the war vets."[33] These leaders were seeking land (as opposed to agri-property) at this stage, and were typically motivated by a nationalist land redistribution ethos as well as the individual's poor economic condition at the time. In practically all instances, however, the group was known to—if not directed by—the CIO, which sought to influence the actions of the groups. However, these groups during the early period could often undertake substantial violence—particularly given the unstable and raw political environment following ZANU-PF's referendum defeat—and it is all but certain that the government lacked the capacity to totally control them.

Farm manager Ketani Makabusi explained that war veterans had "absolute control" over their farm invasion group in the early stages of farm invasions, prior to June 2000.[34] War veteran leaders also had significant flexibility in their decision-making because in the early phases of farm invasions there was little overarching state control or apparatus to guide decisions in the field. Therefore, the experiences of farmers varied considerably because they were dependent in large part on the temperament, strategies, and objectives of the war veteran decision-maker, and therefore there was variation in the behaviors across war veteran groups. As one anonymous farmer survey respondents indicated: "Different gangs did not behave the same."

War veteran leaders sometimes acted as a moderating force, particularly in the early stages. In one instance, Makabusi watched as a young farm invader "abused" some farmers only to be quickly rebuked by the war veteran leader: "Hey you, lighties [youths], you stop that. I'm not going to allow you to do this. . . . You are supposed to be backing up only. You are not supposed to administer violence to that particular commercial farmer. Stop what you are doing."[35] One anonymous farmer survey respondent stated, "Twice violence against me was stopped by other war vets," and another said:

> Only one occurrence of intimidation occurred. A few days later three genuine ZIPRA war vets, whom I knew in the community, visited me to assure me that if any other intimidation took place, I was to send for them and they would get rid of the perpetrators. They told me not to go to the police as they were politicised and would not help me.

In a final example, Makabusi noted how on some occasions genuine war veterans imposed strict rules against farm invasions becoming too violent as long as the farmer cooperated:

> When they were invading, the preservation of human life was part of it. They did make it a point: "We are not really going to go out of hand on this in terms of kill people, but we will discipline you if you don't back us up." They would make a point of that.[36]

Meanwhile, Makabusi spoke about the particular war veteran on the farm where he worked:

> The guy in our particular situation, he did make it a point: "I don't want bloodshed. I have been tasked to clean up this area [evict farmers]. I'm

going to do it, but no bloodshed. . . . There's got to be no bloodshed." And the reason he gave me was that he was under instruction from the local spirit medium to make sure that no blood must be shed during this exercise.[37]

Some farmer respondents also noted that genuine war veteran leaders tended to be easier to negotiate with during the early period—although this was occasional. Farmer Brian Wheeler gave this explanation:

> I found it was much easier to deal with genuine war vets, much easier [than youths or other non-war veterans]. They seemed to have more re-spect and more discipline. . . . In the [local] African language it would be more "respect for blood." They'd actually been through it [during the Lib-eration War] and they'd actually seen dead people and they'd actually seen all this. But these other arseholes had no concept of that at all, and there was much less discipline among them.[38]

Wheeler continued: "A genuine War Vet tended to be, in my experience anyway, to pull back a bit. I found I could talk to them more and reason with them more, while these other guys—their minds were just totally shut." It should be emphasized that this kind of experience tended to occur only during the early period; once farm invasions escalated out of control in about July–August 2000, examples of moderation became far more unusual.

Indeed, Makabusi said the same war veteran in the previous example was far more aggressive with the neighboring farmer: "He [the war veteran leader] was, like, literally, 'I'm giving you 24 hours to pack your bags. I'm giving you literally time to pack your bags, get into your vehicle, and drive off, or tomor-row morning you aren't going to be alive.'"[39] This highlights the subjective variation in how farms were approached by invader groups during the early phases. Makabusi explained it this way: "Our guys [invaders on his farm] were more violent, but the degree with how they went about it just varied with who was actually handling the operation. Our guy was basically like a moderate guy to a degree."

Invasions taking place after June 2000 tended to be far more intensified and violent because there were far more farm invaders frantically seeking land and agri-property before other, competing agents gained the assets. Farm manager Makabusi stated that uncontrolled attacks on farmers—often driven by alco-hol or drugs—were not usually undertaken by genuine war veterans: "That did happen, but it wasn't anyone under the command of a war vet or any group that was led by a true war vet. That was caused by hoodlums. That was caused by thugs."[40] He explained further that the "first groups that came in, the groups who were led by the original war vets—those incidents didn't take place like that. They were generally under control. There was a command. It was systematic." There is little doubt that lines could be blurred between more disciplined war veterans and "thugs," and as has been noted, there were numerous variables at play on each farm. Makabusi differentiated this early period from later takeovers:

[If] there was a prospective farm owner or someone who wanted a piece of land, [the individual] would go along and hire a couple of guys, get them boozed up, go onto a property, and make a whole lot of noise. That was caused by the politicos who went in and tried to get land. . . . Then you got hooliganism just prevailing afterwards and guys misbehaving.

War veterans with more moderate views were deliberately not selected to target farmers. Moreover, war veterans who had committed crimes elsewhere before the land seizure era were told that they would not be charged with these crimes if they undertook successful farm seizures. Mupfure explained that in exchange for not being charged, criminals were told that "'this is payback time. You must follow instructions. Go and kill so and so. Go and beat up so and so. Go and loot and so forth.' And they were very much willing to do so."[41]

War veteran leaders were chosen for their loyalty to ZANU-PF and, according to Mupfure, for their antiwhite and criminal tendencies, but they still demonstrated high levels of discretion in how they selected farms to target and the manner in which they treated farmers and workers. Accordingly, it was not uncommon for neighboring farmers to have markedly different experiences with the same war veteran leader.

As the farm takeovers evolved, the leadership and composition of the farm takeover group began to change. Starting gradually in the period leading up to the June 2000 election, more senior individuals in government became aware that the breakdown in rural security, and the de facto green light given by some ZANU-PF leaders to invade farms, meant that substantial farm wealth was available to anyone willing and able to evict the commercial farmer. While in some cases the existing war veteran leaders continued seeking land for themselves after June 2000, in other instances the farm invasion group was co-opted by more powerful and influential people in order to seize assets for themselves. The shift was shaped by the evolving awareness of the opportunity to seize farm land and assets; the recognition that the strength of law was decreasing most rapidly in rural locations where ZANU-PF held key positions in the state security and legislative infrastructure, which facilitated easier farm takeovers; and by the willingness and ability of individuals to marshal their resources to target farms.

There was no set formula for the leadership of farm invasion groups after June 2000. However, these groups normally included a war veteran in a leadership position, who provided the ability to articulate the ethos justifying the land seizures and could draw upon his wartime military service to mobilize individuals to participate in the invasion. As farm seizures progressed, however, groups were often led by anyone with skills in coordinating individuals in violence, such as members of the state security services.

When farm invasions groups were being orchestrated by a senior politician, prominent businessperson, member of the civil service, or other such individual, this person was usually located in Harare or other urban center where he was permanently employed. For this reason, it was necessary for the primary individual orchestrating the takeover to closely coordinate with the farm invasion group leader. The group leader, who was usually a war veteran working on a contract basis to evict the farmer, was easy to identify because that person was often vociferously coordinating the group and engaging with the farmer, but also often on cell phones communicating with others.[42] For example, farmer Gerry Garner indicated how he identified these coordinators:

> We discovered from time to time that there were plainclothes [members of the] army in amongst the thugs, the guys that were being used [i.e., by other more senior people]. Often you'd pick up a really intelligent guy. He'd be communicating on a cell phone, and we believe those were military guys that were briefing direct with their Ops from wherever that was.[43]

Other farmer survey respondents also provided examples of farm invasion groups operating at the behest of other people. For example, "It appears the settlers were being controlled by an outside political force. Whenever there was a stalemate or a situation that they did not know what to do, it seemed they went to get advice. This advice was put into action when they returned to the farm." In another example the respondent stated: "Four unknown 'minders' were instructed to 'guard' the property and equipment for the future owner. They stole my caravan and took up residence in it, in the garden. They were very likely military personnel—they wore issued boots and had cash to booze and smoke *mbanje* [marijuana]." Farmer survey respondents also gave examples of farm invader groups being supplied by an outside group controlling the overall farm invasion: "Food and alcohol [were] supplied daily to initial squatters in 2000, still being supplied with food by ZANU PF/government even when it is not available to the general public."

Farmers noted that leaders could at times be difficult to identify because these individuals were potentially undertaking criminal activities, or because they were acting surreptitiously on behalf of ZANU-PF and did not want to be identified. For instance, Ronald Jongwe, a member of the army, described how his colleagues in the military sought to discretely participate in farm invasions by changing their clothing: "I know soldiers who were 'away from work' even during elections time. They went there [to farms] 'as campaigners of ZANU-PF,' but they are uniformed forces and they are war veterans."[44] Jongwe explained that Mugabe "probably didn't want to make it appear to the world as if you are sending a uniformed force to invade, but to make it [seem like] a citizen who are going on this *jambanja* [in the context of farm seizures, a rally intended to evict the farmer]."

Early farm invader groups also received different levels of compensation, highlighting how even in the early period (albeit to a lesser extent than after June 2000), the takeover of farms did not occur spontaneously but almost always occurred as part of a campaign orchestrated by powerful individuals. Farm invaders would be rewarded with cash payments, promises of assets from the farm if the farmer was evicted, access to women provided by farm invader leaders for sexual purposes, as well as free alcohol and *mbanje* (marijuana).[45] Some 16.3% of farmer survey respondents witnessed farm invaders being compensated with cash.[46] One anonymous farmer survey respondent stated: "Early occupiers admitted being paid +/− three times the going farm wage to squat on farms. Were paid at the District Administrator's offices in Tsholotsho"; this example of invaders being paid from a government office underscores state orchestration of seizures. Because of logistical costs, farm invasions could not ordinarily be coordinated and achieved by the "rural poor." They had to be undertaken by an individual or group with sufficient resources to maintain pressure on the farmer and repel competitor farm invaders for what could be three years or more of coercion until the farmer left his land. This highlights why more senior individuals in the civil service—and those with access to "free" coercive resources such as state security officials and politicians—tended to gain farms.

Cash was not as commonly used to pay farm invaders because it had obvious cost to the leaders who dispensed it. Other resources on the farm, however, could be promised to youths with no loss to the senior individual coordinating the takeover. Indeed, 33.4% of farmer respondents stated that farm invaders were compensated with promises of land if they were successful in seizing the farm, while 21.2% were promised "spoils" from the farm, such as equipment and fertilizer. It is unlikely that hired youths and other lower level invaders would gain valuable equipment in practice, however, because ultimately such assets would be taken by a more senior individual. In fact, 18.3% were compensated with food and 17.1% were compensated with *mbanje* or alcohol, according to farmer survey respondents. Finally, 3.3% were rewarded by being given access to women to exploit for sexual purposes.

After June 2000 the operations of a farm seizure group were always monitored by the CIO. In most cases, agents operated surreptitiously, insofar as the
farmer and workers were concerned to remove any indication of government
support.[47] Msasa explained that CIO operatives did not want to be identified
by farmers or workers, so they would meet invasion groups at night. In these
meetings, the CIO agent would direct the extent of violence to be deployed in
forthcoming engagements and generally provide organization and management for the effort. He emphasized that individuals who ultimately seized the
farm were not necessarily defined by the CIO, but the CIO did assist in coordinating and controlling the seizures. The CIO's influence also meant that
when other senior ZANU-PF officials were involved, the CIO directly assisted
certain senior officials in seizing farms and agri-property.[48]

Invasion groups preparing to engage farmers or workers would often con-
sume alcohol or smoke *mbanje*. Some 59.2% of farmer survey respondents
stated that invaders were under the influence of alcohol when targeting their
farms, and 55% stated that invaders were under the influence of *mbanje*. Msasa
explained that the use of *mbanje* by members of invasion groups was widespread; in his view 80% used the drug before an operation. Msasa explained
the main reason why drugs and alcohol were used by invaders: "To get cour-
age, because remember you are expecting that someone might die, that you
will kill somebody. Maybe you will end up cutting the head [of a victim], because you have been told that [farm invaders] we need the information tonight.
So if you are told that we need it tonight, the only option is torture."[49] From the
perspective of farmers and workers, who often had to engage with such groups
at night, intoxicated farm invaders brought a new level of volatility and danger
to confrontations. Respondents repeatedly stated that when farm invaders
were intoxicated, they were difficult to restrain and prone to incidental provo-
cations, and if violence did break out, it was likely to be more severe.

These claims from farmer respondents are supported by Msasa, who said
that the CIO did not provide farm invaders with *mbanje*, but that farm invaders would purchase it themselves, especially when operating in rural areas: "I
don't think that they are encouraged to smoke, . . . but mostly the guys when
they are in the bush will end up smoking, so all the guys will smoke."[50]

## Youths in Farm Invasion Groups

"Youths" played an important role in adding numbers to the overall group
size, thereby increasing the intimidatory effect. In the words of senior military
intelligence agent Daniel Inkankezi, "99.9% of them [farm invaders] were not
ex-combatants"; most were youths and other civilians.[51] Youths could be male
or female, but they were usually males aged 18–20, occasionally up to age 24.[52]

According to several sources, if female youths were present, the males in the group usually became more violent because the women tended to urge the males to take more aggressive actions.[53]

In farm invasion groups, a key role for youths was in providing "muscle" in the form of individuals who were willing and able to threaten victims and undertake various tasks assigned by war veteran leaders. In order to create this intimidatory force, farm invader leaders needed a pool of impressionable and unemployed young people who would also be unlikely to claim land and thereby dilute available resources for the leaders. The solution for leaders was to source youths from Mbare and other impoverished areas on the outskirts of Harare.[54] Inkankezi explained: "They were just ordinary thugs hired off or taken from the streets."[55] Hiring youths from Mbare meant that these individuals were already used to some level of violence. Msasa emphasized that unlike youths who "grew up in the villages" and were comparatively unexposed to violence, "those guys who were born in Mbare, you know when you grow up in the ghetto . . . [those individuals] are quite strong, and mostly it's those ex-prisoners as well."[56] Thus, Mbare residents could have both criminal histories and experience growing up amid crime, violence, and poverty, making them ideal candidates to assist in evicting farmers and suppressing the MDC.

Youths from Mbare, who had few other professional or social prospects, were an ideal repository of potential agents to hire for farm takeovers.[57] Those leading the farm invasions would bring their family members (who participated at no cost), and then, depending on their financial resources, hired small or larger numbers of these youths to supplement their numbers over a specified period where they tried to evict a particular farmer.[58] Christian Mucheke, a legal officer in the President's Office, provided insight into why youths and others undertook conflict on behalf of those leading farm invasions. Mucheke stated that with the country's economic problems becoming more severe, participating in invasions "gave them [youths] an opportunity to make money . . . the reward was so tempting because you'd be tempted—5 acres or 10 acres of land in a prime area and that was very tempting. And again, remember, every time on the news, on the radio, music was about taking land and making a person a hero because he has taken land."[59] Mucheke explained that with these kinds of inducements, recruiting agents was not difficult.

Youths from suburbs of Harare could also not easily be identified by rural victims, an additional advantage for the youths and organizers seeking to avoid accountability. Indeed, invaders were often specifically deployed to areas unfamiliar to them so that they would not easily be identified, a specific sign of premeditated criminal intent. For example, when asked why farm invaders did not target areas close to them, thereby minimizing the need for long-distance travel, rose manager Andrew Morfu stated:

> So that you cannot identify the person who hits you. If someone who stays nearby, or maybe in Harare, come and hit me, next day I will see that person [and] know that he just hit me a few days ago, so [then] you create a big [escalation]. So they use people from different areas, the one from north to south, and one from south to north.[60]

Farmer Martin Wilson stated, "Virtually in every case where people went in to do that [evict a farmer], they were unknown people to those that worked on the farms. . . . They [farm invaders] would, in some instances, get the people from one village to go and chase the people of another village out."[61] This was because despite high levels of lawlessness and apparent protection from the state, farmer, worker, and farm invader respondents frequently stated that farm invaders feared prosecution.

An additional aspect that made engaging in violence and intimidation on farms attractive for youths and others was that it gave them a sense of power. In view of their lower socioeconomic status, youths would not normally hold extensive power over individuals in positions of authority. Working as part of a farm invasion group, however, gave them instantaneous authority and control over individuals ranging from farmers to senior workers. Patterson Rukodzi, who trained youths at militia camps, stated: "There were some [youths] who were generally happy. You see, as young people . . . they feel very good to be given powers to assault and harass other people."[62] Further, farm manager Ketani Makabusi explained that there was a lot of "psychological propaganda" undertaken by farm invaders to demonstrate their power to workers.[63] He stated that farm invaders quickly realized that they could use their power to undermine the relationship between workers and the farmer: "'You workers, you see, you idolized this guy [farmer]. He was your employer. Now we are playing games with him. So we can easily play games with him. We can play games with you. You couldn't do anything to this commercial farmer, but *we* can.'" From the workers' perspective, if the farm invaders could easily threaten their powerful employers, then it was reasonable to conclude that they themselves were even more vulnerable.

Given the impoverished status of the youths and the dire prospects many faced as the economy deteriorated, such inducements were especially compelling. From the farm invader leaders' perspective, they could gain motivated agents who were capable of undertaking violence at a low cost, especially when part of the payment could be made in promises of future assets that did not have to ultimately be delivered. Indeed, youths rarely gained significant levels of land and agri-property.

As a means of further motivating youths and giving them a sense of purpose and direction, war veteran leaders conferred upon them the status of "war veteran" because they were ostensibly fighting in the "Third Chimurenga" war—plus it was a moniker that could be given at no tangible cost. It is difficult to overstate the effect this had on youths, who had been living in poverty with few career prospects in Mbare, but whose social status was suddenly raised. Such a title may have ultimately been bogus, but farmer respondents routinely commented that a group of youths claiming to be war veterans and rallying collectively for eviction was a powerful force for a single farmer to face. Youths who had appropriated the war veteran identity were extremely hard to reason with and could quickly become abusive. Whereas genuine war veterans were experienced in using force and understood the long-term consequences of using violence against other people, youths did not have such experience and were eager to demonstrate their newly acquired power.

## Women in Farm Invasion Groups

Women were also key members of farm invasion groups. While some female farm invaders directly engaged with farmers, the main role of most women was usually to urge the invasion group forward. Women served to increase the size and overall intimidatory effect of the farm invasion group, making up 50% of members in some cases.[64] Farmer interview respondents routinely commented that women would encourage their male counterparts to become aggressive and confrontational toward the farmer whose property was being invaded.[65] One rancher stated that female invaders were the "ones egging the men on, getting them to go one step further."[66] Another farmer agreed: "If you get the women in the background, they do all the shouting and make the noise, and basically they make the crowd meaner."[67] Farmers reported that the crowd became increasingly aggressive as women "[broke] out singing and clapping and encouraging the men," and "ululating and shouting and jumping and dancing and spitting."[68] One farmer argued these actions were intended to intimidate farmers and shame the male invaders into taking further action.[69]

Some female invaders also engaged directly with farmers, often encouraging other invaders to directly participate in intimidation. Farmer Rob Dawes stated that "the women would become hysterical and make noises and are very good intimidators."[70] Dawes's wife, Cynthia, reported that female invaders would shout and spit in their faces, and worked to incite other invaders and farm workers to evict the farmer.[71] Farmers found it more difficult to negotiate if women were leading the farm invasion group. One rancher stated: "I can negotiate with the men, but not with the women."[72]

## Breakdown of the Legal System

As soon as invasions began, farmers quickly turned to the legal system for remedy but found that while the courts would often rule in their favor they were unable to implement legal rulings. Bubye pointed out that it was well known that farmers had the legal right to remain on their property, so invaders relied on coercion to circumvent the courts: "They [farm invaders] knew that once they lay a challenge, the constitution was going to be ruling in favor of the farmer. . . . They didn't want that, so OK, fine, what do we do? Drive them out by intimidation. . . . Let's make life difficult for them."[73] In many cases, war veterans possessed sufficient power to simply ignore court orders that directed them to vacate the land they had occupied. Mucheke stated that "people [farmers] would come with a court order and the war vet would look at it at and tear it into three and look at you and smile and tell you to go away and beat you up again and then take everything [from the farm]."[74]

For instance, magistrate Tafadzwa Tegwani stated that after the farm seizures began, "many people who were affected approached the courts to seek protection, get some judgments, in particular white farmers who get their properties invaded—unlawfully invaded. They obtained eviction orders from the courts, but that there was nobody to enforce those, so people had all these judgments that could not be acted on."[75] From his position as magistrate, he saw compelling evidence that "there was violence on a very large scale that had never been seen before. It was quite terrible. Unfortunately it appeared this violence was coming from one side, government supporters against the opposition supporters."

Magistrates such as Tegwani had to contend with an escalating number of court cases brought against farmers by the government and by farm invaders. This was particularly the case after June 2000 when the number of farm invasions escalated. The ever greater number of farm invaders moving onto farms meant that clashes became more likely. This was also the case because farm invaders understood that they could rely upon a politicized legal system in order to gain assets and land from farmers.

For example, rancher George Lyons and his wife Joan related how they were charged in what they believe to be a fabricated case in order to intimidate them and undermine their will to remain on their land.[76] George Lyons, who was elderly when the sentencing occurred, explained that a settler alleged that Lyons had shot and killed one of his goats, but on inspecting the goat "nobody could show any bullet holes." Lyons was taken to court but found that the proceedings, from his perspective, had become highly politicized: "They packed the court with war vets, and the whole thing was just a big put up case." Joan Lyons recounted that "we had the human rights lawyer on the case, and they said it was so packed with war vets that there was no ways [George] was going to get anywhere." George Lyons was sentenced to 105 hours of community service for 8 hours a day. This would have a dire impact on his ability to operate his ranch and fend off land invaders, factors that ultimately led to the couple conceding all 5,300 hectares of their property, except the homestead (at the time of interview).

It is important to emphasize that many people in the civil service, like Magistrate Tegwani, sought to uphold the law and undertake their professional responsibilities despite the overt politicization. For example, an anonymous farmer survey respondent stated, "Some low-ranking police did seem to try and calm things down to no avail, and only at the beginning of the invasions." A different farmer survey respondent gave this example:

> Provincial governor sent army onto my ranch and removed invaders, burnt their huts—local MPs sent them back with youth brigade to burn 22 buildings including 5 chalet-safari lodge, beat-up and looted labour force who fled—some never returned. I was blamed for "bribing the governor." My ranch was part of a wildlife conservancy and therefore "out-of-bounds" for resettlement (government ruling).

The fact that the above example took place in 2001 shows that the willingness and ability of civil servants to carry out their professional responsibilities varied considerably across the country, which accounts for variation in farmers' experiences when dealing with invaders.

Yet pressure escalated on civil servants, particularly after June 2000, to comply with ZANU-PF objectives. Tegwani's superiors demanded explanations for his rulings that went against the government, such as his decision to issue eviction orders against farm invaders.[77] Tegwani reported that he had been "given an order by one of my superiors" to rule a certain way on some cases, and found that superiors reversed his rulings on other cases: "He [the superior] did not have the power to do that, but he just took some papers, consulted and so forth and told the war veterans that the order granted by this magistrate has been overruled, so you can forget about it." War veterans held demonstrations while Tegwani was in session, and the magistrate reported that "threats were made to my life and threats were made to my property, threatening to destroy my property and hang my family." Tegwani was eventually moved to an area where he could have less impact on the government's programs; he noted that war veterans and other government supporters knew he was being transferred before he did.

Farmer Kevin Elbridge highlighted that "the politics was bigger than the law."[78] In his case there was tension prior to 2002 between the courts, which tended to rule in favor of farmers, and war invaders, who established their own rules. Elbridge explained that farm invaders were trying to evict him and moved his possessions off the farm (this was prior to 2002, when new laws were passed that meant that farm invaders could seize farmers' personal possessions as well, such as items in the homestead):

> Our whole house got moved out. Whatever could get chucked on lorries got moved out in six hours and dumped in a yard in Chipinge. We weren't the only farmers at that stage. There were about 16 families that got the same instruction.
>
> I then decided, well, I can't live with this. I need to go and protect myself. . . . We had a hearing coming up in the administration court to hear the status of the farms. . . . Basically everything was withdrawn, and we were told to go back and farm.
>
> We went back. We moved stuff back onto the farm, and ten days later this group of thugs came again—provincial structure [provincial civil servants], district structure [district civil servants], war vets, police, army, prisons [services], and they once again closed up the farm and they told us that we had 24 hours to get off the farm or we faced prosecution.
>
> I had a sleepless night, and I decided that I had to seek the legal recourse again, but before going back to Harare I went and saw the district administrator again and tried to get sense to prevail. It was very obvious that he wasn't interested, and so I had to go back to Harare [to seek legal remedy].
>
> We filed an application in the High Court. It took about 10 days for it to be heard in chambers and I had a lawyer plus an advocate. When I went into the High Court judge's chambers with my legal team, the High Court judge said to me through my legal team that basically I would be embarrassing the minister and chief of police [by pursuing the legal challenge]—the two respondents—and that he would give me an opportunity to withdraw my case. My response to that was I'm doomed if I do—I'm doomed if I don't—and I want to proceed with this matter.
>
> Very quickly it was agreed by consent from the attorney general's office that I should return to the farm, and I got a judgment in the High Court that I should return to the farm, 'and no one will hinder, harass, or interfere with myself, my family, or my workers, and should anyone interfere, the police would intervene and sort the issue out.

However, Elbridge found conditions on the farm untenable due to relentless pressure from farm invaders in the form of trespassing, interfering with workers, theft, and intimidation, and he was eventually forced to leave.

This reality that court orders were increasingly ignored by farm invaders after June 2000 was summed up by farm manager Ketani Makabusi, who stated, "One thing that was not effective [in protecting farmers] was court orders. Court orders were not effective."[79] The view that legal orders were ignored by farm invaders was frequently cited by interview respondents.[80] Similar accounts were also provided by anonymous survey respondents: "Obtained two court orders. When shown they replied, 'That's the law, this is politics.'" A different respondent stated, "High Court judge just wanted my farm because he liked it and desired it for himself," while still another farmer provided an account: "Local Member In Charge tore up [the] High Court order docs. [He] threw docs into dust bin and advised me [that] I would be arrested again and jailed if I returned to the farm."

Phillan Zamchiya also notes several cases where the legal system was undermined. He notes that Chipinge magistrate Walter Chikwanha was assaulted by war veterans in August 2002 after ruling in favor of the MDC in a local court case. Even as late as 2010, war veterans invaded a courtroom to intimidate a judge for ordering the eviction of war veterans and other settlers from a farm.[81]

The government had taken vigorous steps after 2000 either to assert the law or to delegitimize it, depending on the interests of the ruling party. According to Hellum and Derman, the minister of justice, Patrick Chinamasa, stated in 2001 that the colonial-era dispossession of land had taken place outside the court system, as had the struggle for independence during the Liberation War.[82] Therefore, the seizure of farms during the Third Chimurenga would also not be bound by the confines of the law. This statement, of course, served to undermine respect for the country's legal system. Moreover, Hellum and Derman indicate that the minister of justice believed Zimbabwe was governed by "unjust laws" that were subject to "foreign" (i.e., British) influences and that inherently supported the interests of white farmers. As such, these laws were deemed illegitimate by war veterans and could be circumvented.

Similarly, in 2001 Mugabe suggested overt partiality in the courts:

Let it be known that the Courts in Independent Zimbabwe do belong to the people and will, whatever it will take, be placed at the service of those same people for whose convenience and protection they were set up in the first instance. They will not be allowed to go against our quest for full sovereignty; our quest to fulfil the wishes of the vast majority of our people in favour of a mere thousand white racist commercial farmers.[83]

His statement demonstrates that, from ZANU-PF's perspective, the existing legal framework was illegitimate. The government was willing to undercut the courts when rulings went against ZANU-PF's interests. For instance, when the

High Court ordered invaders off farmland in March 2000, Mugabe ordered the police to keep them there.[84] Indeed, as the land seizures unfolded, the nationalist supranarrative would be allowed to trump the rule of law. The irony of course is that this legal framework had been shaped and created in large part by the ruling party itself in the years since independence in 1980.

In 2001, however, Mugabe showed that he was willing to reassert the sanctity of the law once the framework matched the ruling party's political objectives at the time:

> We protect by law all the landless people who occupied commercial farms before 1st March, 2001 to allow government time to complete acquisitions and subsequent settler emplacements on properties which will have been acquired for resettlement. . . . Those demonstrating Zimbabweans who have a legitimate stake in this country [i.e., nonwhites and non-MDC supporters] can only be shifted from where they are presently onto new settlements in the context of government initiated and managed resettlement. I want this message to go clearly to the white commercial farmers.[85]

In this instance Mugabe was directly indicating to farm invaders that their actions would be retroactively protected by law, providing further evidence of his willingness to manipulate the legal system.

Yet what underscores these accounts is that ZANU-PF had a preoccupation with the law. The party wanted to operate "legally" even if laws were flagrantly shaped or undermined to suit the party's interests. Before the seizures escalated uncontrollably, many government supporters doubted that Mugabe would countenance a total departure from the existing legal framework. Sam Moyo, who was generally sympathetic to the land reform agenda, suggested in March 2000 that "they're [the government] not prepared to go to war to take land. They don't really believe in destroying property rights."[86] In fact, Zimbabwe's legal system remained remarkably impartial up until about 2003, when political appointees and intimidation severely undermined the bench, although there had been growing pressure up to this point especially on cases that were important to ZANU-PF's policy objectives, such as land and political violence. This meant that farm invaders and government leaders would have to contend with the real ability of farmers and other citizens to seek legal redress—even if ultimately these efforts did not result in actual satisfaction.

The reason the government so vehemently opposed farmers taking legal action in court was that they were well aware that the farm seizures contravened Zimbabwean law, as the aforementioned statements from Mugabe suggest. Mucheke, who gave Mugabe specific legal advice on the seizures, acknowledged that "legally speaking, the land invasion was illegal."[87] He noted that "assuming there is an outright change of government, the commercial farmers have got a right to claim their farms back despite of whatever the government has given to the invaders."

Mucheke stated that he was a committed member of ZANU-PF. Yet he agreed that the ruling party's insistence that land seizures were justified because the colonial government had "stolen" the land to begin with was an invalid argument. According to Mucheke, "You know we cannot rely on an argument that my forefather owned this farm, and then your forefather came and took over this farm. Look at it. When your forefather came [and] all those things happened—took the farm by force, that happened—there was no farm. It was a forest. He then transformed [forest] into a farm." From a legal perspective, he believed that the transformation of the "forest" into a commercial farm, the amount of time that had lapsed since the farm had first been claimed by early white settlers, the multitude of black workers who earned their livelihoods from the farm, and the fact that farms had been bought and sold many times over were all arguments that supported the property rights of the white farmers: "There is now a beautiful house on that land. You cannot come back . . . 29 decades [*sic*] later and say, 'My grandfather was the owner of this land . . . so the house is mine.' No, no, that's not true." He emphasized that because the farms were commercially traded and were therefore not automatically vestiges of colonial preferential treatment, farmers had true claims and could justifiably file grievances in court.

The government could not, therefore, allow farmers to present their cases in court after having allowed limited, illegal seizures, which ultimately resulted in uncontrolled, widespread illegal activity. According to Mucheke, "There was no way the government was going to allow the courts to give rulings against them when they'd planned it. If you remember, the courts ruled against the government on several issues, and you know what happened? Judges were arrested. Justice Blackie, he was sent to prison. The other judges were fired." There were also international considerations. The government had wanted to frame events as a popular uprising and to distance itself publicly from the seizures. Not only had the scope of the planned seizures been very substantially exceeded, but plausible deniability had been made impossible through the identifiable involvement of senior politicians and members of the state security sector in seizing farms. With their involvement, and with the failure of the police to prevent the very extensive violence then taking place, the government found itself increasingly unable to explain events to the international community. It was therefore important to prevent farmers and others who had grievances against the government from accessing the courts, where legal evidence could be heard and where rulings were already being made against the government.[88]

Farmers who did seek remedy with the courts were often singled out for additional violence, both to punish them and to deter further court challenges. For example, foreman Thomas Rackomechi stated, "The other thing that farmers did wrongly is that when their lands were taken they rushed to court. When you rush to the court, then they say you are resisting, then they attack you there and then."[89] Mucheke stated that legal challenges were also likely to result in violence because farm invaders believed that they operated on a supralegal level based on the "higher" law of nationalism and were thus affronted by legal challenges: "It was like you are challenging our [war veteran] authority. So they didn't want to be challenged [over] their authority."[90]

It must be emphasized, however, that many farm invaders also feared future prosecution. Numerous farmers interviewed for this book stated that farm invaders became volatile and aggressive if they saw farmers photographing them, and sought to destroy any photographic records.[91] Farmer Martin Grover explained that if farmers tried to photograph farm invaders "The guy would immediately take your camera away from you. . . . If you pretended to take a picture of someone close to you, like at the hut outside the gate, . . . the guy would disappear into the hut or try to move out of the way and then there'd be an aggressive reaction to that."[92] Farm invaders interviewed for this book stated that one key reason they did not want to be photographed was that they believed overt government sanctioning of farm seizures would not translate into genuine protection from future prosecution. The fact that farm invaders often tried to conceal their identities strongly suggests that some invaders realized their actions in seizing farms and harassing MDC supporters were criminal in nature, despite government assurances to the contrary. Foreman James Mwengi recounted what he heard from farm invaders on the farm where he worked: "They knew that one day there will be law and order in Zimbabwe."[93] In his view, the records in the legal system would allow for future prosecution.

## Politicization of the State Security Services

The failure of law enforcement bodies to objectively uphold the rule of law after the beginning of the farm seizures has been well documented in existing research.[94] Knox Chitiyo stated that police were given "official instructions not to intervene."[95] Zamchiya also found cases where farmers reported violations on their farms to police but no action was taken.[96] In other instances the police targeted victims of farm invaders' attacks. Game-hunting manager Herbert Nchenchi related an instance where "war vets were busy beating up people. . . . When they [police] got there, the police did nothing. Instead, they were arresting those who were being beaten."[97]

The survey of farmers further corroborates these views. Some 86.9% of survey respondents said that police withheld assistance because the farm seizures were politically motivated, while 59.1% of respondents stated that they were told there was no fuel for police vehicles when they sought police intervention (often this was true, but was also widely used as an excuse not to assist). Another 37.5% were transferred to a supervisor who was never available (another means of avoiding assistance), and 21.9% stated that police officers themselves were active perpetrators. Farmer survey respondents also provided qualitative examples showing that the police failed to undertake their professional responsibilities and in some cases actively evicted farmers:

- "Eight police with AK rifles—30 hours to empty homesteads and seven days to get all livestock off the ranches."
- "We were forcibly given 24 hours to move at gun point by the military, police, the district administrator and CIO."
- "Forcibly evicted from secondary farm with arrest by police."
- "We were physically evicted from our home and farm with the police in attendance—who did nothing, just said they could do nothing as it was political."
- "Arrested by police (for not leaving farm) [and] illegally detained in police cells for three days. Only released at court appearance on condition I did not return to farm. Not charged with any crime."
- "Had no protection from the police or other law enforcement agencies."
- "The war vets were in charge of police."
- "The police were called . . . often to the farm. When dealing with political agitators such as war vets they were powerless to enforce the law. The war vets were immune from prosecution and they knew it!"
- "When called to assist with a case of dissension and work stoppage they [police] led the singing of freedom party songs."
- "Police actively assisted in not prosecuting squatters etc. for theft, stock theft, fence cutting, trespass, etc., etc."
- "Police were witnessed selling 'plots' [of land] and pocketing the proceeds—also were perpetrators of poaching and shooting."
- "Evicted by police and their support unit. They threatened my staff with jail if they did not cease working for me."
- "During the looting spree in August 2001 police vehicles were used to transport offenders to the farm. At one stage a Constable Rutavi and two other armed policemen warned me that if I removed any more claim pegs on the lands I would be arrested."

- "Police generally helped to solve cattle theft problems and thefts but were reluctant to get involved with anything political."
- "The police were very helpful until we were invaded and then were [not] cooperative and even hostile when approached."

The police's tactic of either refusing to enforce the rule of law or actively siding with farm invaders provoked a mixture of anger, disappointment, and despair among farmers and workers. Most respondents recognized that the police themselves had to contend with some level of intimidation. Yet the isolation and fear experienced by farmers and workers was magnified by the willingness of law enforcement officials to allow crimes to be committed in plain sight without attempting to intervene.

The police, however, were facing extreme pressure from farm invaders and the government, a factor that has rarely been acknowledged in previous studies. When asked what response the police made during the farm invasion unrest, farm foreman Telmore Nyakasanga stated, "Fucking nothing. Nothing." When asked to explain why, he stated that it was "because they were given orders from the top: 'Don't arrest anyone. Don't do anything.'"[98]

The police themselves were carefully monitored by the Police Internal Security and Intelligence (PISI), an organization with close ties to the CIO even before the farm seizures began.[99] During the land seizure era, however, the PISI was intensely politicized and became obsessed with stamping out any hint of support for the MDC from within the police force.[100] Over time, police officers who insisted on enforcing the rule of law—especially when doing so went against ZANU-PF's interests—were targeted by PISI.

Interviews with the police gave insight into events from their perspective. Edward Chidembo, a senior member of the Zimbabwe Republic Police, noted a strong shift in the politicization of the police:

Police officers began to be victimized with framed-up charges, being ostracized, being victimized in all sorts of ways as a way of sending messages to the police that if you sympathize with the MDC you'll be in trouble, and that happened on a very, very large scale, and it was very intensive. A lot of police officers left their jobs because of that. They were harassed.[101]

Police officer Edison Bubye identified a similar pattern in the police department where he was employed.[102] He explained that PISI targeted the head of a local police department:

He was the officer in charge, head of the whole [local police department]. His ideas were anti-Mugabe ideas. So they quickly noticed this and they got rid of him. Some will get arrested, some will just disappear. Mugabe's lot made him disappear. So they make sure that all people who are not speaking this language [of ZANU-PF] were uprooted.

Bubye added that PISI was prepared in some cases to take draconian action against noncompliant police in what he called a "cleansing ceremony": "You find people started getting demoted, people started leaving the police, people started getting implicated . . . some jailed, some killed, some disappearing."[103] These points underscore that there were many police who did not support the government's politicization of law enforcement or the abrogation of Zimbabwean law and did their best to remain professional.

Those police officers who did not comply were sent to rural areas, as Chidembo reported: "If you are suspected of being sympathetic [to the MDC] and . . . you were based in Harare, you would be sent to, say, an outpost on the border of Mozambique, a remote place, and that will happen within 24 hours, or quickly you are separated from the [police officer's] family."[104] Jackson Sanyati, a police officer in charge of an eastern district, gave a similar account: "I was now being transferred to remote areas whereby you cannot have any access to media, newspapers to read, no television, nothing."[105] Likewise, Bubye explained that PISI would investigate police officers and would eventually "discover" who was not compliant with ZANU-PF's political objectives:

You'll be reporting to a certain center where you will be monitored, where you don't have to influence other police, you don't have to give orders— basically stripping off the rank. [Or] probably the rank will be there just for the name, but otherwise you don't have the powers, the police powers that you should have.[106]

Chidembo described how promotions were awarded on the basis of party affiliation. Only core supporters of the ruling party were able to rise through the ranks: "Those officers who were seen to be sympathetic to ZANU-PF, when they wanted promotions, even though they were not competent . . . promotions were now based on, on that basis."[107] Sanyati reported that he had passed exams to earn a promotion, but in 2000 he found that "I was one of those people who are being victimized now, being given some fool allegations that I was a member of the MDC."[108] Chidembo added that within this environment of finger-pointing and politicization, personal grudges could be settled by accusations against others of complicity with the MDC: "There was a lot of witch-hunting and so on. If somebody hated somebody . . . he would tell the superiors that so-and-so is sympathetic to the MDC."[109] This process meant that over time the senior ranks of the police became filled with ever more zealous ZANU-PF supporters and officers too intimidated to enforce laws deemed political.

Insofar as land takeovers and events on farms were concerned, the police were told not to get involved in issues that were "political," that is, issues that concerned the political objectives and the well-being of ZANU-PF. For example, MDC supporters could be arrested because such jeopardy suited ZANU-PF, but ZANU-PF supporters were usually able to avoid arrest and prosecution even when engaged in blatant criminality. According to Sanyati, the following was relayed from police provincial headquarters to police stations across the province where he was working:

> If you [police] see such things [politically related criminal activity] happening, don't stand up and don't be bold enough and try to stop anyone. Try, just give it the cold [shoulder] . . . just ignore [it]. . . . This is the situation, this is the phase we are at the moment, but it is going to pass. That is what they say. They say, "Don't involve yourself. Just leave it like that. This is a phase. We are in the war, so just leave it like that."[110]

Sanyati explained that on one occasion he witnessed over 100 cattle being stolen from a farmer. He said that stock theft was an easily prosecuted crime, but in this instance he was forbidden to intervene and he had to allow the farm invader to steal the farmer's assets by "taking it bits and pieces." Sanyati stated that another tactic was simply to never record a reported incident in the "exhibit book" so that, insofar as police legal records were concerned, the incident never took place.

For professional police officers like Sanyati, Limpopo, Bubye, and Chidembo, the situation was intolerable. Many officers who were not prepared to ignore flagrant breaches of the law, or who resented being transferred to remote areas and being passed over for promotions, resigned from the force. The result of these actions was that the police who remained became increasingly radicalized and supportive of ZANU-PF. This encouraged the rapid breakdown of law and order as the farm seizures progressed.

The military also became politicized after 2000. Military intelligence agent Daniel Inkankezi stated that in the 1990s the military was still professional.[111] While ZANLA veterans tended to get preferential treatment, especially over former Rhodesian army soldiers, military leaders emphasized that soldiers must be professional and avoid politics. After 2000, however, according to respondents interviewed for this book, there was a dramatic shift toward overt politicization in support of ZANU-PF.

The soldier Ronald Jongwe recounted one occasion when a military intelligence officer addressed a formal assembly of 500 soldiers over the purported threat to soldiers' interests posed by the MDC.[112] Jongwe reported that the military intelligence officer stated: "'Would you like the land we fought for being returned to the whites?' There was a big 'No, we can't have that.' 'What would you do to people who support such an opposition, who want to give the land back to the whites?' '[The assembled soldiers replied:] They must be chased out of the army—killed. We should have killed such people a long time ago.'" As the meeting progressed, the intelligence officer kept referring to a list he claimed to possess containing the names of soldiers suspected of support- ing the opposition:

> He kept on saying, "But remember, I have a list here which I will announce later on . . . the list of such people whom you say you must kill or must be chucked out of the army without any pension or anything. I've got a list, and some of them were very respectable, high-ranking people." So people [soldiers] were saying, "Come on, come on, we want that list. We want to deal with them."

Jongwe feared that if his name was on the list he would be threatened not just with expulsion from the army without his pension, but with physical harm from the other soldiers.[113]

The mood of the event was intended to polarize soldiers and to shape their political loyalties by claiming that the opposition was specifically seeking to threaten soldiers' apparent interests in the land. It also sought to tie the current land debate to the nationalist objectives in the Liberation War in order to val- idate the seizures and compel soldiers not to let the sacrifices of their forefa- thers be made in vain. Agnes Sengwe, a member of the Zimbabwe National Army, explained that senior military officials would address the rank-and-file troops, speaking of guerrillas who died in the Liberation War.[114] According to Sengwe, military officials told soldiers: "We got this [land and freedoms] through blood, so you mustn't give it away to the white people. It's ours. It be- longs to us."

Voting was also tightly monitored to ensure support for ZANU-PF by sol- diers. Tyson Manyame, a member of the army, said, "When it comes to voting within the ZNA, we as the ZNA do not vote . . . our votes are cast for the ruling party."[115] Agnes Sengwe corroborates this claim by recounting that when she was in the army, she was sent her ballot for the 2000 parliamentary elections with her army identification number printed on the ballot. This triggered fears that if she did not vote for the ruling party, there would be consequences:

> They sent us some envelopes, my name on my envelope, then I will tear [open] my envelope. I will put my X, put it back in the envelope, and then

I will post it. What kind of a voting is that? What would you vote for if you were in the defense forces? So you would be scared that maybe with this [identification] number and my name is there, they will automatically see that I voted for this then.

Sengwe explained that fear over what would happen to her if she was caught voting for the MDC led her to cast her vote for the ruling party.

The politicization of the military went beyond rhetoric. Jongwe reported that after the land seizures began, only ZANU-PF party cardholders were recruited into the military.[116] As the military became more politicized after 2000, it also grew more extreme, with little room left for moderates or those with dissenting views. Senior army officer Steven Sebungwe indicated that the entire state security apparatus was politicized in order to serve the ruling party: "You find all these institutions are now politicized, the army, the police, CIO. They are all working to achieve a certain political objective that benefits ZANU-PF. And I think it's meant to scare everybody who wants to raise a voice of dissent."[117]

Msasa stated that soldiers who had served in the Rhodesian armed forces or for ZIPRA—ZAPU's military wing—decades earlier were increasingly viewed with suspicion by military leaders, even if they did not necessarily show support for the MDC.[118] This happened even if the soldier had an impeccable record of postindependence service. As a result of new suspicions, "You have to show yourself [that] you are now a changed person" and, Msasa noted, had to "show your loyalty."

One way that members of the military could demonstrate their loyalty was in the violent interrogation of political detainees. Msasa explained that there are numerous ways of gaining intelligence from individuals, ranging from talking to the person, what Msasa called "drinking tea" with them, to the use of violence, which was "a shortcut." Military leaders often preferred violent interrogations of detainees—even if a nonviolent method was equally efficacious in gaining intelligence—because it also demonstrated loyalty to ZANU-PF on the part of the interrogator: "They wanted [each soldier in military intelligence] to show them physically [that he was loyal], ja, that's when you are going to be accepted [by leadership]." Msasa elaborated:

If I am given the task of interrogation, they prefer me to kill somebody. So you are now killing somebody for the sake of ZANU-PF government. So that is where they can say this one [the soldier] has changed [i.e., he no longer has loyalties to the Rhodesian government or ZIPRA]. I know certain guys who are still there right now. They were accepted because of such activities like killing people in interrogations and just playing dirty.

Msasa stated that forcing soldiers to participate in violence was a means of inculcation whereby they were bound to their leadership through the joint commission of crimes. No one could claim a moral high ground or easily report their fellow soldiers if they were all guilty of the same crimes: "ZANU is addicted to violence. So if you actually do that type of thing, violence which is part of them, then you are part of them now."

The intense politicization of the military relied on both incentives and threats to keep the security forces loyal to ZANU-PF. For many soldiers, the renewed focus on historical nationalist grievances meant that previous service in the Rhodesian army or the ZIPRA, the military wing of the competing nationalist group ZAPU, cast doubt on their allegiance to ZANU-PF, negating chances of promotion and leaving them viewed with suspicion by superiors. Overt support for the MDC was infeasible; any soldier who was foolish enough to demonstrate such support ran the risk of being expelled from the military or of incurring consequences with military intelligence specialists. Many soldiers found such intense political demands to be unacceptable, leading them to resign and seek civilian jobs.

## CONCLUSION

This chapter has shown that commercial farmers were forced to swim against a rising tide of intimidation and violence as invasion groups began to pour onto farms across the country in 2000. In the initial stages of the seizures, farm invaders were often willing to bypass farms where the owners had good relations with workers and local communities and could count on their support, or if the farmer as an individual put up a robust defense of his claim to the farm. But as competition for land and agri-property increased, the relatively cautious initial approach of genuine war veterans was challenged, and the seizures became more widespread and more violent. The powerful individuals who led many of the seizures had little difficulty in recruiting marginalized youths, who were often bussed in from urban areas to provide the "muscle" behind the invasions. The aggression of these youths was fed by the opportunity to demonstrate power over white farmers, long perceived as a privileged elite; this had an intoxicating effect at least equal to that supplied by alcohol and drugs. Pressure from women, who participated in invasion groups in large numbers, also drove an escalation in violence.

As the rule of law eroded in the countryside and police abandoned their duties of protecting property, farmers were in an increasingly impossible position. This chapter showed some of the strategies used by farmers to mitigate increasing pressure from farm invaders in an attempt to remain on their farms for as long as possible. A forceful response was regarded as extremely risky; yet a willingness to make concessions and even cede control of large parts of their property would only bring a temporary respite.

# 5

## Suppressing the MDC

Previous chapters have shown that the widespread seizure of commercial farm land occurred in an atmosphere of chaos and confusion, particularly in early 2000. The initial five-farms-per-district plan was rapidly exceeded and the government began losing control of takeovers. Yet in consenting to the initial plan for limited seizures, and then deciding, in about June 2000, to co-opt the more extensive takeovers, the government always had a key political goal—suppressing the MDC.

The government blamed its shock defeat in the February 2000 referendum on white commercial farmers, who were believed to have supported the MDC through campaign contributions and by persuading farm workers to support the opposition. Given that in 2000 there were only 4,300 farmers in Zimbabwe, the voting power of farmers in a country of approximately 12 million people was negligible.[1] However, an estimated 325,000 people worked on commercial farms—a sizable voting constituency once families are included.[2] The government recognized that there was widespread support for the MDC among farm workers. Moreover, they feared that farmers would further influence their voting patterns and encourage them to back the opposition in the 2000 parliamentary elections and 2002 presidential polls. In order to suppress this real or imagined source of the MDC's support, ZANU-PF aimed to intimidate workers and evict farmers, a strategy that also allowed the government to placate war veteran demands by providing access to farmers' land and assets.

This chapter begins by exploring patterns of political violence across the country, and why they depended to a large extent on the commercial farming community. In doing so this chapter explores a fundamental puzzle in the land seizure era: why there appeared to be so much violence concentrated in areas where ZANU-PF appeared to enjoy some of the greatest political support. In recognizing the role of commercial farms in this puzzle and the concomitant desire by government to suppress MDC support, the chapter then delves into how the government targeted farmers and workers in order to undermine opposition support.

## WHY WAS POLITICAL VIOLENCE CONCENTRATED IN ZANU-PF'S HEARTLAND?

A key puzzle when examining the dynamics of political violence during the land seizure era is that violence tended to be concentrated in provinces where ZANU-PF had historically enjoyed strong political support.[3] Adrienne LeBas explains that "all available data suggest that violence was more serious and more systematically organised in ZANU-PF strongholds. Mashonaland Central and Mashonaland East, the two provinces that polled the greatest 'yes' (pro-ZANU-PF) votes during the 2000 referendum, accounted for the bulk of the political violence during the 2000 parliamentary campaign."[4] Alexander has also noted that Mashonaland "dominated in terms of numbers of [farm] occupations and violence."[5]

This assertion is confirmed by the violence maps I created for this book.[a] These show that there was comparatively little violence in the most densely populated nonurban provinces: Manicaland and Midlands.[6] There were, however, strong concentrations of violence in the three Mashonaland provinces. Between February 2000 and March 2008, there was a consistent trend for higher concentrations of violence to occur in Mashonaland, whereas outbursts of violence in other areas tended to occur more sporadically.

A closer examination of the referendum result highlights LeBas's point about ZANU-PF enjoying the strongest levels of support in Mashonaland. Table 5.1 shows the breakdown by province, including the urban provinces of Harare and Bulawayo, of the "yes" (pro-ZANU-PF) and "no" (pro-MDC) voting results. The prevailing vote is boldfaced for each province. This table clearly shows that the three Mashonaland provinces voted in favor of ZANU-PF and the constitutional reforms by a sizable margin. It is not necessarily a surprise that ZANU-PF would win these provinces, since the ruling party has historically enjoyed

a. See www.charleslaurie.com for a complete series of color violence maps depicting 21,491 acts of abduction/unlawful arrest, assault, murder, attempted murder, rape, torture, intimidation/verbal threat, and property damage/theft against farmers and workers recorded between 2000 and 2008.

*Table 5.1* CONSTITUTIONAL REFERENDUM RESULTS: FEBRUARY 12–13, 2000

| Province | "Yes" vote (pro-ZANU-PF) | "No" vote (pro-MDC) | Total votes | Difference between "Yes" and "No" |
|---|---|---|---|---|
| Mashonaland Central | 96,661 | 43,385 | 140,046 | 53,276 |
| Mashonaland East | 60,354 | 39,930 | 100,284 | 20,424 |
| Mashonaland West | 75,251 | 53,328 | 128,597 | 21,923 |
| Midlands | 91,587 | 70,572 | 162,159 | 21,015 |
| Masvingo | 61,927 | 49,658 | 111,585 | 12,269 |
| Manicaland | 38,993 | 67,787 | 106,780 | –28,794 |
| Matabeleland North | 26,413 | 31,224 | 57,637 | –4,811 |
| Matabeleland South | 33,606 | 31,759 | 65,365 | 1,847 |
| Bulawayo | 27,737 | 90,422 | 118,159 | –62,685 |
| Harare | 73,410 | 218,298 | 291,708 | –144,888 |
| *Total* | 585,939 | 696,363 | 1,282,302 | –110,424 |

SOURCE: Electoral Institute for Sustainable Democracy in Africa, Zimbabwe Referendum 2000: Results, http://www.eisa.org.za/WEP/zimresults2000r.htm.

political support from this region. For example, army officer Steven Sebungwe reiterated that Mashonaland Central had always been a source of ZANU-PF electoral support.[7] "We have very powerful people coming from Mashonaland Central including Vice President Joyce Mujuru and a lot of other heavyweights in government, Saviour Kasukuwere and all those people, you see."

Table 5.2 shows that the MDC achieved an impressive result in the June 2000 parliamentary election, especially for a party formed only in September 1999. Indeed, the MDC gained 46.7% of the overall vote to ZANU-PF's 48%. Given that the ruling party had received 81.4% of the vote in the 1995 parliamentary election, the surge in support for the MDC is particularly astonishing. The opposition received substantial support in Mashonaland although ZANU-PF still won in all three provinces by relatively large margins. Indeed, the political contest was far closer in Manicaland, the most densely populated rural province, than in Mashonaland. Moreover, it was the overwhelming support for the MDC in the urban centers of Harare and Bulawayo that played a major role in the MDC's strong showing in June 2000.

Given that suppressing the MDC was a key objective for ZANU-PF, it seems surprising and counterintuitive that violence was greatest in areas where the MDC appeared weakest. Logically, one might expect that violence would be concentrated in areas such as Harare, Bulawayo, or Manicaland where the MDC enjoyed strong support. Yet a further analysis of parliamentary election outcome data from the Institute for Security Studies reveals that districts where

*Table 5.2* SUMMARY OF JUNE 2000 PARLIAMENTARY ELECTION RESULTS

| Province | ZANU-PF votes | MDC votes | Other votes | Total votes |
|---|---|---|---|---|
| **Mashonaland Central** | **188,967** | 47,587 | 3,206 | 239,760 |
| **Mashonaland East** | **196,157** | 64,987 | 10,067 | 271,211 |
| **Mashonaland West** | **153,167** | 78,923 | 8,684 | 240,774 |
| **Midlands** | **193,736** | 126,058 | 20,960 | 340,754 |
| **Masvingo** | **163,018** | 92,053 | 21,698 | 276,769 |
| **Manicaland** | 117,232 | **125,908** | 37,274 | 280,414 |
| **Matabeleland North** | 30,064 | **105,492** | 7,826 | 143,382 |
| **Matabeleland South** | 56,166 | **91,825** | 6,226 | 154,217 |
| **Bulawayo** | 22,350 | **142,379** | 5,217 | 169,946 |
| **Harare** | 84,987 | **296,055** | 8,804 | 389,846 |
| *Totals* | *1,205,844* | *1,171,267* | *129,962* | *2,507,073* |

SOURCE: Electoral Institute for Sustainable Democracy in Africa, "Zimbabwe: 2000 House of Assembly Provincial Results," http://www.content.eisa.org.za/old-page/zimbabwe-2000-house-assembly-provincial-results.

there were concentrations of commercial farms tended to support the MDC in far higher numbers, thereby creating pockets of strong MDC support within ZANU-PF's heartland.[8] ZANU-PF could only be sure of consistent support in districts that had few commercial farms but a large rural population. These patterns demonstrated that districts with large populations of commercial farm workers were therefore a rising threat to the ruling party's hegemony.

An important insight into why violence was concentrated in Mashonaland, despite apparently higher levels of ZANU-PF support among nonfarm worker rural constituents in the region, comes from senior CIO agent Hastings Lundi.[9] He highlighted that in the aftermath of the referendum, some voters were optimistic that the June 2000 parliamentary elections would bring substantial electoral change and enable greater MDC representation in government: "When the referendum was lost, there was a real hope in terms of maybe the commercial farming establishment and Zimbabweans in general that when old Mugabe is [weakened], we can actually defeat him [in the June parliamentary elections]." Yet according to Lundi: "They [farmers and other MDC supporters] underestimated the level of violence that was just going to be used and the vote rigging at a national level that Mugabe unfortunately had at his disposal. The MDC won about 97 [seats in the June parliamentary election]. They won 97 seats out of 120 seats, but then they were only given 57." Lundi was adamant about the actual election outcome: "He [Mugabe] lost. They [ZANU-PF] lost the parliamentary elections in 2000. He lost his presidential elections in 2002." Aided by supporters who stood to gain from ZANU-PF remaining in power, elections were simply rigged:

> The people who had benefited, they took his side, like Tobaiwa Mudede, who supervised the elections. He is a beneficiary himself. He has got a vested interest in seeing that Mugabe return to power. All the other guys who were now owners of farms whose houses are on hilltops [in affluent areas], they have enjoyed the trappings of being farmers.[10]

Lundi's insistence that extensive vote rigging accounted for ZANU-PF's victory in the June 2000 parliamentary election was repeatedly echoed by respondents to explain either the June 2000 parliamentary or the March 2002 presidential election results. In addition to Lundi, Tafadzwa Tegwani (a magistrate), Agnes Sengwe and Ronald Jongwe (both members of the army), and Alex Siwaze (a war veteran leader), all whom had privileged insights into ZANU-PF decision-making, stated that elections were rigged in favor of the ruling party.[11] In addition, farmer Nancy Hoover stated that when she visited a polling station in Mashonaland during the 2002 presidential election, "I walked in and found [ZANU-PF minister of housing and public works] Ignatius

Chombo in one of the back rooms rigging the votes, sorting out the paperwork. Getting it all sorted out."[12]

Foreign observers were also aware that elections in the early 2000s had been marred by widespread fraud. An official report into the 2002 poll prepared for South Africa's then president Thabo Mbeki by the country's independent electoral observers was finally made public in 2014. Contradicting South Africa's official declarations that the election met international standards, the "Khampepe report" stated that in the view of the election observers, the vote "cannot be considered free and fair."[13] The veracity of the Khampepe report and strength of its findings is indicated by the fact that the South African government (led by the African National Congress, an ally of ZANU-PF) strongly resisted making it public.

Furthermore, the Forum identified numerous accounts of vote fraud, particularly in the report entitled *"How to Rig an Election": Evidence of a Systematic Campaign to Prevent a Free and Fair Poll*, which assessed voting irregularities in the June 2000 parliamentary election.[14] Brian Raftopoulos also provides evidence of electoral manipulation.[15] Moreover, in describing the 2002 presidential election, a confidential US government diplomatic cable stated:

> A wide variety of reports over the last several days indicate that President Mugabe's ruling party engaged in massive fraud during the March 9–11 presidential poll, enabling him to claim victory. Many of the numbers do not add up, and inflated results in the Mashonaland provinces and other areas correlate with reports of police and ZANU-PF militia detaining MDC polling agents.[16]

The cable then compared the 2002 election results in Mashonaland and Masvingo with those from 2000: "The numbers in many districts of Mashonaland and Masvingo equally defy belief. In 24 constituencies in Mashonaland East, Central, West and Masvingo, ZANU-PF's totals increased by 5,000 to 10,000 votes per constituency over 2000, whereas the MDC's numbers remained mostly unchanged or declined."[17] "ZANU-PF's Mashonaland stronghold" was again referenced in another US diplomatic cable on the 2002 outcome: "The huge increase in Mashonaland numbers (the margin was 15 to 1 in some districts) give[s] rise to suspicions of vote tampering and ballot box stuffing in that province."[18]

This evidence of vote rigging suggests that the official 2000 parliamentary election results presented in table 5.2 are likely to be inaccurate and falsely show support for ZANU-PF. It is plausible—and likely—that the official results exclude numerous MDC votes and exaggerate the actual level of support for ZANU-PF. The ruling party faced a formidable political threat from the MDC and would have needed to substantially manipulate rural results in order to offset the overwhelming MDC support in the cities of Harare and Bulawayo.

Thus, the most logical explanation to the puzzle of why there was so much violence in an area that appeared to be a ZANU-PF stronghold is that the ruling party did not actually have as much support as election results suggest: those results were likely manipulated by the government. Violence was concentrated in the Mashonaland provinces because ZANU-PF *was* facing a serious loss of support in these densely populated and resource-rich areas. The Forum stated that Mashonaland Central "is a region which Zanu (PF) has traditionally claimed as a stronghold and where the party has long insisted that the opposition cannot build support." Yet, according to the report, evidence suggests that "support for the MDC has been growing steadily both before and after the referendum."[19]

Estimates of the number of farmers and workers in each province show the relatively large concentration of potential rural MDC supporters by province. Some 61.3% of farms and 78.8% of workers were concentrated in commercial farming areas in the Mashonaland provinces, according to survey estimates.[20] In view of the potential financial support from the estimated 3,338 farms in the region, and the voting power of the 256,100 permanent workers—especially when spouses and other voting-age family members living on farms are included—it becomes easier to understand why ZANU-PF focused so much violence in suppressing this Mashonaland MDC support base (see also table 6.5 and table 6.6).

Mashonaland was therefore critical to ZANU-PF's continued political success because of the region's historical support for the ruling party and its large numbers of voters. Yet a key threat appeared to emanate from the region, arising from the numerous farmers who allegedly bankrolled the opposition and directed their huge workforces to vote for the MDC. Mupfure explained:

> So if ZANU-PF really wanted to destroy the MDC power base, and they [ZANU-PF] had seen a lot of the farm workers in that area [Bindura]—large concentrations—and they knew that in the event of a vote these are the people who would vote MDC, you would want to fracture that backbone. And so the numbers were there in Mashonaland Central, and so ZANU-PF would really be attracted towards the idea of destroying this power base.

The ruling party and its supporters proved willing and able to resort to violence to regain political control in areas of Mashonaland where large numbers of voters were beginning to move toward the MDC. As Sebungwe put it, "They [predominately the farm workers] were slowly rejecting Mugabe. Now they are known—in a small community, you will know this one is doing this and that one is campaigning for this one. So in order to send that message again, they start killing them to make an example of them."[21]

While ZANU-PF's manipulation of election results was crucial to its political survival, violence also served to consolidate its weakening hold over Mashonaland and to discourage support for the opposition in future elections. The extent of the deterioration in the region is made clear by the Forum, which stated in June 2000, "There is known to be widespread political violence in every single district of Mashonaland Central, with door-to-door campaigns of intimidation and regular beatings of any opposition suspects by Zanu (PF) militias."[22]

Meanwhile, a US government diplomatic cable discussing state-sponsored violence in Mashonaland East in the period just prior to the June 2000 parliamentary elections noted that "incidents of violence against farm workers—as well as threats of punishment if MDC wins here—are extremely numerous."[23] The same report stated: "The 'Mashonalands' are ZANU-PF strongholds, where farm occupations and the war veterans' campaign of violence have been the most aggressive," further suggesting specific and focused concentrations of political violence in the region. The same claim is also made by Sebungwe, who stated that violence was used by the ruling party as a preemptive tool to soften up political opposition. Violence had erupted in Mashonaland "as a result of the opposition putting its foothold into ZANU-PF areas" and was "meant to achieve the same political objective to keep ZANU-PF in power."[24]

## RELIANCE ON MILITIAS TO SUPPRESS THE MDC

There were several ways in which farm invaders organized themselves to suppress the MDC and seize farms. One method was the establishment of youth militias in rural areas. These militias were created after the 2000 referendum with the specific objective of suppressing the MDC in order to allow ZANU-PF to retain power in future elections.

Patterson Rukodzi, a senior instructor at a youth militia training camp, remembered being told, "You ex-soldiers, ex-guerrillas, the British are now coming through the opposition. They want to reverse the gains of our independence, so be careful. If you don't soldier up, you may lose all these gains."[25] He noted that soon after the referendum loss "the regime was very desperate. It was sensing getting out of power—the party. It was sensing getting out of power." Rukodzi explained the purpose for the militias:

It was mid-2000 and by then we were proceeding towards the elections [in June 2000]. . . . I could say that we were told that since the party or the government has lost the referendum there were signs pointing to it that it may also lose the general elections [in June 2000]. So by that time the opposition was going very strong. We were training the youths how to mobilize the masses in the rural areas, to mobilize the masses for the ruling party. And also there were some instances whereby the opposition would be having some—organizing some rallies—so we were also training those guys that if the opposition wants to make some rallies . . . for us to neutralize the movement of the opposition in the rural areas, how they should disrupt the rallies or the meetings of the opposition.

Rukodzi noted that youths could move at a faster rate than the older war veteran leaders, particularly in groups. They could be sent on short notice to disperse a MDC rally or travel long distances to target opposition in adjoining districts.

Yet the key reason, in Rukodzi's view, youths were selected over more experienced war veterans to undertake some operations was that they offered ZANU-PF unquestioning obedience and could easily be persuaded to undertake extremely violent acts: "You [ZANU-PF] don't need somebody who is reasoning because somebody who is reasoning won't do as you like. . . . Some of those things [acts youths were required to undertake], were very, very, very nasty . . . so somebody who is reasoning can't do some nasty things." Rukodzi explained further: "A fresh mind is just as good as a knife. You can use a knife to cut your fruits and vegetables, your meats and everything, and you can also use that knife to cut me. . . . It's flexible . . . but it's a bad tool [if] you are using it against me." Youths offered the government the opportunity to shape impressionable minds through military style training as well as political indoctrination that often sought to inculcate a racially polarized view of society. This would provide an unquestioning "workforce" that could be deployed to secure the ruling party's political objectives.

Militia bases were created all over Zimbabwe, sometimes in schools, sometimes in open plots, and often on farms. Individuals operating from these bases undertook extensive action at the behest of ZANU-PF, as has been identified by Amnesty International.[26] Militias were directly involved in election-related violence during the 2000 parliamentary election, the 2002 presidential election, and various by-elections.[27] Bases served as command, interrogation, training, and accommodation centers for war veterans. They also served to establish a war veteran presence as a kind of "outpost" on farms or other areas where they could undertake surveillance of MDC activities and farm operations. Bases could be small in size, accommodating only a few war veteran leaders and auxiliary youths who provided support for various operations, or large enough for dozens or more war veterans, members of state security, and youths. The link between bases, the militias, and the state is unmistakable, according to Amnesty International, which claimed that militias were organized and supported by state security forces.[28]

Militia members were given extensive powers to commit violence in order to achieve ZANU-PF's objectives. Mupfure stated that youths had been "given a lot of power—immense powers—unregulated powers . . . you can insult anyone. Disrupt a meeting. Rape without consequence."[29] Militias operating from rural and urban bases systematically committed torture and other acts of violence and intimidation against MDC members, as well as perceived MDC supporters, including causing extensive damage to their property.

Youths who committed violence against the opposition rarely faced consequences, despite the severity of some of the violence they committed. Rukodzi stated that youths "were given powers that they can use maximum force against opposition supporters to beat them, to do any whatever, any kind of harassment."[30] In the event of a serious crime, the state security apparatus aggressively deflected criminal complaints and shielded ZANU-PF officials from accountability, often using the crime as an opportunity to further target the opposition: "Let's say if somebody's dead, then it would be said a ZANU-PF supporter was killed by MDC supporters." Rukodzi added that in these kinds of situations, farm invaders "knew that they were well catered for and they were well covered [by state security]."

My own evidence and other NGO reports show that militias had very extensive powers over law enforcement officials. Limpopo explained that, before the land seizure era, youths would be charged if they committed a crime.[31] "In 2000, that's when things started to change because there were a lot of youth brigades." With ZANU-PF making command decisions and youths being trained to undertake political directives, Limpopo recounted,

It was like the police had got nothing to do now because it is now in the hands of ZANU-PF because the government is ZANU-PF there [Bindura, Mashonaland Central]. You cannot go wrong [oppose] with ZANU-PF. If you say anything, a word against, even if you are a policeman, [about] what is happening, if you say anything against ZANU-PF, you were going to be charged for that.

Limpopo emphasized the shift in control after the land seizure era began: "ZANU was controlling everything. It wasn't the government. It was ZANU-PF." According to another police officer: "Many of the police officers are frightened of the war veterans, since they have their own command structure that goes right to the top and that will get them out of jail if they are arrested. Plenty of police officers left the force because of that."[32] With the ruling party exercising complete control, not just of law enforcement structures, but of militias undertaking their directives, they were well positioned to target farms and workers.

Of farmers surveyed for this book, 45.3% reported having a militia base on their farm. However, some provinces reported more militia bases than others.[33]

According to farmer survey data, 11.8% of farmers from Mashonaland Central, 11.3% from Mashonaland West, 10.3% from Mashonaland East, 3.4% from Manicaland, 3.4% from Masvingo, 2.1% from Matabeleland North, 1.7% from the Midlands, and 1.3% of farmers from Matabeleland South reported a militia base on their farm.

LeBas explained that "the location of militia bases in different areas led to a concentration of violent incidents in the immediate proximity of these bases."[34] With this in mind, it is worth investigating where ZANU-PF located its bases and how many existed during the 2000 parliamentary and 2002 presidential elections (data are provided in table 5.3). This evidence shows first that ZANU-PF increased the total number of war veteran militia bases from 2000 to 2002 by over 300%. Total bases in Mashonaland provinces rose from 28 in 2000 to 65 in 2002.

LeBas's assertion that the location of bases led to a concentration of incidents in the proximity of those bases is logical. Bases were located in particular areas in order to assert ZANU-PF's power. A key means of doing so was through the use of violence. For example, table 5.3 shows that a large number of bases were established in Matabeleland North for the 2002 presidential election. The likely reason for this sudden increase in bases probably has to do with the serious defeat ZANU-PF suffered in that province during the 2000 parliamentary election, where ZANU-PF won 30,064 votes and the MDC received 105,492 votes.

*Table 5.3* LOCATION OF MILITIA BASES DURING THE 2000 AND 2002 ELECTIONS

| Province | 2000 parliamentary elections | 2002 presidential elections |
|---|---|---|
| **Mashonaland Central** | 12 | 26 |
| **Mashonaland East** | 12 | 21 |
| **Mashonaland West** | 4 | 18 |
| **Midlands** | 5 | 6 |
| **Masvingo** | 0 | 3 |
| **Manicaland** | 3 | 2 |
| **Matabeleland North** | 0 | 30 |
| **Matabeleland South** | 0 | 0 |
| **Bulawayo** | 0 | 14 |
| **Harare** | 3 | 3 |
| *Total* | *39* | *123* |

SOURCE: A. P. Reeler, "Role of Militia Groups in Maintaining Zanu Pf's Political Power," http://www.kubatana.net/docs/hr/reeler_militia_mar_030331.pdf.

It is impossible to know for certain whether ZANU-PF would have been defeated in Mashonaland in the 2000 parliamentary elections had the ballot not
been rigged. What is clear is that the MDC were gaining ground in an area that
was critical to ZANU-PF's future political success. The large increase in war
veteran bases in Mashonaland ahead of the 2002 presidential election, shown
in table 5.3, suggests that the ruling party was seeking greater control over this
region. Andrew McKinley, a farmer, explained that in the period leading up to
the presidential election in 2002, invaders suddenly appeared on his farm:
"They were all there because they were told this is their job to be there until the
elections for the president. . . . The moment the election result was announced
they just packed their bags and left."[35]

## TARGETING FARMERS TO UNDERMINE THE OPPOSITION

The government and its assortment of supporters, including the youth militias, were willing to resort to extreme measures, including the murder of farmers, in their efforts to retain control over rural areas. While some farmers were
murdered by criminal opportunists operating in a near lawless environment,
others were deliberately murdered by the state in order to influence elections.
According to Msasa:

> Some [farmer murders] were to send a message. An example is the way
> how they killed people. . . . During the elections those are the messages,
> you know: "If you [farmers] vote for the wrong party, this is what we can
> do for you." So it was also a message to the British and to the other farmers
> that we were serious about land invasions. We want our land back.[36]

Another tactic used by war veterans was to initiate high shock-value incidents, such as the besieging and murder of rancher Martin Olds in Nyaman-
dhlovu in Matabeleland North on April 18, 2000, and of his mother, Gloria
Olds, in a nearby area on March 4, 2001. By targeting farmers in this way, farm
invaders were able to intimidate a greater population of farmers in the area.
Indeed, evidence from a Forum report published in 2000 suggests that at least
some war veteran leaders believed that murdering a farmer in Mashonaland
Central would be advantageous to their objectives: "Chitate [the leader of a
farm invasion group] has also threatened that the farmer will be killed as: 'we
are in need of showing off a dead farmer in the Mashonaland Central area.'"[37]
Farm invaders wanted their message to resonate in key farming areas, hence
the concentration of coercion in Mashonaland.

An analysis of the murder dates of farmers (see table 5.4) shows no farmer
murders were recorded in the first two months after the beginning of the land

seizure era in February 2000. This lag before the murder of farmers began can be explained by the fact that the referendum loss was a surprise for most ZANU-PF officials, and it took time to coordinate a response. However, 5 farmers (out of a total of 12 who would die in the eight years of the land seizure era) were murdered in a six-week period between April 15 and May 31, 2000, in the run-up to the June 2000 parliamentary election.

Figure 5.1 demonstrates how close in proximity the three Mashonaland provinces were to the national capital. Figure 5.2 is an example of how violence against workers and farmers tended to be concentrated in the 200-kilometer radius around Harare in the Mashonaland provinces, again illustrating how violence flared in this region. Figure 5.3, in conjunction with table 5.4, shows the location and distance from Harare of all 12 farmer murders that took place between 2000 and 2008. Eight murders were in the Mashonaland provinces, within 100 kilometers of Harare. Two more occurred within 200 kilometers of the capital. Thus, of all murders of farmers during the land seizure era, 67% were in the Mashonaland provinces.

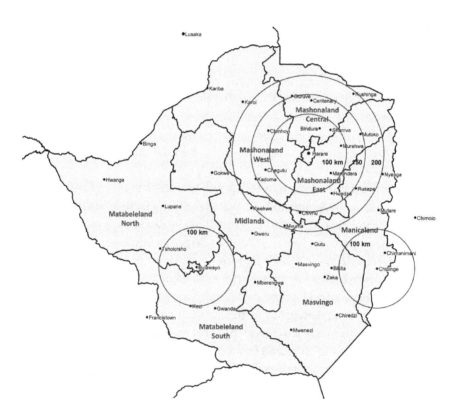

**Figure 5.1** Province Map with Kilometer Markers
SOURCE: Created by author.

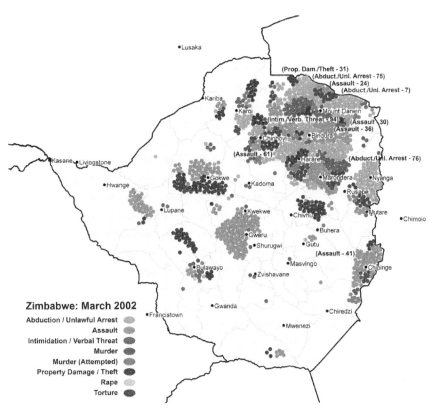

**Figure 5.2** Violence Map, March 2002
NOTE: See www.charleslaurie.com for a complete series of color violence maps depicting 21,491 acts of abduction/unlawful arrest, assault, murder, attempted murder, rape, torture, intimidation/verbal threat, and property damage/theft against farmers and workers recorded between 2000 and 2008.
SOURCE: Created by author.

There were more farmers in the Mashonaland provinces in the first place, so statistically it could be more likely that any murders of farmers in the country would occur in higher numbers in these areas. This explanation is, however, insufficient to fully explain the concentration of murders in Mashonaland. Moreover, two murders occurred in Matabeleland North, a relatively under-populated area insofar as the population of farmers and ranchers is concerned. The fact that both of the Matabeleland North victims (Martin and Gloria Olds) were members of the same family murdered months apart, and that both murders involved the use of AK-47 assault rifles—very rarely owned by civilians in Zimbabwe—suggests coordination in the attacks. Meanwhile, there were no reported murders of farmers in Masvingo or Manicaland provinces, both of which contained sizable farmer populations. This casts further doubt on the suggestion that the pattern of murders simply reflected farmers' population

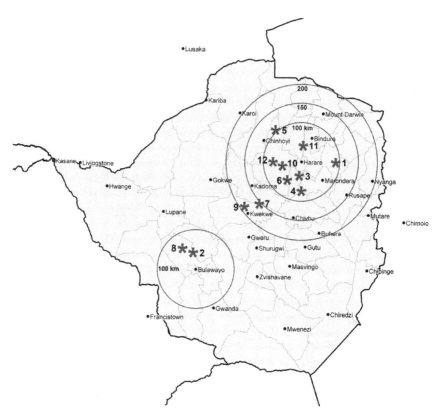

**Figure 5.3** Location of Farmer Murders
NOTE: Table 5.4 lists the farmer names.
SOURCE: Created by author.

distribution. On the contrary, the concentration of murders in Mashonaland is further evidence that the government and its allies were intent on using violence to suppress their opponents in the country's most important political battleground.

In fact, though some murders appeared to stem from the frenzied manner in which farm invaders moved onto farms and sought to end the farmers' resistance, there is evidence to show that the majority of farmer murders during the land seizure era were undertaken at the behest of the state. Legal officer Christian Mucheke estimated that of the 12 farmers murdered, 5 were committed by common criminals—opportunists taking advantage of a lawless period.[38] According to Mucheke, murders undertaken by the CIO at the behest of the state could be identified by the use of firearms. For instance, he stated that the murder of farmer David Stevens,

*Table 5.4* LIST OF MURDERED COMMERCIAL FARMERS: 2000–2008

|    | Farmer | Date of murder | Location |
|----|--------|----------------|----------|
| 1  | **David Stevens** | April 15, 2000 | Murehwa, Mashonaland East |
| 2  | **Martin Olds** | April 18, 2000 | Nyamandhlovu, Matabeleland North |
| 3  | **Allan Dunn** | May 7, 2000 | Beatrice, Mashonaland East |
| 4  | **John Weeks** | May 14, 2000 | Seke, Mashonaland East |
| 5  | **Tony Oates** | May 31, 2000 | Zvimba North, Mashonaland West |
| 6  | **Willem Botha** | July 23, 2000 | Seke, Mashonaland East |
| 7  | **Henry Elsworth** | December 12, 2000 | Kwekwe, Midlands |
| 8  | **Gloria Olds** | March 4, 2001 | Nyamandhlovu, Matabeleland North |
| 9  | **Robert Cobbet** | August 6, 2001 | Kwekwe, Midlands |
| 10 | **Terence Ford** | March 18, 2002 | Norton, Mashonaland West |
| 11 | **Charles Anderson** | June 2, 2002 | Glendale, Mashonaland Central |
| 12 | **Don Stewart** | November 27, 2005 | Norton, Mashonaland West |

NOTE: Included here are farmers who were likely murdered by the government, as well as individuals murdered in an environment where law enforcement was inactive because of political interference. Murders that were not obviously politically related are not included.

which involved Stevens being abducted by farm invaders, taken to a police station, and later shot, was undertaken by the CIO:

> A policeman would not have killed in the police station with a gun. They would torture and beat you up—but he was shot. That was CIO. And the killings of people by guns during these [*sic*] "violence" has been more done by the CIO than by the police. And normally even opposition members have been killed mostly by CIO and not by the police or not by the war veterans per se.

Mucheke's explanation that the use of firearms pointed to state involvement is certainly plausible. For example, court documents show that farmer Charles Anderson was murdered with an AK-47 assault rifle; it is extremely rare for this kind of weapon to be in the possession of civilians in Zimbabwe.[39]

Police officer Samuel Limpopo was also in no doubt that farmers were murdered deliberately by the state, partly in order to warn other farmers by their example.[40] According to Limpopo, victims would be chosen by "big bosses" in each district who would review lists of potential victims, stating, "'This one is a threat, this one is a threat.' So they target. They sit down and ask, 'Do this, do this, do this one.'" Criteria for selection were likely to be based on a perceived threat to ZANU-PF through the farmer's support for the MDC.[41] Indeed, murdered farmer David Stevens was a known MDC supporter in the Mashonaland East province, as was Ian Kay (MDC MP for Marondera Central), who was nearly murdered by ZANU-PF assailants in April 2000 (Kay lived relatively close to murdered farmer David Stevens).

Msasa explained that, while numerous farmers were eventually murdered, the killing of a farmer was a very serious undertaking by the state, and not a casual decision: "I will tell you that one [the order to murder a particular farmer] automatically come from the top . . . and the operatives [agents tasked with murders], they know, the operatives would [be given] an order: 'That farmer must be killed.'"[42] Thus, farmers were murdered in accordance with specific orders from senior government officials and did not occur randomly: "Specifically farmer X [would be murdered] because of maybe the history; they would go check the history of that farmer as well. It's not just any farmer." Msasa further stated that farmers were specifically chosen "just to send the message both to the farmers and to the international world, especially the West." He also pointed out that the murder of a farmer would often have complex objectives. The state would not, for instance, simply murder the most ardent MDC supporting farmer in a given area. Perhaps a non-MDC supporting farmer would be murdered in order to cause confusion within the farming community about who was vulnerable. Agents might also be seeking an international objective so a farmer with a particular background to suit that goal would be chosen. Or the farmer might be killed in a particular way that met certain objectives. Msasa stated that in each murder case, however, a specific set of objectives were established by the CIO with government approval; nothing about the state-sanctioned murder of farmers was haphazard—although not all farm murders were explicitly state sanctioned.

Mucheke provided three criteria that could make a farmer a candidate for murder.[43] First, farmers who were more outspoken against the government and generally communicative about their labors were threatened. Second, farmers who were more supportive of the MDC were at far greater risk. Third, if the farmer resisted or made vocal protests about the actions of farm invaders, then the farmer would be more likely to murdered: "When the farmer resisted and makes a noise and everything, [farm invaders] would withdraw, go back, and plan. Then they are told [by the CIO] to go and shoot him. And the instruction comes from above."[44]

Mucheke agreed that farmer murders were often intended to send a message to the public.[45] In the case of farmer David Stevens, he pointed out that farm invaders first took him to the local police station—where they could have left him if intimidation was their only objective. Mucheke reported that instead they "wanted to show a lesson to others that they shall not resist or they will die, and that was the purpose of killing him." Sebungwe, meanwhile, argued that killing farmers was intended to send a message demonstrating the government's power, particularly because murders served to "distract attention from what is happening in Zimbabwe, because people are very easily swayed about such events. Politicians do it [order murders]. They create a certain scene today to take attention from the real issues that are on the ground and what is actually making news."[46]

State-sanctioned murders were often carried out by a group within the CIO nicknamed the "Dirty Tricks Department." Political opponents were eliminated in a variety of ways that were often made to appear as accidents. According to Sebungwe: "They are executioners. You can use that word. They are used to do that, and they are known. Once you see them coming into an area, then you know something is about to happen."[47]

Intelligence officials interviewed for this book explained that criminals were sometimes used by the state to commit murders, including of farmers.[48] State agents would locate a prisoner serving a long term sentence and offer freedom if the individual committed a murder. If the prisoner happened to be caught, then the state could frame the event as a common crime undertaken by an "escaped prisoner." Respondents stated that in such a scenario, the criminal(s) undertaking the murder would always be accompanied by a CIO agent to ensure the act was completed according to plan. The murder of Charles Anderson appears to have been undertaken in this manner (see extended account in the note).[49]

Farmer Joachim van Vaaden estimated that 10% of a farm seizure group would be made up of a "criminal element."[50] This was particularly the case as farm seizures progressed and individuals with special skills in coercion— learned from illegal activities—were more highly valued in seizing land and associated assets. The use of criminals to undertake state-sanctioned murders may account for the disagreement among interview respondents over whether the murders of farmers were state sanctioned or were common crimes. Indeed, it is intriguing that not everyone in the security forces appeared to have been aware of these "state sanctioned" murders, even though they held senior positions. Lundi claimed that "it was *unheard* of to kill somebody for land. We never really thought it was going to get the extent of someone *dying* for it. I don't think even in Mugabe's book . . . they had envisaged someone being killed for it."[51] Lundi stated that after Stevens was murdered he was personally "actually summoned by our minister saying, 'Go and get those guys and get the police to charge them.'" He added that the murder of Stevens "really kind of shook even your most ardent ZANU-PF people." It is important to keep in mind that, as Lundi noted, the period between the February 2000 referendum and the June 2000 elections had become "lawless" and a "free-for-all," with extreme confusion within the government over its stance toward the farm invasions. Indeed, in this context, it is probable that the killings were undertaken by factions of the state security service of which Lundi was not a part.[52]

It is more likely that the first six or seven murders in table 5.4 were state-sanctioned acts. The involvement of the state security apparatus has been recorded in most of these incidents (for instance, Stevens was taken to the local police station before he was murdered). The fact that the spate of murders occurred within a relatively confined time frame before suddenly ceasing also points to a central mechanism of control, rather than the coincidence of ordinary criminal behavior.

A point repeatedly emphasized by farm invaders interviewed for this book was that the government was concerned about repercussions from the international community for state involvement in the criminal activity occurring on farms. "They don't want anything from outside [media and other political attention]. . . . They don't want the world to know what they are doing," according to Limpopo.[53] While this point is hardly surprising, it does highlight awareness within the government of the stark criminality of events, and it explains why the police treated many of the farm murders as ordinary criminal events. International press coverage of the enormous upsurge in violence against MDC supporters—and especially against commercial farms—was extensive, placing Mugabe and his government in a poor light insofar as Western viewers were concerned. It is one likely reason why the frenzy of farmer murders between April 15 and May 31, 2000, ended after the June 2000 parliamentary election. With ZANU-PF having achieved its election victory, a less overt campaign against farmers and workers was devised. Murders continued, but at a slower rate than was seen in the weeks when ZANU-PF was fighting for survival.

## TARGETING WORKERS TO UNDERMINE MDC SUPPORT

### ZANU-PF's Need to Suppress MDC Support on Farms

The ZANU-PF leadership believed that they could only retain their grip on political power by undermining the influence wielded by commercial farmers over the MDC and their own workforces, and by placating the demands of war veterans. They did not, at the outset, intend to evict all white farmers from their property, but they did seek to weaken white farmers' ability to finance the opposition and to use their authority over their workers to generate support for the MDC. Samuel Limpopo, a police officer, specifically said that the government tended to "target . . . those white farmers who talk to black people."[54] Another police officer, Edison Bubye, emphasized that the government believed that the farmers were "easily influencing" their workers' political views, and "according to Mugabe this is why he lost the referendum."[55]

"It was not just the whites as individuals [who were targeted], but the target was [also] their wealth," according to Thompson Mupfure, a veteran of the Liberation War and senior politician.[56] The government sought "to break the wealth because they [farmers] were being perceived as supporters of the MDC. So if you really wanted to fracture the support base of the MDC, you had to destroy white wealth. . . . You need to destroy the wealth of the whites so they don't have the resources to now fund the MDC."

Limpopo highlighted that ZANU-PF knew that whites constituted a minute voting bloc, but were more concerned with the far greater number of black voters that might be influenced by commercial farmers: "They [ZANU-PF] wanted to teach the African people because they know that white Zimbabweans, they are very few. . . . And how are we going to get our votes? Through the black people."[57] Mupfure agreed that "ZANU-PF knew that the person whose vote will count is the black person, not the white person, and there are a lot of blacks employed by whites who would be influenced to vote for the opposition."[58] As Mupfure put it, farmers would no longer be able to employ workers whom they could turn against ZANU-PF if it could "destroy the [farmers'] wealth." The use of coercion against workers would intimidate them into lining up behind the ruling party, and they would be less able to give active support to the MDC once they lost their employment following the eviction of the farmer. Mupfure explained that once farmers were evicted, "the white farmers' employees would then be rendered eternally displaced persons in their own country. . . . You are talking of 350,000 farm workers." He further added that if there were 350,000 workers and each worker had a spouse and children, the displacement of this many people would severely undermine support for the opposition. These individuals would have lost a key reason for supporting the MDC because they would no longer be employed on farms, and displaced people would have been more vulnerable to hostile government agents.

Many of the officials interviewed for this book made it clear that farms as a whole were targeted for seizure and violence based on the perceived level of support for the MDC on the farm, as discussed in chapter 4. More specifically, senior ZANU-PF leaders targeted farms based on the extent to which they believed that the farmer and farm workers supported the opposition, although as takeovers became a free-for-all, this criterion became less relevant. By early 2000, senior ZANU-PF officials and rank-and-file war veterans were both desperate to stem the growing tide of support for the MDC. The former wanted to preserve their power and to avoid being held to account for past crimes they may have committed, and the latter sought to protect their land claim interests. Thus, farm invaders were vigorous in seeking to thwart MDC support among one of their core constituencies—farm workers.

A war veteran who later seized a farm in Mashonaland, Petros Mzingwane, summed up the perspective of liberation fighters: "They [farmers] are forming the MDC because the MDC was formed to protect the land. And Tsvangirai said he was not going to touch the land—that was one of his promises."[59] Thus, in his view—which was shared by many war veterans and ZANU-PF supporters—the MDC was an illegitimate political party, formed purely for the purpose of protecting white interests. Since, in their view, farmers' interests clashed with those of the ruling party and war veterans, the MDC had to be suppressed.

A senior member of the Zimbabwe Republic Police, Edward Chidembo, explained the process:

> If there is any white commercial farmer who is believed to be sympathetic to MDC, that farm is gone. That was the bottom line. . . . It was also done in a punitive way. . . . Those farmers who were sympathetic to ZANU-PF, their farms were not touched.[60]

Initially, farm invaders were encouraged to seize farms where the farmers and workers were known to support the MDC, and told to leave farms alone when no such support was thought to exist. This view is supported by magistrate Tafadzwa Tegwani, who had exposure to ZANU-PF decision-making as an official in the judicial system: "Anybody at that point [in early 2000] could have been seen to be supporting the opposition, they would certainly fall victim to the government's rage against them."[61] However, as was discussed in chapter 3, the scope of the seizures rapidly escalated. All farmers quickly came to be seen as actual or potential MDC supporters and thus incurred a blanket response from farm invaders. According to Bubye, once the government had lost the referendum in February 2000, "Everyone on the farm was an enemy of the state."[62]

Government officials knew which farms tended to support the MDC because they received intelligence from the CIO and informers on the farms (see chapter 2 for more information on CIO intelligence gathering). For example, Rob Dawes, a farmer from a Mashonaland province, found out several years after the farm seizures began that the bartender of the local country club, where farmers would congregate, was a longtime CIO informant.[63] The bartender had always seemed welcoming, friendly, and nonpartisan and was well liked by the club's members. He had appeared to be part of the country club scene and was never considered by farmers to hold strong political views or to be untrustworthy. Some farmers therefore believed the country club was a safe environment for them to air their political views. Moreover, as the drink flowed, farmers tended to become less guarded about speaking their minds than they might ordinarily be. Through the use of such informants embedded in the farming community, the CIO was able to ascertain even before 2000 which farmers were opposition supporters in that area.

According to Bubye, meanwhile, farm workers were targeted "because they were perceived to be MDC, because they were perceived to be supporting white farmers who are supporting MDC. So everyone who was on the farm was kicked out."[64] In fact, from the beginning of the seizures, farm invaders were quick to distrust workers' political allegiances because they saw them as being easily persuaded by their farmer employers. For example, Mukwa relayed an instance where she was confronted by a farm invader:

> He said we don't trust you because you are working for the party [the MDC]. You are working for the whites. These white men are for the opposition party which we don't want, and we know that you too, just because you are sitting here [i.e., employed on the farm], you are working for the opposition party.[65]

Similarly, manager Herbert Nchenchi was also told by farm invaders that by working on farms they were perceived as de facto opposition supporters: "They were saying we [farm invaders] were supporting the whites and we were wanting to give the country back to the whites because of course then we did support a different political party [i.e., MDC]."[66] According to Msasa, farm invaders would blame workers for helping the farmer to stand his ground. Accordingly, when the farm invaders did eventually take control, they had no inclination to allow workers to remain on the land.[67]

Msasa added that ZANU-PF simply deprived workers of the ability to vote by dispossessing and displacing them: "They [workers] were even told, 'There is no more vote for you.' It's only this year [March 2002] they will not be allowed to vote because they [ZANU-PF] know which party they [workers] are going to vote. So they were dumped [displaced from farms]. . . . The farm workers were treated so badly, very, very badly."[68] Alternatively, farm manager Chesterton Hove stated that farm invaders told him that once they evicted the farmers, ZANU-PF could gain the workers' votes: "It was political trouble because those ZANU-PF they think when they chase the white people [from] the farm, then they can get [political] power as well. And all the people now on the farm [i.e., workers], they can see ZANU-PF is the power here and we can vote for them."[69]

Joyce Mukwa, a farm clerk, believed that farm invaders targeted her employer for his suspected support for the MDC: "They claimed that the owner of the farm was for the opposition party. . . . I think that's why they had to trouble him very much."[70] Imminence Ngiwa, a tractor driver and foreman, found the same situation on the farm where he worked: "They [farm invaders] wanted also to find out if he [the farm owner] is supporting ZANU-PF or the MDC. If they knew that the boss is supporting MDC, that is when they were chasing [him off the farm]."[71] Whether workers were targeted because their employer was a known MDC supporter, or because the workers themselves were known to support the opposition, the majority faced violence from the farm invaders.

### Breaking the MDC Support Nexus by Targeting Senior Workers

Mupfure explained that farm invaders intended to undermine the opposition by targeting the basis of the MDC's financial and popular support: "Number one is to destroy the white wealth, and number two when you destroy this wealth, those who depend on it for employment and salaries would then scatter, and that's exactly what happened."[72]

A key means of forcing farmers off their property—destroying "white wealth"—was to target senior workers. Farmers surveyed for this book were asked whether they believed certain types of workers were targeted more specifically or aggressively than others. A total of 63.7% of respondents believed that foremen or managers, those more senior workers, were targeted specifically or the most aggressively by farm invaders. A smaller proportion of respondents believed tractor drivers (37.0%), laborers (14.3%), domestic workers (5.3%), and horticulture workers (4.7%) were most likely to be targeted. Survey respondents also provided qualitative statements affirming this belief, with one anonymous farmer stating: "Definitely, all management and domestic workers were targeted far more than general labourers." Mucheke agreed that "most of them [senior workers] were killed or displaced, and if you remember some of these senior workers, they had no homes to go to. . . . That farm was their home."[73]

Targeting senior workers achieved both these objectives, since they functioned as the critical bridge between the farmer and the rest of the labor force. According to horticulture manager Andrew Morfu, "From the people to the boss, I would be like the conduit or the party line [telephone line]. So if there are problems, they [employees] come to me. If the boss has got problems, who does he come to? He comes to me."[74] Morfu stated that farm invaders recognized the senior workers' critical knowledge base: "He [the senior worker] knows everything what is happening. He knows where they [the farmer] have been and where they are coming from." Thompson Mbezi, who was in charge of cattle herding on a commercial farm, stated that "they [farm invaders] know the senior workers, they've got experience to talk to us [junior workers]. If we disturb these senior workers, then all these other workers can run away."[75] Manager Chesterton Hove stated that foremen on his farm were treated with particular aggression by farm invaders, who believed that these individuals provided detailed information about farm operations to the farmer, and thus were instrumental to the commercial viability of the business: "They say those foremen have been eyes for their white bosses."[76] According to Hove, foremen were not, however, the only targets. Managers, drivers, and domestic workers were also specifically sought by farm invaders.

The police were also keenly aware of the importance of senior workers in farming operations. According to Limpopo, the strategy of undermining the farmer by targeting senior workers was relatively simple: "Let's dispose the head farm worker. He is the one who manages the people. . . . So if we target him, then nothing is going to be done. They [workers] are not going to work. Let's disturb."[77]

Sebungwe explained that the job of a manager or foreman was a position that ordinary laborers aspired to achieve.[78] These were senior roles that generated respect from other workers. In addition to carrying greater responsibility, senior workers were also better paid. Sebungwe stated that for these reasons, "if they [senior workers] see people coming to evict the farmer, they also stand with him, and . . . they've tried to protect the farmers, but they ended up being killed themselves." Thus, in addition to serving as the "conduit" between the farmer and farm laborers, thereby enabling the farm to operate, senior workers also had a vested personal interest in seeing the farm succeed. Accordingly, they usually worked to preserve their jobs and prevent the invasions from succeeding.

For farm invaders seeking to evict the farmer, a key solution was to break the link between the farmer and the labor force he needed to operate the farm. Senior workers were vulnerable to being targeted for this reason primarily, but according to Mucheke, there were actually three problems facing senior workers.[79] First, because senior workers were better paid, junior workers were "jealous" of them and quick to accuse them of being MDC supporters even if they were not. Second, war veterans did not trust senior workers because they recognized that senior workers had "everything to lose" if the farm was seized and would therefore defend the farmer, the farm, and the other workers. Accordingly, senior workers would not easily comply with the demands of farm invaders. Third, according to Mucheke, senior workers were "loved by the boss, and then they were tainted as traitors on that ground." In fact, farm invaders tended to view all those living and working on farms as legitimate targets. The more senior the worker, the more farm invaders viewed the individual as having unmistakable political and economic ties to the white farmers and hence to the MDC.

Farm workers interviewed for this book recounted that their identities were conflated with those of white farmers by the farm invaders. Foreman and tractor driver Imminence Ngiwa put it succinctly: "We were just treated as a white Zimbabwean."[80] He said they were treated like whites because they shared the same occupation, and therefore were presumed to hold the same political views. He added: "When you are with the whites, they were including you together.... They were just thinking that white and black are the same." Indeed, when the farm that mechanic Chenjerai Mapufuli worked on was seized, "They said I was working for the white farmer, so I was just as bad, like white farmer."[81]

"Most senior employees were regarded as being more loyal to the white commercial farmer, so they were subject to more abuse," recalled farm manager Ketani Makabusi.[82] "We were singled out and as senior management from just foreman level, in fact from middle-management, we were just singled out. 'Guys, whether you were on our side or not, you were close to the former commercial farmer, so we're against you.'" Makabusi did note that in some cases farm invaders sought to use the perceived close relationship between senior workers and the farmer to their advantage, by using the worker's knowledge to seize, for example, agri-property. He related how a farm invader told him, "You know everything about the setup. You can orchestrate theft if you want to. So why not jump on board and be a part of us so we can make this more effective?" He elaborated:

> First they'll abuse you and get you so afraid of them, and then once they get you afraid and all in a panic, then they know quite clearly now, "We've got this guy and he's all afraid and all panicky." And then they come back and try and use you hoping that because you're all afraid, you're going to do what they want for you to try to win back their trust or to get on sides with them.

According to Makabusi, however, in most cases farm invaders simply dismissed senior workers as inherently untrustworthy and sought to remove their influence from the farm as rapidly as possible.

When Mucheke was asked why farm invaders did not see senior workers as a repository of knowledge that should be preserved in order to enable the land claimant to operate the farm after the white farmer was evicted, he explained: "The people who took over the farms were not farmers. Most of them knew nothing about farming, but they have got this false hope that they can do it—it's easy. Some of them were ... farming at a very small scale in their villages, and they think that they will do the same."[83] Accordingly, farm invaders did not believe they needed to retain the knowledge base of senior workers.

Mucheke emphasized that the biggest problem with retaining senior workers was that farm invaders believed they "will mislead the new farmer because they half belong to their old employer and it's always believed that old habits die very hard. And because of that, they [farm invaders] never trusted senior farm workers." This situation was summed up by dairy manager Philip Mahobohobo, who recalled being asked by a farm invader who seized the farm where he worked how long he had worked for his former white boss. When he said that he had worked on the farm for thirty-three years, the farm invader said, "Whew! You have been full of white man. I can't stay with you."[84]

Blair Rutherford accurately describes the relationship between farmers and workers as "domestic government" in which the farmers employed and administered workers.[85] In this system, farmers were expected to provide basic services to workers (which would ordinarily be provided by the state). These benefits included housing and the provision of basic education and healthcare; farmers also provided a kind of unofficial ambulance where workers could request that farmers take sick or injured family members to a nearby clinic. For example, Msasa said that farmers provided food, wages, housing, schools, and healthcare to their workers.[86] Likewise, an anonymous farmer survey respondent stated, "I was fair with my employees and had various schemes in practice which they benefitted from, such as a feeding programme for 60 children under 6 every day, free medicines and good housing." Workers normally received a small piece of land along with associated assistance in cultivation so that they could grow some of their own food. Many farmers would provide commodities produced by the farm at a discounted rate, such as wheat, maize, meat, and dairy products. Other farmers would give more ad hoc assistance, such as providing the farm's welding equipment to repair cooking pots and bicycles. Farmers were expected to provide basic social amenities such as a beer hall, funds for a farm football team, and, at Christmas, a party for the workers and their families. Additionally, farmers would offer basic bereavement support. While these provisions incurred costs for the farmer, this system also meant that they benefited from a highly dependent workforce who might then be more willing to maintain the bonds linking them to their employers.

Working and living conditions on farms were highly variable. Differences depended on the relative wealth and temperament of the farmer, and much less on the capacity of the state to enforce uniform standards. Walter Chambati says that some farm workers experienced "appalling living conditions."[87] It is true that some homes and working environments were of extremely poor quality and sometimes hazardous. Some farmer employers were also abusive. Farm workers interviewed for this book recounted how some farmers were heavy-handed and treated workers very poorly; the spouse of a commercial farmer stated that the neighboring farm owner was "physically very large [and] not known to communicate well with the workers," describing him as a "horror story" insofar as his labor relations were concerned.[88] On the other hand, workers sometimes had progressive employers, lived in brick homes, and had fair and safe working environments. For many people living in rural areas, life on a farm was often far preferable to life in nonfarming communities, which lacked support from farmers. What is certain is that the government bore little burden of the costs incurred by farmers for their workers in providing social support and did not contribute much regulatory oversight of workers.

Employment structures in the agricultural sector dated back to a colonial system that aimed to provide large-scale commercial farms, along with mines and industry, with cheap labor. Rutherford notes that even by 2000, the legal regime was still structured to limit the ability of farm workers to organize themselves.[89] In this respect Sam Moyo is correct in describing the system as "exploitative," although it is certain that some farmers had far greater means to give benefits to workers and their dependents than others.[90] Certainly some farmers faced dire economic conditions prior to the land seizure era and many became insolvent, limiting their ability to provide social support. On the other hand, particularly in the late 1990s, other farmers—especially in Mashonaland—enjoyed unheralded prosperity; but this was not usually passed on to workers in any long-standing and meaningful way.

Poorly paid workers who were dependent on social benefits provided on a voluntary basis by their employer had a lot to lose and almost no recourse if they were deprived of their employment. A dismissed worker faced losing his home and access to basic healthcare and education for his family, and in most cases the worker lacked sufficient financial resources to easily move elsewhere.

For these reasons—and to a lesser extent because of some inherent loyalty to the farmer—workers tended to resist the efforts of ZANU-PF and farm invaders to evict farmers. Most workers were not "sellouts" to any political objective, but were simply looking to maintain their fragile livelihoods. Thus, when farm invaders made demands, workers were reluctant to comply. This reinforced the determination of the farm invaders to use violence and threats in order to gain their acquiescence.

At the same time, farmers were also totally dependent on workers. If workers left, the farmer would be unable to operate. Therefore, farmers vigorously sought to protect their workers and find ways to ensure that they could continue their employment. The MDC also courted workers. Given that the total farm worker population counted about 350,000 people, it is easy to see how the MDC could rise to power so rapidly with their support and also why ZANU-PF felt the need to crush the farm worker voter nexus.[91]

## Framing Farm workers as Illegitimate Outsiders

Another reason workers tended to be targeted both aggressively and punitively was that many had foreign ethnicity. A 1999 survey by the General Agriculture and Plantation Workers' Union of Zimbabwe (GAPWUZ) found that "alien" workers comprised about 30% of the farm worker population.[92] According to Mucheke, "Most of them were of Malawian origin and therefore . . . they were considered as traitors because they were told, you are foreigners who are looking after foreigners in our land, so there was no mercy for them."[93] Malawian and Zambian workers had been brought to work on farms during the Rhodesian era. According to Magaramombe, in 1966 an estimated 54% of male commercial farm workers were from foreign countries.[94] Indeed, Chambati notes that farm workers had faced exclusion even from land redistribution schemes that began at independence in 1980, with farm workers only becoming a recognized category of beneficiary in 1998.[95] By 2000, however, many farm workers were Zimbabwean by birth and their families had lived in Zimbabwe for generations.

The claim that farm workers, as ethnic outsiders, held an "illegitimate" position conveniently served to deprive them of a claim to the land and agri-property sought by farm invaders. It reduced competition for scarce but valuable resources. Thus, by undermining their valid claims to farm assets, farm invaders could increase the supply of the assets for themselves. Accordingly, workers remaining on farms seized by farm invaders also tended to be blamed for any criminal behavior, as farm invaders sought to evict them in order to prevent them from competing for resources.[96] Sam Moyo stated that "some new farmers tended to treat farm workers as thieves, given high levels of stock theft, or as foreigners (although below 30 percent are descendents [sic] of immigrants), and/or as 'reactionaries' who had opposed land reform."[97]

Only ethnic Shonas and, to a lesser extent, Ndebeles were regarded as genuine citizens and ZANU-PF supporters, and therefore as legitimate beneficiaries of seized land and agri-property. This restructuring of identity within the state has, according to Raftopoulos, been "constituted around the centrality of the land question and the contribution of ZANU-PF to the liberation struggle."[98]

In this way, ZANU-PF could delegitimize MDC supporters, legitimize its own support base and tie key nationalist objectives to the seizure of land. Indeed, as Chavunduka and Bromley note, land politics during the land seizure era sought to define who belonged. Those who did could stay and gain benefits, and those who did not were cast out.[99]

## Coercion: The Key to Undermining Workers' Support for the MDC

Workers were more vulnerable than farmers to the very extensive violence and intimidation that was used during the land seizure era.[100] Workers did not benefit from security provided by robust brick homes, fences, firearms, and guard dogs, which farmers usually possessed. Workers also received even less protection from the police and legal system than farmers, since the latter were large-scale employers and business owners, and were capable of recourse to legal counsel in many cases (albeit in decreasing levels as the land seizures escalated). Msasa noted that many farm invaders also feared the technology owned by most farmers, such as cameras, mobile phones, and video recorders, which might capture their identities and be used in court cases.[101] Despite possessing such defenses, farmers were still extensively victimized; farm workers possessed no such defenses and thus the victimization they encountered was even more substantial and severe.

Given that farmers were generally wealthy, they tended to ultimately lose far more in financial terms than workers. However, workers tended to be more vulnerable to violence than farmers, in terms of both the severity and the breadth of different types of physical attacks. Moreover, while workers tended to possess assets with a lower net value than farmers, they tended to be poorer, and therefore these assets were much harder for them to replace. For example, if a farmer experienced the theft of two tractors worth US$50,000, he was more likely to remain financially solvent because of his other assets and savings than a worker who might have lost US$200 worth of assets but was otherwise destitute.

ZANU-PF used systematic violence against workers in order to suppress their support for the MDC and to coerce them into backing the ruling party. Mucheke explained that the extent of severe violence was largely due to ZANU-PF's heightened political vulnerability:

What happened at that time defied logic. Simply in the way to be felt that they [ZANU-PF] should be felt, they had to kill some people. It was a way to exert power, enforce power. As I speak to you now the name "war veteran" in Zimbabwe will send shivers in spines of so many people now.[102]

Mucheke added that violence was a way to "force submission" and demonstrate ZANU-PF's power using strategies, such as public beatings, torture, and murder, that were carried over directly from methods used by ZANU in the Liberation War.

## Pungwes: Intimidation En Masse

On most farms, ZANU-PF's efforts to demonstrate its power were first seen at *pungwes*—political rallies that have a long history in Zimbabwe. During the Liberation War, ZANLA—the military wing of ZANU—used *pungwes* as political education meetings to define and instill loyalty to, and compliance with, ZANU's cause among the local rural communities. Attendance was compulsory, and meetings sometimes lasted days. Attendees were required to be present at political lectures, and the most senior and influential community members in particular were called upon to make public pronouncements of allegiance to ZANU.

The purpose of *pungwes* during the Liberation War, according to veteran of the war Felix Umchabezi, was to ensure the malleability of the civilian population, "to turn people into emotional animals that will do anything. That was a typical approach of ZANU-PF."[103] By exposing local communities to periods of profound fear, in victimizing senior, respected community leaders, and in showing that they were effectively above the law, the militants made sure that community members would realize that they faced an arduous future if they were to resist.

During the Liberation War farm workers had been seen as "sellouts" because of their role in helping white farmers to continue their operations. This was seen as aiding the Rhodesian state by extension. "'Sellouts' were usually killed or beaten publicly," according to Kriger.[104] Welshman Mabhena, a veteran of the war who later became a senior ZANU-PF official and was privy to decision-making in the party's inner circle in the 1990s, explained that the coercion of civilians during the war was effective in ensuring that ZANLA fighters received logistical support.[105] "The guerrillas had gone out killing people. Anybody whom they thought was a 'sell-out' would be killed—never spared. And that was set in the minds of the people." This method was deeply intimidating since many accused "sellouts" in the Liberation War were murdered and tortured by guerrillas.[106]

The tradition of nationalist hostility toward farm workers was revived during the land seizure era. Since black workers were close to their white farmer employers in some cases, there was a racial dimension to the harsh treatment they incurred from farm invaders. Foreman Telmore Nyakasanga summed up his experience: "I'm still working with a white man, so they hate me. So they can fucking come and get me because of that."[107] Workers were seen as enabling farmers to continue operating—and as a result were almost automatically viewed as "sellouts." Makabusi explained that farm invaders claimed to feel betrayed by farm workers: "They would say, 'You are part of us [i.e., black]. How come you have stabbed us in the back?"[108] He recalled, "If you were black and you went out of line [by refusing to comply with ZANU-PF's political objectives], your punishment would be a lot more severe than, let's say, if you are white."

> They [farm invaders] expected more loyalty from blacks. . . . I mean they sort of excused white guys [because] these guys aren't going to be loyal to us anyway because we are taking their land away. There was generally an excuse [for whites not voting for ZANU-PF]. . . but if you [blacks] aren't loyal to us, you don't have a reason not to be loyal to us. We'll gun you down if you aren't loyal to us.

It is difficult to overstate the fear generated by the label of "sellout," which carried over from the Liberation War to the land seizure era. The memory of how sell-outs in the Liberation War had faced extreme violence and intimidation from their own community was part of the living memory of many farm workers in 2000. Violence was a cornerstone of *pungwes* during the Liberation War. Reluctant participants faced being physically assaulted, and suspected traitors were sometimes executed. Draconian punishments like mutilation of lips and noses were not uncommon. Killings of sellouts at *pungwes* were intended to demonstrate the kinds of punishments that would-be "sellouts" might face. Sebungwe gave an example: "He'd [the 'sellout'] get killed in a very gruesome way, when people's hands and legs were being chopped off by axes in the presence of people, and so that thing has always been so. It's a part of the [ZANU political] culture."[109]

During the war, and long after in the public consciousness, *pungwes* remained a hallmark of the intimidation experienced by local communities at the hands of ZANLA forces. The memories of how "sellouts" were treated during the Liberation War made it easy for ZANU-PF and its supporters to remind their victims of the consequences of receiving the label during the land seizure era. Thus, with the escalation of tensions during the land seizure era, the reintroduction of *pungwes* meant that ZANU-PF could recall the deep-seated fear associated with the meetings, thereby achieving a kind of intimidatory head-start. This served to rapidly demonstrate the party's intention to suppress support for the MDC at the community level.

Indeed, before *pungwes* were even held, the intimidatory power of the event would make an impression on many people who had experienced or heard about events during the Liberation War. Msasa emphasized the extreme fear generated during the land seizures when the label of "sellout" was invoked: "The word 'sellout' during the war, it was very, very scary even just to talk about it. So even now if that word 'sellout' started to come out . . . if they said, 'Those people . . . they are sellouts' . . . you are then no longer part of the community. So, you see, that word is so 'scared' to Zimbabweans especially in the rural areas."[110]

*Pungwes* were a logical place for ZANU-PF to begin suppressing the MDC during the land seizure era because they allowed large numbers of people to be intimidated, all at relatively low cost. A key reason accused "sellouts" were so fearful was that the assaults, torture, and murder of victims was undertaken in protracted public displays that fueled gratuitous violence. Moreover, war veterans leading or assisting with farm seizures were able to draw upon firsthand skills and experience in harnessing public displays of violence to intimidate potential opponents. Foreman James Mwengi explained that there was a focused effort at *pungwes* to locate which workers were MDC supporters, and particularly who was a more senior MDC supporter:

> They [farm invaders] had a gathering there to call people for a rally. [They] start chanting slogans, singing, and then they began asking questions concerning how did we deliver politics to the workers and who was the main leader of the opposition at work. And also who was influencing us so that everyone [moves from] from ZANU-PF to support MDC.[111]

Mwengi added that at *pungwes* farm invaders asked "lots of questions" about which workers supported the MDC, while at the same time reminding attendees about the freedoms and opportunities the ruling party had offered voters. Mwengi emphasized that "you have to be in it [ZANU-PF] in order for you to survive." So when attendees were asked who you supported, the answer must be unequivocal: "Which side are you? 'I am the side of the ruling party.'"

*Pungwes* during the land seizure era could easily, and often did, turn violent. Demonstrative violence was frequently deployed against community leaders. Mucheke provided an extended example of how *pungwes* were managed:

> When the war veterans come, they will call all the workers together, call them to a meeting, pick up two who are thought to be traitors [MDC supporters or working in senior positions for a farmer], bring them up in the war style, tie them with their hands at the back, beat them up all over the body, probably kill them. And after killing one or two, all the workers know that death is certain, and therefore the fear of God is thrust into them.[112]

Mucheke explained the effort by farm invaders to involve workers in collective praise of ZANU-PF:

> They [farm invaders] will have all-night vigils singing, praising [Mugabe], other things, praising the war . . . taking the farms as a war. . . . And those who do not participate would be said they are traitors, either killed, beaten up, or evicted [from their homes on the farms].

Msasa detailed methods used to targeted purported "sellouts": "They would take [cut out] your eye or your nose and they [the government] did display that during the elections. It [torture] was still there [many years after the Liberation War]. And they did kill people . . . pour petrol and then fire . . . exactly what they used to do during the war."[113] Msasa explained that this public demonstration of "sellouts" being tortured and murdered in an extreme fashion had a simple aim: "[The purpose was] to send the message to everyone, not the sellout—it's to send the message."

Farm foreman Richard Chipembere elaborated that violence and intimidation were common at *pungwes*, which he perceived with "dread."[114] He explained that the sporadic and unexpected call for workers to attend *pungwes* meant that employees were always on edge. On one occasion he was summoned from his home at 3:00 a.m. by farm invaders and taken to a *pungwe* at the local militia camp: "I was actually pinpointed that I was supporting the opposition and I was the leader of that area." In front of a mass audience of workers from "15 farms," including his wife and children, Chipembere was told to publicly proclaim his support for the ruling party: "Then I addressed it [the crowd], appearing as though I was actually supporting the ruling party." Farm invaders then turned to the gathering and asked "whether I was actually supporting the ruling party or I was the opposition." This public questioning was a means of determining whether Chipembere was telling the truth. "Most people in the area, people liked me anyway, and they actually supported me and said, 'No, he's not opposition.'" Chipembere said he "was happy and grateful I was supported by other people," and because of their support he was taken into a room by the farm invaders, questioned, and then released. The irony was that Chipembere was in fact a known member of the MDC. The willingness of others to come to his defense demonstrates a relatively high level of solidarity among some workers, especially given the likely consequences for supporters of Chipembere who were found to be lying.

Msasa stated that the settling of "scores" by falsely—and in some cases truthfully—accusing workers of supporting white farmers or the MDC was widespread and was also a means through which farm invaders could gain possession of the victim's assets.[115] Anyone accused of being an MDC supporter could be beaten or killed. Foreman Tendayi Garamapudzi explained that "if someone [has] got a grudge with someone, like if someone hits me, that guy could raise a complaint saying that one [person] was not good."[116] Accordingly, accusations could be made purely to settle personal feuds that had nothing to do with politics. Msasa explained that ZANU-PF knew innocent people were being accused.[117] However, the overall framework of terrorizing workers suited political objectives; the innocent were usually not spared.

Having community members publicly select who would be punished by farm invaders at *pungwes*, as Garamapudzi explained, added substantial uncertainty to the events for attendees.[118] Moreover, for individuals to realize that they could be accused and punished while being totally unconnected to the MDC meant there was little safety for anyone at *pungwes*. Especially problematic was the practice of forcing civilians to become stakeholders in ZANU-PF's intimidation through requiring the community to participate in determining the guilt of their fellow villagers and neighbors.

## TARGETING WORKERS' HOMES AND POSSESSIONS

Threats and acts of violence at *pungwes* were often manifested in "compounds," the worker villages on commercial farms. Workers who refused to comply with the farm invaders' demands would usually face threats to their homes and personal belongings. A typical compound may contain some brick buildings with asbestos roofing, but more often homes were huts made of wooden poles and roofed with thatch. There were rarely security fences or other protective devices, and the police routinely ignored transgressions of the law committed by farm invaders. As a result, workers' homes and personal property were routinely attacked by farm invaders.

Hut burnings had a particularly profound effect in intimidating workers. The destruction of a single hut could mean that a worker and his family lost almost everything they owned. The poverty in which many workers lived meant that what possessions they did have could not easily be replaced. Thus, the mere threat of arson in a compound could have great persuasive power for farm invaders.

Adding to the threat of hut burnings was the risk that a family might be burned alive in the hut. Rancher Daniel Fairbanks explained:

When they [farm invaders] arrived, they used this African intimidation that has unbelievable power. . . . You threaten the person's private existence back home. For instance, "We know where you live, and that means we can tie the outside of your hut with wire and set it alight with you and your wife and children inside." Now, if you understand African custom, you'll understand the fear that generates.[119]

The combustibility of a wooden hut with a thatched roof is obvious. Moreover, huts typically have only one door and no windows, limiting opportunities for escape if the structure was set alight. The mere threat of hut burnings, let alone the fact that actual burnings were frequently carried out in villages, served to seriously undermine workers' security.

## ABDUCTION AND UNLAWFUL ARREST

Given that there was an almost total breakdown in the rule of law surrounding events that were deemed "political," farm invaders could also rely on abductions and unlawful arrest to coerce workers. In some cases, abductions did not necessarily involve overt violence, such as when individuals were forced to attend a *pungwe*. Yet in other cases, workers reported experiencing severe beatings and intimidation.

Unlawful arrest was very common. For instance, horticulture manager Andrew Morfu indicated that arrest was a form of intimidation and harassment: "They [police and farm invaders] want to harass us, arrest us, harass us, yes."[120] In other instances workers would be arrested if they reported crimes committed by farm invaders. For example, farm foreman Telmore Nyakasanga recounted a time when cattle were stolen and he went to report the incident to the police, only to find that he himself was then blamed with the theft and threatened with arrest: "Then you just go to the court—the police station—and you tell them about it. 'Eh, fuck, you are to be locked up here,' because they are saying that we have pinched their *mombies* [cattle]."[121]

Arrests would also often come as part of an overall crackdown. For example, farmer Benjamin Colfax reported his experience of his workers being arrested:

> So the police came in and they just arrested people [workers]. If you do anything anti-ZANU-PF, you're going to get arrested. Then they move out and the next guys come in and people are now intimidated and they know they have no support from the police so when they get a hiding from anybody, they don't even go to the police. They don't even try and fight back.[122]

When workers were arrested they usually had little recourse for legal protection, although in some cases the farmer would provide support. In most cases, however, they had to endure several days of jail before being released, often upon payment of a fine.

The result was a rapid breakdown in trust of the police and in willingness to report crimes. Indeed, Thompson Mbezi said that in his experience when workers went to the police to seek help, "Oh, they get very angry" because the police were "scared" to get involved.[123]

## ASSAULT

Farm invaders also relied widely on assault to gain compliance from workers. Assaults were exceptionally common and have been widely documented by groups such as the Zimbabwe Human Rights NGO Forum and Amnesty

International.[124] Assaults ranged from slapping to severe beatings. They were administered with a range of instruments from sticks to whips made of barbed wire. Male and female workers were targeted, and many of my respondents indicated even children and grandparents could be vulnerable to assault from farm invaders.

The following account gives a sense of some of the situations that would bring about assault on workers. Farm clerk Joyce Mukwa describes an occasion where she was forced by farm invaders to enter the farmer's homestead to look for his weapons. At each moment she feared assault:

> They [farm invaders] came direct to my kitchen. It was at lunchtime. They were holding the gun like this [indicates the gun was pointing at her head]. They said stand up quickly. So I had to stand. They said, "Where is your boss?" I said, "He is in town." [They said,] "Today, if you don't show us every weapon in this farm, we are going to kill you." I said, "Where I'm working in my office I have never seen any weapons." They said, "Go and show us."[125]

Mukwa took the war veterans to the homestead but repeatedly stated that she had never seen weapons in the house and did not know where to find any. After being unable to find weapons, "They wanted to beat me by the back of the gun." Mukwa pleaded that she was simply working as a clerk to earn money for her family: "I said, 'Ah, if you beat me for nothing . . . I'm working for my children. I'm not concerned about the [political] party. . . . They had to leave me,'" She added,

> The violence [committed by farm invaders] was every week. At times we were taken to the road to do roadblocks, to check the buses [for MDC supporters]. Plenty things were done there. It was a terrible one, and the owner of the farm was attacked every day—nearly every day—a group of men, not two, a group of men . . . every week, attacking the owner of the farm, every week, every week.

Assaults were also commonly used to force workers to attend *pungwes*. Farm manager Chesterton Hove explained, "They [farm invaders] were violent, yes, because some of the people [workers], they don't want to go [to *pungwes*], and so they [farm invaders] were violent to force the people to go."[126] Hove explained that farm invaders wanted all workers to attend, except those with babies, and the key means of forcing them to attend was the use of assaults and threats.

Many farm workers experienced repeated assaults. Rancher George Lyons stated that "the staff were almost targeted on a daily basis at one stage. They couldn't go out with the cattle without being ambushed and beaten up. . . . They were living in total fear."[127] An anonymous respondent in the farmer survey stated that in his compound there were "beatings with [a] *sjambok* [a thick, heavy whip]," and another respondent stated that "workers and manager [were] beaten on a number of occasions." Similarly, Tendayi Garamapudzi, a farm foreman, explained that laborers on the farm where he worked were repeatedly beaten.[128] While some workers were routinely attacked at meetings, others were targeted in repeat visits to their homes: "I was assaulted each and every time. You know they were coming to my house saying, 'You must leave this place.'" Such beatings only ended when the worker or farmer was evicted.

Interview accounts from workers further convey the frequency and severity of assaults:

- "They [workers] were just *chaiya* [assaulted]. They [farm invaders] were just beating everyone."[129]
- "They [farm invaders] said to me, 'Hey you, come here.' And I started walking, going to them and they said, 'Hey, we said run!' And I said, 'no, I mustn't run. Why should I run? I'm coming there' and they started beating me up . . . the guys who were assaulting . . . they were just enjoying it."[130]
- "They [the government] know they [the people] don't want them, so the only thing is to intimidate them, harass them."[131]
- "There were plenty [of farm invaders intimidating workers].They might come twenty, thirty youth—ZANU-PF youth—and singing, with some *sjamboks* to beat but they didn't beat me, but they were shouting, doing all sorts things for you to be afraid and join the ZANU-PF. They were doing force."[132]

Workers who resisted faced even more severe punishment. An anonymous participant in the farmer survey explained what happened on his farm:

Some [workers] spoke out, but mainly they were too scared as they had been threatened and beaten. Two men (separate occasions) who did not go along with them [farm invaders] were beaten. Trumped up charges of theft were made against them and they were given a community punishment of beatings and after that they disappeared.

Most workers quickly learned not to publicly defy farm invaders.

Assaults occurred in the context of an orchestrated plan to injure and intimidate workers into acquiescing to the farm invaders' demands. Thomas Rackomechi, a farm foreman, explained that assault was just one component in a focused and orchestrated effort to bring about the suppression of the MDC and the eviction of commercial farmers: "The fear is put into people in so many ways. . . . One, by intimidation. Two, by beating them. Three, by promising to kill them."[133]

Adding to the breakdown of security for workers, accounts collected for this book also show how family members were forced to assault each other. Farmer Gerry Garner related an incident on his farm: "We had a scene on our farm when the 91 families arrived. They [farm invaders] took all our senior staff, and they took them into their camp, their war vet camp at the borehole, and they got their own children to beat them—they got [the senior staff's] own children to beat our senior staff."[134] Such instances were part of a multipronged effort to create a totally intolerable situation on farms that would ultimately drive workers away and break their will to support the MDC.

## TORTURE

Workers recounted numerous experiences of torture, a trend also identified by several civil society groups.[135] In one case, farm mechanic Chenjerai Mapufuli was ordered by farmer invaders to burn himself: "They say, 'Eh, just step on the fire!' and then you step because you are scared of killing or beating."[136]

A state security agent, Jackson Sanyati, recounted the use of *falanga*, a method of torture where the sensitive underside of the feet are beaten in order to inflict severe pain: "People were being tortured right in those sensitive areas [soles of their feet]. At the end of the day they were just [exclamation of exhaustion]—a person would be forced to tell something which he or she didn't do . . . off pressure only."[137]

Debbie McKinley, a farmer's wife and a civil society activist, related an experience on her farm:

> On our place, they [farm invaders] used to have these indoctrination sessions [*pungwes*] and march up and down with sticks over their shoulder, and [workers would] be told they were going to be given weapons to kill the whites. In most places they [farm invaders] would use long sticks, often with barbed wire wrapped round it, the usual sort of weapons [to assault the workers].[138]

This evidence of workers being whipped with barbed wire, in order to increase the severity of wounds, was repeatedly relayed in interviews. For example, farmer George Sherman explained what happened to his workers:

> All the laborers and the farmers [were assembled], so the laborers were told to sit there and the farmers were told to sit over there, but the laborers

were being whipped up by the ZANU-PF guys, who actually had sticks with wire on them, who were hitting them and [saying], "You do as you're told and, you know, if you don't cooperate with us, then we are going to get you." And the intimidation was far greater [for the workers] than it ever was towards us [farmers].[139]

Another farmer survey respondent explained: "Senior workers were whipped with barbed wire in front of the whole compound at a *pungwe.*"

In some instances, torture took the form of breaking bones. An anonymous participant in the farmer survey attested that a worker on his farm had "both arms and all fingers broken." A different survey respondent stated that employees were more systematically targeted: "All workers [were forced to] lay flat face down and [were] whipped."

Respondents in state security provided insights into how torture was organized and conducted by the government. Sebungwe reported that the state taught agents associated with militias how to be "cruel" by providing "someone to practice on" while they were still alive in order to replicate the real conditions of a torture session: "They are taught to cut people's limbs when they are still alive, cut people's tongues and so forth. . . . You have to practice it somewhere. You can't just do it even if you are trained to do it, but you need to do it physically so that you have a feel of what it is."[140] Sebungwe explained that torturing a person was not necessarily an easily acquired skill. New recruits often had trouble with handling both the emotional aspect of inflicting extreme harm on another person, and getting used to physically torturing a person. Practicing on prisoners made sense from the perspective of torture trainers, because prisons provided a source of individuals who could be tortured and murdered without friends and family raising the alarm:

> They use prisoners like that. . . . Some of the prisoners who are serving very long sentences, they would actually monitor that you are not receiving any visitors now, for a year, two, because some people are just forgotten about by their relatives. Maybe they are a nuisance to their family and they will just say, "Ah well, good riddance, let him go," and they don't visit that person.

Selected prisoners, sometimes those on death row, were then told to pack their belongings because they were being transferred to another prison, so as not to raise suspicion among other prisoners: "Then they will get into a truck, and then they will be used as, as training aids for those Green Bombers [a youth militia group]. They will be trained to kill them, how to dispose of them." Sebungwe stated that sometimes victims were not dead when their bodies were disposed of:

While they were still alive, [agents would] drive them to Kariba without arms, without other limbs, with maybe missing teeth and . . . a missing tongue. And then they will get there, put cement in there, a bit of concrete and then open up a few holes in the trunk and lock it and then throw the thing in. And then you know if concrete is just [mixed] with water, it just stiffens it hardens and then the trunk box goes down and you'll never be found.

Torture was also undertaken at already established state-run facilities. Lundi stated that underground facilities in the Waterfalls area of Harare—which he said he personally visited on numerous occasions—were used to train security officials in different techniques of torture that were intended to "break you down psychologically and emotionally."[141] He said techniques included the use of methods to make a victim feel as though he were drowning or placing victims in close proximity to aggressive dogs.[142]

Mucheke stated that individuals were tortured and murdered at ZANU-PF bases, which in some cases were called "torture camps."[143] He identified one base on a seized farm: "There was one farm in Beatrice where they used to—I don't know where they took the crocodiles from—and put them in a swimming pool and they would throw people in there. A lot of people died in that swimming pool. They were just thrown in there and the crocodiles would have a feast." It is easy to see how in the land seizure era certain farms that had been seized by government became notorious for the torture and killing of political opponents.

## RAPE

Rape was a widely used means of intimidation and violence. The true scale of rape during the land seizure era is impossible to quantify, as victims were afraid to come forward. Women in farm villages were selected for rape by farm invaders based on their age. According to Hove, farm invaders sought "the young girls, yes they want the eighteen[-year-olds]. . . not older women."[144] Once farm invaders had captured the girls and young women, "They [farm invaders] can take them and they can use them for . . . sexual [purposes], yes. They will give beer and whatever to drink and then can use them [for sex]." Similarly, foreman James Mwengi further identified the prevalence of rape in conjunction with a range of other criminal activity: "You will find that this time [during the land seizure era], there was too much involvement of rape cases, thefts. There are [sic] a lot of thieving which took place during this period up to now, that thieving, nearly everyone knows that this one stole this and this."[145]

Hove's and Mwengi's statements dovetail with an account from Thompson Mupfure, who said that he knew of a ZANU-PF militia base "where girls were being raped."[146] Young women and girls were brought from surrounding villages, farms, and ranches to this base, where they were handed to the Green Bombers and subjected to sexual exploitation. Mupfure elaborated: "[Farm invaders] are spreading HIV/AIDS and also committing crime, a heinous crime forcing children to sleep with people that they don't want to sleep with."

Farmers Chris and Catherine Cleveland stated that in their district "there were a huge number of rapes."[147] They further explained that "there was huge pressure put on the men [male workers], like 'Your wife will be raped, or your sister or grandmother, if you don't do this or you don't do that.'" Farmer Gerry Garner stated that rape was a tool used to break down his workers' resolve to remain on the farms:

> I had one guy [worker] who'd come with me from Centenary [a village in Mashonaland Central] so him and I'd been working together at that stage, probably for 11 or 12 years . . . and they [farm invaders] raped his daughter, and then did another 10 [rapes]. So that night, my senior staff were beaten up by their own children and 11 of my laborers' children were raped in one night.[148]

Rape was also used as a tool to evict farmers. An anonymous participant in the farmer survey explained how he had been threatened by farm invaders: "If we did not move out, they would rape my wife and daughters and kill me." Similarly, another farmer survey respondent stated that there was a "threat of rape to [his] wife." Rancher George Lyons experienced a break-in at his homestead where charcoal figures depicting a rape scenario along with threats of rape were drawn on the walls of the building.[149] Rape was also specifically used to stop farmers from supporting the MDC. After the two daughters of a farmer survey respondent were raped in a single attack, "It was made very clear that this was in retribution for their father's participation with the MDC."

There is no doubt that rape was used explicitly as a weapon of war by ZANU-PF against MDC supporters and their families, a claim repeatedly asserted by interview respondents.[150] While many men were willing to accept higher levels of personal risk, fewer were willing to risk the safety of their wives and children. Threats against family members were, therefore, a brutally effective strategy for farm invaders.

## MURDER AND ATTEMPTED MURDER

Farm invaders also resorted to the murder and attempted murder of workers in order to suppress the MDC. Hove recounted that he was attacked by farm invaders and repeatedly struck across the body with an axe.[151] Critically wounded, he was left for dead.

In another instance, an anonymous farmer survey respondent explains that severe beatings nearly killed some of the workers on his farm: "All of my middle management were assaulted and beaten. Broken legs. Broken arms, unconsciousness." Likewise, a different survey participant also recounted that his farm manager had been badly beaten and left hospitalized in a coma for 10 days. Isolated farm workers were particularly vulnerable; for instance, a farmer survey respondent reported that a worker employed to guard an electric fence for cattle on his farm was murdered during the night.

Debbie McKinley related that her farm guard was beaten to death in front of her son.[152] "I actually took his body out of the mortuary in [Mashonaland East]. It was the most shocking sight I've ever seen in my life, and I've seen lots of dead bodies in mortuaries." Rancher Joachim van Vaaden gave a detailed account of murder on his ranch: "I had a tractor driver that worked for me, a very good, young guy. When we got kicked off, he moved to the neighbor on the property and three months later he was dead, with his head found under the back wheel of a tractor and the tractor switched off. It was stopped."[153] Van Vaaden stated that there was no investigation undertaken by the police, and when he started "asking questions" he was told that it was "under investigation." However, "It never ever was investigated, what happened, who did it." Van Vaaden stated that in such cases as these, "the moment they [police] saw that it was what they called 'political,' anything to do with land and opposing the farmer, they would back off, and the criminal element would take over." However, in van Vaaden's view, "The people around them that were the targets of the intimidation knew exactly why he died. So you had your faceless intimidation, and always the police backed off from investigation."

## INCENTIVES FOR COOPERATION IN FARM SEIZURES

Although farm workers were generally prepared to assist the farmer and were typically distrusted by farm invaders, there were cases where workers actively sought to evict the farmer and worked independently or closely with farm invaders to achieve this goal. This was especially the case after the government began to change its tactics in 2002, by offering incentives to workers who cooperated in removing commercial farmers. The introduction of the Statutory Instrument 6 (SI6) retrenchment requirement in 2002, which compelled employers to provide a remuneration package to retrenched workers (see also chapter 7), was particularly crucial. In effect, the farmer was forced to make a retrenchment payment *if he was evicted*. The exact value of retrenchment packages varied because of uncertainties about the law, poor enforcement, and the willingness and ability of the farmer to pay the package. In general, however, workers received severance pay (three month's salary), wages in lieu of notice (three month's salary), an additional amount based on tenure (two month's salary for each completed year of continuous service), relocation allowance (one month's salary), and cash in lieu of vacation leave (applicable to vacation leave in the year of termination).[154] Therefore, an employee with 10 years of continuous service (but no holiday accrued in the year that service was terminated) would be entitled to a retrenchment package totaling approximately 27 months of pay. Farmers could not budget for the payouts, and few could sustain the financial liability.

The prospect of a financial payout was persuasive for many workers, because by 2002, when the SI6 requirement was implemented, most workers had been subjected to debilitating and long-running harassment from farm invaders, and their economic futures were precarious. The readiness of some workers to concede to the inevitable pressure from ZANU-PF was summed up by a labor officer who said to farmer Rob Dawes: "This [farm invasions] is a wave, and it's going to pass over all of us. You either swim with the wave or you're going to get taken out."[155] In other words, for some workers it made sense to at least gain some financial security from the payout of the farmer rather than resist and ultimately end up with nothing.

The SI6 requirement meant that workers had a clear financial incentive to evict the farmer by 2002. While in many cases workers wanting to evict the farmer were a minority because they could count on government and farm invader support, they could also cause major disruption for the farmer. A handful of disgruntled workers could commit arson, vandalize equipment, leave gates open so livestock would be set loose, and provide intelligence on farmers' and workers' behavior to the state security services. Employers were then left in an invidious position of having to maintain commercial viability with, in some cases, a significant proportion of their workforce clearly trying to undermine them. While the vast majority of farmer survey respondents commented on the support they received from their workers, they also noted that once a farmer was close to being evicted, a tipping point was reached and most workers then vociferously demanded SI6 packages.[156] The Commercial Farmers Union published a document in which it warned, "In practice workers will immediately agitate for a payment of a package in terms of SI 6 of 2002 once they are aware that the employer will no longer be continuing farming. It is not uncommon for workers to hold equipment and livestock to ransom."[157] This is almost certainly because these workers then faced an uncertain economic future and—after years of living in constant fear of violence—wanted to get whatever financial benefits they could.

## CONCLUSION

The evidence presented in this chapter demonstrates the wide range of tactics, including the massive use of violence and intimidation, used by farm invaders to achieve their objective of suppressing the MDC. The farmer and farm worker population was extensively victimized by farm invaders, especially in the three Mashonaland provinces. This region was considered the "heartland" of ZANU-PF's support and was vital to the ruling party's efforts to retain political power. Yet it is probable that senior ZANU-PF officials realized that the MDC's influence was growing steadily in the region by 2000. ZANU-PF's solution was to deploy extensive political violence in order to suppress support for the opposition. By concentrating violence in Mashonaland, farm invaders were focusing their resources on the area in Zimbabwe with the most farm workers and the most desirable land, the highest concentrations of agriproperty, and a large number of farmers who appeared to be sufficiently wealthy that they could donate money in public to the MDC and persuade their workers to vote for the party.

Farm workers, particularly senior workers, bore the brunt of the campaign of terror. Indeed, by targeting these individuals, farm invaders were able to pursue their conflated objectives of suppressing the MDC and seizing land. Committing violence and intimidation against senior workers in public forums in front of workers that the victim would normally oversee was a powerful demonstration that workers, as well as farmers, were powerless to defy the farm invaders. Violence directed against workers on such occasions was often severe, sometimes including murder, torture, and rape. This served to intimidate workers en masse, marking a step in achieving the suppression of any active support for the MDC among farm workers.

Targeting senior workers in this way also hastened the eviction of the farmer. Senior employees served as a "conduit" and connection between the farmer and his workforce. Given the size and complexity of some farms, the role of senior workers was crucial in the successful completion of numerous farm activities. By targeting senior workers, farm invaders undercut the ability of the farmer to operate his business, often resulting in eviction (chapter 7 discusses the eviction of farmers in more detail). Moreover, the attacks on workers—especially those who appeared to be most intimately linked to their white employers—could be justified as a necessary measure to deal with "sellouts." In this way, the nakedly political use of violence against the government's real or imagined opponents could be clothed in the rhetoric of the nationalist struggle to maintain Zimbabwe's independence.

# 6

# Seizing Land and Agri-Property

ZANU-PF's proclaimed justification for the farm seizures was predicated on land-based grievances dating from the colonial era.[1] While some believed that land was illegally seized by "colonials" and thus should be redistributed to the black population, the same could not be said of commercial farmers' movable and personal assets. Indeed, after the farm seizures began, the government had initially planned to compensate farmers for "improvements" to farms, such as buildings and dams.[2] How then, could the later seizure of agri-property be justified?

This chapter analyzes data on the two overarching objectives of most farm invaders—namely the seizure of land and agri-property—in order to understand how these motivations manifested and informed each other. The chapter seeks to establish what kinds of resources farm invaders were targeting, the types of farm invaders who were involved in the seizure of land and agri-property, and the role of violence in these seizures.

Evidence will show that after about June 2000 large-scale farm invasions were fueled by a desire for land, but especially by demand for valuable agri-property—the movable and thus easily salable farm assets such as tractors and other farm equipment. This is of critical importance because the seizure of agri-property, what in essence was state-sanctioned looting, has no colonial-era justification. To shed light on the issue, the chapter shows that the greatest concentrations of violence against farmers and workers occurred in areas with the most valuable land and farm assets. Meanwhile, war veteran beneficiaries—historically the "genuine" claimants to land—declined over time; instead, land and assets were seized by vast numbers of civil servants, who were less able to stake a claim to land based on service in the Liberation War. The proximity of these civil servants right next to some of the richest farming areas in the country was yet another contributing factor to the clamor for farms after about June 2000. Legal mechanisms enabling the seizure of land and assets merely "legalized" what these civil servants were already doing on the ground.

While this chapter seeks to provide a deep-rooted analysis of the key factors motivating farm invaders, experiences on individual farms tended to be highly spontaneous, organic, and complex, varying considerably even within the same district. A single farm invasion group could contain individuals with a wide range of motivations—and sometimes multiple invasion groups competed with each other. Therefore, farmers would often contend with farm invaders who made multiple demands simultaneously.

## NATIONAL DISTRIBUTION OF FARM RESOURCES

### Climatic Indications of Agriculture Resources

The potential of land for use in commercial agriculture is determined by climate, soil geology, and other conditions.[3] Viability for cropping largely depends on the availability and consistency of water access from rainfall or compensatory irrigation. In the 1960s, the Rhodesian government established five different farming regions (called "Natural Regions") across the country, determined by soil quality, temperature, and rainfall consistency (see figure 6.1 and table 6.1). Natural Region II, which exists most extensively in the Mashonaland provinces, was the "most important of the Agro-economic Regions" in economic terms because of its favorable conditions for crop production on fertile soils, as well as "good communications and close proximity to markets."[4]

Farmers based crop choices on climatic conditions and crop management principles (such as crop rotation and the use of beef cattle to graze fallow land). On primary farms, tobacco, cattle, maize, horticulture, wheat, cotton, soybeans, game ranching, coffee, and sugarcane were the primary crops or activities that respondents to the farmer survey conducted for this book most commonly engaged in.[5] The main secondary commodities and agricultural activities were similar: maize, cattle, horticulture, soybeans, wheat, herbs and spices, tobacco, game ranching, citrus, and other livestock. Table 6.2 and Table 6.3 show percentages of these crops and activities produced on farms by survey respondents. These figures demonstrate that the Mashonaland provinces tended toward diversified commodity production with high volumes of

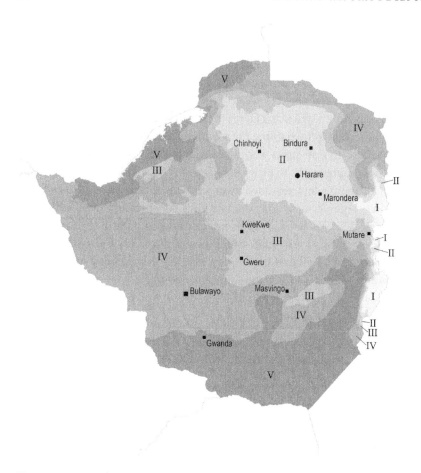

**Figure 6.1** Natural Regions and Commercial Farming Areas
SOURCE: Created by author.

tobacco, grain, cotton, and horticulture crops (as opposed, for example, to specialist coffee production in Manicaland).

What makes the growing of tobacco, wheat, maize, soybeans, cotton, and other similar crops significant, insofar as the behavior of farm invaders is concerned, is that they require extensive high-value equipment to plant, grow, and harvest. The crops also tend to be lucrative and labor intensive, encouraging more extensive investment through irrigation, newer tractors, better farm buildings, and more worker housing. Cattle ranching, on the other hand, requires almost no such equipment and is not as lucrative. Thus, while cropping farms tend to contain extensive agri-property, ranches do not.

*Table 6.1*  NATURAL REGIONS AND COMMERCIAL FARMING AREAS

| Region | % of land | Description |
|---|---|---|
| I | 1.6% | **Specialized and diversified farming.** Extensive, consistent rainfall; higher altitudes, often mountainous; comparatively low temperatures suitable for growing tea, coffee, fruit, and vegetables and for forestry and intensive livestock production. |
| II | 18.7% | **Intensive farming.** Consistent, moderately high rainfall in summer, with infrequent droughts; suitable for intensive crop (e.g., maize, cotton, tobacco, soybeans, horticulture) and livestock production. |
| III | 17.4% | **Semi-intensive farming.** Moderate rainfall with midseason dry spells and higher, often severe temperatures; most rainfall comes in intense showers, reducing effectiveness for agriculture; cropping only possible with drought-resistant varieties; livestock production is favored. |
| IV | 33.0% | **Semi-extensive farming.** Low rainfall with frequent droughts and severe dry spells; cropping of drought-resistant varieties only possible in very favorable locations; predominantly livestock production and game ranching. |
| V | 26.2% | **Extensive livestock farming.** Rainfall is too low and inconsistent for agricultural production; suitable for livestock and game ranching on existing veld (grassland) alone. |

NOTE: Natural Farming Region descriptions are based upon commercial farming uses. Regions described as unsuitable for cropping may still be viable for subsistence agriculture. The 3.1% of land not referenced above is in broken and steep country that precludes agriculture production.

SOURCE: George Kay, *Rhodesia: A Human Geography* (London: University of London Press, 1970), 21.

When considering the volume of agri-property on cropping farms, high-value equipment, such as tractors, combine harvesters, and irrigation pipes, was simply the most prominent movable asset. However, this equipment also indicated the presence of a vast array of other valuable movable assets. For instance, if a farmer had tractors, then he would have a workshop full of valuable tools, stores of diesel and oil, and spare parts. Equipment such as tractors would also indicate the likely presence of ancillary implements used in conjunction with the tractor, such as plows, harrows, and sprayers. Such

*Table 6.2*  PRIMARY AGRICULTURE CROPS OR ACTIVITIES (%)

| | Mash. Central | Mash. East | Mash. West | Mid-lands | Mas-vingo | Manica-land | Mat. North | Mat. South |
|---|---|---|---|---|---|---|---|---|
| **Tobacco** | 25.0 | 26.6 | 38.1 | 1.6 | 0.0 | 8.2 | 0.4 | 0.0 |
| **Cattle** | 6.8 | 20.3 | 6.8 | 18.9 | 16.2 | 0.0 | 16.2 | 14.9 |
| **Maize** | 23.7 | 26.3 | 28.9 | 13.2 | 5.3 | 0.0 | 2.6 | 0.0 |
| **Horticulture** | 20.0 | 20.0 | 5.0 | 10.0 | 5.0 | 20.0 | 15.0 | 5.0 |
| **Wheat** | 23.5 | 23.5 | 35.3 | 0.0 | 0.0 | 11.8 | 5.9 | 0.0 |
| **Cotton** | 75.0 | 6.3 | 18.8 | 0.0 | 0.0 | 0.0 | 0.0 | 0.0 |
| **Soybeans** | 30.8 | 15.4 | 30.8 | 7.7 | 0.0 | 15.4 | 0.0 | 0.0 |
| **Game ranching** | 18.2 | 0.0 | 18.2 | 0.0 | 27.3 | 0.0 | 36.4 | 0.0 |
| **Coffee** | 0.0 | 0.0 | 0.0 | 0.0 | 0.0 | 100.0 | 0.0 | 0.0 |
| **Sugarcane** | 0.0 | 0.0 | 0.0 | 0.0 | 100.0 | 0.0 | 0.0 | 0.0 |

NOTE: A primary commodity is the farmer's principal crop or activity. Although many farmers had secondary commodity crops, almost every farmer could identify one primary crop or activity.

SOURCE: Author's survey of commercial farmers.

*Table 6.3*  SECONDARY AGRICULTURE CROPS OR ACTIVITIES (%)

| | Mash. Central | Mash. East | Mash. West | Mid-lands | Mas-vingo | Manica-land | Mat. North | Mat. South |
|---|---|---|---|---|---|---|---|---|
| **Maize** | 29.9 | 20.9 | 34.8 | 5.7 | 2.0 | 5.3 | 0.8 | 0.4 |
| **Cattle** | 22.6 | 23.1 | 33.2 | 6.3 | 2.4 | 10.1 | 1.4 | 1.0 |
| **Horticulture** | 21.0 | 27.0 | 30.0 | 6.0 | 4.0 | 11.0 | 1.0 | 0.0 |
| **Soybeans** | 32.1 | 11.9 | 42.9 | 7.1 | 2.4 | 3.6 | 0.0 | 0.0 |
| **Wheat** | 41.7 | 15.0 | 31.7 | 5.0 | 1.7 | 3.3 | 1.7 | 0.0 |
| **Herbs and spices** | 21.7 | 28.3 | 25.0 | 3.3 | 3.3 | 11.7 | 5.0 | 1.7 |
| **Tobacco** | 40.0 | 20.0 | 33.3 | 0.0 | 0.0 | 6.7 | 0.0 | 0.0 |
| **Game ranching** | 7.7 | 11.5 | 11.5 | 11.5 | 23.1 | 0.0 | 11.5 | 23.1 |
| **Citrus** | 37.5 | 8.3 | 16.7 | 4.2 | 12.5 | 20.8 | 0.0 | 0.0 |
| **Other livestock** (e.g., pigs, sheep) | 17.4 | 13.0 | 17.4 | 0.0 | 8.7 | 17.4 | 21.7 | 4.3 |

NOTE: Many farmers had more than one secondary crop or activity, so results include multiple answers per respondent.

SOURCE: Author's survey of commercial farmers.

equipment signified other assets that could be targeted by invaders: for instance, sprayers indicated a likely store of chemicals. Farms also usually had
supplies of fertilizer and seed. If livestock was present, the livestock itself was
valuable and would indicate the presence of feed stores, medicines, and vet-
erinary equipment, as well as fencing and gates. Likewise, many farms had
irrigation systems. The pipes and sprayers were valuable, and they indicated
the presence of expensive pumps, switches, electrical fittings, and extensive
wiring. Thus, a single cropping farm with some livestock potentially held a
very valuable repository of agri-property.

## Farm Values and Provincial Farm Seizures

Farmer survey respondents were asked to provide figures showing the total
value of their farm, which included the value of the land itself and immovable
assets (such as irrigation systems), as well as a separate valuation of moveable
agri-property. Figure 6.2 shows the individual farm, irrigation, and implements valuations for each province; figure 6.3 provides the combined asset
totals by province. These data illustrate the considerable value of the agriculture sector in Zimbabwe, as well as the particularly high valuations of Mashonaland assets. Mashonaland farm and asset values were significantly higher
than other provinces and represented a large and accessible source of financial
resources for farm invaders, due to the provinces' proximity to Harare, the
home of many high-level land claimants.

While figure 6.2 and figure 6.3 provide farm and asset values from
survey respondents (values are not projected to the entire farming community), the higher net agri-property valuations for Mashonaland were
not due to smaller quantities of extremely valuable equipment, but rather
to high numbers of mixed-value equipment. Given the soil types predomi-
nating in Mashonaland provinces, these provinces predictably show the
highest totals of tractors and combine harvesters (the research survey
asked respondents only to provide totals for tractors and combines, as
other equipment was too numerous for quantification). In fact, respondents from the three Mashonaland provinces owned the vast majority of
tractors—2,673 of 3,368 (79%)—and combine harvesters—130 out of 149
(87%) among all farmer survey respondents in Zimbabwe (see figure 6.4
and figure 6.5).

Table 6.4 provides totals for farm and equipment valuations, as well as tractors and combine harvester tabulations from the survey. These data show that
the total farmland valuation for the 476 survey respondents was US$510,282,594.
The total valuation for irrigation was US$98,535,598, and for farm implements

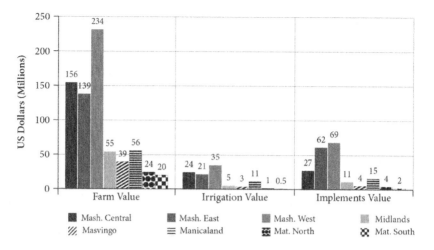

**Figure 6.2** Farm, Irrigation, and Equipment Valuations
SOURCE: Author's survey of commercial farmers.

was US$131,973,777. Thus, the total for the survey sample was US$740,791,969 (survey respondents totaled 476 participants, and there were an estimated 4,300 farmers in Zimbabwe). Thus, the total represented by the survey is only part of the total value of land and assets present on farms in Zimbabwe. Factoring in the 3,368 tractors and 149 combine harvesters represented by survey

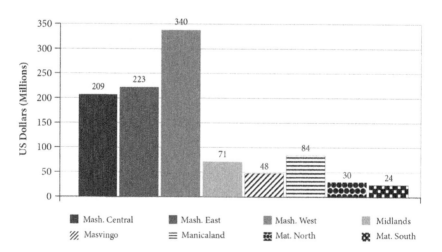

**Figure 6.3** Total Farm, Irrigation, and Implements Valuations
SOURCE: Author's survey of commercial farmers.

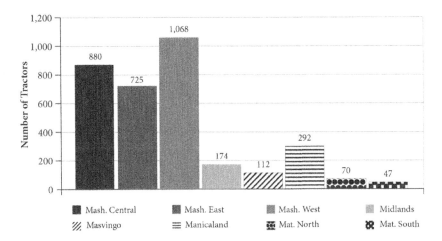

**Figure 6.4** Ownership of Tractors
SOURCE: Author's survey of commercial farmers.

respondents (figure 6.4 and figure 6.5)—along with vast stores of associated supplies—it is easy to see that such extensive agri-property provided a highly lucrative target for farm invaders when the rule of law collapsed.

The value of equipment varied considerably based on characteristics such as brand or age. Not all equipment was new or of high value—one farmer said

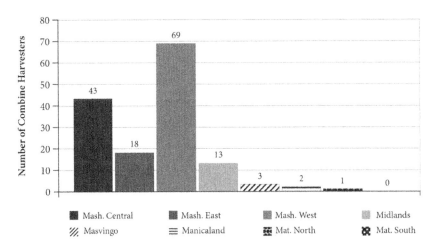

**Figure 6.5** Ownership of Combine Harvesters
SOURCE: Author's survey of commercial farmers.

Table 6.4 TOTAL FARM VALUATIONS AND IMPLEMENT COUNT

| Province | Total farm value (US$) | Total irrigation value (US$) | Total implements value (US$) | Total farm, irrigation and implements value (US$) | Total number of tractors | Total number of combine harvesters |
|---|---|---|---|---|---|---|
| Mashonaland Central | 156,812,251 | 24,485,250 | 27,779,756 | 209,077,257 | 880 | 43 |
| Mashonaland East | 139,744,633 | 21,655,242 | 62,011,208 | 223,411,083 | 725 | 18 |
| Mashonaland West | 234,621,503 | 35,810,744 | 69,228,879 | 339,661,126 | 1,068 | 69 |
| Midlands | 55,174,699 | 5,233,041 | 11,028,061 | 71,435,801 | 174 | 13 |
| Masvingo | 39,631,996 | 3,788,871 | 4,716,774 | 48,137,641 | 112 | 3 |
| Manicaland | 56,993,949 | 11,131,950 | 14,943,654 | 84,069,553 | 292 | 2 |
| Matabeleland North | 24,793,716 | 1,360,500 | 4,116,445 | 30,270,661 | 70 | 1 |
| Matabeleland South | 20,795,603 | 570,000 | 2,149,000 | 23,514,603 | 47 | 0 |
| *Total* | 728,568,350 | 104,035,598 | 196,973,777 | 1,029,577,725 | 3,368 | 149 |

NOTE: *Total farm value* = value of land itself plus immovable assets. Assets such as dams are included; if owned by a consortium, only the farm's portion is included. *Total irrigation value* = movable equipment. Does not include dams. *Total implements value* = movable equipment such as tractors, trailers, plows, etc.

SOURCE: Author's survey of commercial farmers.

that his tractors were "old enough to vote."[6] New Holland machinery was considered midrange and found throughout Zimbabwe, making it a reasonable indicator of average values. In 2009, a small 45-horsepower (hp) (two-wheel drive) tractor cost US$28,000, a midsize 85 hp (two-wheel drive) cost US$42,000, and a large 100 hp (four-wheel drive) cost US$56,000. A New Holland combine harvester with an 18-foot wheat-harvesting attachment cost US$169,000.[7] By comparison, John Deere is considered the "Rolls-Royce" of farm equipment.[8] In 2009, a 45 hp (two-wheel drive) cost US$35,000, an 85 hp (two-wheel drive) cost US$36,700, and the larger 100 hp (four-wheel drive) cost US$60,200. A John Deere combine harvester with an 18-foot wheat-harvesting attachment and 255 hp engine cost US$172,000.[9] To give a sense of scale, however, if all tractors owned in Mashonaland by survey respondents were recently purchased, midsize New Holland machines, there would be US$112,266,000 worth of tractors in the province.[10] This estimate considers only survey respondent data, so actual figures would be higher. Even if this figure was reduced by 75% to account for age and other devaluations, the resultant figure of US$28,066,500 still shows a large repository of valuable tractors in the region.

Overall, Mashonaland was fertile and produced large quantities of high-value cash crops that tended to require larger quantities of agri-property. One farmer summed up the Mashonaland provinces as "a very old farming, established area. . . . They were very well-established properties, very big irrigation setups, a lot of dams, and very, very good infrastructure."[11] Indeed, survey respondents reported that 70% (US$518,800,610) of the total value of the farm, irrigation, and equipment in Zimbabwe was from Mashonaland. These figures indicate that, from the perspective of land claimants, the provinces' farms were a significant repository of easily identifiable, easily seized, and easily sold assets.

## GEOGRAPHICAL DISTRIBUTION OF VIOLENCE AGAINST WORKERS AND FARMERS

In addition to being deployed as a means of suppressing the MDC, violence was widely used against workers and farmers in order to seize land and agri-property. Senior CIO agent Hastings Lundi explained that there were two factors determining the level of violence on farms: "Either 'What's there now [on the farms] that I can really nick [steal] and sell and profit for myself?' or 'Is he [the farmer] in the forefront of the MDC?'"[12] While the second reason relates to the political aspect of farm violence, the first supports the causative connection between violence levels and concentrations of assets. Ronald Jongwe, a member of the army, affirmed this connection: "I think especially the farm invasions, it was so intensified because I think most farms, most good farms are around there [Mashonaland]."[13] Farm foreman Tendayi Garamapudzi also saw a pattern of violence being used to secure resources:

> I understand there were some top guys who wanted some implements from the farms, some farm equipment, and they were irritating the whites [farmers] so that they run away from the farm. Then the top officials will come and steal the things from the farm. That was their aim. . . . They wanted the equipment most.[14]

He added that "they were doing violence, but their aim was theft."

A first step in assessing the violence against farmers and workers on the national level is to gain a clearer understand of the relative distribution of these respective populations. There were clear concentrations of farmers and workers in Mashonaland provinces, as was shown in chapter 5. Table 6.5 further establishes the large numbers of workers in Mashonaland provinces.[a] According to the survey, approximately 78.8% of the permanent farm worker labor

*Table 6.5* PERMANENT AND SEASONAL FARM WORKERS DISTRIBUTION

|  | Mash. Central | Mash. East | Mash. West | Mid-lands | Mas-vingo | Manica-land | Mat. North | Mat. South | Total |
|---|---|---|---|---|---|---|---|---|---|
| **Permanent workers (% of total)** | 28.9 | 21.4 | 28.4 | 4.2 | 4.2 | 9.3 | 2.3 | 1.2 | *100.0* |
| **Permanent workers** | 12,937 | 9,582 | 12,695 | 1,889 | 1,869 | 4,177 | 1,019 | 523 | *44,691* |
| **Seasonal workers** | 16,348 | 8,471 | 13,149 | 1,662 | 2,216 | 6,774 | 744 | 261 | *49,625* |

NOTE: *Permanent workers*: these figures provide a combined total of figures from primary, secondary, and any other farms. Combined data are shown because they represent the total employees corresponding to one farmer. *Seasonal workers*: those employees hired on a part-time basis, such as during harvest time.

a. Analysis of the survey's representativeness of the greater farming community reveals that the survey was robust (see appendix A). Therefore, figures presented in this and subsequent data tables on the survey can be viewed with relative confidence that they generally represent Zimbabwe's commercial farming community.

force was located in the Mashonaland provinces. The higher density of workers in these provinces is not surprising, given that farms in these regions
tended to produce labor-intensive crops.

Figures from the Commercial Farmers Union (CFU) give insight into the
concentrations of commercial farms in the country. Table 6.6 shows that of the
5,446 commercial farms registered by the CFU in 2000, 3,338—61.3%—were
in the three Mashonaland provinces. Similarly, the table shows the number of
farm title deeds in each province, according to government data. Figures show
that of the 8,758 farm title deeds, 4,290 were in Mashonaland provinces (49%).
Similar proportions were represented in survey data, where of the 865 respondent titles, 531 were from Mashonaland (61.4%). Deriving exact numbers
of farmers per province from these data is problematic, because some farmers
had large holdings and few titles, while others had many titles for smaller
holdings.[b] However, the figures at least show that there were large numbers of
farmers in Mashonaland. This claim is further reinforced by the number of
survey respondents from each province, also shown in table 6.6.[15]

There were also concentrations of violence against farmers and workers in
Mashonaland (see also chapter 5). For instance, figure 6.6 shows the distribution of violence and intimidation across each province experienced by survey
respondents.[16] These data demonstrate significantly higher averages of both
violence and intimidation for each of the Mashonaland provinces than the rest
of Zimbabwe. Similarly, table 6.7 provides more detailed insight into the specific types of violence experienced by survey respondents in all eight provinces. These data show that incidents of violence recorded in Mashonaland
accounted for a disproportionately high share of the national total.

## Proximity to Harare and Concentrations of Violence

Favorable climatic conditions for farming and the concentrations of high-
value farm equipment meant that competition for land—and the violence that
accompanied this—was particularly intense in the Mashonaland provinces.
Starting in about June 2000, there was a growing awareness of the lucrative

---

b. In some cases a single title deed included all the land on what was locally considered to be
one farm, while in other cases a locally recognized farm might include several title deeds. For
example, some farmers had separate title deeds for their homesteads and specific agricultural
areas such as horticulture operations that may have had other investors. This meant that legally the farmer had multiple title deeds for what was a single commercial operation. As farm
seizures progressed, the issue of multiple title deeds became contested. Some farm invaders
claimed that farmers had multiple farms as justification for seizure, when in fact the farmer
had several titles for a single commercial operation. However, some farmers genuinely owned
multiple farms.

*Table 6.6* Estimates of National Farmer Distribution

| | Mash. Central | Mash. East | Mash. West | Mid-lands | Mas-vingo | Manica-land | Mat. North | Mat. South | Total |
|---|---|---|---|---|---|---|---|---|---|
| **Total farms in province**[a] | 871 | 1,064 | 1,403 | 426 | 350 | 555 | 719 | 58 | 5,446 |
| **Percent of Farms in Country**[a] | 16 | 19.5 | 25.8 | 7.8 | 6.4 | 10.2 | 13.2 | 1.1 | 100% |
| **Farm Title Deeds: *Totals***[b] | 892 | 1,170 | 2,228 | 1,092 | 657 | 1,299 | 670 | 750 | 8,758 |
| **Farm Title Deeds: *Percentages***[b] | 10.2% | 13.4% | 25.4% | 12.5% | 7.5% | 14.8% | 7.7% | 8.6% | 100% |
| **Farm Title Deeds: *Totals***[c] | 174 | 150 | 207 | 104 | 55 | 74 | 63 | 38 | 865 |
| **Farm Title Deeds: *Percentages***[c] | 20.1% | 17.3% | 23.9% | 12.0% | 6.4% | 8.6% | 7.3% | 4.4% | 100% |
| **Farmer Respondents: *Totals***[c] | 105 | 96 | 131 | 33 | 28 | 48 | 19 | 15 | 475[d] |
| **Farmer Respondents: *Percentages***[c] | 22.1% | 20.2% | 27.6% | 6.9% | 5.9% | 10.1% | 4% | 3.2% | 100% |

NOTE: There were approximately 4,300 commercial farmers in 2000. The CFU data show a total of 5,446 farms because some individuals owned more than one farm.

[a] CFU figures.
[b] Government figures.
[c] Survey figures.
[d] Out of 476 respondents, 1 did not provide a location.

SOURCE: Author's survey; Charles M. B. Utete, "Report of the Presidential Land Review Committee on the Implementation of the Fast Track Land Reform Programme, 2000–2002" (Harare: Presidential Land Review Committee, 2003), 24; CFU figures in Rory Pilossof, *The Unbearable White-ness of Being: Farmers' Voices from Zimbabwe* (Harare: Weaver Press, 2012), 6.

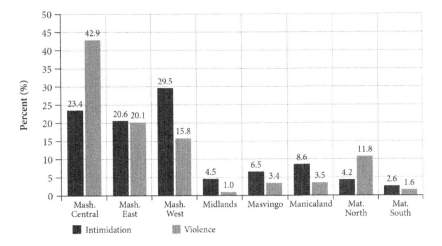

**Figure 6.6**  Violence and Intimidation of Farmers
NOTE: Intimidation and violence calculated by averaging respective variables from the farmer survey. See table 6.7 for these averages. Data reflect respondents who experienced at least one incident between 2000 and when the respondent was evicted or 2008, whichever came first.
SOURCE: Author's survey of commercial farmers.

nature of high-quality land and valuable agri-property in these provinces; this would trigger a shift in the types of invaders seeking to gain control of these resources. Genuine war veterans who had been seeking land in Mashonaland were swamped and outmuscled by the vast number of civil servants whose greater resources and personal influence enabled them to target these assets. The three Mashonaland provinces—and correspondingly a large number, although certainly not all, farms—are easily accessible from Harare in a one- to two-hour drive (see figure 5.1). As a result, all government workers in Harare—such as military personnel, politicians, prison employees, police officers—were in a prime location to move onto some of the wealthiest farms in the country as the farm seizures accelerated in about June 2000. In addition, the convenient location of Mashonaland gave the civil servants the advantage of being able to retain their government jobs while simultaneously seeking farms.

Table 6.8 indicates that genuine war veterans were involved in leading 47.2% of initial farm invasions (the incidents when political violence on farms first occurred). Despite the fact that war veterans spearheaded farm takeovers, only 28.3% of final farm invaders—individuals who led final acts of violence just before the farmer was evicted—were genuine war veterans. Conversely, the total percentage of farm invasions that featured regional and national state

Table 6.7 VIOLENCE AND INTIMIDATION OF FARMERS

| | | Mash. Central | Mash. East | Mash. West | Mid-lands | Mas-vingo | Manica-land | Mat. North | Mat. South |
|---|---|---|---|---|---|---|---|---|---|
| **Intimidation** | Abduction/unlawful arrest | 24.3% | 17.5% | 27.2% | 3.9% | 8.7% | 7.8% | 7.8% | 2.9% |
| | Intimidation/verbal threat | 21.5% | 20.8% | 29.3% | 6.6% | 5.6% | 9.8% | 3.7% | 2.7% |
| | Jambanja | 25.7% | 23.1% | 31.3% | 3.0% | 5.2% | 8.2% | 1.9% | 1.5% |
| | Property damage/theft | 22.2% | 21.0% | 30.2% | 4.6% | 6.5% | 8.6% | 3.4% | 3.4% |
| | *Average by province* | *23.4%* | *20.6%* | *29.5%* | *4.5%* | *6.5%* | *8.6%* | *4.2%* | *2.6%* |
| **Violence** | Assault | 22.8% | 22.1% | 31.5% | 2.7% | 8.1% | 6.0% | 3.4% | 3.4% |
| | Murder (attempted) | 25.0% | 18.2% | 27.3% | 2.3% | 9.1% | 4.5% | 9.1% | 4.5% |
| | Murder | 20.0% | 40.0% | 0.0% | 0.0% | 0.0% | 0.0% | 40.0% | 0.0% |
| | Rape | 100.0% | 0.0% | 0.0% | 0.0% | 0.0% | 0.0% | 0.0% | 0.0% |
| | Torture | 46.7% | 20.0% | 20.0% | 0.0% | 0.0% | 6.7% | 6.7% | 0.0% |
| | *Average by province* | *42.9%* | *20.1%* | *15.8%* | *1.0%* | *3.4%* | *3.5%* | *11.8%* | *1.6%* |

NOTE: Data reflect respondents who experienced at least one incident between 2000 and when the respondent was evicted or 2008, whichever came first.

SOURCE: Author's survey.

*Table 6.8* INITIAL AND FINAL FARM INVADER DATA

|  | Initial farm invaders | Final farm invaders | Percent change |
|---|---|---|---|
| **Genuine war veterans**[a] | 47.1% | 28.3% | *−18.8* |
| **Pseudo-war veterans**[b] | 37.4% | 31.6% | *−5.8* |
| **Respondents' farm workers**[c] | 1.6% | 2.7% | *1.1* |
| **Other farm workers or local civilians**[d] | 4.5% | 2.2% | *2.3* |
| **Regional state agents**[e] | 41.7% | 44.9% | *3.2* |
| **National state agents**[f] | 46.0% | 48.8% | *2.8* |

NOTE: For many farmer survey respondents, more than one farm invader undertook initial and final incidents, so the total exceeds 100%.

[a] War veterans who genuinely served in a combat or support role in the Liberation War.
[b] Individuals claiming to be war veterans but who were too young to have served in the Liberation War. They were normally youths hired to be the "muscle" in an operation.
[c] The farm workers employed on the farm in question.
[d] Farm workers from neighboring farms or general, local civilians.
[e] Local police, district administrators, governors, local government workers, etc.
[f] Military, CIO, President's Office, senior politicians such as ministers and MPs, etc.

In addition to the variables provided in this table, 4.3% of farm invaders leading initial violence were in the "other" category, comprising family members and friends of farm invaders and businessmen; 1.1% of survey respondents indicated that they were unsure of the profession of farm invaders leading final violence.

4.8% of farm invaders leading final violence were in the "other" category, comprising family members and friends of farm invaders, businessmen, and tribal chiefs; 0.5% of survey respondents indicated that they were unsure of the profession of farm invaders leading final violence.

SOURCE: Author's survey.

agents (i.e., midlevel to senior government officials) increased from 87.7% to 93.7%, an increase of six percentage points between the initial and final invasions; this clearly shows that state agents were also involved in farm seizures from the beginning. Thus, a higher percentage of regional and national agents ultimately gained from farm invasions at the expense of genuine war veterans, despite war veterans' Liberation War claims to the land. Not only were many government workers gaining land and assets, but the number of genuine war veterans decreased in the final stage, while the numbers of farm workers and "other" farm invaders stayed consistently low. This meant that land and agri-property were actually being shared among fewer agents in the final, than in the initial, stages of the seizures. Accordingly, this table indicates that, as the land seizure era progressed, genuine war veterans increasingly lost out to claimants who were merely concerned with securing lucrative assets.[17]

Table 6.8 does not indicate what type of individual ultimately took possession of the farm or a portion thereof. This is because many of the commercial farmers had already been evicted when they participated in the survey. It was extremely likely that they would know who had evicted them, but they would not necessarily know who ultimately received the farmland. This is because, as table 6.8 implies, farm invaders often evicted each other in an ongoing process.

The trend for genuine war veterans to increasingly lose out on land as the seizures progressed is recognized by other researchers, such as Sam Moyo: "There is a belief that the liberation war veterans who led the land occupations gained a substantial amount of the transferred land. To the contrary, many war veterans did not get land, and those who did comprised less than eight percent of the land beneficiaries."[18] Moyo then goes on to demonstrate the relative weakness over time of war veteran land claims: "Moreover some members of the ZNLWVA who did get land complain that they were being dispossessed of the land that they had occupied, largely because they were opposed to some elites getting larger plots."

The reason that genuine war veterans were losing out was that, despite claims by the government that land redistribution would primarily benefit war veterans and the landless poor, the seizures were becoming co-opted. The principles supposedly guiding the government's hastily concocted land reform program were soon ignored by the raw opportunists who drove the escalation in the seizures. This meant that war veterans were sidelined as the ability to take control of land and agri-property increasingly came to be dominated by the political and military connections, social networks, and personal funding of regional and national officials.

The government's Utete report confirmed that state officials were predominant among land beneficiaries. Part of the report investigated assistance provided to beneficiaries by the Department of Agriculture and Rural Extension (AREX), a government agricultural support group, but found that "it was difficult to assess this aspect due to the absence of the beneficiaries, the majority being civil servants who tend to miss out on support schemes, which was available during the working days of the week."[19]

Interview respondents agreed that government employees seeking farms close to Harare played a key role in the escalation of farm seizures and violence in Mashonaland. Indeed, military intelligence agent Peter Msasa stated that the farm seizures began slipping out of control because senior individuals—who were mostly located in Harare—began demanding farms for themselves.[20] These individuals were able and willing to use their power and influence to target the conveniently located, wealthy Mashonaland farms. Petros Mzingwane, a war veteran and "new" farmer, explained that "these farms [in Mashonaland] here were hit by proximity [to where senior officials were located]."[21] David Coltart, MP, senator, and Minister for Education, concurred:

> It [Mashonaland Central] was relatively close to Harare, so a very attractive area, very good road communications up to Bindura, and those areas had lots of tarred roads, so were easy to get to in your Merc [Mercedes] from Harare for the weekend. So there was this huge pool of civil servants, army commanders, police commanders based in Harare who would have seen very attractive properties in Mash. Central.[22]

Rancher Daniel Fairbanks also identified that the close proximity of Harare to the Mashonaland provinces allowed farm invaders to easily travel between target farms and their jobs and homes in Harare: "All the ministers and everybody who were involved with all of that stuff [farm seizures] were all Harare-based Central Committee operators. They could rush out in the night, do their stuff, and come back tomorrow morning and be in their office, and there was no problem. Nobody would know that they were doing it."[23] This claim is partially supported by Sam Moyo, who noted that "some elites, during the 2000 to 2002 period, sought land near the more ethnically cosmopolitan towns where they live (particularly Harare and Bulawayo), while others sought land near their communal area 'home' (*kumusha*) districts."[24]

Invaders specifically sought farms in Mashonaland with high-quality homesteads so they could live outside the city in more pleasant, rural conditions and still commute into the capital. Senior police officer Edward Chidembo recalled that "senior police officers or senior army officers, senior CIO officers all wanted farms with a homestead, farms with a nice homestead."[25] Farmer John Hayes said that "certainly really nice houses were more of an attraction" for farm invaders.[26] Another police officer, Samuel Limpopo, corroborated this claim, describing the sentiments of one farm invader: "'There is a beautiful house here [on the farm]. . . . This is a big house. I want this one.'"[27] Rather than just using farms on weekends, according to Chidembo, influential invaders actually lived on farms with large houses: "I'm actually told that a lot of them are commuting from those homesteads to the cities where they work. They are living on those farms."[28]

Farmer Ronald Madison and his wife Penny gave an account of an invader who arrived on his farm with his wife, ostensibly to talk to Madison.[29] While they were all talking on the veranda, the farmer realized that the invader was actually there to decide whether to seize the house:

> PENNY MADISON:   He [the farm invader] saw the home, which was the most beautiful home. [Ronald] had taken eight years to build it for me. . . .[It was] all done out of wood from the farm. . . . They [the farm invader and his wife] sat on our veranda in the Morris chairs . . . saying, "Oh, this is very nice, isn't it?" You know, we weren't even aware, were we [of their intentions]? "Oh, you know, we like these chairs." The next thing was . . .
> RONALD MADISON:   "We [farm invaders] don't just want the chairs, we want the whole house."

That the Madisons' farm, which was located just 30 minutes drive from Harare, was a productive agricultural venture was not as important as the house to the land claimant, who, according to Madison, was looking for a weekend retreat. The problem for Madison was that the claimant's brother-in-law was one of Mugabe's "bodyguards, or maybe his head bodyguard. And so that gave him clout to mess around with us." This point further underscores the competition between Harare-based officials, who relied less on the need to demonstrate farming experience when claiming a farm than the ability to exert influence through powerful connections. The intensity of this competition in the Mashonaland provinces also generated a dynamic in which coercion would be particularly intense as claimants wrestled for access to the area's lucrative land and agri-property.

## FARM INVADERS SEEK FARM ASSETS

The research for this book uncovered numerous accounts of farm invaders being particularly eager to seize agri-property, rather than just land. Senior army officer Steven Sebungwe noted that farm invaders would immediately "sell all the tractors, get maximum profit from what is there on the ground—the farm equipment and farm implements, and then the house is free of charges [to live in]."[30] Joyce Mukwa, a farm clerk, explained the looting on the farm where she worked: "They wanted to grab all his [the farmer's] property like they did. They had some cattle, some sheep, some goats, some horses, some of *everything*, some engines, everything all over the farm. They had to grab everything."[31] Furthermore, a member of the army, Agnes Sengwe, explained that farm invaders were methodical in seizing farm resources: "When there were cows . . . they ate them. They killed them. They slaughtered them. Then they enjoyed the meat. . . . When there's chickens, they ate everything until it's finished. They would stay on one farm as a group. They enjoy the things."[32] She explained that once the resources had been seized, the invaders simply moved to another farm and began the process again.

Indeed, Telmore Nyakasanga, a farm foreman, explained that farm invaders would be disappointed when arriving on a farm with little agri-property: "If he goes and takes where there's not enough equipment, then, 'Ah, here, yes, all we've got is land.'"[33] As military intelligence official Daniel Inkankezi put it, "When the farmers also ran away, they left also all these other things [agri-property], which those guys [farm invaders] could simply grab and make a quick buck. So it was not the land. It was more to see what benefits could accrue immediately."[34] Farmer Kevin Elbridge noted that farm invaders would waste little when stripping a farm of its assets:

It's anything that has a value. It could even be scrap metal. It could even be irrigation pipes, tractors, trailers. Even down at the farm next door to me, they have already taken down two sheds and sold them. He had beautiful workers' accommodation. They've already started collapsing them and selling the bricks, window frames, doorframes and asbestos. They are digging up the irrigation pipes and they are being sold.[35]

Farm foreman Tendayi Garamapudzi recalled how in 1991 the farm where we worked had only one brick house in the compound (worker village). By 2000 the farmer had built 85–90 brick houses for workers.[36] Normally, such a major investment in workers' well-being would have made the farmer a valued employer, but during the land seizure era it made the farmer a target: an occupier could charge tenants rent for living in the houses that the farmer had provided as a benefit in kind; or he could dismantle the housing and sell the materials.

Farm invaders, especially high-ranking officials, tended to locate agri-property on more successful farms. An established farm in a productive area, such as in the Mashonaland provinces, would have good roads, numerous buildings, significant worker housing, and irrigation, and would be well equipped with valuable equipment. According to horticulture manager Andrew Morfu, Mashonaland farms were "established 80 years ago. So all those farms they were well prepared [developed]."[37] Thus, farms in these areas were particularly targeted by well-connected claimants: "All these top guys on this party, they went there because they wanted those farms because they've got much equipment."[38]

Mashonaland's fertility was a particularly conspicuous signal of numerous high-value assets when invaders were considering what farms to seize. Senior politician Thompson Mupfure highlighted the disparity between Mashonaland and Matabeleland: "While you are looking at ranches here [in Matabeleland]

and looking at large tracts of land, it is not so obvious [what assets exist]. . . . But in Mashonaland, as you drive through, there are the patches of green land with beautiful crops of maize, tobacco, whatever you talk about. It's there. It's evident. You can see it."[39] Essentially, even if farms in other areas had extensive assets, Mashonaland resources were more evident.[40]

The nationalist justifications for the land seizures appeared to make little impression on many invaders. In fact, there were instances of black commercial farmers having their land invaded, despite obtaining their farms after independence, as Cliffe et al. have also previously noted.[41] A black commercial farmer interviewed for this research, Arnold Bembezi, was ostensibly an ideal role-model for future, more inclusive agriculture in Zimbabwe, because of his ethnicity, farming experience, and commercial success.[42] Nevertheless, his property was targeted by farm invaders:

> These ZANU-PF people, when they come around and they see there is some modicum of success coming out of there [commercial farm], they will want it. That is the truth—they will want it. And they will go and generate some paper [containing a fraudulent claim] and say, "This is an offer [a bogus government offer letter], and we've been offered this farm, so you can see it has been allocated to us—get moving." If you don't move, they sort you out.

After Bembezi was evicted from his farm he purchased land closer to Harare on which to store his farm equipment, only to find farm invaders arriving there and demanding his assets. Tichafa Ncema, a farm manager, argued that as the land seizures progressed, financial objectives came to far outweigh social and political grievances; it made no difference to farm invaders whether the farmer was white or black, whether he had been kind to his laborers, or whether he had contributed generously to community development.[43] What mattered was the availability of lootable agri-property. This depended largely on the kinds of crops the farm grew—maize and wheat tended to require extensive equipment such as tractors, whereas ranches had fewer such assets—and the success of the farm, which determined whether the venture was likely to agri-property such as irrigation equipment.

A key reason why invaders targeted agri-property is that there were no guarantees that they would retain their newly acquired land if a more powerful invader wanted the farm. In addition, a commitment to engaging in farming was especially inconvenient for farm invaders with paid employment, such as those working for the government. Sengwe gave insight into how the assets on the farms represented more of a financial incentive than the land itself for her colleagues in the military: "[On farms] there were these nice buildings with everything—lights, the pumping machine, boreholes, the pipes, every-thing."[44] While there was symbolic value for some ex-combatants in seizing land, what really mattered to many farm invaders, such as Sengwe's colleagues in the military, was seizing agri-property. Despite its symbolic value, land re-quired labor, capital, and time commitments to yield profits, whereas agri-property provided immediate benefits. Stripping and reselling agri-property yielded immediate financial gain, while land required tilling, seeding, fertil-izing, tending, and harvesting crops before any profits could be realized.

Accordingly, for many farm invaders, the stated objective of obtaining "fer-tile land" simply served as a proxy for their true desire to seize associated farm assets. The perceived injustice of land inequity served as a publicly acceptable justification for seizing farmers' property. It is important to emphasize, how-ever, that while seizing agri-property was a key objective for many farm invad-ers, it was not necessarily exclusive of the objective of seizing land. Yet seizing—and holding—land in an unstable environment brought logistical challenges and cost implications that tended to make agri-property a more ap-pealing target.

This evidence of a "free-for-all" style approach to farm invasions contra-dicts claims by Sam Moyo, who, in a puzzling fashion, paints a rather tranquil—and totally unsubstantiated—picture of farmers willingly leaving their personal assets on the farms, and farm invaders receiving them in a fair and orderly manner: "There were also some 'movables' (machinery, generators, pumps, etc.) which were left by some former farmers. These inherited 'im-provements' are, however, the focus of controversial contests over compensa-tion by former landowners."[45] Moyo then strangely implies that farmers were in the wrong for seeking compensation for these lost assets.

Moyo also focuses on the benefits derived from farmers' assets for farm in-vaders, without mentioning the cost of the coercive process that yielded them: "a range of on-farm infrastructures, called 'improvements' or 'immovables' such as farm houses, barns, bore holes, workshops, sheds, and irrigation piping, and off-farm infrastructures (dams, roads, electricity lines, etc.), that were left on the farms provide additional assets to the beneficiaries."

In contrast to the orderly and seemingly amicable picture that Moyo would have us believe, evidence presented in this book shows that farm seizures were achieved through extreme intimidation and violence, and resulted in pro-found breakdowns of the livelihoods of the farmers and farm workers. Farm-ers did not willingly leave assets on their farms, as Moyo implies, but instead often relinquished them under duress in an environment where legal property rights were worthless. Farmers often had no choice but to abandon their assets because of the absence of protection from state security and in view of the comprehensive collapse of law and order. In some cases this led to the destitution of the farmer, who often retained loan obligations to lending institutions for land and assets.

## Legal Mechanisms Aid in the Seizure of Farms and Assets

The tendency for farmers to relinquish assets became increasingly pronounced as legal mechanisms were gradually passed that prevented farmers from removing their agri-property. The Land Acquisition Amendment Act No. 6 of 2002, which placed a formal structure on the Fast Track Land Reform Programme, allowed for some movable assets to be left on farms (with the farmer's approval), but the value of the assets would be compensated to the farmer; these items included above-ground irrigation equipment, tractors, and combine harvesters.[46] In other words, the government had agreed that farmers would be compensated for seized land, but under this act the value of some equipment would be added to that compensation.[47]

Legal provisions preventing farmers from removing agri-property became even more stringent in 2003 with Statutory Instrument 273 A. This expanded the list of farm equipment that could be acquired by the government to include items such as tractors and plows, as well as materials such as fertilizer and chemicals.[48] Then in 2004 the Acquisition of Farm Equipment and Material Act was introduced; this included provisions to prevent agri-property, such as seed and stock feed, from being removed.[49] These acts criminalized the removal of farmers' personal property from farms and were a major departure from any nationalist-inspired claims to land.

Farmers' accounts underscore the coercion, fear, and loss that encompassed the experience of being forced to leave substantial quantities of agri-property on farms—a starkly different picture from what Moyo seeks to convey.[50] These accounts show that not only did legal provisions gradually restrict the movement of agri-property from farms, but that farm invaders often decided unilaterally what departing farmers could remove from their property (if anything), regardless of more detailed provisions in the law. Moreover, this restriction on the movement of agri-property was taking place in some cases prior to the implementation of the Land Acquisition Amendment Act of 2002, and as the legal mechanisms became more stringent, the framework merely justified what was already happening on the ground.

For example, Elizabeth Shore, the spouse of a farmer, stated:

> There was a window where it was possible to take some stuff into town without questions being asked [by farm invaders]. But as time went on [toward 2002], you couldn't load anything without a bit of bush telegraph

[informal communication] going down the road, and you were prevented from taking it.[51]

In a separate interview Shore's husband, James, explained that he eventually had no choice but to leave much of his agri-property on his farm: "I wasn't able to get everything, by any means, off the farm."[52] Shore said that he faced growing anxiety as he began to gradually lose all his assets, despite his previous faith in the government's commitment to protect property rights. Shore explained that the "enormous amount of intimidation" left him little choice but to comply with farm invader demands.

Farm manager Ketani Makabusi highlighted that in addition to coercion, evictions often happened very quickly, and farmers were forced to leave agri-property on farms: "It was a bit of a mission getting stuff. Some guys lost everything completely. Some guys had to literally [pack] a car and a suitcase and get off the farm or otherwise we're going to kill you tonight."[53] Farmer Thomas Barkley provides a stark illustration of this experience: "I was told literally, I had half an hour to vacate. I managed to push that on to two [hours], but basically all I picked up was my briefcase and my dog."[54] In detailing his losses—and underscoring how farm invaders took advantage of legal provisions that purportedly assured farmers of compensation for agri-property—Barkley stated: "The tractors were left there. The combines were left there. I wasn't allowed to move anything at all . . . the so-called settlers said they were going to be using them and they wanted to buy them, which they haven't done."

Other examples highlight how farm invaders could simply ignore the law, which the police had little inclination or ability to enforce. Makabusi stated that on one occasion a police officer indicated to farm invaders when referring to agri-property, "Listen, these are movable assets. In theory [the farmer has] got the right to take these things off."[55] Makabusi stated that the farm invader disregarded the law and kept the agri-property he wanted. In a different example, Jane Garfield, a farmer's spouse, related that she and her husband Rupert received a court order allowing them to return to their farm to collect some personal property; but on two occasions war veteran youths ignored the court order and prevented them from doing so.

We were then given permission to go back again. When we got back the next time, they were there following us and harassing us. So inevitably we left a whole lot of stuff behind. It just wasn't safe and we started to feel threatened, and we had agreed that it wasn't worth being assaulted or being damaged or hurt or anything like that.[56]

These examples occurred within an overarching context of constant intimidation, in which farmers' ability to carry out commercial operations was severely undermined. From farmers' perspectives, the threats to agri-property were a major concern because of the value of these assets—although this was only one aspect of the overwhelming uncertainty they faced by 2002. For example, farmer George Sherman from Mashonaland East stated that he received a Section 5, a preliminary notice of acquisition and the precursor document to a Section 8, which would have evicted him from the farm.[57] He contested the court order, but although he was entitled to a response from the government, he received none—and then received three Section 8s when he was in fact only supposed to receive one. He explained that at this time his tobacco seedbeds needed for the forthcoming crop were being destroyed by invaders, and his cattle were being "slashed" and "mutilated." As a result, "On [receipt of] the third one [Section 8], I thought, well you know, time to go."[58] Anonymous survey respondents provided further examples of the impossible situations facing farmers:

- "Government acquisition notices, [then] negotiation to retain a part with Ministry of Lands (Mash. West), [then] remained on farm, [then] detained by police, [then] charged, [then] forbidden by magistrate to return except with police escort, [then] bail, [then] three months later charge withdrawn."
- "Forced to pay retrenchment to labour. Financially broke farm. No banks able to lend overdraught due to Section Five on farm."
- "We won our court cases, both Section 5 and 7 were revoked and [we] were entitled to continue farming. This caused increased pressure [by farm invaders] to stop [us from] farming and move off."

These accounts underscore the violent and chaotic scene that compelled many farmers to leave their agri-property on the farms. Agri-property was sought and gained by farm invaders even prior to the passage of legal mechanisms preventing farmers from removing this property, as the above accounts show. The implementation of legal mechanisms simply imposed a veneer of legality to what was already happening on the ground—highlighting how the purportedly nationalist-inspired seizure of land took place alongside the state-sanctioned looting of agri-property that had no historical justification.

## Locating Farm Assets

Valuable assets on farms could often be easily identified by land claimants, even from adjoining farms.[59] Farm wealth, in contrast to other businesses, is easily visible—especially when farms border main transport corridors. Chidembo explained:

> The commercial farms, I mean their wealth is there for everybody to see. You just see those farms—they are massive. They employ a lot of people, and if you went into Zimbabwe during the period when the crops are being nurtured and so on, it was a lovely sight. . . . You'd see huge fields of green maize and so on. So a lot of people admired that.[60]

However, farm invaders had also devised other methods for locating agri-property. One method, primarily undertaken by wealthy senior officials, was to "tour" farming areas in convoys of vehicles. Ministers' convoys would include government-issue Mercedes Benz vehicles and police escorts, whereas military officials used army vehicles accompanied by soldiers.[61] Farmer interview respondents provide evidence of such pretakeover "touring."[62] Indeed, 48.6% of survey respondents indicated that "tours" by officials were specific tipping points that foreshadowed violence and takeover attempts. This statistic strongly suggests that land claimants were using "tours" to choose farms. The fact that they often heralded impending violence indicates a causal link between the decision by an invader to target a farm and the deployment of resources to seize it by force.

Another method for officials to locate farms for themselves was to rely on existing government data in order to select the wealthiest and most productive farms. Lundi stated that rather than being civil servants, some district administrators (DAs) were in fact CIO agents, with the genuine civil servants functioning as deputy DAs.[63] The CIO agents wrote "intelligence reports" on commercial farmers, even in districts where commercial farmers were scarce.[64] Both genuine DAs and CIO imposters were therefore in a strong position to help guide influential politicians in seizing farms, because they had access to government data on farm productivity and to intelligence on the farmers' history of supporting the MDC.[65] Thus, senior officials could remove strong opposition supporters while at the same time seizing the most productive farms.

Influential officials also relied on the Agricultural Technical and Extension Service (Agritex), a government organization providing training and guidance to farmers, in order to access farm data. Given that Agritex officials had personal knowledge of most commercial farmers, they were well placed to guide influential individuals on which farms were most productive and worth seizing.[66]

The ambition to seize movable assets was so strong that it often surpassed the farm invaders' other objective of suppressing the MDC. This became far more common as the farm seizures progressed after about 2001, and invaders with only opportunistic alliances with ZANU-PF joined the farm seizures.

Imminence Ngiwa, a farm foreman and tractor driver, recalled that in many cases, "they [farm invaders] doesn't [sic] bother if he's [the farmer] the MDC or ZANU-PF. What they want is what belongs to the boss there at the farm."[67]

As a result of this strategy, Ngiwa reported that soon after farm invaders arrived, they targeted "just anything," and now "[on the farm] there is nothing there." Free-for-all looting occurred on some occasions, such as in the "trashings" that took place in Mashonaland West.[c] Limpopo explained that once the farmer was removed, farm invaders began fighting among themselves and the mechanized farming infrastructure was dismantled: "Everything was taken away so they are not even producing anything. They took everything away—tractors, machinery, everything was taken away."[68] Ultimately, the farmer and his workers' political affiliation were forgotten in the scramble for agri-property.

## Unused Farmland

Further evidence that agri-property was often more coveted than land comes from the fact that agricultural production levels were not maintained once farms were taken over. If farms were seized primarily for land and not for agri-property, as espoused by war veterans and ZANU-PF, then one would expect farming to have continued. Although the change in operatorship may have produced costs and inexperienced farmers would face a learning curve, farm invaders would in theory benefit from already established water access, infrastructure, and equipment. Overall, "new" farmers should have been able to limit the extent of disruption to production, even if some decline may have been inevitable.

Yet UNDP data show that the drop in agricultural production after the land seizures began was dramatic.[69] Prior to the land seizure era, the agriculture industry "was the largest formal sector employer in the country and made significant contributions to national income and export earnings."[70] Table 6.9 depicts the 1998 and 2007 production levels for major agricultural commodities, indicating that, in 2007, production was just 42% of 1998 levels.[71] Similarly, per capita value added dropped drastically after 2001, and by 2006 had fallen below 1980 levels.[72] It should be kept in mind that these data also reflect some commercial farmer input, especially in the 2000–2002 period, since farmers were only gradually evicted, so the actual input of farms controlled by invaders is likely even lower.

---

c. An act where farm invaders descended en masse, sometimes in groups of 100 or more, onto a farm stealing and destroying nearly all property in one major incident. A trashing was so financially devastating for the farmer and so fundamentally demonstrative of the lack of security, that most farmers left after such an incident.

*Table 6.9* Decline in Production of Major Agricultural Commodities: 1998 and 2007

|      | Maize | Wheat | Soybeans | Cotton | Tobacco | Coffee | Dairy | Beef |
|------|-------|-------|----------|--------|---------|--------|-------|------|
| **1998** | 521 | 270 | 113 | 77 | 210 | 10 | 184 | 350 |
| **2007** | 160 | 62 | 64 | 0 | 65 | 1 | 86 | 120 |

NOTE: In thousands of tons.

SOURCE: United Nations Development Programme, "Comprehensive Economic Recovery in Zimbabwe," 2008.

The decline in agriculture productivity is dramatic, even when allowing for a transition period from existing farmers to "new" farmers. Considering that seized farms were already established and ready for production, the most rational explanation is that much of the land was not used for farming. This claim is supported by the UNDP report, which cited numerous instances of seized land becoming idle.[73] Likewise, a special report published by the Food and Agriculture Organization of the United Nations (FAO) and the World Food Programme (WFP) found that in 2006/2007, just 55% of commercial farmland was being utilized.[74]

Even a government study made similar findings. The 2003 Utete report indicated that A1 allocations (small, single-family holdings given to relatively poor individuals from communal areas in an effort to promote decongestion), had a take-up rate of 97% in 2003.[75] This high rate implies a genuine desire by some farm invaders to put allocated land to use. Yet a different picture is seen on land allocated for commercial farming. Larger, generally more productive A2 plots were intended to create "a cadre of black commercial farmers."[76] Accordingly, A2 beneficiaries were supposed to be assessed through a formal scheme to select "better-off smallholder farmers with demonstrated competency in farming, such as master farmers and agricultural graduates."[77] However, the A2 take-up rate was just 66%, which, according to the government report, "implied [that] a considerable amount of land was lying fallow or unused."[78] The reason for the low rate of uptake is simple. According to the UNDP, "Many of those who had been allocated farms had no farming experience and were in full-time employment, often as civil servants."[79] That is, the invaders who took control of the best land typically had other jobs and often had no reason to become farmers once they had removed the farm's agri-property.

A2 beneficiaries were generally more powerful claimants who, as government officials, had sufficient influence (especially those in state security) to have land allocated to them despite possessing little or no farming skills. This is contrary to official government guidelines.[80] Figure 6.7 shows that more powerful claimants tended to seek more successful farms, well-developed land, and extensive agri-property. Thus, some of the most productive land in the country was sought by powerful—but nonfarming—invaders, who could not easily become farmers even if they wanted to. Nevertheless, these farms could still prove lucrative to A2 beneficiaries, as they could strip the farm of its assets. Zamchiya especially provides a nuanced case study of this scenario in his assessment of the Chipinge district, showing that more influential land claimants tended to get higher-quality agri-property in greater quantities.[81] These assets could then be used directly by the claimant for agricultural purposes or sold for profit. This factor largely explains the large quantities of unused or underutilized land and the concomitant drop in agricultural production.

## What Became of Agri-Property?

Unsurprisingly, the market for farm equipment was rapidly saturated as the farm seizures accelerated. Increased supply was exacerbated by decreased demand: fewer people were willing to buy equipment for fear that it would be seized. To compensate, some equipment was taken to communal areas, while other equipment was peddled to "new" farmers. Equipment that could be transported across the border was sold in neighboring Zambia and Mozambique, as well as other countries. Many pieces of farm equipment were stripped of parts, which were then repurposed. For instance, tractor batteries were used to power radios. Wheels and axles were used for donkey carts. Wiring from tractors, combines, and houses was used for a multitude of purposes, including building chicken coops. Specialized farm equipment often had little resale value or practical use outside of a commercial farm context, and usually this equipment was stripped for parts or deployed for a far more basic use than for which it was designed. Garamapudzi explained that farm invaders repurposed high-value heating equipment used to cure tobacco: "They [farm invaders] wanted to go and do [build] a toilet in the beer hall, so they were taking the heater exchange, taking the bricks to go and build the toilet."[82]

Other agri-property required associated equipment before it could be operated. For instance, a heavy-duty trailer required a medium-sized tractor to pull it, without which the trailer was useful for little more than its wheels. Accordingly, many valuable items had little real value to farm invaders. Other goods were difficult and expensive to maintain, leading many farm invaders to abandon equipment if it malfunctioned or ran out of fuel. Overall, much seized equipment was only somewhat used, often stripped and the parts repurposed, and sold for profit. In some instances equipment was seized, but when found to be impractical or too costly to move, such as in the cases of heavy equipment, it was abandoned. The result was that in many cases equipment worth tens of thousands of dollars or more was stripped and used for parts worth a tiny fraction of that amount.[d]

## LAND AND ASSET-SEEKING FARM INVADERS: WHO WERE THEY?

Farm invaders varied widely in their professions and included top generals and the president himself, to the rural unemployed who eked out a living as subsistence farmers.[83] Leading farm invaders shared one major commonality: almost all were members of ZANU-PF, or at least professed allegiance to the ruling party. Indeed, some 97% of farmer survey respondents reported that the farm invaders leading the initial and final (before farmers were evicted) violence on farms belonged to ZANU-PF. Zamchiya observed similar findings in his study of the Chipinge district, where he identified an overt patronage system in which ZANU-PF supporters received preferential access to land and state agricultural benefits.[84] Accordingly, there was clearly both a practical and political advantage in declaring allegiance to the ruling party.[85]

### Elite Farm Invaders: Senior Party Officials, Leading Politicians, and Families

Some invaders were senior government officials with significant wealth and influence who had access to the resources needed to seize entire farms. These individuals did not personally seize farms in most instances, but after selecting which farm they wanted, they had sufficient financial resources to pay farm invaders to undertake the actual eviction of the farmer and takeover the property.

Unsurprisingly, the elite—or more accurately in most cases, those who had access to patronage—of any given area tended to get the best land and the most agri-property.[86] Indeed, Mandivamba Rukuni and Stig Jensen have found that a large number of A1 farmers were evicted by senior politicians, higher-ranking military officials, and prominent business people.[87] Sadomba concurs:

As soon as the Fast Track Programme took hold, its implementers started to weed out war veterans and other revolutionaries, opening commercial farms for elite settlement. These elites were mainly senior government

d.  See www.charleslaurie.com for photographs of stripped farm equipment.

officials, senior members of the uniformed forces, party loyalists, relatives and the ruling oligarchy, who were given whole farms to themselves measuring hundreds or even thousands of hectares. These "chefs," as the elite are commonly called, chose prime land with good infrastructure and farm houses, chasing away the revolutionaries. In contrast, revolutionaries were allocated A1 plots that were several subdivisions of a farm (as small as six hectares per household) according to official government policy.[88]

Msasa provided another example: "The minister of defense, the minister of finance, those are very influential people. They can do whatever they want. They will just notify you that 'I have got a letter from the Land Minister to take over that farm.'"[89]

### COMPETITIVE ADVANTAGES OF ELITE INVADERS

Senior farm invaders benefited from a competitive advantage when targeting farms because they had influence, access to important logistical supplies such as vehicles, and far greater financial resources than their competitors. Msasa elaborated: "All those nice big farms, they were gone like that and you could see deputy minister taking this [farm], this minister taking this [farm], the police commissioner is taking this [farm], judge this has taken that [farm], and so forth.[90] All those good farms in Mazowe [Mashonaland Central] were taken by judges." Similarly, Edward Chidembo, who as a high-ranking member of the police had firsthand knowledge of his colleagues' behavior, agreed that "a lot of senior old police officers, the majority of them, senior police officers or senior army officers or senior CIO officers, they have got farms."[91]

In addition to strong political influence, a track record of using violence also increased a farm invader's success rate. For example, war veteran Petros Mzingwane, despite being neither a politician nor an active member of the military, was able to seize a high-value farm in Mashonaland Central.[92] This was likely due to his ability to use his fearsome reputation for using violence to ward off rivals for the land. Indeed, military agents deliberately cultivated memories of violence in the Liberation War and *Gukurahundi* during the land seizure era to heighten fear among civilians (see chapter 5). Thus, a farm invader's level of notoriety undoubtedly contributed to a victim's decision on whether to fight, negotiate, or flee.

Among high-ranking farm invaders, military officials were particularly influential. Military officers were specially trained in violence, had access to transport and communications equipment, and could use rank-and-file soldiers to do their bidding. These resources were not officially deployed by the state per se, but powerful military farm invaders could use state resources for personal gain (as subsequent sections will show). Lundi provided an example in which he quoted army commander General Constantine Chiwenga, who had access to military resources and a network of supporters:

> I'm Chiwenga. I have got access to an army truck. I will go and get my boys [supporters] from the countryside because the farm workers have run away. I go and get the farm. My boys from my rural area come over with me. I want you to harvest my stuff [crops], or I just want to flex my muscle to the other guy who also wants this same farm.[93]

Sengwe neatly summed up the advantages enjoyed by members of the military, in stating that despite extensive competition for farms among officials from all over government, "in the end the most people who won were the soldiers."[94]

Meanwhile, Inkankezi, as a senior military intelligence officer, was able to observe that senior individuals could access military assets that were widely used to seize farms and to operate them: "The people who were farmers [working on seized farms], they were all from the army. The driver, everybody was from the army. They were using army personnel."[95] Military privates would work on the farm, reporting to an officer operating as a farm manager. This arrangement ensured the state paid all expenses and the senior officer who "owned" the farm received all profits.

Senior police officers held similar advantages. Many were war veterans and could use their uniforms to coerce farmers into leaving their property. They could also take advantage of their positions to promote their own interests, such as by arresting noncompliant farmers and workers. Chidembo stated that the "majority" of senior officials in the police, army, and CIO had acquired farms.[96]

Underscoring these accounts, farmer survey respondents were asked who led final farm takeovers. A large number of respondents cited regional (44.9%) and national state agents (48.8%), categories comprising state security service officials, politicians, and civil servants (see also table 6.8).[97] Senior officers in the government, army, police, and CIO were frequently mentioned by farmer survey respondents as being responsible. Those cited include Philip Chiyangwa (an MP and Mugabe's cousin), Oppah Muchinguri (governor of Manicaland), and Peter Chanetsa (governor of Mashonaland West) (see endnote for additional detailed examples from farm survey respondents).[98]

There were also a wide variety of farm invaders who were able to exert strong influence through their personal connections. These individuals ranged from family members to bodyguards, friends of powerful officials, and even personal secretaries working for senior individuals. Survey respondents provided extensive insight into the breadth of individuals who did not necessarily possess strong professional credentials or the means to employ violence, but could make use of significant personal or other nonprofessional influence to seize assets. Academics, businessmen, relatives of the president and vice president, and the daughter of a provincial governor were all identified as benefiting from farm seizures. For example, farmer survey respondents cited such individuals as "UZ [University of Zimbabwe] lecturer," "Sabina Mugabe, MP," "Robert Zhuwao, MP," "Patrick Zhuwao, nephew of president," "nephew of [Vice President] Joseph Msika," and "daughter of the Provincial Governor" as having directly seized their farm's assets. Given that these individuals would have been competing with other agents possessing professional influence and perhaps expertise in the use of violence, the importance of having ties with Mugabe and other senior figures is clear.

Interview respondents provide examples of how this influence gave farm invaders the power to ignore the law. A security coordinator hired by farmers in a Mashonaland Central district recounted that on one occasion he had called the police because violence was escalating rapidly.[99] When the police arrived to restore order, the farm invasion group locked the officers in the homestead along with the security coordinator and his spouse. In other cases, the police actively assisted the farm invaders. Farmer George Sherman recalled that a police officer came to his front gate along with the ZANU-PF officials looking to seize his farm.[100] When Sherman asked for copies of the official eviction papers, the officer responded: "We don't have the papers, but I'm a policeman representing the police force and the government."

Similarly, rancher Brian Wheeler in Matabeleland South recounted that war veteran leader Chenjerai Hunzvi came to his property along with the police, a Zimbabwe Broadcasting Corporation television crew, and 28 associates, whom he described as a "typical Matabele impi [armed war party] all coming down the road singing and dancing."[101] Wheeler was forced to confront this group alone, at enormous risk to his safety. Soon afterward the group forcibly entered Wheeler's home and Hunzvi demanded to take possession of Wheeler's weapons, despite having no authority to do so. The accompanying police officer told Wheeler, "Give them [weapons] to Hunzvi. You'll get them back [eventually]." Wheeler stated:

> [In front of the television crew] Hunzvi says, "I've captured this white farmer's weapons." So here he is the great hero and they get back in their vehicle and then off they go, and then the police stay there with me and they reassure me, and some of the head [senior] police come from Bulawayo and they say, "I know these guys [invaders]. It's okay, it's okay. Just go with this thing. It's all political, so you can come up to Nkayi tomorrow and get your weapons back."

According to Msasa, the most important factor determining whether a farm invader was able to secure land was his level of influence with officials in the government and state security.[102]

Figure 6.7 presents a farm invader typology where each farm invader type and its corresponding asset category is defined by a set of behaviors, indicated by data presented in this book. A "farm invader," in this instance, is defined as a category of individuals orchestrating and, to some degree, participating in farm invaders.

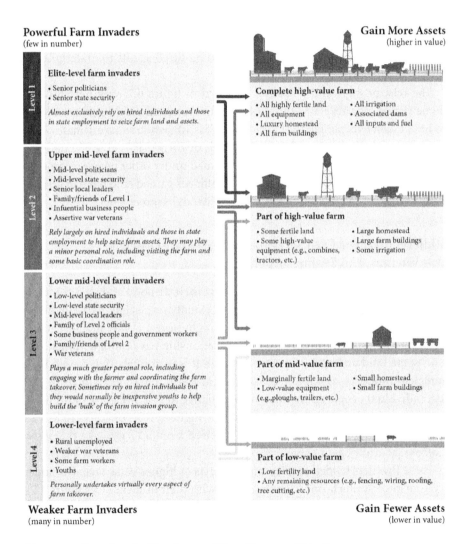

**Powerful Farm Invaders**
(few in number)

**Gain More Assets**
(higher in value)

**Level 1**

**Elite-level farm invaders**

- Senior politicians
- Senior state security

*Almost exclusively rely on hired individuals and those in state employment to seize farm land and assets.*

**Complete high-value farm**

- All highly fertile land
- All equipment
- Luxury homestead
- All farm buildings
- All irrigation
- Associated dams
- All inputs and fuel

**Level 2**

**Upper mid-level farm invaders**

- Mid-level politicians
- Mid-level state security
- Senior local leaders
- Family/friends of Level 1
- Influential business people
- Assertive war veterans

*Rely largely on hired individuals and those in state employment to help seize farm assets. They may play a minor personal role, including visiting the farm and some basic coordination role.*

**Part of high-value farm**

- Some fertile land
- Some high-value equipment (e.g., combines, tractors, etc.)
- Large homestead
- Large farm buildings
- Some irrigation

**Level 3**

**Lower mid-level farm invaders**

- Low-level politicians
- Low-level state security
- Mid-level local leaders
- Family of Level 2 officials
- Some business people and government workers
- Family/friends of Level 2
- War veterans

*Plays a much greater personal role, including engaging with the farmer and coordinating the farm takeover. Sometimes they rely on hired individuals but they would normally be inexpensive youths to help build the 'bulk' of the farm invasion group.*

**Part of mid-value farm**

- Marginally fertile land
- Low-value equipment (e.g., ploughs, trailers, etc.)
- Small homestead
- Small farm buildings

**Level 4**

**Lower-level farm invaders**

- Rural unemployed
- Weaker war veterans
- Some farm workers
- Youths

*Personally undertakes virtually every aspect of farm takeover.*

**Part of low-value farm**

- Low fertility land
- Any remaining resources (e.g., fencing, wiring, roofing, tree cutting, etc.)

**Weaker Farm Invaders**
(many in number)

**Gain Fewer Assets**
(lower in value)

**Figure 6.7** Farm Invader Typology and Farm Resource Objectives
NOTE: Adherence to this pattern was not rigid. Many farm invaders regularly seized land and assets from lower levels but rarely from higher levels.

As Figure 6.7 shows, first, powerful senior officials tended to seize entire farms—and often multiple farms because they had sufficient power to influence the land allocation process and power to deter other claimants.[103] Ironically, while these agents had the greatest ability to employ violence, they were ultimately less likely to use coercive methods because their violent reputations and/or formidable resources led farmers to perceive the circumstances as unwinnable. For example, farmers were unlikely to resist army generals arriving on their farms with soldiers, so takeovers proceeded relatively peacefully. Moreover, these agents had sufficient power to deter competitors; few other farm invaders would have the resources to compete with an army general or government minister, for example. Finally, these individuals rarely undertook actual evictions themselves, relying instead on hired agents to undertake the physical removal of the commercial farmer.

The relationships and objectives outlined in figure 6.7 were not absolute. Some senior officials claimed multiple farms. For example, Mugabe is alleged to have taken over six farms (Lundi stated it is 10), while some estimates indicate that 40% of seized land is in the hands of ZANU-PF's elite.[104] Lundi explained that many of these farms were claimed under other people's names to disguise the true ownership. Other senior officials gained land but had it taken away and given to their rivals following political disagreements.

## Midlevel Invaders: Civil Servants, State Security Officials, War Veterans, and Businesspeople

Midlevel officials who had some resources at their disposal and who could influence the farm allocation process to an extent were active participants in farm invasions. For instance, individuals might have a family member working in the government and through this relationship have enough influence to gain some land and agri-property, although it was unlikely they would have sufficient influence to seize large volumes of assets. Lundi explained: "It was just individual people taking their own initiative to say, 'I've got a ZESA [electricity company] truck.' So I'm probably an engineer, I've got access to a car, I can use that to go and maybe kill a pig [seized from a farm], take the pig to Colcom [abattoir], get the money."

These invaders tended to seize smaller parts of higher-value farms or larger parts of lower-value farms, commensurate with their influence (see figure 6.7). Since these agents did not command such clearly superior resources as elite invaders, they tended to use coercion more frequently. For instance, if an accountant from the Ministry of Education demanded part of a farmer's land the farmer would probably attempt to resist, whereas if a colonel in the army appeared on the farm with two armed soldiers the farmer would probably concede faster. Thus, the accountant would have to be persistent and aggressive in order to seize the farm. Such agents also tended to behave in a predatory manner against weaker invader competitors until their resources ran out. Likewise, midlevel agents tended to lack sufficient power to deter competitors, so these agents had to deploy resources to suppress other farm invaders as well as to evict the farmers. Due to the fact that these agents often had fewer financial resources available to them and had weaker personal ties than more senior individuals, they would often be more personally engaged in farm takeovers. They would personally coordinate logistics, coerce the farmer directly, and motivate groups of hired individuals to threaten the farmer, such as through *jambanja* (rallies to show public support for evicting the farmer), and undermine farming activities, such as though arson and vandalism. Some midlevel invaders would even participate in the actual eviction. Since many of these people were employed in government jobs and therefore unable to visit their target farms on weekdays, violence and intimidation against farmers tended to increase on the weekends.[105]

## Weak Invaders: War Veterans, Rural Unemployed, Farm workers, and Youths

There were also poor farm invaders, such as those from communal areas who would only be sufficiently powerful to gain small pieces of relatively infertile land, or more fertile land but in remote, inaccessible areas (see figure 6.7). Likewise, poorer farm invaders tended to gain low-value agri-property, if they seized any at all. Because of their relative lack of power and influence, these invaders tended to undertake virtually all aspects of farm seizures themselves.

The weakest farm invaders operated like scavengers, seizing what they could. According to Makabusi, weaker farm invaders targeted "just bits and pieces. You know, books, curtains, anything small that could just disappear."[106] Weaker farm invaders would not use violence so frequently, because deploying coercion cost money: youths had to be hired to undertake the violence, and it often took months or years to seize a farm.

## Who Got the "Best" Land and Most Agri-Property?

The relative level of influence and power of a farm invader determined the size and quality of the farm that the individual could target. Yet "cronies" were not the only beneficiaries of land seizures. Indeed, Zamchiya found a broad range of beneficiaries, ranging from high-level ZANU-PF officials to rural peasants.[107] A study conducted by Scoones et al. produced a more contentious claim that "elites" were not the predominant beneficiaries. The researchers state that they have disproven the "myth" that "all the land went to 'Mugabe's cronies'[,] those with access to elite connections and benefiting from political patronage."[108] They go on to say:

> The large group of civil servants, particularly on the A2 plots—and in our sample especially in the sugar estates—were often teachers, agricultural extension workers and local government officials. While not being poor and landless from the communal areas, most could not be regarded as elite, nor often particularly well-connected politically. Indeed, in simple financial terms many were extremely poor, as government wages had effectively ceased during the economic crisis to 2009.

The researchers continue: "The overall picture is complex, but a simple narrative that land reform has been dominated by grabbing by elites is clearly inaccurate."[109]

Yet Scoones and his colleagues fail to take into account several factors that explain how and why individuals of more humble means were able to gain access to land and agri-property. As this book has shown, the seizure of land and agri-property took place in a frenzied atmosphere, and the means and structure of farm seizures evolved organically. Where land and agri-property were of a higher value, more farm invaders would seek it and would apply greater drive and motivation in doing so. Likewise, areas with poorer-quality land and few, high-value assets would see correspondingly fewer claimants using less energy to secure the marginal resources because there was less competition for comparatively lower-value land and agri-property. Assets that had been seized by midlevel and lower-level claimants were usually used or liquidated rapidly, unless a farm invader was very powerful. This was to prevent other invaders from then seizing the assets and leaving the prior claimant with nothing.

So what explains Scoones et al.' findings? There are three factors: misleading land beneficiary data, a timeline issue, and the flaw of a nonrepresentative sample. Indeed, their conclusions largely rest on their findings on percentage profiles of settlers in their study area.[110] According to the researchers, "Our study of 400 households across the 16 sites from Masvingo province showed by far the majority of the new settlers are ordinary people." They then provide evidence showing that "ordinary" people comprised 69.3% of A1 (villagized), 58.1% of A1 (self-contained), 92.3% of informal, and 56.0% of A2 settlers. By contrast, settlers from the security services received 3.6% of A1 (villagized), 5.4% of A1 (self-contained), 3.8% of informal, and 1.8% of A2 plots. For Scoones et al., these figures show that elites (largely in the security services) benefited less, because they comprise a smaller proportion of overall settlers. According to the researchers, this means that the land reform program should be judged as a success.

However, these figures tell an incomplete story. First, Scoones et al.'s definition of "ordinary" is, as the researchers agree, a vague category comprised of "people who had little or very poor land in the communal areas or were unemployed or with very poorly-paid jobs and living in town."[111] Given that the researchers rest so much on this group, greater clarity on who these people were, where they came from, what their political ties were, along with greater depth on their socioeconomic backgrounds, is essential. This is particularly the case given that the "ordinary" categorization is provided by the government—and is therefore of dubious reliability. Moreover, the data presented by Scoones et al. do not differentiate who got what land and to what extent the value of this land and associated assets differed. It is certainly unsafe to conclude, based on these data, that "ordinary" people were able to receive the best land and most of the agri-property at the expense of the security services.

There is also a timeline issue at play which Scoones et al.—as well as Sam Moyo and Hanlon, Manjengwa, and Smart—do not appear to recognize. It is unclear from what data Scoones et al. are making the claim that elites were not the primary beneficiaries of the land seizures, but their study was conducted in 2007 and 2008. The exact year is not as important for the discussion as the general time frame: of the farmers surveyed for this book, 82.8% had been evicted by 2005, and 88.1% had been evicted by 2008. Indeed, Moyo estimates that by 2009 less than 400 of Zimbabwe's 4,300 commercial farms remained.[112] Most of those who continued to farm had conceded the majority of their land and agri-property. So by the time that Scoones et al. conducted their study, the vast majority of farms would already have been stripped of the most valuable agri-property—a process that usually occurred when the commercial farmer was evicted.

This book shows that there was a cascading effect of asset seizures based on the strength of the farm invaders (see figure 6.7). Once stronger land claimants (elites or "cronies") had seized higher-value land and agri-property, less influential farm invaders would only be able to take more marginal land and assets. However, even somewhat senior invaders were evicted by more powerful people on some occasions. Over time, therefore, there were fewer assets available, so by 2007–2008 most farms had been substantially reduced of their original agri-property holdings; for example, farmer Rob Dawes from Mashonaland West, interviewed in 2006, had conceded his second farm and was living on a small section of his primary farm; similarly, rancher George Lyons from Masvingo province had conceded his entire ranch except for the homestead and surrounding garden.[113]

To support their argument that elites did not benefit disproportionately, Scoones et al. detail the beneficiaries in their study site. The researchers note the "large group" of civil servant beneficiaries such as "teachers, agricultural extension workers and local government officials."[114] The researchers insist that these individuals did not constitute an "elite"—and when compared to extremely wealthy and well-connected individuals in Harare, this may be true.[115] However, these professionals would still be relatively well off by local standards and might have some political connections. They had some ability to exercise leverage in order to seize the land and agri-property in their area, perhaps as a result of financial advantages, access to transport and other resources from their workplace, or strong political and family ties. Therefore, they almost certainly constituted a kind of local elite.

Moreover, Scoones et al. also indicate that war veterans held a comparative advantage and thus gained more: "Being influential in the land invasions, war veterans often managed to secure better plots, although not always larger ones."[116] This underscores the point that a local elite, and some war veterans fit in to that category, gained *higher-quality* assets. Therefore, the researchers have actually shown that the "elite" of the given area or with an interest in that area—even if relatively humble by the standards of Harare—did tend to get the better land and agri-property, often at the expense of the nonelite.

Most critical of all, Scoones et al.'s finding that elites were not the primary beneficiaries from land seizures is based on a fundamental flaw, in that their study area is not representative of the broader commercial farming community that their findings purport to represent. They largely undertook their research in former cattle-ranching areas in Masvingo that were relatively dry; this was not land usually used for intensive cropping. Accordingly, these areas would have less valuable land and agri-property than the Mashonaland provinces and would not be a draw for "Mugabe's cronies" and most other national-level elites.[117] Moreover, Masvingo is relatively far from Harare, where most elites were located (as Zamchiya has also pointed out).[118] This made it less likely that high-level officials would target the area—especially given that the much wealthier Mashonaland provinces were more conveniently located nearer to the capital. In fact, Scoones et al. recognize this weakness and indicate that "well-connected elites are few and far between" in their area of study.[119] They continue:

Perhaps because of the distance from Harare, the relatively poorer agro-ecological conditions, the lack of high value infrastructure and the particular local political configurations, in Masvingo province such elite capture is not the dominant story, despite the media assumptions.

When Scoones et al. state that they reject the "myth" that "all the land went to 'Mugabe's cronies'[,] those with access to elite connections and benefiting from political patronage,"[120] in a literal sense they are correct; elites obviously did not get all the land, but no one is really saying that they did. Yet the unrepresentative nature of Scoones et al.' study area means that there is no basis for making a national-level claim that elites were not primary beneficiaries of land seizures.

The real question is not about *land* per se, but about profit and ultimate socioeconomic gain from the massive scale of farm seizures. What is really at stake is not whether elites got a bit more or a bit less land and assets than the rural poor, but who got the high-value assets and who was left with scraps. It is this question—rather than a localized comparison of which groups received the greatest proportion of total land—that is truly fundamental in determining whether the seizure of commercial farms should be regarded as an effort to redistribute the land and correct colonial-era injustices, or as a chaotic asset grab by ZANU-PF supporters.[121]

Moreover, Scoones et al.'s research does show that the "local elite," albeit of lesser stature by Harare standards, did tend to gain comparatively better land and assets.[122] Scoones et al., therefore, have no sound basis to claim they have disproven the so-called myth of elites benefiting disproportionately. In fact, a closer reading of their evidence actually supports the claims that this book makes, that elites gained far more from land seizures than "ordinary" Zimbabweans.

## Competition among Farm Invaders for Resources: Fending Off Rivals

As has been noted, in most, but not all, cases farm invaders were in competition with each other in their efforts to seize farms and agri-property. Evicting the farmer (or at least seizing the farm's assets) was an obvious objective, but it was a goal shared by a great many claimants. With a finite number of farms available, farm invaders routinely competed with each other using professional influence, financial resources, and violence to fend off competitors. For example, an anonymous farmer survey respondent stated, "I was an A2 farm, i.e. for selected party officials. Eventually two party officials were at logger heads as to who would occupy my home. The one broke in and occupied the house."

Sengwe explained how even when farm invaders received official "offer letters" from the government giving them claim to particular farmland, competing farm invaders would still seek the same resources.[123] Despite a farm invader's ostensibly valid claim to the land, in view of the government's post-farm invasion rationalization of land claims, claimants with a competitive advantage easily superseded the "offer letter":

> I remember some people were there on their land with their offer letters, and then soldiers, they would come in. They are not on the waiting list [to claim the land]. . . . They will just say, "I want this area." They look around when they go there [to the farm to see if it is what they want]. If there was someone there, they will say, "Move away with your offer letter. I'm staying here."[124]

Sengwe further noted that because the "offer letter" carried some validity, there was suddenly a proliferation of these letters for the same pieces of land—especially farms that were well stocked with agri-property and natural resources: "We'd have three offer letters on one farm, and I know why they were targeting those farms. [It was those] with the farmhouse, with everything, water, because they [farm invaders] were fighting now with themselves."

Similarly, farmer Rupert Garfield described how the farm invaders engaged in an "open season" to take control over his farm.[125] On one occasion, a group of farm invaders left his property, only for another group to arrive in a vehicle shortly afterward. The logo on the vehicle door had been painted over to hide the company name—this indicated less-affluent farm invaders who had to make use of any available resources to assist in seizing farm assets. The farm invaders said to Garfield: "This is our farm and we're taking it over. So I said, 'Where's your [offer] letter?' They had no documentation whatsoever. So I said, 'Well there's obviously some confusion because you're about the sixth [person] who has come to claim this farm.'"

Zamchiya gave several examples of farm invaders competing with each other for resources.[126] He cited one incident where a local quasi-government committee seized land from a civil servant (who had in turn seized land from a white farmer) under the pretext that the land and its assets (in this case, trees) would be used for community benefit: "War veterans were able to gain the upper hand by arguing that they would use the trees for the greater good and because they were able to use coercive power and threaten other farmers with eviction." Zamchiya witnessed "little development on the farm," but noted that there were allegations from other farmers that the war veterans had sold the trees and kept the proceeds for their own use.

Ultimately a key factor in determining the success of an invader, according to Lundi, was access to sufficient personnel to fend off competitors: "It's a question of numbers. 'I've got more youth who can outfight yours—it's my farm.'"

If farm invaders possessed sufficient wealth and standing, they could hire enough people to secure control of the farm. Lundi elaborated:

> I look at it [the ability to seize a farm] more in terms of power base. If I say I'm a war veteran leader in Goromonzi, I've got maybe 20 followers. Then I've got more clout when it comes to the conferences [where influence could be established]. My district is strong. I've got a strong group of war veterans. Whereas if I'm just a lonely war veteran and I don't have any followers, any other war veterans that I lead, then you don't really have any clout, and you are just like dismissed when it comes to their gatherings up there.

These "numbers" could also come from the ability to rely upon influence and political connections to enable invaders to seize and hold farms. For example, Lundi explained that some senior officials sought cheap labor in order to operate seized farms:

> When the farms were taken over and these guys couldn't pay their workers, that's when they went for the prison labor. But that was only [the] big guys and ministers, the ones who have got access to prison labor. They pay the Prison Service a pittance.[127]

He said the strategy used by farm invaders was to rely upon labor charged at a low rate, but then in practice never pay for the services rendered: "[The prison services] provide labor at a very cheap rate which you don't have to pay now. You can always say, 'I owe the government,' but you might never pay it back!"

Another example of invaders competing with each other comes from an accountant who worked for the state-owned Grain Marketing Board (GMB). Timothy Ngavi said that his boss at the GMB advised him to seize a farm, in order to "supplement your earnings." Ngavi and his boss understood that through his professional connections he could "make a lot of money."[128] Indeed, GMB workers held key advantages in securing crop inputs: "We are controlling the allocation of the seed and fertilizers—get those—go and get a piece of land." Without having to pay for inputs and with the prospect of gaining land for free, farming was an inviting prospect for state employees such as Ngavi.

In order to actually receive confirmation of his "rights" to the land, Ngavi first went to the provincial administrator, who told him to "go and look for any land you want." "I go to find land that is not being used comfortably. I saw the land and I said, 'This is not being used.'" The land he chose had in fact already been seized by a member of the air force from a white commercial farmer. Yet after Ngavi decided that he wanted the land and claimed that it was not being used effectively, an army unit was sent by the provincial administrator to verify Ngavi's choice. Soon thereafter he received an offer letter giving him the right to 300 hectares of land.

The potential for corruption in an arrangement where a prospective farmer chooses his own land by engaging with a provincial government official and the military is obvious. In a twist to the anecdote, Ngavi said that one year later, when he had been visiting overseas, someone else with more "influence" had claimed the land already seized by him. Accordingly, Ngavi's prospects of retaining the property he had claimed looked bleak, leading him to claim ironically, "We really need to do something about property rights in Zimbabwe!"

Cliffe et al. made a similar claim about senior officials using their influence to seize land claimed by other farm invaders: "Some politicians use their muscle to dispossess recipients of land, especially A1 [farmers]; but some 'land grabbers' have in turn been dispossessed of land by war vets and others, so the redistribution continues!"[129]

Sam Moyo, however, paints a more favorable and orderly picture of the land allocation process: "Some elites also illegally occupied land, but most of them relied on state allocations to gain land in an 'A2' Scheme intended to create new middle-sized black-owned commercial farms."[130] This claim is misleading, as while some farm invaders "relied on state allocations," the process of *gaining* the allocations and evicting the farmers was fraught with corruption and violence; it was not a simple, orderly, and transparent bureaucratic exercise of submitting an application and then receiving a determination from an impartial state-sanctioned official, as Moyo implies. Moreover, the senior officials manipulated the "state allocations" system. The *process* was exceptionally corrupt, routinely abused, and prone to manipulation. Senior officials who had the strongest political connections, ties to influential figures, and the financial means to engage in the bureaucratic charade of orderly land allocations were the main beneficiaries.

Competition among farm invaders could result in a periodic respite for farmers whose property was being threatened. Farmers who had trouble determining why their farms were aggressively targeted over a certain period then might receive little attention from land claimants for several weeks. However, Lundi explained that claimants would temporarily stop targeting the farmer until they had resolved among themselves how to divide the farm assets. In doing so, farm invaders would use various tactics, including employing youths to create the "muscle" of a gang-like presence: "I will get my 10 youth, he will get his 10, you will get your 10. So instead of fighting the farmer we were fighting amongst ourselves." Lundi explained that this infighting continued until a victor emerged, at which point the effort to evict the farmer would resume. The victor was often decided by which competing farm invader had sufficient financial resources to bribe a senior ZANU-PF official:

> Probably I [speaking as a hypothetical farm invader] have got protection [a "protection" agreement based on financial payments], so I will go to the minister, and the minister says, "It's your farm." [A competitor] goes, pays more money [to the minister, and the minister says], "It's your farm." He [another competitor] goes, pays more money [to the minister, and the minister says], "It's your farm."

Lundi summed up the competition: "It wasn't so much about maybe harassing you [targeting the farmer all the time]. It was like we are fighting amongst ourselves to see who amongst ourselves is going to get the farm."[131]

Thus, a farm invader's influence and power was directed as much against other land claimants who were in competition for resources as it was against the farmer. Farmer Chris Cleveland provided an example from when he visited the local district administrator's office and saw a map indicating that his farm had been divided into 13 sections, all allocated to "bigwigs."[132] Soon, however, this designation was superseded by "bigger wigs" claiming larger plots than the DA's original subdivisions, and thereby nullifying the claims of other farm invaders. Evidence from Christian Mucheke, a legal officer in the President's Office, supports this claim: "A group of people come and invade the farm. Then tomorrow another senior official comes and invades what is invaded already, so there were victims of the victims of the victims. The main victim was the owner of that farm."[133] These accounts exemplify how in many cases access to land and agri-property was not determined through an orderly process, but rather became a matter of personal influence by which higher-level farm invaders were able to secure better assets.

### Invader Cooperation: "Old-Boys Club" and Profit

Though there was often intense competition among land claimants, in many cases farm invaders proved willing to assist each other. This trend emerged in part from a shared history of service in the military or at least in state security. Lundi explained that there was an "old-boy's club" among state security officials, especially those who had served in the Liberation War or who had lost relatives in the war.[134] Msasa explained that the process had a "trickle-down" effect: "It started from the top. It started with the commanders, then it started going down [the ladder of the hierarchy]."[135] Within this hierarchy the most productive farms were seized by the most senior individuals, who assisted each other in the takeovers: "I remember the wife of the army commander Chiwenga, Jocelyn, who invaded that one [farm]. . . a very productive one. . . . They were going for the most productive farms now . . . the wealthy farms, which they were taking and giving to each other."

Once a method of evicting a farmer or claiming land and agri-property had been devised, farm invaders would "pass word" to friends and colleagues, who would actively assist each other: "I maybe have problems in accessing my farm. Oh, I'll talk to so-and-so. I heard he's got some men for hire, and then I just go and talk to him and then I hire his men." According to Lundi, it was through this means that in part violence and farm seizures proliferated, because a "criminal element" emerged that offered individuals for hire, "smoothing the way for your eventual takeover."[136] It is unsurprising, then, that not only did a market of invaders willing to undertake violent farm invasions emerge, but so did a market for fraudulent land allocation documents and court orders.

A complex system of patronage also came into being (see Zamchiya for two excellent articles on the subject of patronage in Zimbabwe).[137] The patronage system was formed to entrench ZANU-PF's support, but also soon evolved to serve the personal objectives of participants. Individuals of all kinds could leverage family connections and personal networks to gain and retain land and agri-property, and secure agricultural aid from the state, as well as bank loans. Even small-scale beneficiaries and relatively poor people could be part of the patronage system, as Zamchiya has also noted.[138] Such individuals would often operate on a "scavenger" level to seize specific assets. Veteran of the Liberation War Alex Siwaze explained that during farm seizures, the poor would take anything they could find, even small items: "This was a free-for-all that if you don't have a spanner, it is now up to you to get that spanner. If they [invaders] are going to a farmhouse, somebody was coming out with a teaspoon, somebody was coming out with a cup, a teacup, or bucket."[139]

## CONCLUSION

While land was the stated objective for many farm invaders, the findings of this chapter indicate that asset-seeking was also a key driver of the land seizure era. Some invaders were indeed pursuing land, most notably poor war veterans and those in congested communal areas. Yet many others, especially government workers in paid employment, were not genuinely interested in land. They were looking for farm assets that they could easily sell for immediate financial gain without making a long-term commitment to farming.

This claim is demonstrated in part by the large quantities of seized farmland that were never used for farming. It is also supported by the data indicating that it was not the poor and landless who were largely driving the effort to seize farm-related resources, but rather midlevel government workers and especially senior party members who by comparison were already wealthy. In addition, interview data show that through internal networks, senior political officials and members of state security used their influence to secure the distribution of farms to friends, family members, and colleagues. The poor could also benefit from these networks, although they would usually gain lower-value assets.

This desire of farm invaders for equipment resulted from the overall legal and economic instability in Zimbabwe during the land seizure era, in addition to disorder within ZANU-PF. Enforcement of the law had ceased to occur with any impartiality during 2000. With so many officials using their positions in the civil service and state security apparatus to enhance their own financial status, ownership claims did not rest on legal titles but on an individual's ability to protect his claim to assets. Msasa reaffirms this point:

> You won't be secured—if you are not someone influential—if you take a farm, because someone is coming to take it from you again. . . . They [powerful officials] will just see who you are. Who you are, how influential are you? If you are not influential [with ZANU-PF], that farm will be gone [seized by a competing agent].[140]

In such an environment, protecting immovable land was far more difficult than secreting farm equipment. A large piece of land would inevitably draw other claimants. Moreover, the government claimed ownership over farmland and eventually nationalized it. While 99-year leases would be granted, former legal titles became a source of contention, and the notion of landownership became contestable. It would be extremely risky for someone to invest in an expensive farm in an environment where other invaders needed only to use influence or bribery to claim the land themselves.

In the absence of strong protection of property and personal rights, a large number of competitors were able to seek assets. However, with so much competition and with law enforcement barely functioning, the time horizon for most farm invaders was very short. They had to take what they could get, when they could get it. Thus, most farm invaders opted to seize lower-net-value assets—agri-property—but at least gain resources that could be removed and sold for an immediate finical gain, rather than opt for higher-value farmland that then had to be defended from other invaders. Only officials with major financial resources, as well as the ability to deploy extensive violence, could realistically feel secure in seizing control over land as well as agri-property.

This chapter has also demonstrated that the land seizures were concentrated in an area within a 200-kilometer radius of Harare, an area that includes most of the Mashonaland provinces. This region contained the most valuable land and agri-property and could be easily accessed by influential officials, who could summon considerable resources to fight for control over farms and farm assets. It is no coincidence, therefore, that violence was concentrated in this region during the land seizure era. The convenient proximity to some of the most valuable land and agri-property in Zimbabwe for a large pool of government-employed farm invaders is a convincing explanation for high levels of violence in Mashonaland.

The fact that many farm invaders were so motivated by agri-property rather than land has important implications. It reveals that ZANU-PF misrepresented land demands from citizens, and that these purported land demands were largely confined to some war veterans and the communal area poor—individuals who ironically received the least land and agri-property in the end. While war veterans and their demands were undoubtedly influential, there is no doubt that ZANU-PF polarized and radicalized the land issue, manipulating this important constituency so that it supported the ruling party against the MDC.[141] It appears that the Helen Suzman Foundation's survey, which found that only 9% of Zimbabweans believed land reform was the most important issue in the 2000 parliamentary elections, and CIO agent Hasting Lundi's assertion that land redistribution was not widely supported (see chapter 2), are more accurate than ZANU-PF insistence that there was widespread demand for land.[142] The land issue was a political red herring.

# Moving onto Farms

*The Emergence of Extortion and "Protection" Schemes*

Chapter 6 showed that extensive conflict existed among both farm invaders and farmers over farmland and agri-property and that armed invaders possessed varying levels of financial, political, and social power. Some influential officials possessed sufficient resources to allow them to take control over farmland, which could then be operated as a commercial enterprise. Other farm invaders, comprising in large part the rural poor, were relegated to theft of agri-property, which would generally offer only a short-term cash boost. Yet farm invaders of all types were seeking at least some financial resources and were not purely looking to achieve political or ideological objectives in their search for land and agri-property.

It is important to bear in mind that the seizure of farms were rarely completed rapidly. Farmers would typically attempt to negotiate with the invaders in order to be able to remain on their property. This chapter looks at the initial consequences of farm invaders moving onto farms by examining two main types of interactions between invaders and farmers: the existence of short-term theft and extortion practices, and the emergence of long-term protection schemes. These two types of interactions were used by farmers as a means of trying to cope with invaders, while the invaders used them to extract the greatest financial return from farmers. Short-term extortion practices occurred when invaders engaged with farmers over a limited time frame in order to extort money and agri-property, usually in exchange for the promise of protection from further harassment, intimidation, and violence. While the invaders involved in this practice were often the cause of coercion against the farmer to begin with, the potential for some respite was attractive to many farmers. Farm invaders engaged in short-term arrangements would attempt to gain as many assets from farmers as quickly as they could before other claimants with greater coercive power superseded their own claims. Indeed, it is difficult to draw the line between this method of extortion and outright theft or looting. Farm invaders involved in short-term engagements were usually weaker because they lacked the power to simply evict the farmer and to suppress asset-seeking from other claimants. Typically, such extortion practices resulted in fewer financial gains for farm invaders than if they could engage in a long-term extortion agreement with the farmer.

Long-term protection agreements occurred when more powerful farm invaders made an agreement with the farmer, whereby the farmer would pay a fee to the invader for ongoing "protection" from other farm invaders, and in return the invader would profit from the farmer's continued crop production. In this way the farmer could keep producing with some level of security and continuity because he, theoretically, possessed sufficient protection from other land invaders to safeguard his assets and investment. Invaders, however, would need to possess sufficient power to suppress other competitors' efforts to seize the farm and agri-property in order to provide genuine protection and would need to suppress any short-term inclination to seize the farmers' assets for themselves. Their protection needed to be sufficient for at least one full growing season in order for the sustained operation of the farm to be viable from the farmer's point of view.

Short-term extortion offered few benefits to farmers because invaders usually offered only bogus protection and sought as much of the farmers' assets as possible even if it rendered continued production impossible. However, theoretically speaking, long-term protection agreements—which were much less common—offered some advantages in that the fee usually imposed on farmers was sustainable because it was in the racket's interest to keep the farmer producing. Farm invaders in such agreements stood to gain more by benefiting from fees earned over a long time horizon, and farmers in such agreements gained from at least being able to remain on their land and reap some financial benefit without further harassment from other invaders.

## SHORT-TERM EXTORTION IN THE LAND SEIZURE ERA

There was a rapid proliferation of short-term theft and extortion across Zimbabwe soon after the land seizures began. This kind of theft and extortion had no precursor in preexisting criminal behavior. Extortion tended to occur

"spontaneously" as ordinary farm invaders saw an opportunity to gain financial resources (agri-property and sometimes land) and material assets when
the government sanctioned the takeover of commercial farms. Thus, the
number of people engaging in this practice—ranging from senior officials to
landless peasants from the communal areas—was very extensive. Ordinary
people could easily participate.

Within two months of the land seizure era beginning, extortion of farmers
by invaders was being practiced widely.[1] Farmers would initially face demands
for money and agri-property, such as foodstuffs, in return for the extortionist
claiming to protect the farmer from theft or physical harm to his family and
farm workers. Initially, extortion rather than theft, which was more blatantly
illegal, proliferated because the breakdown of law enforcement was gradual
and it took time for farm invaders to realize that outright and overt theft would
not be prosecuted. According to Daniel Inkankezi, a senior military intelligence agent, awareness of very lucrative extortion opportunities spread rapidly
among farm invaders: "People were motivated by the quest to go and get
money there [from farms]. . . . It was what can you [the farmer] do for us [farm
invaders]."[2] As more invaders realized the opportunities for extortion and
theft, there was increased pressure on land claimants to seize assets before
competing farm invaders seized them. This pressure was exacerbated as awareness of the available resources increased.

Facing a sudden breakdown in February 2000 in the enforcement of property rights and an influx of large numbers of predating invaders, farmers were
vulnerable and had few options to protect themselves and their assets. Initially, some farmers made deals with extortionists in the mistaken belief that
by conceding assets they would be given a reprieve from further predation.
Indeed, when invasions began in February 2000, farmers had no way of knowing how long the pressure would last; as chapter 3 highlighted, even Mugabe
initially believed that invasions would be limited in scope. While variables
differed on each farm and depended, for example, on the strategies and attitudes of farm invaders, the value of the farm, and the farmer's response to extortion, farmers obviously tried to remain on their properties for as long as
they felt it made sense to do so. For instance, one anonymous farmer survey
respondent stated: "Firstly, I was (and still am) a farmer and didn't want to give
up doing what I loved, as I believed that the storm would blow over." Another
respondent said, "I believed that being a primary producer I would survive,
and having had comms [communications] with Mugabe and others, and done
everything legally, like a bad smell it would blow away." A different respondent
stated, "Realising I was in a no win situation I adopted a policy of appeasement
and a certain degree of concession [to farm invaders]." This perception—
particularly prior to August 2002 when legal measures were implemented that

made it extraordinarily difficult for farmers to remain on their land—meant that farmers often sought to "buy time" and try to navigate farm invasions by appeasing invaders.

Senior CIO agent Hastings Lundi described the process by which the practice came about: "There was a lot of extortion which happened during that time. Some farmers after realizing, 'We've lost,' they were actually paying the war veterans some protection money. Some people who were actually making money off the farmers were actually getting some protection money and were saying they were kind of protecting them."[3] Thompson Mupfure, a veteran of the Liberation War and senior politician, identified farmers seeking to buy "protection" from invaders in order to secure a reprieve for their farms and homes: "There are some whites who must have succumbed at that point either by giving some of the . . . land invaders some money, buying protection, paying protection fees, and this become [sic] such a common [practice]—this thing to give protection fees, so that then the [farm invasion] commander can say, 'No, we are leaving this farm now.'"[4] Thus, in the early period of the land seizure era, farmers initially believed they could purchase "protection" from predating land invaders to substitute for the breakdown in law enforcement. However, this protection was rarely substantive. Dealmaking merely served to encourage other invaders to target these seemingly pliant farmers, in the hope of seizing assets for themselves.

It is important to emphasize how quickly farm invaders became aware of an opportunity to make money. This led to a frenzy among them to seize a share of the resources available on a farm before their competitors moved in. War veteran and "new" farmer Petros Mzingwane described an extremely rapid proliferation of farm invaders seeking money and agri-property from farmers.[5] Inkankezi stated that the sudden demand for farm assets led to a dramatic increase in corruption as farmers desperately sought to protect their position:

> Why it really got out of control was that was a lot of corruption and bribes going on. Some farmers thought that if they gave these people who are coming to intimidate them some money, they would [leave], and it happened really quick, so these people, like [Chenjerai] Hunzvis and [Jonathan] Moyos, . . . and quite a few other guys who were literally in charge of the [farm seizure] operation per se [were paid]. When they go to farms and threaten this farmer, this farmer says, "No, no, no, no, Mr. Hunzvi, come in here [to negotiate]" [and gives him] a back hander.[6]

Inkankezi explained further that farm invaders were quickly in competition with each other: "Most of the people [farm invaders] that have moved there [onto farms], they almost got into a situation where there is competition [among themselves] to get to this farm or to that farm." Alex Siwaze, another veteran of the Liberation War, recalled that many poor farm invaders saw the seizures as their only chance in life to gain some financial windfall, so they were quick to take advantage of the growing opportunity for bribes and theft: "You might have a poor person without even a kitten, who actually thought that if he grabs four or five beasts of head of cattle, or donkeys there or sheep or goats, at least he will be rich."[7]

Schemes by farm invaders to extort money and agri-property were soon widespread. Inkankezi explained that there was "a lot of money changing hands at the time."[8] He noted that vulnerable farmers were uncertain of how to handle invaders, because although the extortionists were making unlawful demands, they had government backing and clear support from state security officials, who were reluctant to prosecute them.

Many farmers decided to protect themselves through cash payments to threatening farm invaders. Thus, some farmers were "coerced into parting with the money," while others made a conscious choice to do so, "thinking this problem would ease" and that the land seizures "could just be a passing phase."[9] Handing out cash payments or giving away commodities from the farm were relatively attractive to farmers because they were easy to do, did not result in the loss of valuable land or agri-property that might have future value, and tended to avoid binding farmers into relationships with extortionists that might prove even more costly and predatory in the future.

For example, farmer Gerry Garner from Mashonaland West stated that farm invaders would visit him seeking livestock.[10] "They come and try and force the farmers to give them a couple of pigs, and the intimidation would increase with the promise that 'if you give us a pig, we'll pull the thugs off.'" Garner noted that it was often easier to simply concede and give, in this example, a pig rather than face escalating intimidation that would cause even greater disruption and financial loss on the farm.

However, paying out to extortionists did not mean that violence would necessarily cease, and it often encouraged escalating financial demands on the farmer. "If you [the farmer] parted with one or two [hundred thousand dollars] (at that time a hundred thousand was a lot of money in Zimbabwe and a farmer could easily afford that)," recounted Inkankezi, "maybe that would keep you safe for two weeks—you never know."[11] Indeed, farm invaders operating as short-term extortionists offered insubstantial protection and would simply return in the future with new demands and concomitant threats because they knew the farmer was financially able and willing to engage in such transactions. Farm foreman Imminence Ngiwa said that in the district where he worked, even farmers with a history of maintaining good community and labor relations would soon face demands for cash or agri-property from farm invaders: "When you give them [farm invaders] things, then they come after you. Never mind you are doing good or bad."[12] The prospect of financial gain rapidly superseded political objectives.

Extortion quickly became routine. Cash payments resulted in more demands with little recognition of the farmer's finite ability to pay them. Inkankezi noted further:

> Chances are everyone else who was going to the farms, especially the second month or so [March 2000], knew that there's money to be made there. Because the guys that came from there the previous day, or two weeks ago, they were loaded [with money]. So people were motivated by the quest to go and get money there.[13]

This account gives insight into the short-term outlook and competitive predation among farm invaders. Beton Mopane, a farm mechanic, provided an account of the relative ease with which farm invaders could seize agri-property: "I saw some of the war vets, if they come to a white man and start complaining about the farm, if that white man, if he says, 'No, what I'm going to do for you guys, I will give you that bullock. I know you want meat. Then I will give you some bags of mealie meal [ground maize] for you to feed yourselves.'[14] Then they will leave him. They will just take their things, and they will go." Successful invaders returned with relatively large amounts of money, encouraging others to participate before competitors took all the money. Payments therefore had the unintended consequence of fueling additional demands and generating a massive extortion enterprise among farm invaders.[15]

Basic formulas for theft and extortion soon developed, with some invaders relying on aggression, while others sought a more cooperative approach—but with both seeking assets through coercion. War veterans understood that their reputation for violence gave them a key advantage in coercing farmers. Other farm invaders including some war veterans tried a less brazen approach. Christian Mucheke, a legal officer in the President's Office, explained: "Some of them, the war veterans, were more civil. They will come and say, 'Oh, my friend, listen, I need your farm. Let's talk.'"[16] Some invaders would say that they believed they had a right to the land and agri-property, but were willing to be reasonable with the farmer and only take a portion, emphasizing that other farm invaders would be less cooperative, so the farmer would be better off dealing with them. Mucheke explained that by seeming reasonable, some short-term extortionists hoped to gain assets more easily. However, whether through violence or with apparent civility, the ultimate intention of many farm invaders was to gain the greatest wealth possible given the individual's capacity, resources, and time available.

Inkankezi explained what happened when farmers did not concede to farm invaders' demands: "If you've [farmer] got nothing to do [give], the chances are, then, there's a bit of coercion."[17] For instance, the farmer and workers would likely be the focus of threats and violence, livestock and irrigation equipment would be stolen, and crops could be destroyed. This descent into widespread extortion is precisely the reason why the government lost control over the limited farm seizure program that it had originally intended to implement.

Roving extortion gangs were formed soon after the farm seizures began to proliferate. Farmer Eric Fillmore describes a prototypical scenario where extorting farm invaders roamed rural areas seeking farmers to target.[18] Fillmore's workers had wanted him evicted so they could get SI6 worker termination compensation packages, payable by the farmer (as opposed to the government) when the farmer was evicted. Workers had already threatened Fillmore and his family, converging on his homestead in an attempt to intimidate him into leaving: "There was every single woman from the compound [worker village], and they all carried axes and *badzas* [hoes] and machetes." When this strategy failed, the workers brought in a gang of farm invaders to help evict Fillmore from the farm.

Fillmore told of how he was confronted by "six leaders of the big gang." He explained that the "Super Six" was made up of "real thugs . . . two of them I think have been responsible for murders." Fillmore emphasized that "they operated with, I would say, with almost total immunity," suggesting the gang had connections in ZANU-PF or with state security. As a way of making their reputation for violence clear, "They bragged about it [murders in Kariba and Karoi] and said, 'You know, we're bulletproof. We've actually killed people. Have you not read about it in the paper?'" The leaders demanded alcohol from Fillmore and then explained the extortion arrangement: "If I looked after them, they would look after me." Ironically, although the gang had been hired by the workers to evict the farmer, the gang members were actually double-crossing the workers and offering to protect the farmer from his employees in exchange for a fee.

Although Fillmore's farm had not been designated by the government for seizure, the gang had the power through their government connections to target his land holdings. He finally chose not to pay the gang and was "designated [for seizure] soon after that." Fillmore contacted local police to ascertain if this designation was legitimate, to which the police responded that "my name was down for arrest if we were still on the farm [after the eviction date]," a demonstration of the power of roving invasion gangs with government and state security connections.

Fillmore noted that he had paid small sums to the group and provided small amounts of *mealie meal* (ground maize) during negotiations to keep the peace.

While he never paid the higher sums demanded in order for the farm invaders to provide the services they claimed to offer, he also had to keep on good terms with workers through additional small payments to some worker leaders. Thus, while the farmer never conceded to major extortion demands, he was perpetually harassed for small payments in order to try to facilitate a more favorable outcome for himself.

This account underscores the short-term horizon and extensive competition among farm invaders to seize land and agri-property. The farmer initially tried to "buy time" with small payments to the gang and worker leaders, but these provided scant protection and probably only encouraged other extortionists to view Fillmore as pliant. The farmer in this case then recognized he had no viable options to remain on his land, and so he left, reducing his agricultural productivity to zero. Thus, the case offers an example of how short-term extortionists and attempted extortionists so extensively predated on farmers that they were unable to continue production. A long-term protection agreement would, in theory, have allowed the farmer to continue operating, albeit with a heavy fee imposed by the extortionists.

In another example of short-term extorting agents seeking money, farm invaders would temporarily evict a farmer and then use extortion to allow him back on the farm. For instance, farm invaders made their power known to dairy farm manager Philip Mahobohobo by saying, "We are the ones who did this job first [evicted the farmer], and we are the ones who can take him back again. So we want 50 million [Zimbabwean dollars]," about US$9,000 at the time. "Our boss, he said, 'It is too much.'"[19] The farmer eventually paid the figure because he owned a dairy herd and had to attend to the cows regularly. Yet rather than stopping further harassment, the payment only encouraged greater demands—in this case for an expensive farm vehicle. Despite conceding to repeated demands because of his concern for his livestock, the farmer was soon evicted anyway by a different invader.

Another instance of extortion for cash is recounted by Lundi.[20] To a large extent, various lands committees controlled which farms were designated for seizure. In one case, Lundi explained that farmers "used to give Karimanzira [the head of a lands committee] lots of money," in exchange for Karimanzira saying, "We'll leave that farm, we'll leave that farm."[21] Initially, some farmers had approached the lands committee seeking these types of concessions, but the situation changed when violence became commonplace. Lands committee members then realized there was a lot of money to be made in manipulating the farm takeover list. Rather than wait for farmers to approach them, "Some people in the lands committee would go [to farmers] and say, 'Give me so much and then I can give you some protection.'"[22] Lundi stated that "protection" schemes offered by senior ZANU-PF officials provided temporary relief to farmers, in exchange for a payment of money or agri-property to ward off other farm invaders.

From the farmer's perspective, the problem with these schemes was that if too many farmers participated, there would be insufficient quantities of land and agri-property for invaders. Thus, there was a need for exclusivity. Since approaching the lands committee was a particularly successful strategy for farmers in protecting their assets, it became a popular approach, with the competition driving up the demanded price. However, there was no mechanism in place for lands committee members to honor one another's agreements with farmers, so farmers had no recourse or guarantees. Indeed, there were incentives for other committee members to break these agreements in order to try to strike their own deals with farmers. It is obvious, then, that any "protection" would be temporary, with predation eventually destroying all incentives for the farmer to continue to produce.

The opportunism of the lands committees and the propensity for manipulation and corruption is given a light touch by some researchers. However, farmers interviewed for this book, who actually had to engage with these individuals routinely, relayed the nearly overwhelming corruption of the lands committees and incessant, unsustainable demands made by them for kickbacks and illegal payments.

Many short-term extortionists also sought agri-property. One respondent described how farm invaders forced farmers to hold auctions so large quantities of agri-property could be "bought" for almost nothing by farm invaders. Mucheke explained the process: "A lawyer would just come to your farm and say, 'There is a problem here. Your workers are complaining.'"[23] Under the pretext of addressing worker revenues, the invader would then tell the farmer: "I have come to sell your beasts, and it's an auction. And people will be coming to buy now and the money is going to pay your workers, and you must leave tomorrow." Ostensibly the money for the auction would be used to pay workers.

According to Mucheke, auctions were not widely publicized so as to limit competition among farm invaders, and the farmer was not allowed to bid. To make the auction appear more plausible, "There are lorries coming with war veterans with money. They will be buying a cow for as cheap as one [dollar]. They will buy a tractor for two dollars [and] twenty cents in those days, and they say the money is going to pay the workers and then those guys pocketed the money or paid the workers and then pocketed the rest."[24]

In reality, farm invaders were often representatives of a senior official and were "buying" the agri-property on this official's behalf. Mucheke explained that "after four days you will see that farm has been taken by a [government] minister. I have personally gone to farms. I have personally done auctions, and

I have personally witnessed ministers, army commanders taking over those farms."[25] With an auction arrangement, however, the process would appear legal, so that the senior official could not be accused of theft. Mucheke explained that senior ministers easily dealt with protesting farmers in this scenario:

> They have a plan where the following morning you can go and dump a package of drugs and then charge the farmer with drug trafficking, and then tell him that you can go to prison for twenty years or leave the farm. Or kill one worker and then say to the farmer, "You are the one who killed him," even if he is not, and then tell him to leave. Or first tell him all of the rest of the people are angry outside there because their colleague has been killed. And a lot of racial connotations were raised in order to enflame the people.

Any of these threats would be plausible and would be extremely threatening to the farmer who already knew that he could not rely on an impartial police force and legal system. Especially noteworthy is Mucheke's awareness that people could be easily fomented by race-baiting, exacerbating the farmer's vulnerabilities. Under these threats, the farmer would have little choice but to leave his farm without his assets.[26]

In other instances invaders could profit from desperate farmers who needed to quickly sell agri-property because they were facing eviction or, in the case of livestock owners, could not continue supporting their animals. For example, farmer James Shore from Mashonaland Central said that when he moved from his farm he no longer had anywhere for his cattle to graze, so he had to sell 800 head of cattle "at rock-bottom prices because the slaughterhouses were absolutely inundated."[27] Similarly, farmer Gerald Burr from Mashonaland West also highlighted that, because of a saturated market, livestock only commanded very low prices: "We sold all our cattle at low prices. I mean we gave them away, but at least we got rid of them."[28]

As for farm invaders with fewer resources to seize land and agri-property outright, farm manager Ketani Makabusi reported that when invasion groups first moved onto a farm they told the laborers: "We are going to remove these commercial farmers so we can give *you* guys this land."[29] With this assurance, workers would get more enthusiastic and believe they had an interest in protecting the agri-property. Workers were told to "cling onto everything" and not let anyone take it. The problem for the workers was that once the farmer was evicted, the leading farm invader or the senior person who was orchestrating and paying the invasion group simply arrived on the farm, evicted the workers, and kept the land and agri-property for himself: "In other words the people [workers] were basically used."

Short-term extortion schemes predominantly sought money and agri-property. Occasionally, however, political support was exchanged for protection. Siwaze related that an arrangement developed on one ranch that exchanged workers' votes for protection of the property: "A ballot box was given to a farmer and the ballot box was actually monitored by the farm laborers. And all the voters of that farm voted for this Obert Mpofu.[30] To prove that there is not even one person who is voting for the opposition, that ballot box was counted alone—which is not existing [not allowed] in the laws of the electoral system."[31] In exchange for a ballot box of votes, the farmer and workers would not be harassed: "They [farm invaders] don't have any means of accusing him [farmer]. He's an employer giving work to blacks. He is actually assisting the government of the ZANU-PF to win the elections, right? So how can he be removed from that farm?"[32]

This trading of farm votes for protection had obvious limitations. First, protection could only be secured during election periods. After Mpofu was elected, there would be no mechanism for the farmer to ensure continued protection. Moreover, the votes did not have constant value, so there was no guarantee that the service would continue to motivate the war veterans. For example, if Mpofu was confident of his election prospects, the votes would lose value and he might seize the farm anyway. Thus, at best, such an arrangement would only be of temporary benefit.

From the farmer's perspective, the prevalence of short-term extortion presented three options. First, acceding to the invaders' demands usually resulted in no real gains for the farmer and only emboldened invaders to seek more assets. Second, the farmer could try to ignore extortion demands, but this usually resulted in a serious increase in harassment, which most farmers eventually found unsustainable. A third option was for the farmer to engage in a long-term protection scheme with an invader.

One seemingly logical solution was for farmers to work together against invaders to control protection prices and provide collective solutions. Yet collective action rarely occurs in large groups, because in order for the cooperative benefit to be achieved, some individuals will be unable to advance their personal interests. These individuals then decide to pursue their own interests despite—and at the cost of—group welfare, thereby undermining the collective action. During the land seizure era, not all farmers had the same number of assets at stake or faced the same threats from invaders. The variation of farmer assets is indicated by the survey data, where farm valuations ranged from US$25,000 to about US$24,000,000, and valuations of equipment ranged from US$250 to approximately US$1,000,000. While some farmers faced severe violence in the first few months of the land seizure era, others were not threatened until 2001 or 2002 or even later. Individuals facing extreme violence or with large holdings at stake—or indeed those with little at stake—might seek their own solutions, potentially at the cost of a collective arrangement. Indeed, it should not be assumed that farmers were a homogenous group that would act collectively. Angus Selby shows that farmers have historically been fractious and prone to individual action, even on seemingly trivial matters.[33] It would have been difficult to persuade some farmers to operate against their self-interest, given the extensive personal and financial commitments that they had to their land, which was bound up with their homes, entire livelihoods, and the safety of their family and workers. Thus, collective action among large numbers of farmers did not emerge during the land seizure era.

## LONG-TERM PROTECTION SCHEMES IN THE LAND SEIZURE ERA

Given the weakness of the strategy of either conceding to extortion demands or trying to ignore them, it could be reasonably assumed that there would be widespread attempts among farmers to engage with farm invaders offering long-term protection schemes. These schemes involved invaders who had sufficient strength to claim an entire farm outright and sufficient resources to deter other invader claimants. They could then offer the farmer protection to enable him to continue operations (see chapter 6 for a discussion about farm invader typology). The invader would not gain profit from the outright seizure of the farm but would get a steady income over many years, which would result in a far greater overall financial gain without the need to actually run the farm.

In many respects, the long-term model appears to be a logical fit during the land seizure era. There were vast numbers of senior politicians and members of state security with sufficient power to become long-term protection agents, and there were 4,300 farms under threat. The scheme seems especially attractive given the numbers of senior officials living in Harare who had other jobs or lacked the resources or inclination to be farmers and so would benefit from the experienced farmer's continued operations. Indeed, it has been widely noted that many invaders possessed almost no farming skills. Lundi explained the problems faced by one minister: "I talked to [the governor of Harare, David] Karimanzira at times. . . . He can't even farm himself and he has six farms. He is a minister but he can't farm."[34] Lundi explained that Karimanzira lacked the working capital, expertise, and willingness to personally be a farmer, so his seized land remained unused. Msasa made similar claims about politicians who seized land.[35] Similarly, Jane Garfield, a farmer's spouse, noted that invaders in her area came to the farm only on weekends, indicating they had other jobs.[36] Farms require almost daily attention, so attending to farm duties only on weekends would not be commercially viable. Moreover, many invaders lacked working capital, making commercial farming even more unlikely.[37]

Farm workers gave numerous similar accounts. For example, mechanic Beton Mopane said that invaders assumed they could farm but quickly realized they needed skills and capital: "They were thinking that farming is easy, but when they started they realized it was very difficult, just from not even paying their workers. They were failing to get their tractors serviced. They were failing even to buy the tractor. They were failing to do that, so they [were] finding that it is difficult to have a farm."[38] Foreman Telmore Nyakasanga said bluntly:

> The problem is that these people [farm invaders], they don't know farming. They don't know farming. If they were people who know what they're doing, yes of course if you help them this year, then next year they will be able to do [farming] on their own. But now it's [been] almost five years. . . . They just come by the gate and say, "Hey, we need assistance. We need assistance. We need assistance."[39]

Accordingly, it would have been logical for these kinds of powerful agents to adopt the long-term protection model.

By 2009, however, less than 400 farmers of the original 4,300 remained; some 88.1% of respondents surveyed for this book had left their farms by 2008.[40] The widespread eviction of farmers is both an indication and a cause of the fact that long-term schemes with farm invaders could not usually survive for an extended period.

Farm invaders had to be able to meet several conditions in order to engage in long-term agreements with farmers. They had to stop short-term extortionists from seizing the farmer's land and agri-property. They had to provide sufficient stability, security, and predictability on the farm to enable production for at least one full growing season. They had to demonstrate some modicum of trustworthiness and "reasonableness" to the farmer. For example, they could not agree to a fee and then constantly try to renegotiate the terms or make other demands of the farmer that would render the arrangement unsustainable. Finally, they had to find a farmer willing to make a deal with a long-term protection racket.

While evidence from numerous farmer interviews suggests that only a small minority of farmers were willing to come to such an arrangement, some farmers did engage in dealmaking with invaders in order to stay on their farms.

Police officer Edison Bubye said that one way to identify which farmers had protection arrangements was to look at farms where there was an absence of coercion:

> The farmers who managed to stay, they've entered into deals with people like the police chiefs, the army chiefs, the air force chiefs, whoever, even a senior government official, even the minister, then to say, "Look here, this is your farm. I'll work for you, or we're in a partnership." Those were the farmers that were not touched because you find that there are farmers where there was police presence protecting that farm.[41]

Peter Msasa, a military intelligence agent, stated that some farmers had an attitude of "If you can't beat them, join them."[42] He explained that the farmers who remained on their property late into the land seizure era were able to do so because "they are doing something. Either they pay the provincial governor or something. They are not only there for professional reasons, no." Msasa also gave evidence of the strength of some of these protection arrangements, citing a farm in Manicaland that even had a delegation of farm invaders who went to see Mugabe personally to advocate that the farmer should remain. This supply of "protection" services by extortionists to farmers in exchange for fees was compared by Msasa to a criminal syndicate operating in a space where ordinary law enforcement no longer functioned: "It's like now they [farm invaders] are operating like Mafia. They have to pay something, you see. That is how they [farmers] are surviving there."

Farmer respondents also asserted that some farmers engaged in dealmaking with invaders in order to remain on their farms. Debbie McKinley, a farmer's spouse and activist, identified farms in Mashonaland East where the farmers made arrangements to remain on their farms.[43] These farmers were also making large profits because the scarcity of other farmers, most of whom had been evicted, had driven up commodity prices. Farmer Thomas Barkley also stated that he knew some people who had made long-term protection arrangements.[44] Barkley indicated that the components of this deal were simple: the farmer had to be "100% party line [a ZANU-PF advocate] and paying them off, and doing everything [all the work on the farm]." Barkley added, however, that the "very controversial subject" of farmers engaging in long-term dealmaking with farm invaders caused "bitterness" among those farmers who had not made such arrangements.

It is therefore reasonable to conclude that many, if not all, of the less than 400 farmers remaining on their land in 2009 (Moyo's estimate)—approximately 9% of farmers on their land in 2000—were engaged in some kind of protection arrangement with one or more state official.[45] Scoones et al. suggest the same in their study of Masvingo province: "New deals have to be struck with new neighbors on the resettlement schemes, and securing alliances with key officials is always important."[46]

Two examples of long-term schemes were identified during the research for this book: one in Mashonaland Central, and one in Manicaland. In the Mashonaland Central case, farmer James Adams was approached by a farm invader from the military with an "offer letter" for the Adams farm: "He [the farm invader] had been given an offer letter that would never stand up in court because he hadn't even got the title deed name right, but I just kept quiet about that."[47] Adams could see that a takeover was inevitable, indicative of the highly competitive short-term extortionist environment. Although he could have contested the letter in court, he decided upon a different strategy. By making an agreement with a particularly powerful invader whom he perceived to be less violent, and who could provide stability through his military connections, he was effectively choosing his own takeover agent. Adams made it clear that this decision was a last resort, with his only other option being to leave the farm.

The arrangement involved the military official taking formal possession of the entire farm. According to ZANU-PF documentation, therefore, the farm was no longer the property of the farmer but was owned and controlled by the invader. While the farmer appeared to outsiders as simply the manager, he in fact operated the farm much as he had done in the past. The protection agent clearly benefited from the deal, as he was appointed as a paid director of the farm company controlled by the farmer. Adams explained that he proactively gave the military official a high profile in the arrangement and asked him to attend managers' meetings. As a result, the invader had more personal interactions with the farm and indeed became somewhat integrated with it, giving him a vested interest in its continued operations.

The primary reason Adams's situation was initially workable was that the invader possessed sufficient coercive power to deter competing claimants. There are three secondary explanations. First, Adams made sure to raise awareness in the community about the military connections of the official offering protection, which served to publicly identify the invader and dissuade short-term extortionist competitors. Second, Adams cultivated the military official's involvement and interest in the farm's success, thereby encouraging his continued support. Third, for the arrangement to work, the invader had to be integrated into farm operations in order to see that farm resources were finite, that he could not simply extort the farmer until the business collapsed, and to recognize that the farm's survival would yield him long-term profits.

In addition to protecting the farm from other invaders and allowing him to run the entire operation much as he had done before, Adams explained another benefit that became more relevant as the overall agriculture industry collapsed and farm inputs and fuel became harder to purchase. The farmer realized that the invader had useful contacts in government and could use his influence to help procure fuel and other supplies. Thus, in addition to providing a "front" for the business, making it appear black-owned and under the control of a member of the military, the relationship had a secondary function: the invader supported the regular operation of the farm during the land seizure era when certain scarce commodities could only be reliably purchased through the influence of senior officials.

Over time, three constraints emerged in Adams's arrangement, which the invader could not prevent. First, although the invader could stop competitors from seizing the property, he could not protect the farmer from constant harassment through requests for handouts and free assistance (such as the preparation of farmland for seed planting) from "new" farmers, neighboring invaders, and invaders passing by the area. Adams explained that on a given day there would be "20 guys" coming to him seeking help with their crops, asking him to fix equipment or to give them cash loans, or requesting free inputs such as seed, fertilizer, and chemicals. The constant requests proved costly. According to Adams, approximately "20%" of the requests were met in order to maintain tranquility, but the cost of these contributions became burdensome as they were made in addition to the proceeds being directed to the military official in return for protection.

Strong invaders might deter competitors who either arrived on the farm to make a claim or, more likely, promoted their claims to the district land committees or the ZANU-PF elite; these were direct confrontations that were easy to identify and confront if the strong invader had sufficient influence. But small, informal requests such as from farm workers, "new" farmer neighbors, or individuals from the local community approaching the farmer directly were not a threat to the farm operation. They were calls for favors, assistance, and handouts that could easily be made but had a drag on the farmer's time and resources. Farmers also faced rampant theft. For the farm invader, who usually lived in a nearby city such as Harare and whose influence was largely political, their power to stop stem the relentless tide of small yet debilitating interruptions was limited. Thus, even a relatively strong farm invader struggled to offer meaningful protection in a context where the basic rule of law had ceased to apply. Only exceptionally powerful invaders with extensive resources could provide complete protection for the farmer.

A second constraint in Adams's case was that while the invader could provide basic stability, he could not prevent the breakdown of the farmer's community.[48] Because long-term protection schemes were rare, most other farmers and their families were evicted over time. So while Adams remained on his farm and had sufficient income for his family, he had no nearby friends, community, local clubs, or social occasions. Nearly all white farmers were un-comfortable socializing with the "new" farmers, most of whom were invaders who had seized the property belonging to the farmer's neighbors and friends. Given the racial and political tensions, as well as the pervasive violence and intimidation used in farm seizures, the remaining white farmers felt even more isolated given that most "new" farmers were core ZANU-PF members, many of whom served in government or in state security. Adams emphasized that while he still retained some aspect of his farm and a much-reduced income, he and his family felt totally isolated and continually contemplated leaving.

A related social problem was criticism from fellow farmers. Elizabeth Shore, a farmer's spouse, described such farmers as essentially being collaborators with the farm invaders.[49] She felt that these kinds of farmers made it worse for others who stood by their principles—and property rights—and left their farms rather than strike deals with criminals. Shore agreed that bargaining would have allowed her to stay on her farm for some additional period of time. However, she said:

> It is not within my conscience. We have never lived like that. We don't think that way. And you know, at the end of the day it is our farm—why should we bargain? I don't go into somebody's house down there and say, "I am going to occupy your spare bedroom unless you pay me whatever." It is the same thing. We don't do it. There is nothing wrong with owning something.

It is clear was that farmers who entered into long-term protection arrange-ments faced serious stigma from within the farming community. This was es-pecially the case because many evicted farmers were facing dire hardships and viewed those staying on their farms as profiteers. Indeed, these dealmaking farmers have been referred to as "white war vets," a deeply unflattering label. An International Crisis Group report stated that many farmers were "embar-rassed" by engaging in deals with invaders.[50] Accordingly, farmers would likely have been deterred from engaging in arrangements with long-term pro-tection schemes as a result of these kinds of social consequences.

The third constraint was that Adams's arrangement gave only imperfect se-curity to the farmer. While the arrangement may have been preferable to evic-tion or harassment by short-term extortionists, the farmer was still subject to a myriad of threats, even from the military official with whom Adams had made an arrangement. Adams cited one instance where the invader's son was urging his father to take over the farm entirely. While the farmer was able to suppress the son's demands, the threat of outright eviction was ever present.

The long-term protection agent was in effect always threatening to become a short-term extortionist and seize all of Adams's assets. For example, it was possible that if the invader had been threatened by a more powerful individual, he may have quickly resorted to seizing the whole farm in order to gain something before the stronger individual seized it. Thus, the farmer could continue making a modest profit, while sharing much of it with the long-term agent, but he was very unlikely to make further investments in the farm. At best, production would remain at current levels, but it would not increase because there was insufficient trust between Adams and the invader.

From the perspective of the invader providing protection, however, Adams's arrangement was beneficial. Undertaking nominal work and relying extensively on his reputation for violence through his position in the military, the invader on Adams's farm gained substantial financial rewards. He did not have to work the land, worry about the crops, or undertake daily work duties. He simply came to some meetings and occasionally used his influence to help the farm operations. For that nominal effort, he was rewarded with a large portion of the farm's profits.

Yet a fourth constraint—which was the responsibility of the invader—was the ever escalating level of fees he demanded from the farmer. In the case of Adams, the invader's son had constantly urged his father to take a greater percentage of the farm's profits.[51] The increase in fees at some point reached a level where it was no longer financially viable for the farmer to remain. Lundi commented on this threshold when discussing the diminishing number of farmers who remained on their land after March 2002: "Those few [farmers] who were there, they were probably they were paying too much protection fees to the influential ministers and probably to the soldiers as well."[52] Constant threats to increase fees had the consequence of weakening trust between farmers and farm invaders, and farmers would become unwilling to invest more than the minimum to continue operations. This had the effect of constraining growth and preventing possibly greater profits for both the farmer and the invader who provided protection.

## THE PREVALENCE OF SHORT-TERM EXTORTION
## AND LONG-TERM PROTECTION SCHEMES

It should not be assumed that all farmers only chose a short-term or long-term option although many, if not most, farmers experienced at least some short-term extortion. Farmers would engage with extortionists merely as a matter of survival, and often for relatively small losses such as some beef or a crate of alcoholic drinks. Protection arrangements also existed for farm invaders who had seized property from former white owners. Lundi explained that payments were made by farm invaders to more senior individuals who possessed more "clout" and could provide protection from competing farm invaders: "If you [a farm invader on a seized farm] harvest, then you say if it wasn't for him [the powerful protecting agent], then I wouldn't be here. He has 10% of my earnings."[53]

What is clear, however, is that genuine and successful long-term schemes were very rare. There are three key reasons why short-term extortion was far more prolific. First, there was an enormous market for farms and agri-property for a large number of potential extortionists to target. Second, short-term extortion did not require locating a farmer willing to make a long-term agreement with an invader. Third, short-term extortion avoided the major political problem for the invader of having to do business with white farmers, most of whom were suspected by ZANU-PF of being MDC supporters. There was a very extensive pool of agents available to participate in seizures of land and assets. Given the serious deterioration in the economy, with inflation reaching 404% and unemployment topping 60% by 2002, it is easy to see why these individuals would be motivated to target farms in this way.[54]

At the same time, there was a large market of land and agri-property to be seized. Large-scale commercial farms made up 11.8 million hectares of land in June 2000.[55] Given that both gazetted (designated by government for seizure) and nongazetted farms would ultimately be targeted, all of the 11.8 million hectares was theoretically available for invaders to seize. Chapter 6 detailed the enormous value of equipment that was available. Theoretically, all of the equipment and livestock on all the farms was also accessible for theft.[56] Given the pool of agents and availability of land and agri-property, it is easy to understand how short-term extortion became rampant.

Recognizing the relative value of earnings in relation to the value of agri-property can give a sense of the incentive for ordinary people to engage in short-term extortion. In 2000, a civil servant in education was earning US$3,779 per annum, whereas a farm worker was earning US$309 per annum.[57] Figure 7.1 and Table 7.1 show this relative decline in average per annum earnings for the public services in the period leading up to the 2000 farm seizures, and a substantial fall in relative earnings of civil service positions (agriculture earnings are provided for comparison) after farm invasions began. For instance, public administration, education, and healthcare workers earned less than half as much in 1995 as they did in 1980.

For civil servants earning comparatively low salaries, the prospect of procuring almost immediate wealth by targeting farms proved immensely attractive. Inkankezi explained that "there was a lot of money there [on farms]. I tell you, a lot of people became millionaires overnight at that period."[58] A civil servant extorting just one tractor from a farmer would have gained the

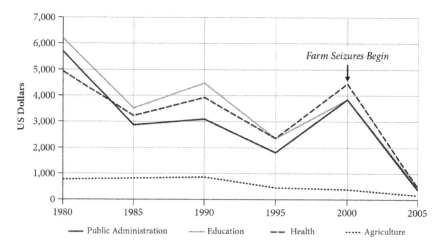

**Figure 7.1** Civil Servant and Farm worker Earning Data

*Table 7.1* CIVIL SERVANT AND AGRICULTURAL WORKER EARNING DATA

|      | Public administration | Education | Healthcare | Agriculture |
|------|-----------------------|-----------|------------|-------------|
| 1980 | 5,668                 | 6,144     | 4,894      | 701         |
| 1985 | 2,782                 | 3,457     | 3,171      | 733         |
| 1990 | 3,015                 | 4,423     | 3,865      | 803         |
| 1995 | 1,748                 | 2,261     | 2,288      | 368         |
| 2000 | 3,800                 | 3,779     | 4,417      | 309         |
| 2005 | 293                   | 385       | 382        | 71          |

NOTE: All figures in US dollars.

SOURCE: John Robertson, "General Zimbabwe Statistics," email to author, 2008; calculations by Tara McIndoe Calder, letter to author about the land seizure era.

equivalent of more than five years' pay.[59] Even if a civil servant could not manage to access such a high-value item, a more attainable goal might be 10 beef cattle, valued at US$300 each.[60] These cattle equaled nine months' earnings for a civil servant, and 10 years' earnings for an agricultural worker. These substantial gains inspired intense and unqualified competition, both among farm invaders and with farmers.

In addition, law enforcement activity was negligible. Thus, the conditions for extortion by thousands of ordinary but opportunistic people were optimal. In fact, the prospect for rapid gains in personal wealth meant there was a frenzy of asset seeking. Inkankezi noted that "there was actually a rush for this one [farm invader] to get to that farm so he can get the money before you [another farm invader] can get it."[61] A key underlying reason for this scramble was that short-term extortion was relatively easy and cheap to undertake, and required no working capital, expertise, or long-term commitments. With large numbers of willing farm invaders, large quantities of land and agri-property to target, nominal law enforcement interference, and an urgency to seize assets before competitors did so, short-term extortion became rife.

Farm invaders providing long-term protection had only limited power that existed within the confines of the farm. Farmers had the option of engaging in an agreement with these farm invaders and thus being subject to this power, or leaving their farms and avoiding all arrangements with farm invaders altogether. Therefore, long-term relationships required both an invader willing to offer long-term protection and to work with the farmer, and a farmer willing to work with the invader. This made the agreement, in effect, a working relationship between the two, despite the presence of coercion. It was fundamentally also difficult for two such individuals to ever find out about each other.

For many senior invaders, farming was very much a secondary or even irrelevant concern. They wanted the homestead, land, rents charged from former farm workers, and benefits from the sale, use, or rent of any farm equipment. The fact that many invaders were not looking to be farmers might suggest that it would be logical to allow the lawful owner to continue running the farm. Indeed, some invaders would undoubtedly have preferred the income from a long-term relationship with the farmer. Yet the relationship carried the problem of who would supply working capital, and it raised challenges when other, more powerful invaders, sought justification to seize the land.

It must also be remembered that many senior invaders had multiple considerations and objectives—both financial and political. If these senior invaders only sought a financial objective, then it is logical they should choose the most lucrative option, which was to engage in a long-term protection scheme. However, many powerful farm invaders had no interest in working with farmers, and not all farmers would work with invaders—as was shown in the account from Elizabeth Shore.[62] In fact, farmers and farm invaders alike were often deeply opposed—morally, socially, and politically—to working with each other. From the perspective of farmers, invaders were simply stealing their assets and those of their neighbors, so working with them raised issues of ethics and trust.

Similarly, white farmers were an avowed political enemy for many farm invaders, so there was little incentive to make long-term business arrangements with them when there was an opportunity to seize their assets outright.

ZANU-PF's primary objective during the land seizure era was to retain political power, which was being threatened by the MDC and its purported farmer supporters. To suppress the MDC, ZANU-PF invoked an extensive and pernicious antiwhite, anticolonial, and anti-Western agenda. For senior politicians, their livelihoods, power, and potentially their personal freedom (since some could likely be prosecuted for *Gukurahundi* crimes) were at stake if the MDC gained power. Suppressing the MDC was therefore of great importance for invaders with ties to the government.

Moreover, many officials were also ex-combatants who fought the Rhodesian military and were likely to carry ongoing animosity toward white farmers and their descendants. Even if a high-level farm invader was indifferent to white farmers or even sympathetic to their losing their property, officials had to appear to their colleagues to be toeing the ZANU-PF political line. Given the political conditions, it would have been difficult to make business deals with the white "enemy," despite the potential for profit. Indeed, these invaders running protection rackets were in fact *protecting* white farmers. Senior officials in long-term protection schemes with farmers had difficulty concealing the arrangement from other ZANU-PF officials and competing invaders who might cite the arrangement as justification for themselves seizing the farm. Thus, many were reluctant to engage in long-term arrangements with a white farmer and suspected MDC supporter.[63]

The following examples show how political concerns informed and often supplanted economic considerations. Farm foreman Telmore Nyakasanga said invaders would have meetings during which farmers remaining in an area were identified: "We [farm invaders] can see there are still three [or] four bosses [farmers] there. What are they still doing in your area?"[64] The farm invaders in charge of a certain area would then feel greater pressure to evict the farmers, while other invaders would be aware of exactly which farmers were remaining in case they were interested in seizing the properties. Nyakasanga's account indicates that the farmer's presence drew scrutiny, leading invaders who were offering protection to face pressure from multiple angles: pressure to conform to party values, and pressure to withstand competitors who knew exactly where the protector's farm was located. Only a motivated and powerful official could withstand these challenges and protect the farmer.

Mupfure explained more fundamentally why long-term protection arrangements were unlikely: "This strategy [farm seizures] was never meant to address the land issue. It was a strategy to address a political issue."[65] What was at stake for ZANU-PF was a power shift toward an emerging opposition party that they needed to permanently stop: "When you camp at the white man's house, you're not so much saying, 'I want land,' but you are saying, 'For you to defy me by supporting a different political party, it means that probably I should kill you, and probably you leave or you begin to support ZANU-PF.'"[66] Mupfure's point is fundamental in explaining the paucity of long-term protection schemes. Ordinary people could become short-term extortionists and steal from farmers because they had no overriding political agenda with which compliance was compulsory, but senior officials had to abide by ZANU-PF's primary objective—suppressing the MDC. Working with whites would be hard to justify given the racial tensions, and therefore it was rational for senior officials to avoid these kinds of deals.

## CONCLUSION

By March 2000, farmers faced extortion from multiple claimants demanding tracts of land or access to agri-property. Given farmers' comparative wealth and extreme vulnerability, it could have been assumed that long-term protection schemes would have been more common, as these would have ultimately yielded greater gains for farm invaders. These agreements, however, were comparatively rare, as demonstrated by the fact that the overwhelming majority of commercial farmers had been evicted by the end of the land seizure era in 2008.

There were three main reasons that short-term extortion was much more widespread than any long-term protection arrangements. First, there were vast farm resources available for individuals to easily target, and extensive demand for these resources from large numbers of ordinary people. Second, short-term extortion was a relatively simple practice of threatening victims into relinquishing their property, and it required no specialist skills. It also did not require the cooperation of a powerful official willing to do business with a white farmer, and a farmer willing to do business with a threatening and predatory invader, which was a rare occurrence. Third, invaders carrying out short-term extortion did not have to contend with competing financial and political objectives. While invaders running protection rackets would gain more financially from a long-term relationship with a farmer, they would also then be engaging in business with ZANU-PF's political, and purportedly historical, enemy. Short-term extortion did not test these competing prospects and obligations and simply offered large prospective financial rewards.

The actual protection offered under long-term protection agreements was imperfect, and the arrangements themselves were unstable. Farmers were still susceptible to invaders changing the terms of the agreement and potentially seizing all the farmer's assets—in effect reverting to short-term extortion. While the officials running protection schemes provided some macro-level protection from other predatory farm invaders, they could not stop constant micro-level harassment and demands from local ZANU-PF officials, "new" farmers, workers, and other farm invaders. Furthermore, a deal to gain long-term protection brought some financial security for the farmer, but he was still left socially isolated. This isolation was a serious problem given that farmers often had families and were living in deeply rural areas against the backdrop of an extremely hostile political environment.

In any event, powerful officials with the capacity to provide long-term protection rarely did so. This is because, in practice, officials engaged in farm seizures had multiple, competing considerations, in addition to seeking financial gain. For many farm invaders with links to ZANU-PF, making a business arrangement with white farmers was personally, socially, and, above all, politically unfeasible. So while financial objectives alone would have compelled the invader to engage in schemes that allowed him to profit while the farmer remained on the land, other considerations prevented these schemes from taking effect.

As it gradually became apparent that protection schemes would be untenable in the long term, farmers were faced with an exceptionally difficult position as invaders sought to force them off the land. Chapter 8 analyzes the methods used to evict farmers and seize their land and assets. It assesses how the breakdown in rural security created conditions of chronic insecurity that undermined the ability of farmers to operate their farms commercially, as well as their willingness to continue living on farms as their families and workers became increasingly vulnerable.

# Farmer Eviction Methods

The two key objectives underlying the farm invasions were the suppression of the MDC political opposition and the seizure of farmland and agri-property. The use of very extensive violence against both farm workers and their farmer employers was key to farm invaders as they sought to achieve these goals.

The use of violence against farmers had a seemingly common-sense result: farmers would eventually capitulate to the invaders and leave their farms. The problem with this supposition is that while some farmers were forcibly evicted, others faced extensive, ongoing violence but did not immediately leave. Indeed, numerous farmers still remained on their properties even in 2002, two years after the land seizure era began and after they had been subjected to sustained violence and intimidation.[1] It is not immediately clear why some farmers remained on their farms longer than others.

The existing literature does not explain which methods of evicting farmers were most successful, how farmers managed risks associated with farm invaders, and what explicit aspects of violence and intimidation were the most important in informing farmers' decision-making on whether to remain on their properties. While some farmers were forcibly evicted, almost all farmers sustained a period of intimidation and possibly violence before they left their farms.

This chapter seeks to demonstrate the extent of violence experienced by farmers as they resisted eviction and how it informed their decision to remain on their farms. Farm invaders employed various different methods as they sought to take control, ranging from forcible removal to sustained intimidation that eventually prompted farmers to leave. At the same time as farmers faced this barrage of violence and intimidation, the breakdown in law and order and property rights, and the country's economic collapse, also played important roles in forcing farmers to leave.

## EFFECTIVENESS OF COERCION IN EVICTING FARMERS

Evidence collected for this book shows that very extensive violence was widespread during the land seizure era. Comprehensive threats to personal and property rights resulted in a condition of chronic vulnerabilities for farmers. These vulnerabilities were especially serious when farmers producing tobacco and food crops such as wheat and maize reached the critical point in August of each year when they would have to commit enormous expenditure for the next year's crop. Were conditions sufficiently stable for them to commit to this enormous capital outlay? The lack of long-term stability would play a critical role in informing farmers' decisions on investment and production—and ultimately on whether to remain on their farm.

### Violence and Eviction

Violence toward farmers was intended to bring about compliance with the demands of farm invaders.[2] In theory, severe violence, or the threat of it, would cause farmers to leave their farms. Indeed, 77.4% of farmer survey respondents reported that threats were the primary reason for eviction. On closer examination, however, the causal link between violence and eviction is less clear.

Figure 8.1 shows that while 46.6% of farmer survey respondents first experienced violence in 2000, the majority (51.2%) were only evicted in 2002. The reason for this delay in eviction is not initially clear. One possible explanation is that the overall volume of violence increased until it reached a threshold where farmers were sufficiently fearful and decided to abandon resistance.

Figure 8.2 shows that in 2000, when a large proportion of farmers first experienced violence and intimidation, the majority of respondents experienced the first incidents in the March–April 2000 period, rather than toward the end of the year. These data, showing that farmers began to experience coercion almost as soon as the farm seizures began, support Petros Mzingwane's assertion that there was a sudden "eruption" of conflict on the farms.[3] Moreover, there is regional consistency in survey data

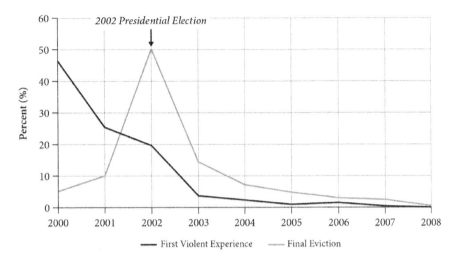

**Figure 8.1**  Year Farmers Experienced First Acts of Violence and Final Eviction
SOURCE: Author's survey of commercial farmers.

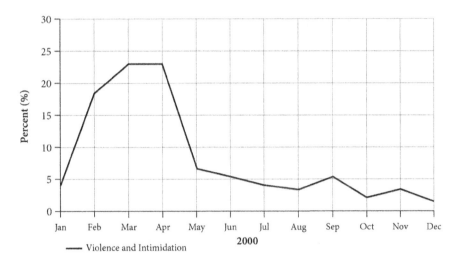

**Figure 8.2**  Month in 2000 when Farmers First Experienced Coercion
SOURCE: Author's survey of commercial farmers.

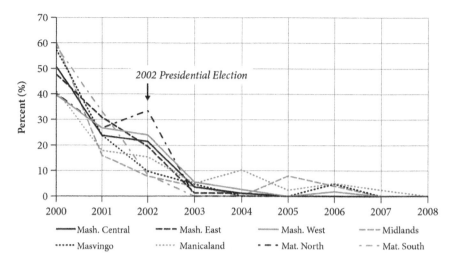

Figure 8.3 Year Farmers First Experienced Coercion
SOURCE: Author's survey of commercial farmers.

depicting when farmers first experienced violence. Figure 8.3 shows a province-level breakdown of when farmer survey respondents first experienced violence and intimidation. These data show a similar national profile of most farmer survey respondents experiencing coercion for the first time in 2000.

Relationships between violence and eviction can be further explained by examining levels of national violence longitudinally. Violence maps created for this book record the national proliferation of violence from 2000 to 2008.[a] The data show that 2002 had the highest levels of violence recorded during the land seizure era. However, counterintuitively, farmers did not typically leave during periods when violence was at its peak. It is impossible to conclude, therefore, that high aggregate levels of violence correlate with increased evictions.

Mapping data show that March 2002, the month of the presidential election, was the most violent month of the land seizure era, with 1,673 incidents recorded (see figure 5.2 and figure 8.5); figure 8.4 shows that farmers

a. See www.charleslaurie.com for a complete series of color violence maps depicting 21,491 acts of abduction/unlawful arrest, assault, murder, attempted murder, rape, torture, intimidation/verbal threat, and property damage/theft against farmers and workers recorded between 2000 and 2008.

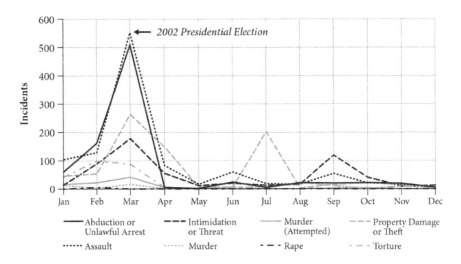

**Figure 8.4** Political Violence in 2002
SOURCE: Mapping data set. See appendix A for additional information.

and workers faced a variety of threats, but despite violence being widely anticipated during this election, only 1.2% of all survey respondents left their properties in March 2002.[4] Nor did high levels of violence result in a delayed effect, as farmers made plans to leave, because only 4.1% of survey respondents left in April 2002. It seems reasonable that if farmers were leaving only because of violence, they would have left *before* the widely anticipated violence of the March 2002 election and avoid the conflict. Failing that, they would have left during the escalation of violence, or soon after, when it became clear Mugabe had managed to remain in power.

Survey data (see figure 8.5) show a very substantial peak of evictions in August 2002, with 12.1% of survey respondents leaving in that month. This figure is substantially higher than the 1.1% per month average eviction recorded for the January 2001 to July 2002 period. Interestingly, only 83 incidents of violence were reported in August 2002, just 5% of March 2002 levels (according to the mapping data). While there is some evidence of a correlation between higher levels of violence and eviction, as shown in July 2001, September 2001, and June 2003, mapping data show that for many other farmers, violence alone was not a direct cause of eviction.

It may be assumed that it would take several months for farmers to pack and leave their farms. Yet a farm invader could in some cases simply threaten the farmer sufficiently to cause him to leave within as little as a

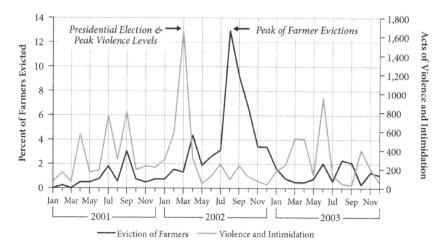

**Figure 8.5** Violence and Farmer Evictions: 2001–2003
SOURCE: Author's survey of commercial farmers and mapping data set.

few hours.[5] Meanwhile, the escalation in violence beginning in 2000 meant that most farmers had already removed personal valuables and whatever other assets they could remove long before eviction, leaving only essential items on the farm (although since farm operations required agri-property, substantial quantities would have remained on farms). As the land seizure era progressed, farm invaders became far more assertive in preventing the farmer from removing agri-property and personal assets; the more the farmer left, the more the invader gained.[6] Therefore, after about 2001, farmers were sometimes unable to remove anything at all when they left the farm. This meant that farmers were as ready as they could be to leave, which allowed them to make a relatively rapid departure from the farm when evicted.

The assumption of a direct relationship between high levels of overall violence and farmer evictions does not hold. While farmers were certainly influenced by violence, data suggest that violence was not the only consideration for farmers about whether to leave or remain on their land: there were other variables that also influenced farmers' decision-making.

## Methods to Evict Farmers

Examining methods used to evict farmers gives deeper insight into farmers' decision-making on when to leave their farms. When survey respondents were asked about the reasons for permanently leaving their farms, 77.4% cited verbal and written threats to safety, property, and livelihoods. Another 32.9% left because they believed there was no economic future for farmers, and 12.3% cited the impossibility of operating the farm as a business—a direct reflection of a breakdown of property rights. Meanwhile, 19.5% believed there was no social future because of the breakdown of their local community, and 11.8% left because their friends and neighbors had been evicted. As farmers became more isolated and vulnerable and their safety, property and livelihood became increasingly threatened, they did not want to be the only farmers left in the area. Smaller numbers of respondents also cited other reasons: too much pressure on workers; no support from state authorities; deteriorating prospects for their children; pressure on their family; the threat of being jailed—particularly when faced with the eviction orders under Section 8 of the Land Acquisition Act in August 2002—or when facing other legal pressures such as from the "offer letters" delivered by invaders to establish their claim to the farm.

It is clear, then, that farmers had numerous reasons for leaving, but most were at least partially influenced by threats. Reframing "threats" to include economic, social, and legal vulnerabilities (including false arrest), of which physical safety was but one—albeit major—consideration, more accurately reflects the complexity of farmers' reasons for leaving their property. Fundamentally, extensive instability and chronic vulnerability motivated most farmers to leave their farms.

Counterintuitively, only 11.3% of survey respondents left their property explicitly because they were physically forced to do so by state agents. This relatively low figure shows that many farmers could choose, to some degree, when they would leave, and that violence was just one of many considerations. This helps to explain why the data fail to show a direct correlation between violence levels and eviction levels.

Interviews with farmers provides further evidence to show that most farmers were evicted through multiple financial and social pressures, rather than explicitly through violence. One farmer explained that "wearing down is a definite tactic, because to them [farm invaders], time is no object. Time is no object to them [farm invaders] at all. To us [farmers] it is enormous."[7] The farmer highlights a key difference in the responsibilities of farmers and farm invaders. Farm invaders, who were often unemployed youths from Harare or the local rural areas, could afford to spend extended periods disrupting farm activities, and in fact were often paid to do so. Farmers, on the other hand, had a time-sensitive business to operate and could often not accommodate disruption to the farm's operation.

## VIOLENCE AGAINST FARMERS AND THEIR FAMILY MEMBERS

Coercion against farmers and their families was a specific and widely employed tool to evict farmers. As figure 8.1 and figure 8.2 demonstrate, violence and intimation were used from the earliest days of the land seizure era and did not cease until farmers left their properties. Accordingly, farmers who resisted eviction sometimes experienced periods of intensive coercion that spanned multiple years. Moreover, the intensity of violence often escalated the more the farmer resisted. According to farm clerk Joyce Mukwa, farm invaders "wanted the owner of the farm to move straightaway, but if the owner of the farm was still there, that's why they [were] making more violence."[8]

The survey of commercial farmers sheds light on the extent of coercion experienced by farmers from invaders seeking to evict them. The overwhelming majority (88.1%) of survey respondents or their families experienced verbal threats. For example, one respondent stated that he was told by farm invaders, "If we did not move out they would rape my wife and daughters and kill me." These threats were often accompanied by the brandishing of weapons, significantly raising the potential for a life-threatening situation to occur. One survey respondent recalled that farm invaders had cocked an AK-47 and pointed it into his wife's face. Indeed, while farmers tended to experience most threats themselves because they would normally face invaders alone, threats against the farmers' families were a widely practiced means of undermining the farmer's resolve to remain on his property.

Another 21.8% of survey respondents experienced at least one act of abduction or unlawful arrest. Arrest was a key means of intimidating farmers into complying with government and farm invaders directives. For example, there were a series of arrests in August 2002 when Section 8—the compulsory eviction order—of the 2002 Land Acquisition Act was more systematically enforced by the police. Kathy Grover stated that her husband, Martin, spent two nights in jail for not meeting the requirements of the eviction order and refusing to leave his farm.[9] These instances almost always involved the direct participation of the police in arresting farmers (and, less commonly, their family members) and holding them at the behest of senior or influential figures seeking to evict the farmer. Arrests would often take place on a Friday afternoon because by that time in the week the local magistrate was usually no longer available. The farmers would be jailed until the following Monday, when they were usually released by the magistrate for lack of evidence; this was a means of manipulating the legal system to intimidate farmers and workforce. For example, a farmer survey respondent stated, "We found that we were targeted on Thursdays and Fridays because they would like to try and arrest us over the weekend because the courts were closed over the weekend. So we had a lot of problems having to be away from the farms on Thursdays and Fridays [in order to avoid arrest]."

For the farmers and their families, the prospect of spending any time in a Zimbabwean jail was very threatening. Jails were often overcrowded, cold, and extremely unsanitary. On being taken to jail, farmer Nancy Hoover found messages written in human feces on the wall and the floor covered in feces.[10] She also stated that while she initially had her own cell, a "drunk" prisoner was then placed in the cell with her, an experience she said she found "intimidating."

The police were also often complicit in abductions by farm invaders and in most cases simply sought to prevent overt violence against the farmer. In such cases, farmers and their family members were often assaulted, severely intimidated, and subjected to humiliating treatment. A farmer survey respondent told of how his wife was made to dance in the center of the crowd while singing a ZANU-PF song.

Farmers were also evicted through a practice called *jambanja*. This is a Shona word for "rally" and indicates a form of intimidation in which there is little or no physical contact, but the victim is relentlessly intimidated for an extended period, ranging from several days to half a year or more, until he leaves his property.[11] Human rights activist Archbishop Pius Ncube stated that "the whole idea . . . [was] to cause these farmers to be scared and to leave [their farms]."[12]

*Jambanja* was widely practiced, with 56.8% of survey respondents indicating that they experienced this form of intimidation. One survey respondent provided an insight into what a *jambanja* was like: "Farm invaded by group of about 50, I was alone in the house. Broke through security gate, surrounded house armed with sticks, choppers, etc. Beat up gardener because he locked the gate when he saw them coming." In other cases *jambanjas* involved farmers having to engage groups of agitated farm invaders in close proximity. For example, a farmer survey respondent, reported "having to wipe spittle off [his] face" following a "severe *jambanja*."

*Jambanjas* could often be deeply intimidating and exerted a grave emotional toll on the farmer. For example, Martin Wilson from Mashonaland East reported that, on one occasion, "about 100" farm invaders broke into his home after they "bashed the [front] door down, smashed it down."[13] Wilson stated that the invaders were already intoxicated but began cooking food in his kitchen, drinking his alcohol, sitting on his sofa, watching his television, and moving around the house—this while Wilson and his wife were in the home: "Some of the youths [were] dancing in the middle of the room, all singing songs like 'down with the MDC' and all sorts of things." Wilson stated that "there were a hundred of these guys and they were everywhere, taking stuff out of the deep freeze and helping themselves. And you'd go into the dining room and they were all sitting around the table. They're eating your apples and drinking beer." Wilson reported that after five hours, in which the invaders kept asking if he was harboring MDC officials and paraphernalia, the invaders left. Wilson said that the invaders "never laid a hand on me" but that the confrontation was nevertheless designed to "try and violate your personal space as much as possible."

Similarly, as part of a *jambanja* or as an independent act to undermine the farmer's ability to remain on his farm, animals were targeted by farm invaders. 48.8% of survey respondents cited deliberate injury or death to their livestock, and 16.2% of respondents indicated harm to their pets. "Oh, it was horrific," stated farmer Joan Lyons. "Our cattle were axed here on the tail and on the spines, killing the cattle."[14] In another case, farm invaders were unable to evict the farmer, so they stacked hay around his daughter's horse and set fire to the hay, killing the animal.[15] Elizabeth Shore, the wife of a farmer, related an incident where invaders killed her pet calf by shooting it with blasts of a shotgun.[16] She recounted that the knowledge that the calf died in a slow and brutal manner, despite her efforts to bargain with the invaders, made her despair at any prospect of remaining on her farm. These methods and the continual presence of farm invaders outside the homestead caused extensive distress to isolated farmer families.

Assault was also prolific, with 31.8% of survey respondents indicating that they experienced assault. Survey respondents gave numerous examples:

- "Settlers assaulted us constantly and family members too. Tried to kill one of my sons."
- "They held my daughter's arms through the burglar bars on the back door and beat them."
- "Tied up and beaten with my parents, tried to electrocute my father and held hostage. Held hostage for +/– eight hours. Wife and I barricaded in our home +/– three days."
- "Assault followed by abduction of daughter."

In some instances farmers experienced only a single attack, but many faced repeated assaults. For example, Mukwa explained how her employer "was terribly attacked—every day—nearly every day."[17]

The police were often present during both mass demonstrations on farms and during incidents of violence against farmers and workers. Yet—with some noteworthy exceptions—they usually intervened only to stop life-threatening incidents of violence. For example, manager Herbert Nchenchi described an incident where although the police were present during the beating of his boss, they prevented him from being murdered: "When they were beating this farm owner . . . when they hit him on the head with the back of an axe and then when he went down, then that's when the police said, 'No, no, no. You are going to kill him. Stop. Stop. Stop. Stop.'"[18]

Other types of violence were also practiced. Torture of farmers or of their family members was reported by 3.2% of survey respondents. For example, dairy foreman Philip Mahobohobo described an incident where a farmer was nearly murdered: "There was another woman [a farmer's wife] from Karoi. . . . Her husband was put in the mud, the whole body, the whole head [was submerged] . . . even the white man, they will torture them."[19] Meanwhile, 9.4% of survey respondents reported at least one incident of attempted murder, and 1.1% of survey respondents reported a politically motivated murder in their family. Indeed, the threat of murder was ever present, with farm workers also told that they should target their employers.[20]

Violence and intimidation tended to escalate in severity the longer the farmer remained on his property. Initial contacts between farmers and farm invaders were rarely violent. These encounters normally consisted of threats against the farmer in conjunction with a series of justifications of why the farmer should leave, normally hinging on nationalist grievances. Farmers interviewed for this book recounted instances where initial contacts with invaders could at times be devoid of overt threats; instead the invaders would try to persuade the farmer to leave, normally by indicating that there was no hope in resisting advances, which would only intensify. For example, Nchenchi stated that "the first time they came in it was just the farm invasions [to occupy the land], and there was a [later] time when they came in and they attacked the owner to a degree that he was close to death."[21]

These methods of relentlessly employing different types of coercion undermined the farmer's willingness to remain on his property. While major episodes of violence did occur—such as the murder of farmers discussed in chapter 5—the far more common means was to place such psychological strain on the farmer over time that he would eventually leave on his own. Jackson Sanyati, a police officer in charge of an eastern district, neatly summed up the process: "They just wanted to give pressure—to give pressure."[22]

The reason less life-threatening methods were often used was that while government institutions like the state security services and state-owned enterprises were rapidly politicized after the land seizures began and soon became unprofessional, the legal system was more gradually compromised until about 2003 when it was largely a ZANU-PF-dominated institution. It was more difficult for ZANU-PF to intimidate judges, and it took several years for political appointees to enter the legal system in large numbers. Especially in the early phase of the seizures, invaders feared legal consequences, even if court orders

were rarely enforced by the politicized police force. Invaders therefore preferred intimidation because it was less likely that many smaller acts of longer-
term intimidation could directly implicate invaders. Felix Umchabezi, a
veteran of the Liberation War, explained:

> If they took him [farmer], lifted him bodily out of his house, they would
> be accused of having actually done so. But if they created an environment
> that was intolerable to the farmer and the farmer eventually leaves, you
> cannot accuse anybody. They will say, "[He] left on his own. He was not
> harmed by anybody. Did you say he was harmed by anybody? No, he
> wasn't harmed. . . ." But sometimes they would become violent. They
> would kill a cat, cut them open and . . . hang them in the door of the
> farmer's house. And maybe throw another cat on the bonnet of the farm-
> er's car.[23]

The survey of commercial farmers sought to gain data on the effects of intimidation and violence of farmers and their families in order to shed light on
the severity of the coercion they experienced. The requirement of medical
care acts as an instrument for assessing the severity of an injury. Emotional
injuries, such as chronic stress and anxiety, were often perceived by farmer
survey respondents to be sufficiently serious to require medical attention.
Some 60.6% of farmers and their families who experienced emotional injuries
sought medical treatment. The widespread negative emotional consequences
of intimidation for the farmer and his family are illustrated by the fact that
32.4% of male heads of household, 34.3% of female heads of households,
20.2% of children, and 0.5% of grandparents sought medical treatment for
emotional injuries.

The serious emotional injuries experienced by a farmer's family had a major
effect on a farmer's willingness and ability to remain on his farm. This is indicated by the fact that 77.4% of survey respondents cited threats to safety, property, and livelihoods as the key reason for leaving their farms. A farmer would
have to contend with the knowledge that his family was suffering as a result of
his efforts to remain on the farm. Moreover, numerous interview respondents
indicated that while male farmers tended to want to remain on their farms,
their families were often more willing to leave. Thus, in addition to the pressure inflicted by farm invaders, a farmer would also to some extent face pressure from his family to leave the farm, almost always due to safety concerns.
If a farmer removed his family to the safety of an urban area, which usually
happened when threats escalated, the farmer was then faced with the additional emotional burden of living apart from his family—and being alone on
the farm—for what would be an indefinite period.

Farmer survey respondents were also asked whether they sought medical treatment for injuries. Of the survey respondents, 46.2% of farmers and their families who experienced physical injuries believed these were sufficiently serious to seek medical treatment. The survey also demonstrated that adult men (i.e., farmers in almost all cases) were targeted far more frequently with more serious physical violence, with 34.3% of male heads of household seeking medical attention, compared to 7.0% of female heads of households, 7.7% of children, and 0.7% of grandparents.

These data show that male farmers were targeted for violence by farm invaders far more often than other family members. This is unsurprising given that the farmer would interact with invaders during his work on the farm more often, and that the invaders' objective was to remove the farmer. While targeting family members might also intimidate farmers into accepting eviction, it made sense that resources were concentrated where they would have the most direct effect.

## Violence against Workers and Their Family Members

Workers were also targeted by farm invaders in order to undermine the farmers' ability to operate the farm as a commercial enterprise. In this context, threats against workers can be seen in terms of how they informed the farmer's overall decision-making on whether to try to remain and operate the farm as a business.

When invaders arrived on the farm, they faced farm workers who roughly fitted in two categories: those who wanted the farmer evicted and those who did not. Unsurprisingly the more senior farm workers, such as managers, foremen, tractor drivers, and other specialists, tended to be better paid and often received additional benefits, such as better homes because many would have lived and worked on them for many years. As discussed in chapter 5, these workers tended to support the farmer and worked to prevent his eviction. For example, foreman Richard Chipembere stated that workers on the farm where he was employed "knew if the ruling party, the government, takes the land, then they are going to suffer. . . . They knew it was going to be a disaster."[24]

Going down the scale, the less skilled and experienced workers tended to be paid less and therefore had fewer incentives to support the farmer. There were a large number of additional variables. Whether workers had lived on the farm for a long time (many families had lived on the same farm for generations) and if they had dependents played a part in their decision-making. In addition, the reputation of the farmer as an employer was a critical factor. If he paid better wages, treated workers fairly, did not hold racist views, and was generally reasonable, then workers were more likely to support the farmer.

It is worth keeping in mind that the accounts from workers in this section come from those who tended to be closest to farmers and had the most to lose if the farm was seized. As such, they were, with few exceptions, opposed to the farmer's eviction, although almost all indicated that they believed that some kind of additional land reform program was necessary, and some were critical of their current or former bosses and other commercial farmers.

The mechanism of undermining the farmer by undermining his workforce is neatly captured by Umchabezi, who as ZAPU's director of publicity had extensive contact with farm invaders:

> Black farm workers were, as it were, resources for the white farmers. You frighten them and you leave the farmer alone, and he cannot go and till the land himself. Driving black workers away from, out of, the farms, and the farms will remain unproductive and the white farmer will eventually also find it impossible to continue living on unproductive land.[25]

The strategy was simple: preventing employees from going to work would cause the farm—too large for the farmer to operate alone—to soon become economically unviable. This would ultimately force the farmer off the land, which farm invaders would then seize.

As discussed in chapter 5, farm invaders often distrusted farm workers, who were seen as collaborators with the white enemy and as a support base for the hated MDC. Yet, particularly in the early stages of the seizures, many farm invaders recognized the utility of attempting to co-opt farm workers. This strategy of separating farmers and workers was routinely identified by workers interviewed for this book. Thompson Mbezi, who was a livestock foreman, stated that farm invaders told him and others workers on the farm where he was employed, "We mustn't work for him [the farmer], number one. Number two, they say, 'We don't want to see him in here in this farm. We don't want to see him!'"[26]

Farm manager Ketani Makabusi said that the process of using labor to evict a farmer usually began with the arrival of a war veteran and his associated rabble of youths, who would announce their intention of evicting the farmer:

> There was the one senior guy who was a Liberation War hero. He was a proper war vet . . . and he had about five or six youths with him. . . . They would round up the labor, saying, "Right, farm workers, we are here to liberate you. You need to earn, get paid your total benefits [SI6 compensation packages from the farmer]. We are removing this commercial farmer from the farm. This farm is now going to go to an indigenous person. You are now going to work for an indigenous person."[27]

Similarly, Mbezi stated that farm invaders initially sought to gain his support by seeking to incite racial grievances against the farmer: "'Why are you wasting your time working for a white man? Because it's better to work to us.'"[28]

In employing this strategy, farm invaders promised benefits to entice the workers into voluntarily relinquishing support for the farmer. Such an approach was usually the first method used by farm invaders, since promising the spoils of the farm to workers required little commitment of their own resources and time.

Promises of major gains for farm workers were easy for farm invaders to make, since the assets being promised did not belong to them and few farm invaders actually carried through on delivering on promises if assets were seized. Foreman Tendayi Garamapudzi said that where he worked the farm invaders told workers they would "get everything on the farm" if they helped to evict the farmer.[29] In another instance, Garamapudzi said that workers were told they would get specific possessions from the farmer: "'As soon as your boss goes, you will be all right,' meaning everyone will be having the car. That's what they were told. . . . They were thinking that, 'Wow, we are going to be rich.'" In this example, the prospect of gaining the farmer's car seems to have overridden the practical side of how it would be shared among several people, but the appeal of the easy promise made by the farm invader is clear. Some farm invaders also sought to gain workers' support by highlighting the prospect of workers gaining SI6 worker retrenchment packages if the farmer terminated their employment (see also chapter 5). As has been noted previously, violence and coercion also raised some risks of prosecution, as well as potentially problematic social implications, and was not usually a first-choice method for farm invaders seeking to evict the farmer.

If workers were not receptive, then farm invaders would take steps to prevent them from engaging in labor on the farms. For example, foreman Zacharia Nyembwi stated: "When they [farm invaders] come, they come to boss boy [foreman] and says, 'Tell your workers to stop. We don't want them to go to work. If they go to work, you will be punished.'"[30] Similarly, mechanic Chenjerai Mapufuli was told, "No, no, no. You are not at work today because we are taking over that farm."[31]

Workers reported being told that their continued employment on the farm was against the law, a worrying threat for many workers given how the police were increasingly politicized after 2000 and grew willing to use their authority to enforce ZANU-PF objectives. For example, Mapufuli was told that it was against the law to work for white people.[32] Quoting a farm invader, he said, "You black people [who] worked under white people, you are against the law." If workers—particularly the key senior employees—were not receptive, farm invaders would become more coercive and use threats to gain compliance. Chapter 5 details the extreme intimidation and violence that workers experienced at the hands of farm invaders. Farm invaders engaged in relentless, systematic intimidation and violence, for example, through *pungwes*.

As discussed in chapter 6, farm invaders would not always remain on the farm permanently—although in many cases they did—but would come on weekends. This was because most senior officials involved in the farm seizures held government jobs or other permanent professional positions that only gave them time on weekends to try to seize a farm. This meant that workers had to experience a roller coaster effect of fearing the return of farm invaders. This severely undermined productivity. Mbezi explained that farm invaders "used to come once a week, especially the weekend, between Saturday and Sunday.... We are always staying worried. You don't even feel [like we can] work nicely."[33]

Farm invaders could also rely on a range of other measures to coerce workers into compliance. According to Mucheke, some farm invaders would starve workers into complying or leaving the farm: "They went into the storerooms, farming storerooms, took all the food which was stored for the farm workers, was taken away. At the end of a week or two there was no food for the farm workers, so they couldn't stay long and they left."[34]

Ultimately however, violence and intimidation were the most widely practiced means of targeting workers, as detailed in chapter 5. The targeting of workers' property could be either a punitive measure to punish workers for perceived noncompliance with the farm invaders' demands, or a preemptive measure to "soften up" a workforce in preparation for escalating demands. For example, activist and farmer's spouse Debbie McKinley reported that on one occasion farm invaders burned 14 workers' homes to the ground.[35] Rancher Henry Monroe detailed his experience: "We could hear the action in my workers' quarters where they [farm invaders] were starting to break down doors, remove property, and throw all their property out. And this [violence] started agitating our workers because they felt that they didn't know what was going on."[36]

Such instances obviously impacted workers most directly and severely. Some workers lost almost all of their possessions and had no financial means to replace them. However, they also directly undermined the farmers' resolve to remain on the farm in some cases, thereby bringing about the eviction the farm invaders were seeking. Indeed, Monroe decided to acquiesce to the farm invaders' demands and leave his property following the violence against his workers: "I decided that enough was enough. If we continued in this vein, it would just get worse."[37]

Workers were told that they would experience violence if they supported their white farmer employer. For example, mechanic Mapufuli was told by farm invaders: "If our boss [is] kept away [from the farm], there's no murder."[38] Mahobohobo explained that black workers experienced "more violence because they [farm invaders] said you must suffer. . . . It [violence] was a way of stopping you to support the white people."[39]

The scale and scope of violence experienced by workers has been covered in chapter 5. However, a poignant example of the punishment the workers experienced when they refused to leave the farmers' employ comes once again from Mukwa:

> The violence was every occasion, every day—every day—and we had to sleep in the bush for about two weeks [to avoid it]. . . . We had to sleep there during the rainy season, afraid of those war veterans. And one of our guys was beaten terribly and left naked. . . . He came back to the farm naked. They had taken all his clothes for no apparent reason, just because we were working for the whites.[40]

Workers were told that if the farmer was evicted the violence would end. Mechanic Beton Mopane said that the longer a farmer persisted remaining on his property, the more violence workers experienced.[41]

As noted previously in this chapter, violence against workers severely undermined both the practical ability of the farmer to continue farming and the farmer's emotional resolve to remain on his property when his presence clearly resulted in greater coercion of his workforce. Farmers such as Shore, Hendricks, Elbridge, Kennedy, McKinley, Taylor, Knox, Coolidge, Wheeler, and Morton all cited violence against workers as a major consideration in leaving their farms.[42]

## INTERFERENCE WITH FARM OPERATIONS

A key strategy to evict farmers was to interfere with their ability to operate the farm as a business. Tobacco farming provides an example of farmers' exceptional vulnerability to interference with their crops. The growing process begins with seedlings that are grown in seedbeds, then transplanted into the larger fields where the main tobacco crop is grown. Farmer Tim Sherman indicated that his seedbeds were destroyed by farm invaders, leaving him unable to plant the entire year's tobacco crop.[43] Sherman's example reveals the impact of interference on key aspects of cropping. The result of this type of interference were substantial financial losses for the farmer, who was unable to plant the year's tobacco crop.

This was not an isolated incident. One farmer from Mashonaland West reported 96 work stoppages between January 2001 and May 2005.[44] In another case, farmer Thomas Barkley described how farm invaders took over land on which he had installed an advanced center-pivot irrigation system costing between US$35,000 and US$45,000 for 50 hectares coverage.[45] This system was rendered unusable when farm invaders began building huts around the system. Barkley believed this was deliberate provocation: "You know that they're not going to be able to utilize that facility [the center pivot], that it was done straight as an intimidation tactic, a 'stuff you' tactic."[46] However, "It didn't matter how much reporting we did or how much, you know, complaining we did to the authorities. They [the farm invaders] would just take over."

As well as being subjected to relentless violence and intimidation, laborers were at times physically prevented from working. This tactic was widely deployed and frequently used at critical times in the crop cycle. Farmer Kevin Elbridge explained: "We were trying to pick coffee in one of the lands, and the new settlers came and chased my labor away and threatened that they would kill them."[47] As a result, "The coffee ended up—well we weren't able to pick it. The new settler picked a little bit, but the majority just rotted, and that coffee is totally dead now. And I received not one cent back on my investment." Farmers often borrowed money from the bank to invest in each year's crop and repay with the proceeds. Even if their inability to make repayments was the fault of the farm invaders, the farmers were still responsible for the loan, and many faced bankruptcy.

Another strategy was to build huts in the middle of a field to block the farmer's access. If the farmer attempted to plow the field, thereby destroying the huts, the farmer would face severe consequences from the farm invaders and the police. Sherman explained: "We were not able to use the land without reprisals against our cattle. I had a couple of cattle mutilated. They'd slash them. They'd just leave it alive, slash the tendons, and just wait for your response. 'Are you going to move or aren't you going to move?'"[48]

Theft was another critical problem for farmers and was experienced by 68.6% of survey respondents. Sometimes, eviction through theft was passive or unintentional: a farm invader stole for his own gain, and over time this forced the farmer to leave. For instance, an anonymous farmer survey respondent said that he had had 81 head of cattle stolen in one week. Other farmer survey respondents provided different examples:

- "Cattle stolen, 100 bags (×50 kg) reaped maize stolen."
- "Cattle taken, dog and ducks taken."
- "Attempted to burn crops, stealing fencing and irrigation equipment."
- "Theft of cattle, motors, switches, miniature circuit breakers (MCBs), anything."

This level of theft made it difficult for farmers to operate, even if invaders were not forcibly evicting them.

Vandalism was also an active means of coercing farmers to abandon their property. While theft offered invaders the prospect of immediate gain, vandalism provided the potential of a much greater benefit if it was sufficient to drive the farmer off his land, thereby potentially making land and much larger quantities of agri-property available. One farmer from Mashonaland East recounted how farm invaders stole a four-wheel-drive tractor and ran over a stack of expensive irrigation pipes, destroying the pipes. Other types of vandalism included oil being drained from specialist freezer units, and ball bearings being dropped into tractor gearboxes, both of which caused very costly damage.[49] Anonymous farmer survey respondents provided additional examples:

- "Cattle hamstrung, burning of plantations, slashing of crops (tobacco seedbeds)."
- "Burnt all grazing for 600 head beef cattle [i.e., so cattle could no longer be fed from this source]."
- "Livestock theft, burnt wheat (standing), compound burnt."
- "All three homesteads were ransacked and trashed while briefly unoccupied."

Given the size of most commercial farms, it was nearly impossible for farmers to protect their agri-property. This therefore provided a relatively easy means for farm invaders to cripple farm operations and force the farmer to incur potentially major losses.

The ability of farm invaders to exploit crops' time sensitivity meant that farmers could easily be forced off their land through prolonged economic pressures induced by disrupting production. Thus, farmers faced two kinds of vulnerabilities: acute and chronic. Acute vulnerabilities were those comprised of explicit, targeted, and focused acts of violence. "Trashings," where farm invaders descended en masse onto a farm, stealing and destroying nearly all property, are examples of acute vulnerabilities, alongside physical attacks.

### TARGETING HARVESTS

Many farmers believed that farm invaders intentionally raided farms during harvest time in order to secure profits for themselves. Farm invaders would identify a farm for seizure but would not actually take over the property until the crop was ready. Thus the farmer would use his skills and capital to prepare the crop for harvest, and the farm invader would then time the seizure to gain the maximum possible financial gain—the profits of the entire season's crop—with no expenditure of capital or expertise. Mucheke explained:

Some of them [farm invaders] would fool you [the farmer] and say, "OK, I want you to finish your crop, and after you sell your crop I'll come and take your farm." And so when you're just about to sell your crop, they'll come and take over and the courts would rule in favor of the commercial farmer owner, but still no one could implement it. So lawlessness came.[50]

Farmer Al Jensen provided corroborating evidence of this strategy, stating that farm invaders "timed it to perfection" and arrived just when his orange crop was ready for harvesting: "These guys were everywhere, and they started to reap my crop there and then and bring in their own blokes [to harvest]."[51]

Timothy Ngavi, an accountant for the Grain Marketing Board (GMB), a state-owned enterprise to which farmers were required to sell their maize, provided insight that senior officials timed seizures to maximize financial returns by targeting crops at harvest: "The first harvest on the good land, the very good land . . . would go to people who had the power. . . . It was government, or the police force, or the army."[52] Once these individuals had taken the crop, the commercial farmer would rarely attempt another year of farming. The loss of crops and the waste of investment clearly had a powerful influence in persuading farmers that they had no future if they remained on the land.

In interviews farmers repeatedly identified this behavior of invaders timing seizures to coincide with the harvesting of crops. For example, an anonymous farmer survey respondent stated, "Local MP allocated my banana plantation to the ZANU-PF youth wing for their gain and I was prevented from reaping the crop." Another survey respondent stated: "The Zhuwao's [relatives of Robert Mugabe] commandeered my tractors and eventually reaped my crop of tobacco." In another example, Elizabeth Shore, the spouse of a farmer, spoke about how some invaders moved from farm to farm stripping the homestead of fittings and the farm of crops: "What they have also done is they will go to a farm with a nice house and a crop ready to reap. They haven't done anything [to earn those assets]. You strip the house and reap the crop and move on to the next one."[53]

In an extended example, farmer Al Jensen described how farm invaders—with support from the police—violently seized his citrus crop as it was being prepared for market:

We're in the middle of reaping our citrus, and I told him [farm invader] he could go and get lost [after he arrived on the farm claiming the citrus]. You know, get the hell out of there and they had cops there, armed—two armed cops with him. They eventually drove off. You know, your adrenalin boosts—you hear what's going on around the country [i.e., violent encounters with farm invaders].

They came back that afternoon about three o'clock I suppose. [The citrus] pack shed was running, and I had all my staff there, and they came back, four of these people plus more police this time. They ran through my shed armed with iron bars and just beat the hell into my labor. I was watching them. They had these cops there. And they went berserk. And I said to the cops, "What the hell are you allowing this for?" And they did—they did nothing. . . . You know they [farm invaders] warned me and they said, "Look, we're taking this place here. If you're going to carry on working here, someone's going to get killed."[54]

Jensen said, "I'd only reaped not even a quarter of my crop," so the value of assets seized by the invaders was considerable.

Ngavi gave additional insights into the way farmers were defrauded by the government-owned GMB so that the financial gains of harvested crops could be transferred to farm invaders.[55] Ngavi stated, "You could see that there was a lot of 'new' farmers who had come in at the time of harvest, because we could see that some people, someone has just come in to do the harvest, they deliver, and they go." The farm invader would seize the crop from the farmer, deliver it to the GMB, and receive payment. Ngavi explained that the invaders did not intend to farm, but only to profit from the opportunity of seizing crops from one farm after another: "They were moving to other farms or whatever, but . . . they were coming in order to get quick money. They were paid and then they start something new."

Ngavi described two other ways by which farmers were ultimately defrauded of money by farm invaders manipulating the GMB, which had become a highly political organization soon after the land seizures began. The first was that when a farm invader had seized a farm, but the farmer had already sent his crop to the GMB, the invader who had recently seized the farm would still be the one who was paid the value of the delivered crop. The second was for the GMB to manipulate the time frame of farmer payments.[56] Ngavi explained that GMB officials clearly understood that farmers had to be paid on time so as to be ready for the next cropping season. Amid the country's economic collapse, however, the GMB had limited funds. With no money for payments because of corruption and the failing economy, Ngavi stated, "You have to manage the paying of the farmers." In other words, payment was delayed so that the GMB could capitalize on rapid currency inflation, thereby devaluing farmers' payments. Even at lower inflation rates, the GMB's delayed payments nearly eliminated farmers' earnings.

These examples demonstrate the range of economic pressures that beleaguered farmers were faced with. Attempting even basic functions, such as securing payments from the GMB, meant financial ruination. Many farmers did not have funds to purchase inputs for the next cropping season. Those who did would rarely risk making an investment given the industry's overwhelming instability.

### Targeting Farms by Manipulating the Law

Provisions already existed prior to the land seizure era that allowed the government to purchase commercial farms legally, thereby enabling land redistribution programs to exist while preserving farmers' property rights and the stability of the agriculture industry. The Land Acquisition Act of 1985 mandated that all farmers wanting to sell their land had to first offer the land to the government, the core of the "willing seller, willing buyer" arrangement. If the government did not want to purchase an available farm, a "certificate of no present interest" was issued, allowing the farmer to sell to any other buyer. This mechanism allowed a market for farms to exist alongside land redistribution programs. The problem for the government was that legislation required the government to purchase farms—given that they were the personal property of the farmers—rather than seize them outright. This resulted in the effort during the February 2000 referendum to give the government the power to seize land without compensating farmers.

Once invaders began moving onto farms during the land seizure era, especially when the government lost control over seizures, legislation was rapidly enacted to legalize farm takeovers. A raft of new measures were enacted to legalize farm takeovers, decriminalize acts such as trespassing on farms, give amnesty to those undertaking human rights violations,[57] and give coherence to the overall land redistribution program. Chapter 6 identified the Land Acquisition Amendment Act No. 6 of 2002, the Statutory Instrument 273 A (2003), and the Acquisition of Farm Equipment and Material Act (2004), which gradually constrained the ability of farmers to remain on their land and retain ownership of their property. Other measures included the "fast track" land reform program of July 2000, the Land Occupiers (Protection from Eviction) Act of 2001, and Mugabe's use of presidential powers in November 2001 to effectively nationalize farmland.[58] Moreover, behavior that was politically motivated was given explicit protection; Mugabe's clemency order of October 2000 "granted indemnity to every person liable to criminal prosecution for any politically motivated crime committed during the period from 1 January 2000 to 31 July 2000," including grievous bodily harm.[59]

These laws served the state's objective of seizing farmland by directly undermining farmers' property rights. Accordingly, they have been contested by farmers and are said to violate international standards regarding the protection of property rights and due process of law.[60] The legal assault on property rights also undermined the value of farms on the market, disrupting farmers' ability to borrow against the value of their land for the next growing season or to fund new projects.[61] Likewise, laws essentially criminalized the act of a farmer remaining on his property once the property had been identified for seizure. Thus, legislation served as an explicit tool of expropriation and intimidation. If farmers remained on their property after certain eviction notices were presented, they could be jailed—and many were.[62]

Another legal means of forcing an eviction was to cause unrest among labor by offering incentives for workers to evict their farmer employers. As discussed in chapter 5, the introduction of SI6 retrenchment packages meant that workers stood to gain what in some instances was a sizable cash payout if their employer left the farm. Farm invaders seized upon the promise of this payout to incite workers to defy their employer. Farm foreman Tendayi Garamapudzi stated that farm invaders told him and his colleagues, "You guys will be rich as soon as these white farmers go. You will get everything on the farm."[63] Therefore, through this legal mechanism, workers had a financial interest in evicting the farmer, thereby becoming tools for farm invaders. Farmers therefore faced losing the crucial support of their laborers, a government strategy described by one anonymous farmer survey respondent as a "clever move to divert attention and keep labor happy."

Although farmer survey respondents reported that most workers did not seek their eviction, this only applied to the early period of farm invasions, prior to the SI6 retrenchment packages coming into effect. During this early period workers stood to lose their homes and livelihoods if the farmer was evicted, so in most cases the farmer could rely on their support. By 2002, however—and in an environment of dramatically weakening property rights and escalating coercion of farmers—the SI6 package offered beleaguered workers the prospect of immediate financial rewards. Once the possibility of these payouts was clear, farmers noted that some workers rapidly became more hostile and less compliant. For instance, one anonymous survey respondent stated, "Our workers (or some contractors) only became hostile over 'severance packages.'"[64] As already noted, even a small number of noncompliant workers agitating and undermining the rest of the workforce could be extremely disruptive; so the strategy of encouraging workers to evict the farmer by no means required the participation of the entire workforce.[65]

The prospect of financial payouts under the SI6 requirements did not lead to all workers turning against their employers. Given that many farmers had workforces of 100 or more, there would obviously be variation in the attitudes of workers on each farm. The role of farm workers would depend in part on the effectiveness of farm invaders in persuading workers to assist them, the levels of coercion applied to workers, labor relations on the farm, the relative wealth of the workers and farmer, the prospects for alternative housing and employment once the farmer was evicted, and other social variables such as family responsibilities. An example of the interplay between workers seeking to balance pressures exhibited by farm invaders and their need for continued employment comes from an anonymous farmer survey respondent: "[I] feel I had a good relationship with workers, e.g., [the workers] threatened me to pay retrenchment, [but] once out of sight of war vets all weapons discarded, had normal meeting."

The SI6 requirement also meant that farmer employers had a major financial liability to pay for retrenchment. The retrenchment package requirements were financially disastrous for farmers, "utterly punitive" in the words of one farmer's spouse, who reported a sudden liability of US$818,000 for retrenchment payments.[66] Exacerbating the problem, the government ordered a pay increase for workers that "doubled the [workers'] salary," according to farmer Eric Fillmore.[67] The consequence of this legislation was that workers became much more eager to evict their farmer employers so they could gain the retrenchment payments: "They all wanted to be laid off, terminated," according to Fillmore. He explained further: "All they wanted was the money because they saw everybody getting enough money to go and buy nice shirts and bicycles and a radiograms [music playing device]. It was a large amount of money." Fillmore believed that these workers did not realize that once they received their termination packages, there were only scarce opportunities to find other jobs. Indeed, unemployment levels reached 60% in 2002.[68]

The strategy of requiring farmers to pay retrenchment packages served to break the financial dependence of workers on the farmer employer. It then gave workers a vested interest in evicting the farmer. Some workers then became de facto ZANU-PF agents and began using violence and intimidation against their employers. For example, Makabusi said that workers were directly incentivized with promises of retrenchment packages if they helped evict the farmer.[69] Quoting farm invaders, he said, "We've got to make sure we can get what we can out of this person [farmer] before they leave, because you are owed a lot of money, so the equipment mustn't move. Because if this person fails to pay you terminal benefits, we have to sell this equipment to compensate you."

Fillmore explained that workers on his farm quickly became aggressive toward him and his family: "It was our guys, my own labor, who performed [coercion] for two to three months. They barricaded us in and locked us up, and all they wanted was money, money, money, money all the time."[70] It should be emphasized, however, that while in some instances a few workers, out of 100 or more employees in some cases, sought to evict their farmer employers, workers rarely targeted their employers in large numbers. A far more common pattern was workers and farmers being covictimized and seeking to support each other for their mutual common good.

For example, farmer Shore stated that on his farm in Mashonaland Central almost no members of his general labor force of about 100 people were outwardly hostile to him.[71] He reported that these workers tended to be extremely fearful of invaders. However, his "rose workers," a group of 90 who specialized in operating his rose horticulture operation, were almost all hostile and sometimes aggressive and threatening. He attributed the difference to the ability of some avid ZANU-PF workers in that specific workforce to have a lot of influence, and because almost all of these specialist workers were relatively new hires with few long-standing ties to the farm and to Shore as an employer.

The requirement to pay retrenchment had a second and arguably more important objective for ZANU-PF: it bankrupted the farmer so he was unable to provide further financial support for the MDC. The financial outlay was enormous. Respondents reported being nearly bankrupted after paying retrenchment packages.[72] Fillmore gave a sense of the financial impact on farmers: "It was huge. It was an iniquitous package. It mean that's what basically broke everybody, really."[73] Given that farmers were simultaneously losing their livelihoods, being forced to move home, and incurring unexpected costs of eviction, few were in a financial position to make donations to any political party.

Farmers reported facing extreme challenges in meeting the costs, and for many farmers it resulted in major economic hardship if not insolvency. Still, many interview respondents indicated that because they hoped to one day return to their farms and were concerned about violating the law, they met the SI6 requirement. However, disputes over the payouts between farmers and workers became protracted in some instances. For example, George Sherman stated that some workers located his new address when he moved from his farm to Harare and started to *jambanja* his new home in order to gain retrenchment.[74] He indicated that the disputes arose over workers who claimed more senior positions than they actually worked, longer tenures of employment, or additional bonus packages.

For farm invaders, and the ZANU-PF government that implemented the SI6 law, the strategy of mobilizing workers against the farmer was a low-cost means of undermining commercial operations on the farm. Any financial payouts made by the farmer to workers were likely no loss to invaders, because they were not eligible to receive them anyway. In practice, relatively few workers would ultimately gain agri-property and higher-quality farmland—the objective of many invaders. Workers could easily be sidelined, so the strategy did not typically lead to invaders facing greater competition for resources. For workers, who often experienced severe coercion from invaders, the prospect of aiding in the eviction of their farmer employers was rarely an invitation to ally with invaders. Instead, it was an opportunity for workers, who were often relatively poor, to gain some financial benefit in an employment scenario that was increasingly uncertain if not bleak.

As chapter 3 detailed, a final means of using strategies through the legal system to evict farmers was to break the ability of the farmer to access legal protection from the police. For farmers this meant that when there were breakdowns on farms, they could not rely on the police to enforce the law and come to their aid. This resulted in the severe weakening of farmer morale and of farmers' practical ability to continue operating their farms. In other instances the police actively assisted farm invaders in evicting farmers, becoming practically indistinguishable from the evicting farm invaders. Farmer survey respondents provided some examples:

- "Eight police with AK rifles—[told me I had] 30 hours to empty homesteads and seven days to get all livestock off the ranches."
- "Threatened to be arrested for not moving off the farm. Put in 'holding cell' when I had to appear in court. Prison guard very threatening but did not become violent."
- "Local Member-In-Charge [commanding officer] tore up High Court order documents. Threw documents into dust bin & advised me I would be arrested again & jailed if I returned to the farm."
- "Some of the invaders are policemen and CID members, also Army and Airforce."
- "Local member in charge became a 'settler' on the farm, along with a magistrate and army officer."
- "Most (not all) policemen encouraged and promoted violence and intimidation."
- "The police were called in often and often to the farm. When dealing with political agitators such as war vets they were powerless to enforce the law. The war vets were immune from prosecution and they knew it!"
- "Police were witnessed selling 'plots' and pocketing the proceeds—also were perpetrators of poaching and shooting."

In another case, farm manager Herbert Nchenchi stated that "about 150 war vets" arrived with police and requested to meet with the farmer.[75] The farmer was assured of his safety and so was unarmed, but when he met the police, "the War Vets came in and the police just stood by when the War Vets attacked him." According to Nchenchi, although the farmer had been badly beaten, he was treated as the criminal: "He was detained. They took him up to the police station and he was hurt. He was badly hurt, and they had to take him to hospital."

Rancher Henry Monroe detailed his experience of law enforcement officials being subject to farm invaders' demands:

> They [farm invaders] surrounded us and all our labor was inside the [homestead] security fence, and, ja, they demanded that we get off [the farm]. The local police inspector was there himself, but he did nothing to try to quell things, and this must have gone on from early morning until late afternoon. And then we understood [that our effort to remain on the farm was futile], because we couldn't get in or out [of the homestead][76]

Few farmers could find means to repeatedly navigate these kinds of incidents.

At the same time, farm workers provided numerous examples of the police failing to enforce the law. Foreman James Mwengi explained that after being severely beaten and having his property destroyed by farm invaders, he went to the police seeking remedy, only to be told, "'No, no, no, you go and confront them yourselves.'"[77] In an extraordinary account, farm clerk Joyce Mukwa recounted witnessing war veterans attack police who were not complying with their demands.[78] She stated that violence had reached serious levels on the ranch where she worked, causing police to come and calm the situation. When the five officers arrived, they were angrily confronted by war veterans, who objected to the police enforcing the rule of law on the ranch: "'You are not allowed to come and guard this white man. You must guard us. Go away.' They had to beat them terrible. Then the police had to run away. They [war veterans] grabbed their guns. They kept them [the police] from our place." The incident highlights the extent to which the rule of law had been undermined and farm invaders had been allowed to take on a supralegal position. The rancher and workers witnessing such an incident would hardly have felt they had any protection from state security and would have felt less able to resist farm invaders' demands.

## CHRONIC BREAKDOWN OF FARMER SECURITY

A final key method used to evict farmers was to engender a chronic breakdown of security on their farms. This strategy simply involved imparting a sense of perpetual vulnerability on the farmer and his family—even if no direct violence ensued. With this method, farmers were always left guessing what would happen to them, their workers, and their property. Farmer George Sherman explained that the strategy was not to "pull the rug from under the farmer" in a single dramatic act, but rather to take a gradual piece-by-piece approach where "they're just pulling the hair out of the rug to see whether and when you were actually going to pull off [leave the farm]."[79] What made this strategy so effective was that violations of farmers' security were deep-seated, leaving victims with little sense of control over their personal lives.

Survey data provide many examples of chronic vulnerability. One survey respondent bluntly stated, "Theft—Theft—Theft" in response to a question about losses and intimidation on his farm. The respondent was referencing chronic vulnerability, not an acute, catastrophic loss. Likewise, another survey respondent noted, "Attempted to burn crops, stealing fencing and irrigation equipment." They, too, were highlighting continual losses. As farmers were relatively asset-rich, they could sustain these losses for some time, but not indefinitely—although variations in wealth among different farms meant that some farms could last far longer than others.

A poignant extended example of the chronic breakdown in security comes from Eric Mifflin, a missionary in a farming community in Mashonaland West, who related an experience of a neighboring farmer:

> He drove up to his house, and there were 30 people [farm invaders] still in his house. They were cooking eggs on the stove and watching TV. They were in his swimming pool. There were people lying on his bed. They had just taken over the house, and they kind of sniggered as he came and got something and walked out of the house and left again and realized this was not going to be a pretty picture to hang around.[80]

For the farmer to face 30 people in his home was in itself deeply threatening, but Mifflin stated that what really made the farmer realize that his situation was untenable was the blatant violation of his home, including his bedroom where an orgy involving invaders and their female companions had taken place, and his total inability to do anything about it. Mifflin stated that the scope of the violation was humiliating. "It's one thing to be stolen from when they didn't know you were in the house and they came and stole something. . . . Here you've been violated and they're actually laughing at you. They're sitting in your chair laughing, and there's just nothing you can do about it."

This kind of violation of personal space meant that farming families rarely experienced periods of tranquility. Jane Garfield, the spouse of a farmer, discussed how invaders at their homestead would eventually leave late at night: "It would go on until about four in the morning. Then you'd sort of creep out in the morning and think, 'Now what am I going to find?'"[81] This kind of 24-hour harassment proved deeply undermining to farmers over time, especially when farming neighbors had left, farm operations were increasingly interrupted, and personal invasions increased in severity. Uncertainty was reported by survey respondents to be a major consideration in when to leave their farms.

The data in table 8.1 come from farmer Rupert Garfield and his wife, a largely typical farming couple, who owned a mixed-use farm in Mashonaland Central. The following account is only a brief three-month portion of their

*Table 8.1* THREE-MONTH CHRONOLOGY OF COERCION ON A COMMERCIAL FARM

| Date | Event |
| --- | --- |
| July 9, 2002 | An all-night visit by nine settlers and the Land Technician who gained unauthorised access to homesteads and forcibly and "inventorised" residential properties. The illegality of entry was established by the Ministry and the local MP. Intention to take over all operations, again made clear, bearing in mind "all operations" included not just the basic farming operations but the trading store, the butchery, the bakery and the milk. |
| July 10, 2002 | The settlers forcibly closed the premises and made clear their intentions to take over all operations. |
| July 12, 2002 | The MP and Assistant DA came to our house, ate our food and assured us that everything was quite fine and went out and assured the staff, the whole labour force that everything was quite fine and that we were going nowhere. |
| July 15, 2002 | There was a further extension of time applied and submitted to the Ministry. |
| July 18, 2002 | Attempt to meet the Governor at Mazowe. The meeting, despite an appointment, was unsuccessful [the governor was not available for the meeting]. |
| July 30, 2002 | We had a meeting on the 30th of July in the Ministry in Harare and were referred to some other individual in Bindura. |
| July 31, 2002 | Meeting with this fellow in Bindura who informed us that it was too late for anything and referred us to the Provincial Administrator. |
| August 1, 2002 | First [telephoned] the DA in Concession to arrange a meeting, organised and an appointment made on 2nd August. Suddenly "the DA becomes unavailable." Phoned the fellow in Bindura, referred to another fellow in the Ministry in Harare. |
| August 3, 2002 | We met the DA and the Land's Officer, the latter quite helpful suggested we again draw up the sub-division proposal which we did on the 4th August. |
| August 4, 2002 | Drew up sub-division proposal. |
| August 5, 2002 | Attempted to present the DA with the proposal, "he became unavailable." The other fellow in Harare referred us back to Bindura. The sub-division proposal lodged with Governor, Provincial Administrator, the MP and the Ministry of Lands. |
| August 6, 2002 | Met the DA. Told again "it was too late." Agritex official was interested in the proposal and persuaded the DA to put it before the Provincial Lands Committee. |
| August 7, 2002 | High Court Order was issued allowing us to continue farming and all related activities. |

*(Continued)*

*Table 8.1* Continued

| Date | Event |
| --- | --- |
| August 8, 2002 | Copies of the High Court Order served on the Police, the Ministry and settlers. The settlers just stamped on the order in the wheat land. |
| August 12, 2002 | The settler put padlocks on our son's gate and refuses to move claiming the property for himself. |
| August 14, 2002 | Letter written to the local MP and attempted to phone the member-in-charge [police] who was "unavailable." |
| August 17, 2002 | Settler and four colleagues entered the homestead area and issued death threats. |
| August 18, 2002 | The two Green Bombers [youth militia group] broke into [the] house. Police informed with no response. |
| August 19, 2002 | Settlers and Agritex moved the irrigation pump from main block and secured their own in position. |
| August 26, 2002 | The second High Court Order was granted for the eviction of the settlers and the restraining order. |
| August 27, 2002 | Copy of the eviction and the restraining order served on [local] police with no response whatsoever. Letter was written to the main settler and also to the local MP. |
| September 9, 2002 | My elder son was arrested by the local member-in-charge with the so-called Task Force, then released but all [farm] operations closed down. |
| September 10, 2002 | There was a message to call the [local] member-in-charge. |
| September 11, 2002 | The member-in-charge was contacted who spoke to the DA and instructed all operations to open again on the farm. |
| September 12, 2002 | Prevented by the settlers to open all [farm] operations. So now we immediately had a conflict between the so-called settlers and the so-called administration, actually the member-in-charge and the DA. |
| September 13, 2002 | Saw Assistant Police Inspector . . . and went to the Green Bombers. They backed down and bakery and mill were re-opened. The major incumbent, the 5th Brigade[a] Presidential Guard Major arrived and came there with conditions regarding the running down of stocks in the store stocks and butchery stocks. No conditions were ever discussed. |
| September 14, 2002 | He [Presidential Guard Major] attempted more conditions—wanted the bakery to sell bread to him at wholesale and he sells it retail. The woman who was a DDF [government department] employee in Bindura, she arrived with a DDF tractor and asked for the keys to the bakery manager's house, which was denied. |

*Table 8.1* Continued

| Date | Event |
|---|---|
| September 26, 2002 | The main 5th Brigade individual telephoned concerned about the movement of assets. In the meantime the crane truck and a lorry had been stopped for moving equipment. The mill was closed and the bakery and the police called. During negotiations we made it clear that we were running down store and butchery stocks but we were not prepared to do any deals. Again keys to the bakery manager's house were demanded and refused. |
| September 29, 2002 | The Major, this 5th Brigade individual, telephones on the morning of the 29th that unless he was contacted that night, the Green Bombers were informed that we were persistent but they were going to sell all the bread through the store the following day. The following day the Green Bombers informed all customers that they were only to purchase bread at the store which they had commandeered. The kiosk at the bakery was kept closed and the customers reacted [responded negatively to the closure]. DA phoned and asked for a meeting. |
| October 1, 2002 | Met with the Acting President and Minister for Home Affairs and the MP. Telephoned the current governor and again. The maximum farm size proposal was put to him. |
| October 2, 2002 | Met with the current governor, re-submitted the Land Sub Division Proposal aware that our farm was always 650 hectares and the maximum farm size was 400. So we submitted this very detailed proposal for keeping the 400 hectares and suggested subdividing the balance and letting beneficial settlers in whom we would assist and train, but the 400 hectares was obviously the core of the operation and this is why it was rejected. |
| October 10, 2002 | They [farm invaders] broke in [to the homestead]. |
| October 14, 2002 | Then it was just a succession of padlocks on the gates, breaking their padlocks and putting our padlocks back on. Having those padlocks broken. The woman, the DDF woman broke into the bakery manager's house. . . . It was a very unhealthy so-called agreement which [included] all our inputs and their gain. Then this 5th Brigade individual refused to allow us to combine other wheat because "his" wasn't dry. He hadn't a clue. All wheat has got to dry on the same day. So as far as he was concerned, why were we putting the machine on our lands and not on his wheat. As a result, he actually stopped the combines, threatened the drivers to set fire to the combines and as a result it rained and buggered up the whole wheat crop. |

NOTE: Excerpts have been slightly adapted in order to more prominently identify the dates in question.

[a]The Fifth Brigade was a unit of the Zimbabwe National Army notorious for atrocities committed during the *Gukurahundi* era. The unit was formed in 1981 and disbanded in 1988.

SOURCE: Author's correspondence with respondent.

overall experience. Many farmers experienced multiple years of interference and threats. What is most conspicuous in this account was the Garfields' frequent attempts to comply with purported "requirements" and seek remedy from senior officials. However, a pattern of officials ignoring requests for assistance from farmers is clearly evident.

In July 2000 a document entitled "On the White Farmers and Opposition" was created and circulated among war veterans addressing a purported operation called "Give Up And Leave." A copy of this document was provided to the author from a well-known and reliable anonymous activist respondent.[b] Moreover, the existence of the document has been identified in existing literature, such as by Selby.[82] The document and accompanying operation are probably genuine, both because of the reliability of sources and because the methods of evicting farmers and suppressing the MDC outlined in this book are almost identical to those defined in this document. The following is a transcription of the document:

*25 July 2000*
*ON THE WHITE FARMERS & OPPOSITION*

- The opposition should be systematically infiltrated with highly paid people to destabilize and cause divisions and infighting in the party. This should be from branch/cell level to national.
- Methods should be devised to create negative press reports about the opposition and white farmers regionally and internationally.
- Operation "Give-Up-And-Leave" should be thoroughly investigated and planned so that farmers are systematically harassed and mentally tortured and their farms destabilized until they "give in" and "give up."
- Some farmers should not be included in (3) above. The "Pamire-Silencing-Method" should be used. It should never be pointed to anyone other than the victim him/herself.
- "Sell-Outs" in the farms should be made to vanish with no trace whatsoever.
- There should be a massive secret recruitment of unemployed party faithfulls [*sic*] (to be used/trained?).
- The State President "To Assure Us"

    a) Top Jobs (for Ex Combatants)
    b) No going back on the farm seizures.

---

b. The document was provided to the author on the condition that the respondent's identity not be revealed.

c) Big rewards if the opposition and white farmers are brought to their knees.

d) No more prosecution for any "politically" motivated crimes and readily available, state and party lawyers for those already in the courts

The third bullet point referencing "Operation 'Give Up and Leave'" starkly sums up the methods identified in this chapter. Indeed, farmers were "systematically harassed and mentally tortured," and farms were destabilized until they were no longer commercially viable. The "Pamire Silencing Method" means the murder of an individual that is made to appear as an accident. The term comes from a car crash in 1996 involving businessman Peter Pamire. Army officer Steven Sebungwe explained: "He was killed in an accident when he was coming from the airport. He had gone to South Africa. People believed that he was having an affair with Grace Mugabe. So I don't know what happened to his car. I think they cut one of his brake pipes. So when he was driving home at night he was involved in an accident. He died on the spot."[83] As accounts documented in this book have demonstrated, some farmers were allegedly murdered by the state, and these murders were made to appear not as accidents but as ordinary crimes in which the state had little or no direct involvement.

The fifth bullet point referencing the elimination of "sellouts" has also been identified in this book. This chapter and chapter 5 discussed the targeting of senior farm workers and those accused by the state of assisting farmers. While these individuals did not "vanish with no trace," they were systematically targeted with intimidation and violence, including murder, until this group ended its political support of the MDC and its practical support of commercial farmers. The recruitment of party loyalists also occurred in the form of rallying youths and unemployed people in communal areas. Finally, the sixth bullet point also occurred, with farm seizures being made permanent and war veterans gaining senior positions throughout the government.

The planning by the state to target farms and MDC supporters suggested by this document is important, because it provides further evidence of strong state complicity in a range of extralegal activities. Prior to July 25, 2000, when this document was written, large-scale farm seizures were unplanned, but after the June 2000 parliamentary election—which evidence overwhelmingly suggests ZANU-PF lost by a large margin, prior to the results being doctored—the government realized it had to take focused and urgent action or it would also lose the 2002 presidential election. The document is also important because it demonstrates that farmers were treated more carefully than workers. Rather than murdering large numbers of farmers, most were "mentally tortured" into leaving their property. Large-scale murders of farmers would have gained enormous international news media and political attention that the government did not want, and would likely have cost Mugabe some African political support. However, farmers leaving from "harassment" in a purported popular uprising achieved Mugabe's political aims with fewer negative political consequences.

## CUMULATIVE EFFECT OF REPEATED PRESSURES TO EVICT FARMERS

Threats, violence, and other methods to evict farmers had a cumulative effect on farmers' decision-making on whether to remain on their property. Farmer Chris Cleveland explained:

> They'd [farm invaders] come back and back and back on that same issue [eviction], hoping that you might do something [i.e., leave the farm]. In the meantime, they'll be intimidating the labor and trying to get them on their side, and trying to get them to start to build huts outside their areas on various parts of the farm, trying to show that they had come to take the land.[84]

Given that 45.3% of farmer survey respondents reported having a war veteran militia base on their farms, farm invaders could undertake relentless operations against farmers and workers with relative ease.

This methodical approach to wearing down farmers was often necessary for farm invaders to overcome farmers' emotional and financial attachments to their properties. Farmers lived and derived their livelihoods from farms and raised their children on the land. As a result, many farmers were extremely devoted to their farms and were only evicted after continual and multipronged attacks on their property and aggressive erosion of their personal security.[85]

### Resistance to Eviction

Farmers derived emotional and social value from their farm life, rather than merely economic value. Farmers interviewed for this book spoke often about investing in their farms over the course of many years, often at great personal cost. Kevin Elbridge discussed his efforts to develop the farm into a flourishing business:

> From 1990 to 2000, in 10 years, from a farm with nothing, I developed it to where we had 197 hectares of coffee, 220 hectares of timber, 100 hectares of macadamia nuts. We had a dairy herd of 100 cows and we were starting to develop an avocado pear plantation. . . . We had started building this dam. We had already spent US$300,000 on this dam.[86]

Despite this extensive capital investment, Elbridge's legal title and a decade of labor, the farm was simply taken over: "It was very emotional when these guys came with their 'offer letters' for my plantations, which I'd never recouped any money from. Basically everything was develop, develop, develop, and now it was all taken away."[87]

Farmer James Shore found it difficult to leave what he considered how his farm had been his life's work.[88] He had invested all farm proceeds into further agricultural development on the farm—which benefited the local and national economy—because he had confidence in the government upholding the rule of law:

> I was under extreme stress because I could see that I was in the process of losing everything that I'd worked for 45 years to build up. And I had enough confidence in this government to carry on investing very, very heavily rather than diversifying out of agriculture. As I was gradually having everything taken from me and I was going to be left very, very badly off [financially], which of course I was, and that was the situation we were left in.

Many farmers reported being in Shore's predicament; they were asset wealthy but had few investments outside of their farms. For example, rancher George Lyons stated, "Financially it was devastating on us because we do not have any reserves. We do not have any other means of income and I'm past an employable age now, so it was disastrous for us from a financial point of view."[89] This focus on agricultural investments occurred for many farmers because farming in Zimbabwe had few government incentives and was very capital intensive, so farmers had little choice but to reinvest most profits to further develop the farms. With agriculture being a risky profession, prone to climatic and pest problems, the famers' persistent reinvestment conflated their financial and emotional attachments to the land, fueling a determination to hold onto their land for as long as they could. An anonymous farm survey respondent echoes this view: "I had built this farm up from virgin bush with no boreholes, dams and my wife and I were determined never to leave or sell the farm." The result of the continual reinvestment was that many farmers had few savings, which led some farmers to persist in trying to retain their farms and agri-property.

Cindy Anderson described a similar story, and how in an effort to retain his livelihood, her husband lost his life to farm invaders:

> We had developed our farm from nothing. There was absolutely nothing there [when they first arrived]. Our first thing was to put up a brick

compound for the labor with the electricity and borehole [for water]. We had a shed. We had a drier. . . . All that we did ourselves, and I think my husband had spent, what, about 18 years farming, and we never went on holidays or spent money on the house. Everything always went into the farm that he bought.[90]

Anderson explained that as violence increased, her husband remained attached to the financial and emotional investment he had made on the farm: "I felt angry because I felt that we were endangering our lives and it was money involved. You can also understand when somebody, their whole working life is gone into something, and they don't want to give it up." Anderson's husband, Charles, was murdered in the homestead on June 2, 2002, while Cindy Anderson and their children were held on the lawn at gunpoint.

## The Weakening of Resolve to Remain on the Land

Farmer survey respondents repeatedly identified being exhausted over time by a wide variety of events, particularly by the breakdown of economic security, property rights, and of their social community:

- "A combination of an uncertain social future for my children, a very uncertain economic future, the difficulty of procuring inputs without resorting to backdoor deals and the increasing pressure from settlers to do land prep[aration] for which they supplied the diesel, but tried to evade the monetary payment."
- "August 2002, couldn't take the constant terrorism and how livestock and trees, crops were mangled and our lives threatened."
- "I could not farm. There was no law. They [farm invaders] shot or snared all the game, netted the dams, cut all the trees down, burnt the farm, stole everything, intimidated my labour."
- "I WAS the last farmer in the immediate area on my land and it became frightening being alone, and the community was falling apart with lack of safety at the farm over weekends, and no church operating anymore."
- "Friends and neighbours had left or had been killed. I left because my property had been coveted by a relation of a member of the ZANU-PF party and was ordered to do so—resistance would have been futile."
- "Over two years too many people had been moved on. The lands were pegged [by war veterans]—and it just became impossible to operate, and I was not prepared to co-operate."

- "Four years of uncertainty, looked as though we had no future, 'offer' letter to 'new' owner with persistent farm visits, labour lost will to work, high ranking official who had an interest in my farm, endless meetings with police, DA etc. take their toll."
- "It became unviable as we were down-sized to a point that you could no longer ranch. Theft was uncontrollable. Labourers were not allowed to work. Could no longer cope with emotional and sociological [*sic*] stress."
- "I was advised by my District Administrator that I was fighting a losing battle and that I should get off with what I can before I lose the lot. I took her advice."
- "The biggest reason I left the farm was an economic one. Inputs had to be bought at black market rates and I was unable to trade forex [foreign currency] from flower exports at the same rate—as well as witnessing first hand horrendous intimidation against my neighbours."

Concern among farmers over the breakdown of their community was repeatedly cited by farmers. The attitude was neatly summed up by one rancher in Matabeleland South who said that he "didn't want to be left sitting high and dry with no neighbours."[91] This concern was multifaceted. It was a social concern in not wanting to be the only white farmer remaining in an environment of "new" farmers closely allied to ZANU-PF and likely to be antiwhite, but there were also economic concerns in that farmer neighbors helped each other resolve problems on farms. Cooperation among neighbors to control stray livestock, mitigate fire damage, and prevent theft was very important.

Farmer Thomas Barkley explained that the tipping point for him in deciding to leave his farm was reached when he was given an ultimatum to leave by a group of farm invaders and police.[92] He explained that he had three farms and had agreed to give up two, but invaders had then begun demanding portions of his last farm. Barkley had already experienced a very extensive breakdown of his ability to operate the farm, having had his irrigation system rendered inoperable. For security reasons, he had moved his family off the farm, which left him alone on the property. He explained the tipping point came when his personal safety was threatened: "They [farm invaders] arrived with about three or four policemen armed, which was—I was quite scared . . . that was very intimidatory. I was told, literally, I had half an hour to vacate." Barkley explained that facing an armed and intoxicated group of farm invaders alone gave him a sense of the hopelessness about remaining on his land:

The scary part of that . . . they arrived with one of those mini buses full of youths. Now you're talking about illegal substances. These guys were goofed [intoxicated] out of their heads, absolutely. They'd just mixed Chibuku [beer] with *mbanje* [marijuana], and they were goofed and they were in a tight circle around me. . . . They were just waiting for instructions to beat the hell out of me. So I said, 'ja, OK, fine, I'll move now. I've been fighting this for bloody 18 months or more'. . . The threat of violence was always there, the whole time. With anyone and everyone.

Barkley had faced similar situations before and had been able to navigate them, but the crippling operating environment and perpetual risks to his safety and that of his workers brought him to a tipping point. Similarly, farmer Rupert Garfield summed up the psychological consequences of farmers experiencing these kinds of chronic vulnerabilities:

> We could see that the die was cast and whether we managed to stay on another week or a month or a year, the die was cast and they [ZANU-PF and farm invaders] had it in for us. We did what we could within the confines of a very diminishing social and legal framework because . . . one's got to appreciate that our whole community was crumbling. . . . And we could just see it [crumbling]. We had a radio and in desperation we left it on, but if you called for help, there was no response [from other farmers, because they had been evicted].[93]

Garfield's testimony highlights how farmers came to appreciate the futility of resisting the government's efforts to evict them. Likewise, rancher Daniel Fairbanks highlighted how farmers' psychological ability to resist farm invaders was gradually undermined:

> It's a continuous attack on you—the way they attack the wildlife. . . . They've been to some people and then they chop all the beautiful trees in their garden or they kill their goldfish or they smash their dog's brains in or something like that. That is a psychological war. Now, they're not physically attacking you, but they're attacking your mind.[94]

Fairbanks emphasized that the efforts by some farm invaders to make deals with farmers, such as through entering into bargains to end coercion in exchange for agri-property, or to concede some land if the invaders promised not to pursue the remaining assets, had the effect of raising hopes for farmers. Ultimately, as chapter 7 has described, these deals rarely lasted. This left the farmer even more desperate, as he realized that the few apparent means of recourse available to him provided no positive long-term results.

James Shore explained how his home environment, his ability to operate the farm, and his physical security were comprehensively broken down.[95] Most important of all was the apparently bleak prospects for a future improvement in law and order and the impossibility of protecting his property rights.

> I had reached the stage on that last day, when I was surrounded by about . . . 15 or 20 people . . . at my garage at the house and they were shouting at me and I was shouting at them. Halfway through it I thought, whatever are you doing here? I had been living in the house. I had my cattle . . . squashed in one corner of the farm, and nothing else was happening on my side. They [farm invaders] were all over the place, and I thought, well, is it really worthwhile pursuing this? I mean, I've got no law to support me, no work for people on the farm who I know sympathized and hoped that I wouldn't be booted out, but they were physically afraid of coming to my assistance in many ways, and I thought, well, you know, what's the use of it?

Shore elaborated on the attritional aspect of farm invaders' constant threats: "It just gradually wearing one down . . . not physically touching you or anything like that, but just intimidating you to a point that after a period of months and months, one eventually gave in."

Most farmers in situations such as Shore's eventually recognized that there was no hope of a favorable resolution to the farm invasions for them, and the best option available was to leave their farms. Only a fraction of farmers were able to remain. Chapter 7 highlighted relatively rare cases of successful long-term protection agreements. In extremely unusual cases, farmers were able to successfully thwart farm invaders' efforts to seize their land and assets. In these situations, the farmer had to be exceptionally hardy and willing to accept severe curtailments to his freedom and lifestyle. Ranchers such as Fairbanks were willing to endure imprisonment for several days at a time until bogus charges were eventually dropped.[96] Fairbanks had to accept that on release from prison he might come home to find the homestead ransacked. He devised methods to avoid facing farm invaders as much as was possible, such as by gaining intelligence from his workers on the invaders' whereabouts and pretending he was not at home when invaders arrived at his homestead. This made it difficult for invaders to directly threaten him. Fairbanks also expended extensive financial resources to protect his labor in order to retain their support. With this kind of commitment, farmers could sometimes deter farm invaders for a lengthy period. However, farmer's individual circumstances differed considerably. Some farmers needed to protect families that included small children, and other families contended that farm invaders actually moved into the homestead with them. Most farmers were unable or unwilling to accept such invasive conditions and the concomitant severe threat to their security, and simply left their farms.

Makabusi further underscores these accounts with a summation of what he witnessed in Mashonaland East.[97] He explained that the invaders on the farm believed he was sympathetic to ZANU-PF and confided in him their strategy for removing the farmer. This essentially involved wearing down the farmer and engendering a sense of hopelessness: "You [farm invaders] get your own band of guys, get them boozed up, offer them money, and you go [to the farm]. You go and cause a racket." He said that over time the farmer would reflect to himself on the fate of other farmers in his district: "This has happened to guys [other farmers] before. In the past two years, this has been happening to people, so it's now happening to me. Let me just pack up and go because I'm not going to win." Seeing that there was no likelihood of success, Makabusi said in most cases the farmer would then leave his property.

Finally, insight into the extent of psychological pressure experienced by farmers and the high levels of anxiety and uncertainty they experienced when seeking to remain on their farms comes from Thomas Barkley.[98] He stated that he knew that negotiations on subdividing his property would last several months, but as no previous agreements with farm invaders had ever been honored, he felt the final result of eviction was inevitable. Barkley explained his feelings the moment he decided to leave his property:

> Eventually it wears you down to such a degree that you just say, "Okay, enough now." When I eventually got the boot and I was given that half hour [to vacate, Barkley's wife] was in town [Harare], and I said, "Don't come back home. I'm out of here. . . . I'm not going back there because of those bloody youths and that lot that had come out from Harare," and she burst into tears. . . . I never felt that. I just felt enormous relief. I just felt *phew*, it's over and I'll just move on. . . . I just felt now I don't have to deal with all that shit any more.

Barkley added that when the emotional pressure had diminished a short time in the future, he experienced "bitterness" over the loss of his agri-property and land. However, he believed the eviction was inevitable and felt relief after being evicted, because he would no longer have to cope with the daily uncertainty of farm invaders' behavior.

## Financial Tipping Points

Chronic vulnerability had important effects on farmers' financial considerations. It helps explain why more farmer survey respondents left in August 2002, when violence levels were relatively low, than in March 2002, when violence reached its highest point in the land seizure era. The reason points to a key difference for farmers between acute and chronic vulnerability. Acute vulnerability can, to some extent, be endured because the victim knows the event will soon pass (for instance, the presidential election period had a definitive end). Chronic vulnerability, however, broke down hope that tranquility and an environment in which commercial farmers could operate would ever be restored.

Farmers left in August 2002 for a multitude of reasons. By this month some 2,900 remaining farmers were subject to eviction under Section 8 of the 2002 Land Acquisition Act, with violators subject to a large fine and jail term of two years, or both. The International Crisis Group recorded 300 farmers being jailed in 2002 "for defying orders to vacate their farms."[99] However, at the time the constitutionality of the eviction orders was questioned. Indeed, news media articles stated that 60% of farmers were remaining on their properties "waiting to see if the government would enforce the order" and underscored the willingness of some farmers to defy the eviction orders.[100] There is no doubt that arrest or the threat of arrest was a major concern for many farmers who feared conditions in Zimbabwe's jails. Some 21.8% of farmer survey respondents experienced at least one act of abduction or unlawful arrest. Interview accounts underscore that farmers were highly aware that the prospect of arrest was real, given that their colleagues were being jailed, and they feared both the uncertainty of arrests that could occur on short notice as well as the unsanitary conditions in Zimbabwe's notorious jails.[101]

More tobacco and food-crop farmers left in August 2002 than in any other month because—within this overarching environment of uncertainty that included widespread coercion, breakdowns of law and order, and risks of arrest—it was the last month in the farming calendar before farmers had to make a financial commitment to the next season's crop. By August of each year, farmers largely needed to have committed to purchasing seed, fertilizer, fuel supplies, and chemicals to be ready when rainfall and soil temperatures were optimal for planting the tobacco crop in September or October of each year. Accordingly, farmers faced rigid time constraints imposed by seasonal growing conditions. This commitment to the next growing season required an enormous financial outlay before the crop was even planted. For a 50-hectare tobacco crop (and most farms were much larger than 50 hectares), the total cost from planting seedbeds to final sale would be approximately US$8,000 per hectare, or US$400,000 in total.[102] When the crop was planted, farmers still had to grow and protect the crop 24 hours a day for the entire season (four to five months for tobacco and six to seven months for maize), then harvest and process the crop before selling it and gaining any profit. Only when the crop was sold did farmers recoup their initial investment—often made several months prior—making this commitment especially risky when farmers were already facing myriad threats. Moreover, crops obviously cannot be moved or hidden during the growing season to protect them from threats. Farms of several hundred hectares and larger were almost impossible to protect from farm invaders, who could simply burn an entire crop. In sum, farmers faced an extremely risky investment climate in August 2002.[103]

Obviously, farmers were affected by violence, as data herein indicate. Yet it also appears that the 77.4% of survey respondents who indicated that threats were the primary reason for eviction were not simply referring to physical threats. In fact, survey data have shown that ultimately the balance tipped for many farmers because of the need to make immense financial commitments to crops that, in all likelihood, would simply be stolen or destroyed by farm invaders. If farmers did not intend to plant crops, there was little reason to remain on the farm and endure violent invaders, who would likely intensify their efforts if faced with farmers who decided to forgo planting. For most farmers in August 2002, when contemplating another year's crop, the position was untenable.

Therefore, two causes explain the timing of farmers growing tobacco and food crops being evicted in August 2002. Farmers' devotion to their property and reliance on the farm for their livelihood meant that it took time for the cumulative effect of threats and violence to reach levels that were sufficient to dislodge farmers. Farmers had an enormous amount to lose if evicted, so although victims of acute, extremely violent encounters might leave, most victims of chronic violence persevered on their farms long past 2000, when, according to the survey, 46.6% of farmers experienced violence or intimidation for the first time. Over time, friends and neighbors would have been attacked, along with workers, often in shocking and brutal ways. Farmers likely hoped the situation would improve and, given that farms were their homes and livelihoods, took all possible measures to remain. This was especially so for the many farmers who faced financial destitution if they left. Still, violence levels increased from 2000, reaching a peak in March 2002. By that stage, it became clear that farm invaders could simply walk into a homestead and engage in theft and other crimes, not only with police acquiescence but sometimes with their direct assistance. Although many farmers were likely to be emotionally and financially defeated by this point, it appears that many persisted until the last possible moment—August 2002—when they would be required to commit to inputs for the next growing season. The need to commit to the next season's crops led farmers to re-evaluate the situation, with many deciding to capitulate. The majority of farmers in the survey, 51.2%, left their farms in 2002, and 12.1%

of all farmers left in August 2002, the greatest proportion to leave in any one month during the land seizure era.

The survey data clearly indicate that individual threats alone were insufficient to evict all farmers. On the contrary, the most effective means of evicting a farmer was to deprive him of hope for farming in the future. The creation of a pervasive, persistent atmosphere of violence and intimidation that threatened farmers' economic and social, as well as physical, well-being was necessary to achieve universal eviction. Multiple, long-term, low-level assaults and threats fundamentally shattered the victim's hope for the future. Once the farmer realized he had no hope, no friends and neighbors, no viable business, no property rights, and no personal safety, then he would almost always leave his farm. Acute incidents could leave the farmer with the hope that it was just "bad luck" and so there may still be hope, or that other positive aspects made staying on the farm worthwhile. The obvious exception was a "trashing," which was so financially devastating for the farmer and so fundamentally demonstrative of the lack of security, that most farmers left after such an incident. Usually, however, farm invaders were ultimately most effective when they relentlessly applied pressure on multiple fronts, thereby conveying to the farmer their ability to break the law with impunity over extended periods. This left farmers with no hope for the future and therefore no reason to remain and endure the risks.

## CONCLUSION

Farmers were frequently subjected to violence during the land seizure era, as has been extensively documented in existing literature and in this book.[104] However, it was relatively unusual for farmers to be forcibly evicted in single, violent attacks. Other means of intimidating farmers, such as interference in the operation of their farms, theft of resources and arson against farm buildings, were not explicitly violent, but over time often forced the farmer to abandon his property.

While many farmers left purely because of physical threats, most were evicted through a comprehensive and chronic breakdown in security and disrespect for property rights. The timing and intensity of violence, as well as the methods through which violence was deployed, were partly responsible for creating a sense of "chronic vulnerability." This drew farmers into a war of attrition in which the farm invaders almost always emerged as the victors.

This "chronic vulnerability" had emotional consequences for the farmer, but also significantly undermined his ability to operate his farm as a business. By 2002, when violence and lawlessness was widespread, many farmers were unwilling to undertake the financial commitment to growing the next season's crop. These farmers recognized that it was economically unfeasible to protect a large crop 24 hours a day for the several-month-long cropping cycle, at a time when Zimbabwe was experiencing widespread political violence. In that environment, despite the fact that the farmers could protect themselves physically to some extent, the financial risks of farming when faced with comprehensive threats was too great to ignore.

# Impact on Commercial Agriculture Production

This final chapter shows that the land seizure era has had a profound impact on Zimbabwe's economy and society. The chapter explores the consequences for commercial agriculture through documenting levels of crop production and analyzing why cropping was severely impacted by the breakdown of farmers' property rights. The chapter examines existing research on the agriculture sector after the farm invasion period to understand how other researchers have concluded that the sector has largely recovered from farm invasions. In fact, the evidence shows that the negative impact on the agribusiness sector continues to affect the national economy. Meanwhile, the chapter discusses how the erosion of personal and property rights had serious consequences for farmers seeking to remain on their land.

## DECLINE IN NATIONAL AGRICULTURE PRODUCTION

Bill Kinsey has noted that in any radical reform there will be a transitional phase as markets and production systems adjust.[1] Zimbabwe's transitional phase has been long and costly. Evidence showing a severe fall in Zimbabwe's agriculture production after February 2000, when the land seizure era began, is consistent. Figure 9.1 demonstrates that, beginning in 2000, there was a clear drop in agricultural production in Zimbabwe. By contrast, production increased both in neighboring South Africa and worldwide during the same 2000 to 2009 period. Likewise, farm production in Zimbabwe can also be seen in agriculture value-added data, which show that agriculture generated 22% of GDP in 1998, but just 14% in 2002.[2] Annual growth in the agriculture industry fell from 3.2% in 2000, when the invasions began, to –22.7% in 2002, when violence was most intense.[3] The economy as a whole grew by 2.9% in 1998, but contracted by 9.8% in 2002 and by 17.2% in 2003.[4] Moreover, Professor Tony Hawkins has indicated that "food and livestock production (excluding beef) collapsed from three million tonnes in 2000 to 1.3 million tonnes 12 years later."[5]

The enormous decline in production, and overall knock-on effect on the national economy, was a direct consequence of the farm takeovers.[6] Trained, well-capitalized farmers were evicted, resulting in loss of established expertise, which undermined the ability of the agricultural sector to maintain stable production levels.[7] Experienced farmers left their land and were replaced, in most instances, with invaders who had little or no commercial farming experiences, which then meant that farms no longer produced sufficient quantities of the national staple foods. Moreover, disputes over landownership claims among different invaders and with the government, along with insufficient

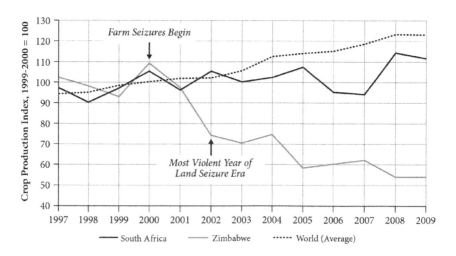

**Figure 9.1** Crop Production Index
NOTE: World Bank crop production index based on production values in USD. Data reflect all crops except fodder crops.
SOURCE: World Bank, "Zimbabwe Crop Production Index."

capital, have resulted in large tracts of land being unused.[8] For instance, a 2008 report found that only 55% of commercial farmland was being used.[9] Similarly, the 2003 Utete report for the government identified that just 66% of A2 beneficiaries (commercial farmers) had actually taken their land.[10] Meanwhile, the commercial farmers who had not yet left, as well as many "new" farmers who faced competition to hold onto the land that they had seized, were still experiencing severe threats to their personal and property rights by 2005—a problem that in some areas still persists at the time of publication; land claims in Zimbabwe remain political and thus subject to continual change. It is reasonable to expect that farmers facing such threats would hide their assets to the greatest extent possible and minimize future production in order to mitigate anticipated losses.

Food scarcity, caused by the breakdown of the commercial farming sector, lasted long after the early farm seizures of 2000. Food insecurity could be attributed to droughts, and while droughts have obviously had a major detrimental effect, Zimbabwe's commercial farming sector prior to 2000 had historically provided sufficient food for the country. For example, according to Godfrey Mudimu at the Overseas Development Institute, "Zimbabwe has been food self-sufficient [e.g., during the droughts of 1982, 1987, and 1992] and even exported surpluses to fellow SADC countries and others (such as Ethiopia)."[11] He noted that prior to 2000 the country even maintained stores of food: "Before 1999, the country had produced surplus and maintained a strategic grain reserve that covered six–nine months."

The International Federation of the Red Cross (IFRC) stated in a 2009 report that Zimbabwe was the most food aid-dependent country in the world.[12] That same year, the World Food Programme reported that nearly 7 million Zimbabweans needed food aid, about 75% of the population.[13] In 2012, the IFRC made an emergency appeal for food aid in Zimbabwe.[14] Similarly, in 2014 the IFRC reported that some rural Zimbabweans were trading sexual favors for food.[15]

The breakdown of the commercial farming sector also caused widespread socioeconomic dislocation. The UNDP estimated that between 200,000 and 400,000 workers were displaced, agricultural markets failed, institutional knowledge on commercial farms was lost, major strains were put on commercial lending institutions, and the ensuing collapse of the national economy caused a severe breakdown in social service institutions.[16] Thus, food insecurity stems not just from the failure of actual crop production, but a collapse in the complex socioeconomic system of which agriculture was an integral part. While some researchers have recorded production increases, they are often referring to specific, individual cases and not the agricultural system as a whole.

## SHIFT FROM PROFESSIONAL COMMERCIAL PRODUCTION
## TO AGRICULTURAL PATRONAGE

The key aspect of this breakdown was the transformation from an established, organized, and market-based agricultural sector to a system of patronage. While this book disputes many of the findings made by Scoones and his colleagues, it is indisputable that some land beneficiaries have achieved notable production results.[17] However, the overarching agriculture sector—from land allocation, to government aid for agricultural inputs—has become highly political.[18] This means that the criteria for success, insofar as the ability of farmers to retain land and receive government aid is concerned, are dictated less by market forces than by political ties; the most politically connected—not the most skilled—farmers tended to get the most land and farming assistance from the state. The distorting effects of this patrimonial system have a negative overall impact on production, even if it is possible to identify some well-connected beneficiaries.

For instance, Zamchiya gave an example where the government initiated a "Champion Farmer Programme" whereby the most skilled "new" farmers would be given preferential access to the limited supply of agricultural inputs such as seed and fertilizer.[19] He found that over time the process had become politicized, resulting in patronage, rather than skill, functioning as the criterion for awarding the valuable inputs. While in some instances this resulted in a few farmers having more productive harvests, it also allowed the allocated inputs to be sold for profit: "The Agritex officials were not happy with the politicized identification of champion farmers as they felt their technical roles had been usurped and that such a process resulted in bad harvests."

This kind of politicization and corruption was widespread after about 2005. The GMB accountant Timothy Ngavi commented that after the farm seizures began, there were numerous new personnel assigned to senior positions in the GMB.[20] Appointees in some cases had no practical experience but instead relied upon political connections to gain top positions: "I know someone who was, for example, a forklift driver of the company, but he was so strong politically that when he joined [the GMB] he was made the provincial manager for the province." Ngavi explained that at the time the GMB was responsible for the distribution of inputs for new farmers, "So these political appointees were supposed to supervise this, the issuing of maize, grain, seed, and fertilizers."[21] Ngavi reiterated that these individuals had special powers over what were deemed "political decisions," which were not subject to conventional professional considerations. The quality of decision-making at the GMB rapidly deteriorated: "The maize seed would go to relatives and friends, and it would be kept by a few people for the seasons to come, and meanwhile others don't have anything. This is what happened. So it was a deliberate attempt to try and solve this [problem of new farmers having no inputs], but it did not work. It did not work."

The breakdown of professionalism in the commercial farming sector was critical, since so much of agri-business functions on trust and networks of cooperation. Patronage meant that individuals could bypass conventional channels and create market distortions that ultimately undermined productivity. For example, farmer William Shore stated that commercial seed suppliers had historically allowed farmers to purchase an excess of seed in case it was needed at short notice during planting time; any unused seed could be returned for a refund.[22] After 2000, however, commercial seed suppliers found that in some cases returned seed bags had been adulterated, so the program was canceled and henceforth all farmers lost the community benefit of the program. Similarly, Zamchiya gave an example from the GMB's program for subsidized seed and fertilizer:

[The war veteran] benefited from the Grain Marketing Board's (GMB) subsidised fertiliser and seeds. He did not wait in the long queue to obtain these items but, like many war veterans and traditional leaders, he simply produced his war veteran card and then jumped the queue. According to a GMB worker, "it was difficult to control the amount of seed and fertiliser war veterans and senior ZANU(PF) officials would get because they were very aggressive."[23]

In another example, Ngavi stated that he was aware of a practice whereby a new farmer would send a lorry to the GMB to deliver a load of maize.[24] Once the lorry's cargo was weighed and the "new" farmer given a payment receipt, the vehicle would depart—without delivering the load. It would then circle the GMB facility and return again, ostensibly delivering another load of grain. This process would happen numerous times before the cargo was ultimately delivered, allowing the farmer to claim multiple payments from a single delivery. The consequences for the GMB was that the state-owned enterprise rapidly faced profound financial difficulties, while the state lost revenue from tax receipts and was unable to accurately calculate the harvesting of the nation's staple food crops.

The practice required the cooperation of GMB officials, providing further evidence of how a partisan patronage system undermined economic rationality. After 2000, key stakeholders in the agricultural sector increasingly relied upon personal ties to further their objectives. In gaining land, inputs, and bank loans, patronage and personal ties replaced professional, objective criteria. This opened the door for rampant corruption, which undermined productivity: "Agricultural extension officers also blamed political claims to land for undermining agricultural production. The extension officer held the view that some new farmers were able to legitimate their stay on the land through politics rather than through agricultural production."[25] Personal ties meant that favors could be given and withheld.

The breakdown of commercial agriculture also meant that where farmers had previously been almost totally self-sufficient, new farmers were often highly dependent on the state for assistance. This introduced obvious inefficiencies and had a high cost for the state, and encouraged major opportunities for corruption. For example, government fuel trucks would sometimes dispense diesel to self-proclaimed farmers.[26] Individuals of every description, including children, would claim some of this diesel, before promptly going to the local petrol station where it could be resold. Corruption also meant that those who were allocated resources could claim kickbacks from beneficiaries, further distorting the agribusiness sector and introducing not only a major drag on production, but a major red flag that tended to drive away commercial investors.

The dependence of new farmers on state assistance also meant that ZANU-PF could rely upon the cadre of new farmers for political support. During election times there was an increase in the provision of aid to rural communities. In the Lupane area, for instance, the government promised to bring electrification to rural villages. As the election neared, some basic power lines would be put up, but once the election was over the project was shelved and rural communities still had little access to the power grid. Similar strategies were used with the dispensing of fertilizer and seed.

Senior CIO agent Hastings Lundi stated that during the land seizure era there was such a frenzy to seize farms that there was little "forward planning" on the part of claimants—who, in his view, were largely civil servants:

> It was your poorly paid civil servants, some of them taking on a 2,000-hectare farm. Where are you going to get the money from? There wasn't any foresight in terms of, "Do I really want to be a farmer myself?" It was just, "OK, I've got a farm. It's going to farm itself." . . . There wasn't really any sort of forward planning to say, "Well, where am I going to get the finance from?"

With productive and well-organized farms taken over by individuals with no agricultural background or capital, the government found itself responsible for having to support these farmers in order to mitigate the collapse of the agriculture sector.

Yet the reality that agricultural production fell substantially is not universally recognized. Scoones et al. claim that, in some areas, and with some commodities, there were increases in production.[27] However, there is no evidence to support claims that agriculture production has increased more broadly. Even data supplied by Sam Moyo in table 9.1 show that most agricultural commodities were produced in lower quantities in 2010–2011 than in the 1990s; this is especially the case for wheat and maize, which are the main food staples.[28]

As noted previously, the findings from Scoones et al. and Hanlon, Manjengwa, and Smart are localized and not generalizable.[29] They show that, in some cases, the specific experiences of some farmers led to improvements, but they do not pay sufficient attention to the greater dislocation of the agribusiness sector—and this is what really impacted the national economy.

Large-scale agriculture production enables the development of agribusiness, the business of agricultural production. Agribusiness includes commercial farms as well as the broad range of associated businesses that support agricultural production, including companies that provide farm machinery, livestock, feed, seed, and agrichemicals, transportation and distribution businesses, crop specialists such as agronomists, and a host of other less agri-focused businesses such as those engaged in marketing, sales, and accounting. It is these businesses that depend largely on commercial farms and that generate enormous levels of employment and tax revenue. Accordingly, the breakdown of commercial farms in Zimbabwe did not simply lead to farmers and workers being evicted and displaced; it resulted in the collapse of a complex sector of interconnected businesses. This is what led directly to the catastrophic collapse of the national economy.

There was also the loss of enormous skill, experience, and expertise of farmers and workers who had developed their institutional knowledge over multiple generations. "The former white farmers knew what they were doing," acknowledged Tongai Muzenda, deputy public service, labor, and social welfare minister in 2014: "This area of Gutu West used to have a [cattle] herd of close to 60,000—but now all is history. We want to return to those golden days when the country was among the best beef producers and exporters in southern Africa."[30] Muzenda is also reported to have said, "The former white farmers knew very well that there is no crop you can produce in this part of the country hence they concentrated on cattle production," further pointing to an awareness of institutional knowledge on the part of commercial farmers and workers.[31]

Muzenda was certainly not calling for a return to the agriculture structure that had existed prior to the land seizure era. Few people, even many commercial farmers, would disagree with the claim that major land reform had to occur. What is important to highlight is that the picture of successful land

*Table 9.1* COMPARISON OF AGRICULTURAL PRODUCTION: 1990S TO 2010/11

| Crop | 1990s (avg.) | 2002/3 | 2005/6 | 2006/7 | 2007/8 | 2009/10 | 2010/11 | % Change: 1990s–2010/11 |
|---|---|---|---|---|---|---|---|---|
| Maize | 1,685.6 | 1,058.8 | 1,484.8 | 952.6 | 575.0 | 1,322.7 | 1,451.6 | −13.9 |
| Wheat | 248.4 | 122.4 | 241.9 | 149.1 | 34.8 | 41.5 | 164.8 | −33.7 |
| Small grains | 164.8 | 112.8 | 163.9 | 120 | 80.1 | 193.9 | 13.1 | −92.1 |
| Edible dry beans | 5.3 | 7.1 | 21.5 | 30 | 3.8 | 17.2 | — | N/A |
| Groundnuts (shelled) | 86 | 86.5 | 83.2 | 100.2 | 131.5 | 186.2 | 230.5 | 168.0 |
| Soybeans | 92.8 | 41.1 | 70.3 | 112.3 | 48.3 | 70.2 | 84.2 | −9.3 |
| Sunflower | 41.2 | 16.9 | 16.7 | 25.7 | 5.5 | 14 | 11.5 | −72.1 |
| Tobacco | 198.3 | 93.5 | 44.5 | 79 | 69.8 | 123 | 177.8 | −10.3 |
| Cotton | 207.8 | 159.5 | 207.9 | 235.0 | 226.4 | 260 | 220.1 | 5.9 |
| Sugar | 438.9 | 502 | 446 | 349 | 259 | 350 | 450 | 2.5 |
| Tea | 10.6 | 22.0 | 22.0 | 13.5 | 8.3 | 14 | | N/A |
| Coffee | 8.4 | 8 | 1.3 | 0.7 | 0.8 | 0.3 | | N/A |
| Citrus | 90 | 130 | 123 | 123 | | | | N/A |
| Noncitrus fruit and vegetables | 149 | 180 | 161 | 162 | | | | N/A |

NOTE: Figures are in thousands of tons.

SOURCE: Sam Moyo, "Three Decades of Agrarian Reform in Zimbabwe," *Journal of Peasant Studies* 38, no. 3 (2011): 519. Sam Moyo lists his sources as the Ministry of Agriculture, Mechanisation and Irrigation Development, World Bank, Gain Report, and Zimbabwe Tea Growers Association.

beneficiaries put forward by researchers such as Hanlon, Manjengwa, and Smart is not supported by evidence of agriculture crop production supplied by impartial research institutions.[32] Their findings also do not seek to account for the enormous loss of expertise, for example on animal husbandry, which takes decades to develop.

A major contribution of the research of Sam Moyo and Scoones et al. is that they have shown that small-scale producers can—in select cases—make up some ground for specific commodities.[33] For example, Zimbabwe's tobacco production levels have nearly recovered to 2000 levels. Thousands of small-scale producers are now engaged in tobacco farming, which tends to be far more lucrative than other crops. There is clearly a place for small-scale production, since it provides employment and benefits livelihoods, and their productivity is impressive. However, the production of nearly all other crops is well below 2000 levels. There is practically no evidence to support claims that small-scale production exceeds large-scale production and that it could make up for the shortfall in output. Economies of scale, the benefits of (expensive) advanced technology, familiarity with the latest techniques, and the ability to capitalize on crop rotation mean that commercial production in almost all cases will lead to higher productivity. As important, large-scale commercial production is also a critical engine for the economy through the network of dependent professions that make up the agribusiness sector.

Some researchers have attempted to downplay perspectives that base their analysis on productivity data. Sam Moyo states that an overt focus on linear agricultural production "detaches the analysis of land reform from the broader question of agrarian transformation, leading to flawed conclusions about the relationship between land ownership, land reform, and agricultural development."[34] Moyo's focus on "transforming the role of various agrarian classes" points to the breakup of the white-dominated commercial farming sector. In Moyo's view, there is value not just in enabling agricultural production but in dislocating the "legacy of colonialism" that many perceive to have been inherent in the commercial farming structure prior to the land seizure era.

This perspective is also open to criticism. Since 1980 Zimbabwean law had operated under a "willing buyer, willing seller" program for the transactions of farms. The government had legal right of first refusal when farms were placed on the market, thereby ensuring the government has the mechanism to purchase farms for land redistribution. Zimbabwe's successful land redistribution program in the 1980s attests to the effectiveness of these legal provisions in making land available for government programs. Indeed, numerous farmer respondents indicated that they engaged with the government through this mechanism when they sold their farms.[35] There were other, far less "radical" ways of transforming the commercial farming sector—if that was indeed a priority.

As evidence in this book has shown, however, it had not been Mugabe's initial intention to allow the widespread and destructive farm seizures that occurred between 2000 and 2008. When land claimants began to pour onto farms, all the government could do was hastily apply the label of "land redistribution" in order to mask its loss of control. The ultimate collapse of a highly successful agricultural industry demonstrates that Mugabe was correct in his original belief that a violent and disorderly campaign of farm seizures would jeopardize Zimbabwe's socioeconomic well-being.

# Conclusion

Three major findings emerge from this book, some of which contradict established literature and long-standing assumptions about Zimbabwe's land seizure era. First, the government never intended mass large-scale farm takeovers; in fact, the state lost control over the small-scale, extralegal farm seizures that it had initially authorized. Second, ZANU-PF's primary focus was on preserving its political power during the land seizure era, rather than engaging in a genuine effort to reform the inequities that existed in access to land. Third, extensive violence was deployed against an unarmed population both as a punitive measure to suppress suspected supporters of the MDC opposition, and in an effort to evict farmers and seize land, associated assets, or both before competitors took them.

A key finding, absent from previous literature, is that Mugabe initially opposed large-scale farm takeovers. Prior to the land seizure era, Mugabe needed the financial resources generated by commercial agriculture and funding from international donors, neither of which would be forthcoming if the government was seen to be destroying the commercial farming industry. In recognizing that large-scale seizures would be detrimental to the economy, Mugabe initially sought to prevent them. The need to protect agriculture is one explanation for the lack of large-scale land reform in the 20 years after independence, despite the legal mechanisms allowing the government to undertake comprehensive reform earlier. Thus, despite his public, pro-seizure posturing in pursuit of war veteran political support, Mugabe took steps to protect commercial agriculture.

This position became less tenable as government intelligence reports and public demonstrations by farmers gave the impression that most farmers were supporting the MDC. In fact, support for the MDC among commercial farmers was not nearly as widespread as ZANU-PF claimed. Still, farmers' public and financial involvement in opposition politics triggered a furious response from ZANU-PF officials and war veterans, who recalled their conflict with the Rhodesian state. The ruling party believed that white farmers were not only ungrateful to ZANU-PF for not seizing farms after independence, but were now mobilizing to retain colonial-era privileges. Moreover, farmers' financial support for the MDC was evidently still sufficient, even if it was provided by a smaller number of farmers than ZANU-PF claimed, to threaten the ruling party. As a result, Mugabe could no longer privately defend commercial farmers in front of the enraged war veteran constituency whose support he so vitally needed. While public support for the MDC among farmers was actually far less than portrayed by ZANU-PF, the anecdotal evidence showing a relationship between the MDC and the white farmers enabled ZANU-PF to characterize all farmers as disloyal neocolonials and thus as political and historical enemies. The racial and colonial dimension further stiffened war veteran and ZANU-PF resolve to target farms.

The initial plan, however, was merely to fire a warning shot to farmers and workers by seizing a small number of farms that would then be used to appease war veterans' land demands. The evidence presented from interviews with intelligence agents, police officers, senior politicians, state security officials, and war veterans have demonstrated that the violent takeovers of farms occurring after ZANU-PF's defeat in the February 2000 referendum was part of a hastily arranged, *small-scale*—and illegal—farm seizure operation, which was supposed to have been limited to just five farms per district. Alexander, Tendi, and Compagnon have shown that land had been repeatedly promised to war veterans by ZANU-PF, to the extent that many no longer believed the ruling party's promises on the issue by 1999.[1] From the point of view of war veterans, it appeared unlikely that ZANU-PF was genuinely committed to extensive and long-promised land redistribution. Meanwhile, the economy began to seriously decline in the late 1990s, forcing many war veterans into poverty. As a result, war veterans became ever more fervent in demanding land, because land was the one asset that held its value and would provide direct returns. A vicious spiral ensued, where the more the economy deteriorated, the more war veterans demanded land that would hold its value. After ZANU-PF's defeat in the February 2000 referendum, the alarming prospect of another MDC win at the June 2000 parliamentary elections began to emerge. If the MDC won, senior ruling party officials could lose power and face prosecution for a host of illegal acts performed on behalf of ZANU-PF since independence. This sudden threat to the government's senior leadership, along with the threat that a victorious MDC would pose to war veteran prospects for securing land, triggered the initial plan to illegally seize five farms per district.

Yet as war veterans, with direct assistance from the state security services, began moving onto farms to undertake these highly politicized but small-scale seizures, the willingness of police to enforce farmers' and workers' personal and property rights broke down. This collapse of the rule of law occurred because many senior police officials were war veterans themselves and identified with fellow war veterans who were seizing land and agri-property. Senior police were often ZANU-PF members and followed direct instructions that farm takeovers were a "political" event and should not be interfered with. Therefore, the very officials meant to be restraining and controlling the war veterans were deliberately allowing them to seize farms and agri-property without consequences. Moreover, many police, soldiers, and ZANU-PF politicians also began participating in the seizures themselves, usually using state resources to do so.

Farm invaders realized, therefore, that a relatively large number of farms—along with very extensive and valuable agri-property—were essentially undefended. The emergence of an enormous supply of farms and agri-property brought about a similarly substantial demand by farm invaders for control over these resources. As more invaders became involved, competition for resources increased, dramatically escalating levels of violence. In this way the small-scale, extralegal seizures initially authorized by the government escalated rapidly into a frenzy of takeovers directly aided and supported by state security officials. The government was then powerless to reign in the forces that it had unleashed.

The seizure of commercial farms was not part of a genuine land reform program. The initial seizure of five farms per district would not have occurred if ZANU-PF had not needed to placate restive war veterans. Evidence from interviews with politicians, state security agents, war veterans, and one of Mugabe's legal advisors strongly demonstrates that the farm seizures were primarily a ploy to preserve ZANU-PF's political power. The plan was hastily concocted when ZANU-PF faced a direct political challenge from the MDC after the referendum defeat, in order to warn farmers against giving further aid to the MDC, and to placate war veterans with seized land.

Seizing a small number of farms satisfied three important functions for ZANU-PF officials and war veterans. It would provide land to reinvigorate war veterans' support for ZANU-PF and financially benefit senior officials; it would destroy the MDC's purported financial base by frightening commercial

farmers into closing their checkbooks; and it would disrupt a key MDC constituency of farm workers because, if they would or could not be co-opted,
displacing them and depriving them of their livelihood meant they could not
financially support the opposition or easily protect themselves from ZANU-
PF coercion. All three of these considerations were overtly political.

The large-scale takeover of commercial farms, however, were neither
planned nor controlled. With farm takeovers rapidly exceeding the initial
planned scope of five farms per district, and with state security agents unwilling to enforce the law on farms, ZANU-PF had to redefine what was happening in order to regain its authority. When seizures accelerated beyond what
had been intended, Mugabe came out publicly in support of the effort, framing
the movement in nationalist, populist, anticolonial terms, so as not to reveal
that the government—and he in particular—had lost control. Only when the
government amended the regulatory framework to legalize the takeovers and
bring order to what had essentially become a frenzied "free-for-all" were the
seizures subsumed into what could be described as a land reform program. At
best, the takeover of farms was political expediency masked as an ex post facto
land reform program.

Reframing the seizures as an exercise in confronting colonial-era disparities
in access to land served to popularize and rationalize takeovers, bringing the
farm seizures in line with historical ZANU-PF political rhetoric on land redistribution. Masking takeovers in the nationalist language of the Liberation War
was, however, purely a political gimmick intended to deceive and manipulate
unemployed youths and war veterans into helping ZANU-PF pursue its political objectives. Interview accounts show that although ZANU-PF had spoken
vociferously about land redistribution since independence, large-scale, extralegal takeovers were never planned or intended.

Researchers such as Sam Moyo have given too much weight to the nationalist motivations behind the land seizures, at the expense of the political exigen-
cies.[2] Assuming that the land seizures were driven by the effort to redistribute
land is intuitive, given the long history of land debate in Zimbabwe. Indeed the
widespread media coverage of war veterans moving onto farms lends a natural
assumption that the driving factor behind the seizures was land hunger among
the country's black majority. The evidence presented in this book, showing
that political considerations were of primary importance in driving the seizures, has fundamental implications for the validity of ZANU-PF's claims that
the seizures were genuinely undertaken in order to further the nationalist
cause of land redistribution.

In reality, it is questionable that demand for land was as widespread as is
often assumed prior to the seizures. There is no doubt that many rural Zimbabweans wanted land and that for some people, including many war veterans,

there was undeniable historical significance in reclaiming land. For the majority, however, gaining better jobs and access to improved social provisions was a far more important priority than taking up farming. The government's own assessment of demand for land among rural villagers demonstrated that people were really seeking better livelihoods. Calls for land were in some cases genuine, but in all likelihood demands for land were largely a proxy for a range of frustrations.

Alongside suppressing the MDC, farm invasions were driven by demand for financial resources achieved through seizing farms and agri-property. It is a relatively unsurprising fact that farm invaders targeted more successful, productive, and wealthy farms. However, the evidence that farm invaders tended to seek agri-property on farms over the land itself is an unexpected and more important finding. This undermines assertions in the current debates, and claims by ZANU-PF, that there was a widespread demand for land redistribution prior to the seizures; it also severely undermines nationalist motivations for farm seizures.[3] Undoubtedly, some farm invaders were seeking land on which to practice agriculture. However, seizing farms with valuable assets presented invaders with opportunities for substantial—and immediate—financial gains. The more fertile farms tended to have larger quantities of agri-property, because they were more financially successful and produced crops that required more farm equipment. Accordingly, when invaders moved onto "fertile farms" they were often really seeking agri-property that could be stripped and sold—without actually being used to undertake farming.

This behavior in seeking comparatively low-value farm assets that would provide only short-term gains, over high-value land that would deliver a long-term return, initially appears counterintuitive. Yet data from my survey and maps, as well as my interviews with workers, farmers, and farm invaders, show that the land seizure era was an intensely volatile and unstable period. Land and agri-property were sought by competing claimants from all levels of government, and as legal mechanisms broke down and official means of undertaking transactions and defending property collapsed, the retention of these assets became a contest of power: the more powerful the invader, the more likely he could control the assets over an extended period of time. Since few had the power to exclude competitors in this way, the solution for other invaders was to become short-term extortionists, seeking assets that could be easily removed and sold before they could be taken over by competitors. The initial puzzle of why farm invaders decided to forgo greater long-term gains in the interest of lower-value but more certain, immediate prizes is then explained as being a consequence of the existence of numerous weak competitors seeking control over the same assets.

A small number of very powerful invaders could potentially seize entire farms with fertile soil and high-value agri-property—either as short-term extortionists or long-term protection agents entering into agreements with the existing farmer. Moving down the scale of influence, less powerful farm invaders targeted only parts of fertile farms and lower-value agri-property—and only as short-term extortionists. The least powerful invaders gained only marginal land and a few, minor assets.

These claims contradict the findings of Scoones et al., who studied what they call the "myths" of land reform.[4] Their research makes important contributions to the development of agriculture in one part of Zimbabwe after 2000, yet their overall claims are too sweeping and based on too little evidence. Their research was undertaken largely on cattle ranching land that was drier and relatively lacking in agri-property. Their conclusion that few beneficiaries of the land seizures were political "cronies" is unsurprising, because the more powerful farm invaders would be unlikely to seek the low-value land in the area where their study was conducted. Indeed, Scoones et al. demonstrated that where land was more fertile within their study area, there were more government-employed invaders seeking it.[5] However, they assume that the relatively small number of government-employed beneficiaries, compared to the large number of ordinary civilian beneficiaries, is a nationwide pattern. Accordingly, they conclude that the beneficiaries of land seizures in general were not largely political "cronies."[6] It has never been in question that poorer invaders also gained some land and potentially some agri-property; what is salient is which invaders got what assets. That is, did the land seizure era bring about an equitable and fair redistribution of assets along the lines of the nationalist agenda espoused in public by ZANU-PF? Or did the most powerful, well-connected, and influential farm invaders seize the most lucrative property—regardless of nationalist credentials and economic need? The evidence presented in this book demonstrates that it was the latter.

Interviews and survey data show that many invaders who received A2 holdings (larger, commercial plots) were not the landless poor extolled by ZANU-PF, but government workers, particularly those employed in state security. These individuals were already in paid employment and did not, in general, want to become farmers. Farming required long-term capital investment and necessitated engaging in the undesirable land competition previously described. Thus, it made little sense for these kinds of invaders to seek land. Given that their state employment gave them access to the political power and resources necessary for successful evictions, many of these invaders became short-term extortionists, seeking agri-property for immediate profit. Ironically, ZANU-PF's "land redistribution" scheme thus tended to provide additional wealth to those who were already employed and relatively well off, and less to those who were weak and poor.

Violence has been an integral—indeed fundamental—part of ZANU-PF's governance structure since the party's formation. As a nationalist organization fighting to end white rule, ZANU discovered the efficacy of violence in its earliest days. Violence became a reliable tool by which to achieve and maintain political power. After taking power in 1980, ZANU-PF dealt with political threats in the same manner that it had dealt with military threats during the Liberation War—with the use of force to assert control. The party's rule remained benign, although corrupt, only as long as its political power was not threatened.

ZANU-PF's response to the formation of a powerful opposition threat in the form of the MDC in 1999 was simply a continuation of a long and well-established strategy, where violence formed a cornerstone of governance. Seen in this context, the catastrophic events of the land seizure era are easy to understand. When the MDC emerged, ZANU-PF faced its most viable political threat since independence. Rather than honor its stated democratic ideals or undertake genuine and meaningful land redistribution, the party leadership was ultimately prepared to risk the nation's dominant industry in an effort to retain power. This decision was standard ZANU-PF strategizing: proclaimed virtues and objectives masked an essentially self-serving party, which risked the national economy and well-being of the population to retain political power.

The key problem for ZANU-PF at the outset of the land seizure era was that, by 2000, the party had exhausted its nationalist credentials and credibility. While it continued to promote the threadbare nationalist message, this dogma was more relevant in the 1970s, during which a colonial government existed, or even the 1980s as the colonial institutional apparatus was being dismantled. By 2000, many Zimbabweans were looking for new political leadership with new ideas and a more progressive agenda. In espousing these kinds of messages, the MDC rapidly achieved popularity. Indeed, state intelligence agents interviewed for this book explicitly stated that ZANU-PF won elections after the beginning of the land seizure era only by manipulating the vote count.[7] Fundamentally threatened, ZANU-PF believed it needed to resort to violence once again in order to protect its power.

The critical issue that ZANU-PF faced is that by deploying extremely brutal violence to retain power, including massacres of women and children as occurred during *Gukurahundi* in the 1980s, a normalization of coercion occurs. Mugabe once famously stated that he had "many degrees in violence," and Nathan Shamuyarira, a senior ZANU-PF official, boasted that "the area of violence is an area where ZANU-PF has a very strong, long and successful history."[8]

Practitioners of violence in such regimes are rewarded for their actions with ever greater levels of power; the most violent and criminally minded individuals rise to the top. With these individuals in leadership positions, the regime becomes even more willing to forcibly resist political opposition, because its officials are accustomed to coercion and they fear prosecution for past offenses. The normalization of violence provides an efficacious way to stay in power, making resistance to change easy and familiar. In its efforts to protect personal interests above all else, the leaders cross a threshold after which they are delegitimized by their excessive violence and blatantly self-serving, extralegal actions. Without legitimacy, the remaining public accountability collapses, and the leadership becomes even more predatory, corrupt, and entrenched.

Accordingly, senior officials became bound to each other through the commission of crime and extortion, including in the land seizure era.[9] These individuals then had a vested interest in protecting each other and ensuring that existing political power structures were upheld in order to avoid prosecution and loss of assets. Thompson Mupfure, a veteran of the Liberation War and senior politician, explained:

> A lot of ZANU-PF people in top positions are aware that all this looting they have been doing around the country at the end of the day [can be] reduced to a personal affair. And when it becomes a personal affair, all the money they have amassed, the wealth that they have amassed, they stand to lose it. And that is why they remain captives of Mugabe, because they are so much afraid that should you allow for a new dispensation to set . . ., even if you realize that this person is a liability . . . A lot of them realize that Mugabe is a liability, so what then should you do? You [senior ZANU-PF official] would rather die clinging onto his [Mugabe's] aprons than allow a system that will then prejudice you as an individual. I think this is a predicament a lot of them are into that they don't know then what to do.

Thus, through rewards and threats, networks of patronage and the use of violence, an authoritarian political system has survived for more than three decades.

Underscoring this system is the pervasive use of violence and fear—used against both enemies and allies. Edward Chidembo, a senior police officer, gave an example by stating that throughout the police force, officers feared opposing Mugabe:

> My own experience in the police force is that right from the beginning a lot of people respected him [Mugabe] because they feared him and that we also

felt that in the police as well. There was always this fear, and that fear applied to his ministers, police force, and the army, everybody—people feared him. . . . People feared Mugabe, and nobody wanted to be seen as if he is opposing Mugabe, so a lot of people would support him through fear.[10]

These bonds of fear—which as this book has shown, were based on widespread torture, murder, and targeting of families—have allowed ZANU-PF to survive during the land seizure era, and withstand the threat posed by more law-abiding and democratically inclined opposition parties.

ZANU-PF's normalization of violence and its reliance on extralegal means of retaining power have led the regime to increasingly operate for its own benefit, irrespective of consequences for the general population. ZANU-PF has little incentive to comply with demands of Western governments and NGOs; hence, the government has expanded its "Look east" policy, where countries like China provide investment without requiring accountability in government or respect for human rights.[11] While some politically powerful neighboring countries like South Africa may have intermittent influence, the ZANU-PF regime is not subject to continuous and strong international constraints. This is a consequence of the regime's political isolation, and also because as the economy started to fail, economic ties with the outside world were weakened, which served to reduce the tangible bases for international relationships.

ZANU-PF came to power based on the agenda of promoting benefits for the black majority in Zimbabwe. There is no doubt that it achieved some important objectives. Over time, however, ZANU-PF's preoccupation with holding power became the first priority, and serving the people was relegated to a secondary concern. Resentment against a leadership that sought personal benefits over national well-being, a major contradiction to the aims of the Liberation War, was frequently raised by both farm workers and farm invaders interviewed for this book.

Mugabe and his officials operated as a predatory government—senior officials benefited very extensively by seizing farms and agri-property for themselves. The most critical example of this predation was the risk Mugabe and other senior officials took with the national economy, and the rule of law, in initiating the limited five-farms-per-district seizure plan. The strategy was devised and undertaken only as a means of preserving ZANU-PF's hold on power, and it enabled senior ruling party officials to retain their lucrative and powerful positions as well as evade potential criminal prosecution. Moreover, senior officials targeted the livelihoods and homes, and personal safety, of large numbers of people for the benefit of the ruling elite.

The consequences for the nation were disastrous. Chidembo explains how the failure of the farm seizure plan became self-perpetuating:

He [Mugabe] thought he would deal with the opposition. Then having secured the opposition, he would have wanted to strengthen the economy so
that he could gain more support and so on. But the opposition was getting
stronger, so in order to deal with the opposition he used tactics that undermined the economy, like seizing farms. And the more he undermined the
economy, the stronger the opposition became. It's a vicious circle because the
opposition is getting stronger, and in order to deal with them he has to further
undermine the economy . . . and everything just spiraled out of control.[12]

The irony is that at the end of the land seizure era, most senior officials were
still in power and had benefited substantially from the takeovers, while living
standards for most Zimbabweans have fallen dramatically. Mupfure noted
that "the land issue in this country is just being bartered for political purposes," while political rhetoric after the land seizure era has simply sought to
justify the "looting."[13]

Mupfure spoke about the government's predatory nature, arguing that war
veterans had been "used" by ZANU-PF and became tools for senior officials.
Mupfure especially identified how war veterans simply listened to political
propaganda broadcast on state-owned media outlets. From this messaging the
war veterans "became usable material, I mean these comrades of mine, they
became usable material in this whole carnage." This claim that war veterans
were "used" to achieve ZANU-PF's objectives was affirmed in interviews with
other farm invaders, such as the intelligence agent Peter Msasa.[14]

More fundamentally, in allowing themselves to be misled by "incitement"
and political propaganda, war veterans lost sight of their original Liberation
War political, social, and economic objectives and socialist ethos. Mupfure
believed that losing sight of the objectives occurred because war veterans allowed themselves to become fixated on the emotive land issue:

Once you isolate land and you say we were land fighters, you in fact have
distorted your original objectives. And that is why I wanted to detail, to talk
about the original conviction that in 2000 Mugabe bastardized the whole
Liberation objectives and now apparently because of the levels, the low
levels of education amongst most of the fighters, people easily accepted the
fact that we were fighting for land, that you know [is a] distortion.

Mupfure emphasized that the Liberation War was not only about land; the
land issue was one of many objectives. Mupfure believed that ultimately war
veterans allowed themselves to believe they were fighting for freedoms when
in fact they enabled the longevity of an authoritarian government that curtailed their rights:

A lot of them [war veterans] did not understand the interconnectedness of land, freedoms, rights, democracy, and all this, that you are not fighting for an individual. You are not fighting for an individual party. You are fighting for a new dispensation that will guarantee you the rights, the freedoms, the land and so forth regardless of who is in power—a new constitution, for instance, which is one of the things that we're fighting for, a new constitution that will contain a bill of rights that will guarantee every Zimbabwean regardless of their race, their creed, their ethnic grouping and so forth and so forth and so forth. But because people did not understand fully . . . they became usable material in the year 2000. They became available for abuse, and my understanding is that these former comrades of mine were abused by Mugabe's system then in the year 2000.

In the face of its weak performance in delivering benefits to the Zimbabwean people, ZANU-PF constantly sought to sharpen racial divisions in order to polarize political debate and win support for the land seizures. This was a strategy used by ZANU-PF to discredit the MDC as auxiliaries of a "white" political agenda. It was also a means of strengthening the bond with the war veteran constituency, by connecting contemporary economic and social discontent with historic injustices. That this strategy was still being successfully used just prior to the referendum in 2000, when ZANU-PF had been in power for 20 years, gives insight into ZANU-PF's skill in manipulating the political agenda.

The implications of the farm seizures, especially for white farmers, are emerging elsewhere in southern Africa. Observers and critics fall into two camps: those who see dire lessons in following the Zimbabwean model of illegal seizures, and those who are inspired by the apparently definitive steps to end the vestiges of colonial privilege and Western interference in Africa. The former cite practical social and economic concerns, such as the need to maintain the rule of law in order to attract investors and maintain the economic basis for social institutions such as healthcare and education. The latter invoke nationalist calls for short-term sacrifice, through withstanding some temporary disruption to the economy, in order to achieve the greater, long-term good of returning land to black Africans. Caught between these two lines of thought are countries like South Africa, which has a large and overwhelmingly white-owned commercial farming sector. While South Africa has a far more diversified economy than Zimbabwe, parallels between the white-dominated agricultural communities of Zimbabwe's neighboring countries have rapidly brought into question to what extent white South African farmers should relinquish land before they meet the same fate as Zimbabwe's farmers.[15]

Farming in Zimbabwe will be a combination of some large-scale commercial and smallholder operations for the foreseeable future. While Scoones et al.'s research is problematic in various ways, there is no doubt that smallholder farming has a major place in the agriculture sector. Yet here too, his findings are far too generalized and optimistic. Smallholder operations will remain central both for food production and for employment, but in the long term the country will once again shift toward a reliance on commercial farming for food production, rural employment, tax revenues, and exportable commodities. The World Bank believes that a business-focused, commercially motivated agriculture sector is a necessity for countries like Zimbabwe.[16] This is a trend throughout Africa, and there is no reason to believe that Zimbabwe will be any different once the government can move past politics and focus on economic growth. However, this will require a solid, stable, and predictable property rights policy, something ZANU-PF is currently unable to deliver with any credibility.[17]

This book has sought to present a balanced enquiry into the land seizure era. The evidence presented here reveals that the land seizures brought about severe social, political, and economic consequences for the country. Despite ZANU-PF's public protestations to the contrary, the ruling party never sought to target commercial farming to the extent that ultimately transpired. Thus, for those international observers who laud the "Zimbabwe model" of land reform, it should be emphasized that even Mugabe and some senior ZANU-PF hardliners initially sought to prevent farm seizures because the obvious consequences were disastrous.

The reality that ZANU-PF operates, first and foremost, for the personal gain of its leadership rather than for the benefit of the Zimbabwean people is now beyond dispute. Indeed, it is clear from this book that the threat of losing political power was a sufficiently serious prospect for senior officials that they chose to gamble the country's economic and social well-being and future by putting their own needs before that of their country.

# Appendix A

## Research Methodology

The timing and scale of conflict during the land seizure era raise profound questions about the motivations driving the Zimbabwean government's large-scale seizure of commercial farms that began in 2000. The seizures ushered in a highly dynamic period marked by intense violence, the breakdown of law and order, the fragmentation of state institutions, and the collapse of the national economy. It also marked a period of chronic political insecurity for the ruling ZANU-PF party, manifested in broad crackdowns on the political opposition, the intensification of surveillance, and an era of suspicion, mistrust, and political polarization.

Indeed, much of the existing academic research on this period is contested and charged. The continuing polarization of the sociopolitical environment in Zimbabwe makes objective analysis and academic debate very difficult. It is for this reason that there may not be as much critical examination of the taken-for-granted assumptions in the existing literature about the land seizure era as one might expect; these assumptions include the notion that the land takeovers were planned in advance, and that the aim was to redistribute land for the benefit of the black majority.

Within this environment there were understandably few definitive answers—supported by evidence—into the fundamental questions that my research has sought to explore. This paucity of evidence has occurred because collecting data on government decision-making, violence, potential violations of the law by state agents, and the suppression of political opposition is obviously extremely difficult and harrowing to undertake.

The questions that *The Land Reform Deception* seeks to explore go to the heart of ZANU-PF's right to hold power in Zimbabwe, the legality of the farm seizures, and the culpability of lawbreakers in widespread acts of violence. Accordingly, I have sought to rely upon multiple broad-based data sets that complement each other and provide a range of new evidence-based insights into Zimbabwe's land seizure era.

The findings in this study rely upon three separate major data sets: quantitative mapping data, qualitative interviews, and quantitative survey data. With this approach, the study has benefited from the strengths, while mitigating the weaknesses, of each method.

This research began with a longitudinal quantitative mapping data set that allowed for violence to be analyzed from 2000 to 2008. The data set was compiled by coding 90 reports from the Zimbabwe Human Rights NGO Forum ("Forum"), a civil society group that tracked incidents of violence nationwide throughout the land seizure era.[1] Forum data were the only source of systematic monthly violence information spanning most of the land seizure era; it is of sufficient quality to have been used by the US Department of State, for example.[2] From these reports I derived 21,491 individual acts of political violence nationwide (including urban violence) according to the following types: abduction/unlawful arrest; assault; murder; attempted murder; rape; torture; intimidation/verbal threat; property damage/theft. I then depicted each act of conflict on a geographical map according to the type of incident, the month it occurred, and the geographical location. Through this process I created 92 violence maps from February 2000, the month when large-scale violence began, to March 2008, when large-scale farm violence and thus the land seizure era had largely ended.[a,3]

These violence maps served as a starting point into my further research on Zimbabwe. Given that there had been little systematic research at the time on the key drivers of the land seizure era, violence maps provided me with a unique perspective into when violence proliferated and dissipated over time, which areas were consistent "hot spots," and in what ways hotspots were tied to key political events. In this way, the violence maps served to inform in which geographic areas I sought interview respondents and in part served as a basis of further discussion about respondents' experiences during the land seizure era.

My interviews with respondents who were directly involved in the land seizure era provided rich, in-depth perspectives on the experience of violence in Zimbabwe. These interviews helped to shed light on the experiences of respondents as well as their perspectives of these experiences. The interviews were particularly useful for investigating the "unknown" phenomena of the land seizure era, because new questions and lines of enquiry could be further explored as they opened up in interviews. However, it took considerable effort and resources to locate respondents, schedule and conduct interviews, and then painstakingly analyze the evidence that they provided.

a. See www.charleslaurie.com for a complete series of color violence maps depicting 21,491 acts of abduction/unlawful arrest, assault, murder, attempted murder, rape, torture, intimidation/verbal threat, and property damage/theft against farmers and workers recorded between 2000 and 2008.

The qualitative interviews for this research focused on three key stakeholder groups—a total of 111 in-depth interviews. I interviewed 24 farm workers and local village leaders because they were a key focus of government and farm invader initiatives during the land seizure era. Workers were presumed by the government to support the opposition MDC. Due to the large number of workers employed on commercial farms, they constituted a critical voting constituency that ZANU-PF sought to influence.

I also conducted 55 interviews with commercial farmers. Commercial farmers, who were almost all white, were the primary focus for evictions because in order for the government to undermine farm worker votes it was imperative for the government to evict white farmers and disrupt the farm community nexus. This nexus was comprised of white farmers who owned land that, for some individuals, was associated with historical land grievances. Farmers were also suspected of supporting the MDC and of influencing their workers to vote for the MDC. Given that in this research I was primarily seeking to put forward an economic and political argument for why events occurred during the land seizure era, I sought a higher number of interviews of farmers because they were a focal point of farm conflict.

I also sought to gain insights into the motivations of the government and of farm invaders in order to have a well-rounded interview data set that benefited from the perspectives from all key stakeholders. I conducted 32 interviews with individuals such as war veterans, members of ZANU-PF, the opposition MDC party, those employed in the army and police, individuals in the Central Intelligence Organisation (CIO) (the state secret service), as well as members of NGOs who could give insight into government decision-making.

I conducted all interviews myself and in person. Ninety-four interviews were held in Zimbabwe, 13 in the UK, and one each in Spain and South Africa. I conducted two interviews personally but over the telephone with a respondent in Australia and one in South Africa.

Given that one of ZANU-PF's key objectives was to break the farm community nexus, of which commercial farmers were the core, I undertook a large-scale survey of commercial farmers. The final survey sample of 1,442 respondents represented 34% of the farmers operating in 2000 when large-scale farm seizures began.[4] Given that when the survey was conducted many farmers had been evicted and had moved to other countries, the survey became global. Current and former Zimbabwean farmers from 24 countries worldwide participated.

The surveys had the advantage of being easier to conduct on a larger scale and enabled me to undertake statistical analysis of the data. The method was particularly effective for exploring "known" phenomena in greater depth statistically, such as the greater victimization of MDC supporters and proliferation of violence in the Mashonaland provinces. However, the surveys did not easily allow me to investigate the nuanced, "human" experiences that I explored during the interviews, or to ask follow-up questions into new and interesting pathways.

I made every effort to finds means of including workers in the survey; indeed, the inclusion of their views would have strengthened the findings. However, the resources required to conduct a systematic study of this population of an estimated 325,000 people, many of whom were displaced and jobless, would have required substantially more resources than were available for this project. Moreover, workers were the most at-risk population from the state security services, so a large-scale survey would have required extensive resources to be undertaken safely.

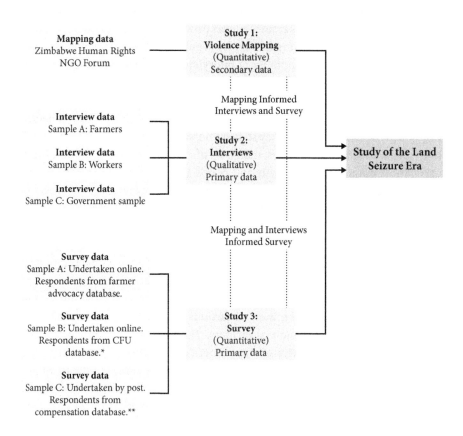

Figure A.1 Mixed-Methods Flowchart
*Commercial Farmers Union (CFU) sent an appeal for survey respondents to their farmer database.
**A farmer support organization provided a database of farmers.

Conditions for conducting fieldwork in dynamic and complex environments such as Zimbabwe are rarely ideal. Of course, given unlimited resources, there are many more interesting and valuable additional dimensions that could be explored. However, the focus of farm invaders on disrupting the farm community nexus, of which farmers were the core, means that the survey remains a useful contribution to our knowledge of events on farms.

The mixed-methods flowchart (figure A.1) illustrates the three-part approach taken for the data collection underpinning this study. The chart highlights the complimentary assistance of the mixed-methodology approach and how the different data sets overlap and co-inform each other.

# Appendix B

## Overview of Interview Respondents

*Farm worker Interview Respondents*

| | Race | Foreman | Manager | Game manager | Tractor driver | Mechanic | Clerk | Domestic worker | Livestock foreman | Head of compound[a] | Local village leader | Headmaster |
|---|---|---|---|---|---|---|---|---|---|---|---|---|
| Thomas Rackomechi | B | ✓ | | | | | | | | | | |
| James Mwengi | B | ✓ | | | | | | | | | | |
| Fortunate Marula | B | | | | | | | | | | ✓ | |
| Richardson Banongwe | B | ✓ | | | | | | | | | | |
| Jefferson Idzuyu | B | | | | | | | | | | | ✓ |
| Phillipson Marodzi | B | ✓ | | | | | | | | | | |
| Isaac Shiri | B | ✓ | | | | | | | | | | |
| Philip Mahobohobo | B | ✓ | | | | | | | | | | |
| Richard Chipembere | B | ✓ | | | | | | | | | | |
| Takemore Makuti | B | | ✓ | | | | | | | | | |
| Beton Mopane | B | | | | | ✓ | | | | | | |
| Telmore Nyakasanga | B | ✓ | | | | | | | | | | |
| Chenjerai Mapufuli | B | | | | | ✓ | | | | | | |
| Tichafa Ncema | B | | ✓ | | | | | | | | | |
| Tendayi Garamapudzi | B | ✓ | | | | | | | | | | |
| Andrew Morfu | B | | ✓ | | | | | | | | | |
| Ronald Nyerere | B | | | | ✓ | | | | | | | |
| Imminence Ngiwa | B | ✓ | | | ✓ | | | | | | | |
| Joyce Mukwa | B | | | | | | ✓ | | | | | |
| Chesterton Hove | B | | ✓ | | | | | | | | | |
| Chipo Nyuchi | B | | | | | | | | ✓ | | | |

*Farm worker Interview Respondents (Continued)*

| | Race | Foreman | Manager | Game manager | Tractor driver | Mechanic | Clerk | Domestic worker | Livestock foreman | Head of compound[a] | Local village leader | Headmaster |
|---|---|---|---|---|---|---|---|---|---|---|---|---|
| Zacharia Nyembwi | B | ✓ | | | | | | | | ✓ | | |
| Thompson Mbezi | B | | | | | | | | ✓ | | | |
| Herbert Nchenchi | B | | | ✓ | | | | | | | | |

NOTE: All respondents were anonymized using Zimbabwean river, animal, and plant names. These names do not necessarily correspond with the respondent's geographical location.

[a]"Compound" refers to a worker village located on a commercial farm.

*Commercial Farmer Interview Respondents*

| | Race | Male farmer | Female farmer | Wife of farmer | Security consultant | Wife of security consultant | Missionary | Member of parliament | Leader of farmer advocacy group |
|---|---|---|---|---|---|---|---|---|---|
| Elizabeth Shore | W | | | ✓ | | | | | |
| James Adams | W | ✓ | | | | | | | |
| Ronald Madison | W | ✓ | | | | | | | |
| Penny Madison | W | | | ✓ | | | | | |
| Aaron Buchanan | W | ✓ | | | | | | | |
| William Thackeray | W | ✓ | | | | | | | |
| Thomas Barker | W | ✓ | | | | | | | |
| James Shore | W | ✓ | | | | | | | ✓ |
| Eric Fillmore | W | ✓ | | | | | | | |
| Arthur Breckinridge | W | | | | ✓ | | | | |
| Joan Breckinridge | W | | | | | ✓ | | | |
| John Hendricks | W | ✓ | | | | | | | |
| George Sherman | W | ✓ | | | | | | | |

*(Continued)*

*Commercial Farmer Interview Respondents (Continued)*

| | Race | Male farmer | Female farmer | Wife of farmer | Security consultant | Wife of security consultant | Missionary | Member of parliament | Leader of farmer advocacy group |
|---|---|---|---|---|---|---|---|---|---|
| **Tim Sherman** | W | ✓ | | | | | | | |
| **Chris Cleveland** | W | ✓ | | | | | | | |
| **Catherine Cleveland** | W | | | ✓ | | | | | |
| **Martin Wilson** | W | ✓ | | | | | | | ✓ |
| **Joachem van Vaaden** | W | ✓ | | | | | | | |
| **Eric Mifflin** | W | | | | | | ✓ | | |
| **Rob Dawes** | W | ✓ | | | | | | | ✓ |
| **Cynthia Dawes** | W | | | ✓ | | | | | |
| **Martin Grover** | W | ✓ | | | | | | | |
| **Kathy Grover** | W | | | ✓ | | | | | |
| **William Shore** | W | ✓ | | | | | | | |
| **Harriet Shore** | W | | | ✓ | | | | | |
| **Gerald Burr** | W | ✓ | | | | | | | ✓ |
| **Trudy Grant** | W | | | ✓ | | | | | |
| **Nancy Hoover** | W | | ✓ | | | | | | |
| **Andrew McKinley** | W | ✓ | | | | | | | |
| **Debbie McKinley** | W | | | ✓ | | | | | |
| **John Taylor** | W | ✓ | | | | | | | |
| **Rupert Garfield** | W | ✓ | | | | | | | |
| **Jane Garfield** | W | | | ✓ | | | | | |
| **Benjamin Colfax** | W | ✓ | | | | | | | |
| **George Harding** | W | ✓ | | | | | | | ✓ |
| **John Hayes** | W | ✓ | | | | | | | |
| **Thomas Barkley** | W | ✓ | | | | | | | |
| **James Knox** | W | ✓ | | | | | | | |
| **Brian Wheeler** | W | ✓ | | | | | | | |
| **Martin Sutherland** | W | ✓ | | | | | | | ✓ |
| **Al Jensen** | W | ✓ | | | | | | | |
| **Kevin Elbridge** | W | ✓ | | | | | | | ✓ |

*Commercial Farmer Interview Respondents (Continued)*

| | Race | Male farmer | Female farmer | Wife of farmer | Security consultant | Wife of security consultant | Missionary | Member of parliament | Leader of farmer advocacy group |
|---|---|---|---|---|---|---|---|---|---|
| **Edwin Kennedy** | W | ✓ | | | | | | | |
| **Charles Morton** | W | ✓ | | | | | | | |
| **Henry Monroe** | W | ✓ | | | | | | | |
| **Daniel Fairbanks** | W | ✓ | | | | | | | |
| **George Lyons** | W | ✓ | | | | | | | |
| **Joan Lyons** | W | | | ✓ | | | | | |
| **Matthew Coolidge** | W | ✓ | | | | | | | ✓ |
| **Gerry Garner** | W | ✓ | | | | | | | |
| **Arnold Bembezi** | B | ✓ | | | | | | | |
| **Roy Bennett\*** | W | ✓ | | | | | | ✓ | |
| **Elaine Oates\*** | W | | | ✓ | | | | | |
| **Maria Stevens\*** | W | | | ✓ | | | | | |
| **Cindy Anderson\*** | W | | | ✓ | | | | | |

\*Actual name. All others names are anonymized.

Respondents Who Gave Insight into Government and War Veteran Activities

| | Race | Vice president of Zimbabwe | ZANU-PF minister | MDC minister | Politburo member | Member of parliament | Governor | Senator | ZANU-PF official | MDC official | CIO[a] | Police | Army[b] | War veteran involved in seizures[c] | War veteran not involved in seizures[d] | Magistrate/legal advisor | Leader of war veteran association | Leader of youth training camp | Tribal chief | Member of clergy | Human rights activist/attorney | Lancaster House attendee | "New" farmer | Employee of state-owned enterprise |
|---|---|---|---|---|---|---|---|---|---|---|---|---|---|---|---|---|---|---|---|---|---|---|---|---|
| Welshman Mabhena* | B | | | | ✓ | | ✓ | | ✓ | ✓ | | | | | ✓ | | | | | | | | | |
| Archbishop Pius Ncube* | B | | | | | | | | | ✓ | | | | | | | | | | ✓ | ✓ | | | |
| Thompson Mupfure* | B | | | | | ✓ | | | | ✓ | | | | | ✓ | | | | | | | | | |
| Chief Nyati | B | | | | | | | | | | | | | | | | | | ✓ | | | | | |
| Akim Ndlovu*[f] | B | | | | | | | | | | | | | | ✓ | | | | | | | ✓ | | |
| Joan Pierce | W | | | | | | | | | | | | | | | | | | | | ✓ | | | |
| Alex Siwaze | B | | | | | | | | | | | | | | ✓ | | ✓ | | | | | | | |
| Felix Umchabezi[g] | B | | | | | | | | | | | | | | ✓ | | | | | | | | | |
| Jabulani Sibanda* | B | | | | ✓ | | | | ✓ | | | | | ✓ | | | ✓ | | | | | | ✓ | |
| Nicholas Panhane | B | | | | | | | | ✓ | | | | | ✓ | | | | | | | | | | |
| John Nkomo*[h] | B | ✓ | ✓ | | ✓ | | | ✓ | ✓ | | | | | | ✓ | | | | | | | ✓ | ✓ | |
| Denton Masumu[i] | B | | | | | | | | ✓ | | | | | | ✓ | | | | | | | | | |
| Dumiso Dabengwa*[j] | B | | ✓ | | | | | | | | | | | | ✓ | | | | | | | ✓ | | |
| Patterson Rukodzi | B | | | | | | | | | | | | | ✓ | | | | ✓ | | | | | ✓ | |

Respondents Who Gave Insight into Government and War Veteran Activities (Continued)

| | Race | Vice president of Zimbabwe | ZANU-PF minister | MDC minister | Politburo member | Member of parliament | Governor | Senator | ZANU-PF official | MDC official | CIO[a] | Police | Army[b] | War veteran involved in seizures[c] | War veteran not involved in seizures[d] | Magistrate/legal advisor | Leader of war veteran association | Leader of youth training camp | Tribal chief | Member of clergy | Human rights activist/attorney | Lancaster House attendee | "New" farmer | Employee of state-owned enterprise |
|---|---|---|---|---|---|---|---|---|---|---|---|---|---|---|---|---|---|---|---|---|---|---|---|---|
| Petros Mzingwane* | B | | | | | | | | | | | | | ✓ | | | | | | | | | ✓ | |
| Ketani Makabusi[k] | B | | | | | | | | | | | | | | | | | | | | | | ✓ | |
| Tafadzwa Tegwani | B | | | | | | | | | | | | | | | ✓ | | | | | | | | |
| Chief Negomo* | B | | | | | | | ✓ | | | | | | | | | | | ✓ | | | | | |
| David Coltart*[l] | W | | | ✓ | | ✓ | | | | ✓ | | | | | | | | | | | ✓ | | | |
| Edison Bubye | B | | | | | | | | | | | ✓ | | | | | | | | | | | | |
| Jackson Sanyati | B | | | | | | | | | | | ✓ | | | | | | | | | | | | |
| Samuel Limpopo | B | | | | | | | | | | | ✓ | | | | | | | | | | | | |
| Ronald Jongwe | B | | | | | | | | | | ✓ | | ✓ | | | | | | | | | | | |
| Peter Msasa | B | | | | | | | | | | | | ✓ | | | | | | | | | | | |
| Edward Chidembo | B | | | | | | | | | ✓ | | ✓ | | | | | | | | | | | | |
| Timothy Ngavi | B | | | | | | | | | | | | | | | | | | | | | | ✓ | ✓ |
| Agnes Sengwe | B | | | | | | | | | | | | ✓ | | | | | | | | | | | |

(Continued)

Respondents Who Gave Insight into Government and War Veteran Activities (Continued)

| | Race | Vice president of Zimbabwe | ZANU-PF minister | MDC minister | Politburo member | Member of parliament | Governor | Senator | ZANU-PF official | MDC official | CIO[a] | Police | Army[b] | War veteran involved in seizures[c] | War veteran not involved in seizures[d] | Magistrate/legal advisor | Leader of war veteran association | Leader of youth training camp | Tribal chief | Member of clergy | Human rights activist/attorney | Lancaster House attendee | "New" farmer[e] | Employee of state-owned enterprise |
|---|---|---|---|---|---|---|---|---|---|---|---|---|---|---|---|---|---|---|---|---|---|---|---|---|
| Steven Sebungwe | B | | | | | | | | | | | | ✓ | | | | | | | | | | | |
| Hastings Lundi | B | | | | | | | | | | ✓ | | | | | | | | | | | | | |
| Daniel Inkankezi | B | | | | | | | | | | ✓ | | ✓ | | | | | | | | | | | |
| Christian Mucheke[m] | B | | | | | | | | | | | | | | ✓ | ✓ | | | | | | | | |
| Tyson Manyame | B | | | | | | | | | | | | ✓ | | | | | | | | | | | |

NOTE: Positions held before and/or after farm seizures in 2000.

* Actual name. All other names are anonymized using Zimbabwean river, animal, and tree names.

[a] Including military intelligence and President's Office.

[b] An individual who served in Zimbabwe's army at any time since independence.

[c] Personally involved in seizing land and assets or committing acts of violence at the behest of government during the land seizure era. These genuine war veterans do not include those who may have given orders or allowed others to commit violence, only those who were "on the ground" seizing farms.

[d] A genuine veteran of the Liberation War who was not involved in the violent seizure of commercial farms. All individuals classified as "veterans" are ZANLA or ZIPRA.

[e] An individual who took possession of a farm seized from a commercial farmer.

f A member of ZIPRA's War Council; ZIPRA's first commander; briefly a ZAPU MP soon after independence; forced to flee into exile with Joshua Nkomo in March 1983 during the *Gukurahundi* period.

g Former senior member of ZAPU.

h ZANU-PF national chairman; Speaker of parliament; Minister for Lands, Land Reform and Resettlement; Minister of Home Affairs (during the height of the land seizure era); Lancaster House signatory; appointed minister of state in the President's Office in 2009 and then became Vice President of Zimbabwe.

i Political affairs officer in the Liberation War.

j ZIPRA's chief of intelligence; member of ZIPRA's War Council, its supreme body; Lancaster House delegate (see HMSO, "Southern Rhodesia—Report of the Constitutional Conference, Lancaster House, London, September–December 1979" [London: Lancaster House, December 21, 1979], 1); Minister of Home Affairs (1992–2000); Politburo senior committee member. Dabengwa was also charged with treason in 1982 at the beginning of *Gukurahundi* with Lookout Masuku and four others. He was released then redetained soon after for nearly four years.

k Elsewhere in the study, Makabusi is described as a "farm manager." Although he was a farm manager, farm invaders thought he was a fellow farm invader. He claimed land as a "new" farmer but continued working on behalf of his former white farmer employer.

l MDC MP for Bulawayo South; MDC senator; MDC-M Minister for Education. Coltart is also an attorney and human rights activist.

m Indicated that he was a legal officer in the President's Office.

# Appendix C

Land Seizure Era Flowcharts

# Flowchart Depicting Key Events Leading to the Land Seizure Era

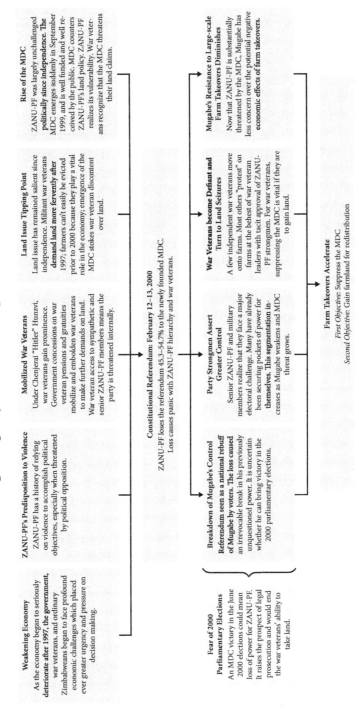

Figure C.1  Flowchart of Key Events Leading to the Land Seizure Era

The following flowcharts illustrate the key farmer and worker stakeholders and their decision-making processes during farm takeovers. The flowcharts are presented in chronological order. **Phase I** flowcharts detail events in the prereferendum period. They provide a basic chronology of the rise of the war veterans and MDC and explain the relationship between these groups and ZANU-PF during the 2000 constitutional referendum. **Phase II** flowcharts outline initial land invasions. These flowcharts outline the process through which war veterans politicized and/or targeted members of the local farming communities, farm laborers, and farmers. Flowcharts depict decision-making by farm invaders, workers, and farmers. **Phase III** flowcharts show the types of farm invaders involved in farm invasions, how farm invaders decided who received agri-property, and how victim groups were targeted in order to ultimately gain land and agri-property. **Phase IV** flowcharts explain the post-commercial-farming era, at which point the majority of Zimbabwe's land had been seized by farm invaders.

These flowcharts are not intended to rigidly define the process of decision-making and seizures in all cases; indeed, this research has shown that the process of seizing farms varied considerably. However, the flowcharts define a general process that was common and generally followed in most farms seizures.

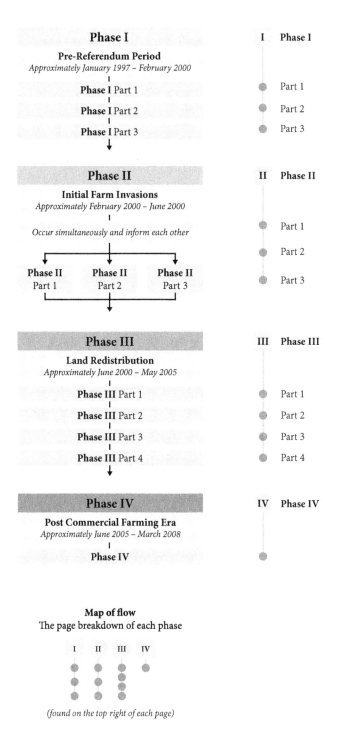

**Phase I**

**Pre-Referendum Period**
*Approximately January 1997 – February 2000*

Phase I Part 1

Phase I Part 2

Phase I Part 3

**Phase II**

**Initial Farm Invasions**
*Approximately February 2000 – June 2000*

*Occur simultaneously and inform each other*

| Phase II Part 1 | Phase II Part 2 | Phase II Part 3 |

**Phase III**

**Land Redistribution**
*Approximately June 2000 – May 2005*

Phase III Part 1

Phase III Part 2

Phase III Part 3

Phase III Part 4

**Phase IV**

**Post Commercial Farming Era**
*Approximately June 2005 – March 2008*

Phase IV

I   Phase I
    Part 1
    Part 2
    Part 3

II   Phase II
    Part 1
    Part 2
    Part 3

III   Phase III
    Part 1
    Part 2
    Part 3
    Part 4

IV   Phase IV

**Map of flow**
The page breakdown of each phase

I    II    III    IV

*(found on the top right of each page)*

**Figure C.2** Land Seizure Era Flowcharts: Overview

# Phase I

## Part 1

### Pre-Referendum Period Flowchart:
Early 1997 – February 2000

**Duration:**

38 months

**Key Characteristics:**

- ZANU-PF in-fighting and rise of the war veterans and MDC.
- Some basic organisation emerges as war veterans gain credibility and socio-political power.

---

**Early 1997**
War veterans are relatively inactive

↓

**Late 1997**

- Under the charismatic Chenjerai 'Hitler' Hunzvi, the war veterans begin gaining substantial strength and national prominence.
- War veterans demand greater benefits and rally support from fellow veterans within ZANU-PF, civil service and the state security services.
- September 1997: Government concedes and agrees to pay each war veteran ZWD$50,000 (US$2,778) plus ZWD$2,000 (US$111) per month for life.
- 6 November 1997: Clare Short, as British Secretary of State for International Development, re-defines British responsibility over land. Remarks are taken as Britain reneging on 'colonial' responsibilities.
- War veterans become prominent, influential, and emboldened. Payouts initiate collapse of the economy.

↓

**Early 1998**

- War veterans increase demands for land.
- Government is already facing severe economic hardships and cannot afford land purchases for war veterans.
- Government increases politicisation of land issue and turns to international donors, particularly Britain, for support due to its colonial history.
- June 1998: Government publishes Land Reform and Resettlement Programme Phase II framework outlining compulsory farm purchase.

↓

**Late 1998**

- 'Farm invasions' prior to a donor conference are controlled by CIO to manipulate international perception of land crisis.
- September 1998: 48 countries and donor organisations attend government-run donor conference; they largely agree to poverty reduction and some land redistribution; funding is limited and most aid is in the form of technical support.

**Figure C.3** Prereferendum Period Flowchart: Early 1997–February 2000

# Phase I

## Part 2

### Early 1999

- War veteran agitation continues as its prominence increases. This exposes ZANU-PF's political vulnerability and divergent interests between war veteran and non-war veteran members of the ruling party.
- Limited farm occupations take place with government knowledge.
- Senior ZANU-PF members recognize that placating war veterans with seized commercial farmland will potentially worsen the already deteriorating economy.
- Sporadic and minor farm occupations continue, often called "demonsstrations," occur on some farms "listed" for acquisition. Government instructs war veterans not to disrupt farming activities.

↓

### Late 1999

- September 1999: Movement for Democratic Change (MDC) is formed as ZANU-PF's popularity wanes. The new party gains support from commercial farmers due to the party's opposition to compulsory farm takeovers.
- Despite initially underestimating the MDC's power, ZANU-PF launches a racially charged political counter attack, framing MDC as a "puppet" party of the West and white commercial farmers.
- November 1999: First official "farm invasions" are staged in Svosve, near Marondera, to "scare" white farmers into withdrawing financial support from the MDC. "Invasions" are promoted by Vice President Muzenda and Minister Emmerson Mnangagwa.
- Mugabe initially resists invasions: Described as "really angry" by one CIO operative about the staged invasions, Mugabe orders the staged invasions to cease so they do not undermine the recovering Zimbabwean dollar and anticipated financial support from the IMF.

↓

### Early 2000

- Government states that it will hold a constitutional referendum to give power to seize commercial farmers *without compensation* to farmers. The proposal circumvents the need for funding farm purchases for land redistribution. The proposal also satisfies war veteran demands for more land.
- Farmers rally support for MDC to protect their property.
- MDC grows dramatically in popularity and it is recognized as a genuine contender to defeat ZANU-PF.

↓

### February 12–13, 2000

- Constitutional referendum is defeated 45–55%. Defeat is seen as a triumph for the MDC and rebuff by voters of Mugabe and ZANU-PF, their first major political defeat since 1980.
- The unexpected ZANU-PF defeat causes near panic in the ruling party and suggests that the MDC could likely win the June 2000 parliamentary elections.
- For war veterans, the defeat is a turning point. An MDC win would end their land ownership aspirations, so suppressing the MDC becomes a priority. To this end, many begin invading farms with the *de facto* authorization of some senior officials and military figures.

↓ ↓

| **War Veterans** | **Senior ZANU-PF Officials** |
|---|---|
| • More militant war veterans defy Mugabe's official statement recognizing the referendum defeat.<br>• Some war veterans begin farm invasions, with security chiefs' tacit approval. | • Recognizing that the political environment has changed, senior officials ally themselves more closely with war veterans.<br>• Suppressing the MDC has become a priority.<br>• Senior officials take matters into their own hands and invade farms using war veterans; most others coordinate with Hunzvi. |

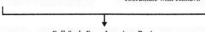

**Full-Scale Farm Invasions Begin**

Figure C.3  (*continued*)

# Phase II

### Part 1
### Asserting Control over Local Community

**Initial Farm Invasions Flowchart:**

February – June 2000

**Duration:**

1-5 months

**Key Characteristics:**

- Initial invasions are usually carried out by unemployed war veterans.
- Some individuals are seeking land for themselves, many are paid by local ZANU-PF offices which also provide logistical support.
- Command structure based on military structures from Liberation War.

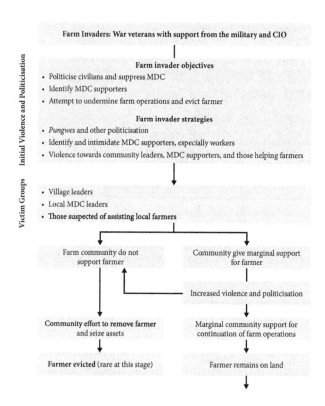

Figure C.4  Initial Farm Invasions Flowchart: February–June 2000

# Phase II

## Part 2

### Asserting Control over Farm Workers

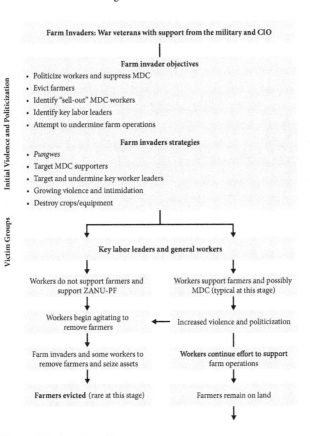

**Farm Invaders: War veterans with support from the military and CIO**

**Farm invader objectives**
- Politicize workers and suppress MDC
- Evict farmers
- Identify "sell-out" MDC workers
- Identify key labor leaders
- Attempt to undermine farm operations

**Farm invaders strategies**
- *Pungwes*
- Target MDC supporters
- Target and undermine key worker leaders
- Growing violence and intimidation
- Destroy crops/equipment

**Initial Violence and Politicization**

**Victim Groups**

**Key labor leaders and general workers**

Workers do not support farmers and support ZANU-PF

Workers support farmers and possibly MDC (typical at this stage)

Workers begin agitating to remove farmers ← Increased violence and politicization

Farm invaders and some workers to remove farmers and seize assets

**Workers continue effort to support** farm operations

**Farmers evicted** (rare at this stage)

Farmers remain on land

Figure C.4  (*continued*)

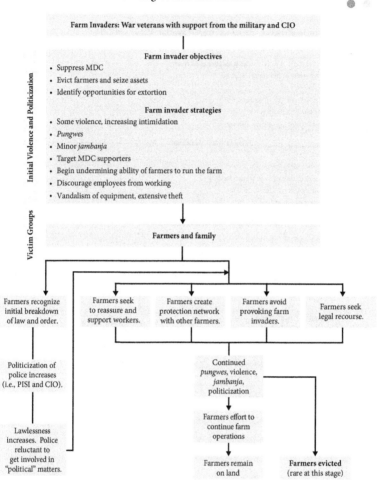

# Phase II

### Part 3
### Asserting Control over Farmers

**Initial Violence and Politicization**

**Victim Groups**

Farm Invaders: War veterans with support from the military and CIO

**Farm invader objectives**
- Suppress MDC
- Evict farmers and seize assets
- Identify opportunities for extortion

**Farm invader strategies**
- Some violence, increasing intimidation
- *Pungwes*
- Minor *jambanja*
- Target MDC supporters
- Begin undermining ability of farmers to run the farm
- Discourage employees from working
- Vandalism of equipment, extensive theft

**Farmers and family**

| Farmers recognize initial breakdown of law and order. | Farmers seek to reassure and support workers. | Farmers create protection network with other farmers. | Farmers avoid provoking farm invaders. | Farmers seek legal recourse. |

Politicization of police increases (i.e., PISI and CIO).

Continued *pungwes*, violence, *jambanja*, politicization

Lawlessness increases. Police reluctant to get involved in "political" matters.

Farmers effort to continue farm operations

Farmers remain on land

**Farmers evicted** (rare at this stage)

Figure C.4  (*continued*)

# Phase III

## Part 1

## Land Redistribution and Formation of Invasion Groups

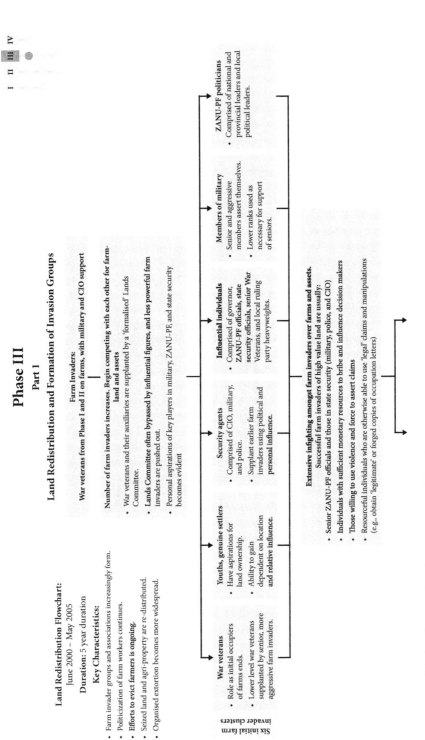

**Land Redistribution Flowchart:**
June 2000 – May 2005
**Duration:** 5 year duration
**Key Characteristics:**

- Farm invader groups and associations increasingly form.
- Politicization of farm workers continues.
- **Efforts to evict farmers is ongoing.**
- Seized land and agri-property are re-distributed.
- Organised extortion becomes more widespread.

**Farm Invaders:**
War veterans from Phase I and II on farms, with military and CIO support

**Number of farm invaders increases. Begin competing with each other for farm-land and assets**

- War veterans and their auxiliaries are supplanted by a 'formalised' Lands Committee.
- Lands Committee often bypassed by influential figures, and less powerful farm invaders are pushed out.
- Personal aspirations of key players in military, ZANU-PF, and state security becomes evident

**Six initial farm invader clusters**

**War veterans**
- Role as initial occupiers of farms ends.
- Lower level war veterans supplanted by senior, more aggressive farm invaders.

**Youths, genuine settlers**
- Have aspirations for land ownership.
- Ability to gain dependent on location and relative influence.

**Security agents**
- Comprised of CIO, military, and police.
- Supplant earlier farm invaders using political and personal influence.

**Influential individuals**
- Comprised of governor, ZANU-PF officials, state security officials, senior War Veterans, and local ruling party heavyweights.

**Members of military**
- Senior and aggressive members assert themselves.
- Lower ranks used as necessary for support of seniors.

**ZANU-PF politicians**
- Comprised of national and provincial leaders and local political leaders.

**Extensive infighting amongst farm invaders over farms and assets.**
**Successful farm invaders of high value land are usually:**
- Senior ZANU-PF officials and those in state security (military, police, and CIO)
- Individuals with sufficient monetary resources to bribe and influence decision makers
- Those willing to use violence and force to assert claims
- Resourceful individuals who are otherwise able to use 'legal' claims and manipulations (e.g., obtain 'legitimate' or forged copies of occupation letters)

Figure C.5 Land Redistribution Flowchart: June 2000–May 2005

I II III IV

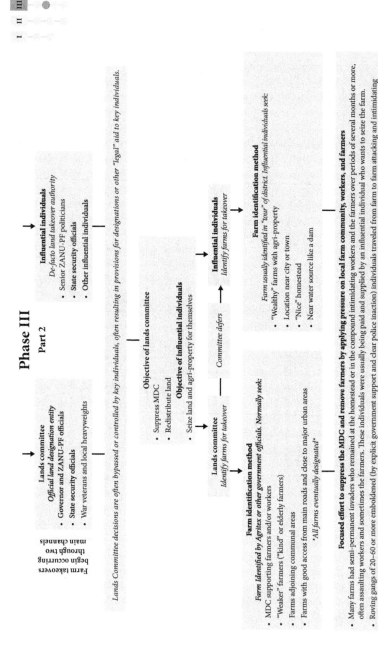

Figure C.5 (continued)

# Phase III

## Part 3

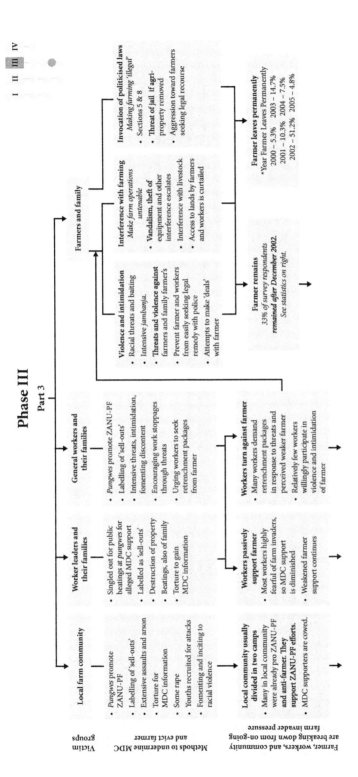

I II III IV

**Victim groups**

- Local farm community
- Worker leaders and their families
- General workers and their families
- Farmers and family

**Methods to undermine MDC and evict farmer**

**Local farm community**
- *Pungwes* promote ZANU-PF
- Labelling of 'sell-outs'
- Extensive assaults and arson
- Torture for MDC information
- Some rape
- Youths recruited for attacks
- Fomenting and inciting to racial violence

**Worker leaders and their families**
- Singled out for public beatings at *pungwes* for alleged MDC support
- Labelled as 'sell-outs'
- Destruction of property
- Beatings, also of family
- Torture to gain MDC information

**General workers and their families**
- *Pungwes* promote ZANU-PF
- Labelling of 'sell-outs'
- Intensive threats, intimidation, fomenting discontent
- Encouraging work stoppages through threats
- Urging workers to seek retrenchment packages from farmer

**Farmers and family**

**Violence and intimidation**
- Racial threats and baiting
- Intensive *jambanja*.
- **Threats and violence against farmers and family farmer's**
- Prevent farmer and workers from easily seeking legal remedy with police
- Attempts to make 'deals' with farmer

**Interference with farming**
*Make farm operations untenable*
- **Vandalism, theft of equipment and other interference escalates**
- Interference with livestock
- Access to lands by farmers and workers is curtailed

**Invocation of politicised laws**
*Making farming 'illegal'*
- Sections 5 & 8
- **Threat of jail if agri-property removed**
- Aggression toward farmers seeking legal recourse

**Farmer, workers, and community are breaking down from on-going farm invader pressure**

**Local community usually divided in two camps**
- Many in local community were already pro ZANU-PF and anti-farmer. They **support ZANU-PF efforts.**
- MDC supporters are cowed.

**Workers passively support farmer**
- Most workers highly fearful of farm invaders, so MDC support is diminished
- Weakened farmer support continues

**Workers turn against farmer**
- Many workers demand retrenchment packages in response to threats and perceived weaker farmer
- Relatively few workers willingly participate in violence and intimidation of farmer

**Farmer remains**
33% of survey respondents *remained after December 2002.*
See statistics on right.

**Farmer leaves permanently**
*Year Farmer Leaves Permanently
2000 – 5.3%   2003 – 14.7%
2001 – 10.3% 2004 – 7.5%
2002 – 51.2% 2005 – 4.8%*

*According to survey from this study

Figure C.5 *(continued)*

319

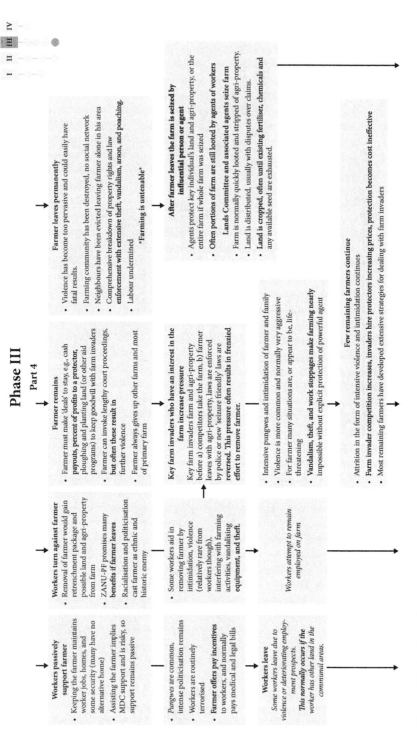

# Phase III

## Part 4

I  II  III  IV

**Workers passively support farmer**
- Keeping the farmer maintains worker jobs, homes, and some security (many have no alternative home)
- Assisting the farmer implies MDC support and is risky, so support remains passive

**Workers turn against farmer**
- Removal of farmer would gain retrenchment package and possible land and agri-property from farm
- ZANU-PF promises many **benefits if farmer leaves**
- Racialisation and politicisation cast farmer as ethnic and historic enemy

**Farmer remains**
- Farmer must make 'deals' to stay, e.g., cash **payouts, percent of profits to a protector,** ploughing and planting land (or other aid programs) to keep goodwill with farm invaders
- Farmer can invoke lengthy court proceedings, **but often these result in** further violence
- Farmer always gives up other farms and most of primary farm

**Farmer leaves permanently**
- Violence has become too pervasive and could easily have fatal results.
- Farming community has been destroyed, no social network
- Neighbours have been evicted leaving farmer alone in his area
- Comprehensive breakdown of property rights and law enforcement with extensive theft, **vandalism, arson, and poaching.**
- Labour undermined

"Farming is untenable"

- *Pungwes are common, intense politicisation remains*
- Workers are routinely terrorised
- **Farmer offers pay incentives** to workers, and normally pays medical and legal bills

- Some workers aid in removing farmer by intimidation, violence (relatively rare from workers though), interfering with farming activities, vandalisation of **equipment, and theft.**

**Key farm invaders who have an interest in the farm increase pressure**
Key farm invaders want farm and agri-property before a) competitors take the farm, b) farmer leaves with agri-property, laws are enforced by police or new 'seizure friendly' laws are reversed. This pressure often results in frenzied effort to remove farmer.

**After farmer leaves the farm is seized by influential person or agent**
- Agents protect key individual's land and agri-property, or the entire farm if whole farm was seized
- **Often portions of farm are still looted by agents of workers**
Lands Committee and associated agents seize farm
- Farm is normally quickly looted and stripped of agri-property.
- Land is distributed, usually with disputes over claims.
- Land is cropped, often until existing fertiliser, chemicals and any available seed are exhausted.

**Workers leave**
*Some workers leave due to violence or deteriorating employment prospects.*
*This normally occurs if the worker has other land in the communal areas.*

*Workers attempt to remain employed on farm*

- Intensive pungwes and intimidation of farmer and family
- Violence is more common and normally very aggressive
- For farmer many situations are, or appear to be, life-threatening
- **Vandalism, theft, and work stoppages make farming nearly impossible without explicit protection of powerful agent**

**Few remaining farmers continue**
- Attrition in the form of intensive violence and intimidation continues
- Farm invader competition increases, invaders hire protectors increasing prices, protection becomes cost ineffective
- Most remaining farmers have developed extensive strategies for dealing with farm invaders

**Figure C.5** (*continued*)

320

# Phase IV

**Post Commercial Farming Era Flowchart:**

June 2005–March 2008

**Duration:** 2.5-year duration

**Key Characteristics:**

- Large numbers of farm workers are displaced.
- Most farmers have been evicted, and few workers remain on farms.
- With most land and agri-property redistributed, violence on farms tends to diminish and remains only where farmers resist.
- Violence is largely deployed against urban and peri-urban MDC areas.

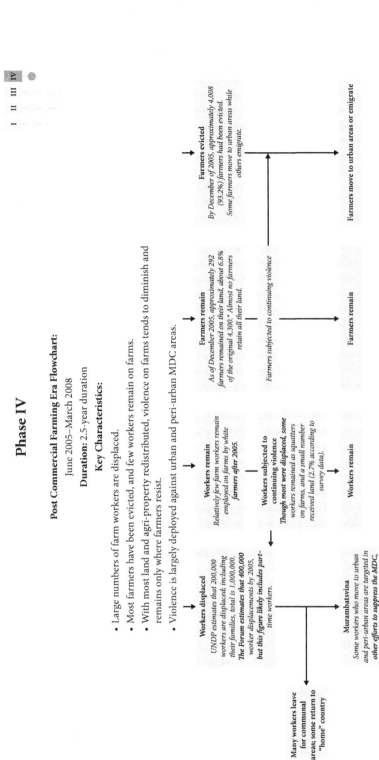

**Farmers evicted**
By December of 2005, approximately 4,008 (93.2%) farmers had been evicted. Some farmers move to urban areas while others emigrate.

**Farmers remain**
As of December 2005, approximately 292 farmers remained on their land, about 6.8% of the original 4,300.* Almost no farmers retain all their land.

*Farmers subjected to continuing violence*

**Workers remain**
Relatively few farm workers remain employed on farms by white farmers after 2005.

**Workers subjected to continuing violence**
*Though most were displaced, some workers remained as squatters on farms, and a small number received land (2.7% according to survey data).*

**Workers displaced**
UNDP estimates that 200,000 workers are displaced; including their families, total is 1,000,000. The Forum estimates that 400,000 worker displacements by 2005, but this figure likely includes part-time workers.

**Murambatsvina**
*Some workers who move to urban and peri-urban areas are targeted in other efforts to suppress the MDC, such as Operation Murambatsvina.*

Farmers move to urban areas or emigrate

Farmers remain

Workers remain

Many workers leave for communal areas; some return to "home" country

*Estimates made from survey data. Figures assume 4,300 farmers in 2000.

**Figure C.6** Post-Commercial-Farming Era Flowchart: June 2005–March 2008

# Notes

1. The "land seizure era" is a term I coined to define the period from February 2000, just before farm takeovers began, to March 2008, when most farmers had been evicted and little farm violence remained. Terminology for this period is enormously contested. For example, Sam Moyo states that the term "land seizures" is used mainly by the independent media to "emphasise the negative political action of the ZANU (PF) and the war veterans" (Sam Moyo, "The Land Occupation Movement and Democratisation in Zimbabwe: Contradictions of Neoliberalism," *Millennium: Journal of International Studies* 30 [2001]: 320). I considered a range of terms. "Land occupier" implied a temporary holding of land, which is not reflected in how events unfolded during the land seizure era. "Land takeover" implies an orderly and somewhat legal process, which also is not indicative of the experience on most commercial farms. Cliffe et al. note that the terms "incursions," "invasions," and "occupations" are all "partisan" (Lionel Cliffe, Jocelyn Alexander, Ben Cousins, and Rudo Gaidzanwa, "An Overview of Fast Track Land Reform in Zimbabwe: Editorial Introduction," *Journal of Peasant Studies* 38, no. 5 [2011]: 913). I ultimately selected "land seizure" because it appropriately conveyed a robust and forceful taking of farms, often with violence and coercion. I believe also that the term appropriately frames how many war veterans would see events during the period of study, a "taking back" of land they viewed as being rightfully theirs.

2. A "war veteran" is a nationalist veteran of the Liberation War, a term that carries significant political and social status. This label has frequently been appropriated—including during the land seizure era—by others to capitalize on the perceived right of war veterans to claim farm land. Accordingly, many individuals with no military background claimed to be war veterans, as did youths in support of farm takeovers. The term "war veteran" is contested and politically charged. Accordingly, wherever possible this book seeks to identify relevant clarifying details when using the term. The term "Liberation War" is more commonly used in research on the war waged by nationalists in the 1960s and 1970s against the Rhodesian government, and is a term usually

preferred along with "Second Chimurenga" by nationalist war veterans of the conflict. The term "Rhodesian Bush War" is more commonly used by those outside Zimbabwe.

3.  In this book "ZANU-PF" and "government," when referring to the government of Zimbabwe, are used interchangeably since the Zimbabwe government was, and continues to be, dominated by ZANU-PF and had its resources used for party objectives.

4.  Sam Moyo, "Land and Natural Resource Redistribution in Zimbabwe: Access, Equity and Conflict," *African and Asian Studies* 4, nos. 1–2 (2005): 210.

5.  A "commercial farm" is defined in this book as a large commercial farm where the primary beneficiaries are members of a family rather than absentee landlords, shareholders, or commercial partners. The operating objective of these farmers is profit or utility maximization through market sales (definition adapted from www.FAO.com). Sam Moyo, "Three Decades of Agrarian Reform in Zimbabwe," *Journal of Peasant Studies* 38, no. 3 (2011): 496.

6.  Food and Agriculture Organization of the United Nations, "Future Energy Requirements for Africa's Agriculture," http://www.fao.org/docrep/V9766E/v9766e05.htm#4.6.%20zimbabwe.

7.  Annual growth rate for agricultural value added based on constant local currency. World Bank, "Zimbabwe Statistics," http://data.worldbank.org/country/zimbabwe.

8.  United Nations Development Programme, "Comprehensive Economic Recovery in Zimbabwe" (2008).

9.  International Federation of Red Cross and Red Crescent, "100,000 Cases: The Spectre of Cholera Remains in Zimbabwe" (2009), 5.

10.  UNDP, "Comprehensive Economic Recovery in Zimbabwe," 155.

11.  John Robertson, "General Zimbabwe Statistics," email to author, 2008.

12.  *The Economist*, "Bags of Bricks," http://www.economist.com/node/7843601; John Robertson, "Zimbabwe's Hyperinflation," *Harvard International Review*, http://hir.harvard.edu/zimbabwe-s-hyperinflation.

13.  Steve H. Hanke, "R.I.P. Zimbabwe Dollar," CATO Institute, http://www.cato.org/zimbabwe.

14.  World Bank, "Sub-Saharan Africa Country Statistics," http://databank.worldbank.org/data/views/reports/tableview.aspx?isshared=true#.

15.  Many current literary sources use the term "black" and "white," so the author will adopt the convention. However, the author maintains awareness of the racial sensitivities under discussion in this book.

16.  Moyo, "Land and Natural Resource Redistribution"; Moyo, "Land Occupation Movement"; Sam Moyo, "The Land and Agrarian Question in Zimbabwe," presented to the conference "The Agrarian Constraint and Poverty Reduction: Macroeconomic Lessons for Africa," Addis Ababa, 2004; Ian Scoones, Nelson Marongwe, Blasio Mavedzenge, Jacob Mahenehene, Felix Murimbarimba, and Chrispen Sukume, *Zimbabwe's Land Reform: Myths and Realities* (Woodbridge: James Currey, 2010); Mahmood Mamdani, "Lessons of Zimbabwe," *London Review of Books* 30, no. 23 (2008); Prosper

B. Matondi, "Understanding Fast Track Land Reforms in Zimbabwe," in *Zimbabwe's Fast-Track Land Reform* (London: Zed Books, 2012); Joseph Hanlon, Jeanette Manjengwa, and Teresa Smart, *Zimbabwe Takes Back Its Land* (Sterling, VA: Kumarian Press, 2013). *Zimbabwe Takes Back Its Land* has an overt bias in support of the government's policy platform and appears to be an attempt at agenda-setting.

17. Cliffe et al., "Overview," 912.
18. Sam Moyo and Paris Yeros, "Land Occupations and Land Reform in Zimbabwe: Towards the National Democratic Revolution," in *Reclaiming the Land: The Resurgence of Rural Movements in Africa, Asia and Latin America*, ed. Sam Moyo and Paris Yeros (London: Zed Books, 2005).
19. This is supported by Amanda Hammar, "A Measure of Just Demand? A Response to Mamdani," Association of Concerned African Scholars, http://concernedafricascholars.org/docs/acasbulletin82-8hammar.pdf.
20. Matondi, "Fast Track Land Reforms," 3.
21. Dan Weiner, Sam Moyo, Barry Munslow, and Phil O'Keefe, "Land Use and Agricultural Productivity in Zimbabwe," *Journal of Modern African Studies* 23, no. 2 (1985): 251–52; Angus Selby, "Commercial Farmers and the State: Interest Group Politics and Land Reform in Zimbabwe," University of Oxford, 2006, 115.
22. Bill H. Kinsey, "Land Reform, Growth and Equity: Emerging Evidence from Zimbabwe's Resettlement Programme," *Journal of Southern African Studies* 25, no. 2 (1999): 178.
23. Robin Palmer, "Land Reform in Zimbabwe, 1980–1990," *African Affairs* 89, no. 355 (1990): 169.
24. Cliffe et al., "Overview," 910.
25. Qtd. in Ibid.
26. Palmer, "Land Reform in Zimbabwe," 169.
27. The agreement signed in 1979 between ZAPU, ZANU, and the Rhodesian government that brought independence to Zimbabwe in 1980.
28. Rory Pilossof, "Possibilities and Constraints of Market-Led Land Reforms in Southern Africa: An Analysis of Transfers of Commercial Farmland in Postcolonial Zimbabwe, 1980–2000," *Journal of Agrarian Change* (2014), http://onlinelibrary.wiley.com/doi/10.1111/joac.12090/full.
29. Clare Short, "Letter to Minister Kangai," *Guardian*, http://politics.guardian.co.uk/foi/images/0,9069,1015120,00.html.
30. Moyo, "Land and Natural Resource Redistribution," 203.
31. Zvakanyorwa Wilbert Sadomba, "A Decade of Zimbabwe's Land Revolution: The Politics of the War Veteran Vanguard," in *Land and Agrarian Reform in Zimbabwe*, ed. Sam Moyo and Walter Chambati (Dakar: Codesria, 2013), 83.
32. Miles Tendi, "Sundayview: What If 'Yes' Vote Had Won in 2000 Referendum?," *Standard*, http://www.thestandard.co.zw/opinion/27903-sundayview-what-if-yes-vote-had-won-in-2000-referendum.html.
33. Not all veterans participated. Many disagreed with takeovers and were members of the MDC.

34.  Jocelyn Alexander, "'Squatters', Veterans and the State in Zimbabwe," in
     *Zimbabwe's Unfinished Business*, ed. Amanda Hammar, Brian Raftopoulos,
     and Stig Jensen (Harare: Weaver Press, 2003), 101; Brian Raftopoulos, "The
     State in Crisis: Authoritarian Nationalism, Selective Citizenship and Distor-
     tions of Democracy in Zimbabwe," in Hammar, Raftopoulos, and Jensen,
     *Zimbabwe's Unfinished Business*, 231.

35.  Nelson Marongwe, "Farm Occupations and Occupiers in the New Politics of
     Land in Zimbabwe," in Hammar, Raftopoulos, and Jensen, *Zimbabwe's Un-
     finished Business*, 165; Jocelyn Alexander, *Unsettled Land: State-Making and
     the Politics of Land in Zimbabwe 1893–2003* (Oxford: James Currey, 2006),
     185; Raftopoulos, "The State in Crisis," 231.

36.  Jocelyn Alexander and JoAnn McGregor, "Elections, Land and the Politics
     of Opposition in Matabeleland," *Journal of Agrarian Change* 1, no. 4 (2001):
     511; Moyo, "Land and Natural Resource Redistribution," 202.

37.  Steven Sebungwe, senior army officer, Zimbabwe National Army, interview,
     March 30, 2009.

38.  Mandivamba Rukuni and Stig Jensen, "Land, Growth and Governance:
     Tenure Reform and Visions of Progress in Zimbabwe," in Hammar, Rafto-
     poulos, and Jensen, *Zimbabwe's Unfinished Business*, 246.

39.  Alexander and McGregor, "Elections, Land," 511.

40.  Norma Kriger, "From Patriotic Memories to 'Patriotic History' in Zimba-
     bwe, 1990–2005," *Third World Quarterly* 27, no. 6 (2006): 1151.

41.  NGO reports include Zimbabwe Human Rights NGO Forum, "Torture by
     State Agents in Zimbabwe: January 2001 to August 2002" (Harare: Zimba-
     bwe Human Rights NGO Forum, 2003); Amnesty International, "Toll of
     Impunity," http://www.amnesty.org/en/library/asset/AFR46/034/2002/en/
     dom-AFR460342002en.pdf; Zimbabwe Human Rights NGO Forum,
     "Only Bruises on the Soles of Their Feet! Torture and Falanga in Zimba-
     bwe" (Harare: Zimbabwe Human Rights NGO Forum, 2009); Zimbabwe
     Human Rights NGO Forum and Justice for Agriculture Trust in Zimba-
     bwe, "Adding Insult to Injury" (Harare: Zimbabwe Human Rights NGO
     Forum and the Justice for Agriculture Trust in Zimbabwe, 2007); Zimba-
     bwe Human Rights NGO Forum, "Monthly Violence Reports," in *Monthly
     Violence Reports* (Harare: Zimbabwe Human Rights NGO Forum, 2001–
     2008); Amnesty International, "Time for Accountability" (London: Am-
     nesty International, 2008); Zimbabwe Human Rights NGO Forum, "Who
     Is Responsible? A Preliminary Analysis of Pre-election Violence in Zim-
     babwe" (Harare: Zimbabwe Human Rights NGO Forum, 2000); "Politi-
     cally Motivated Violence in Zimbabwe, 2000–2001" (Harare: Zimbabwe
     Human Rights NGO Forum, 2001); "Political Violence Report, May 2006"
     (Harare: Zimbabwe Human Rights NGO Forum, 2006). News media re-
     ports include BBC, "Meagre Harvest in Zimbabwe," *BBC News*, http://
     news.bbc.co.uk/1/hi/business/1818263.stm; Michael Wines, "Corruption
     and Despair Choke Zimbabwe," *New York Times*, http://www.nytimes.
     com/2003/10/19/world/corruption-and-despair-choke-zimbabwe.html?s
     cp=11&sq=zimbabwe&st=nyt; Scott Baldauf, "Mugabe Using Police to

Crush Opposition, MDC Says," *Christian Science Monitor*, http://www.cs-monitor.com/World/Africa/2009/0820/p06s08-woaf.html.

42. Amnesty International, "Toll of Impunity"; Alexander, *Unsettled Land*, 186; Amnesty International, "Time for Accountability," 11.

43. E.g., Stathis N. Kalyvas, *The Logic of Violence in Civil War*, ed. Margaret Levi (New York: Cambridge University Press, 2006); Doug McAdam, Sidney Tarrow, and Charles Tilly, eds., *Dynamics of Contention* (Cambridge: Cambridge University Press, 2001); Paul R. Brass, *Theft of an Idol* (Princeton, NJ: Princeton University Press, 1997); Roger D. Petersen, *Understanding Ethnic Violence* (Cambridge: Cambridge University Press, 2002); Mary Kaldor, *New and Old Wars*, 2nd ed. (Cambridge: Polity Press, 2006); Kalevi J. Holsti, *The State, War, and the State of War* (Cambridge: Cambridge University Press, 1996); Charles Tilly, *Politics of Collective Violence* (Cambridge: Cambridge University Press, 2003); Mark R. Beissinger, *Nationalist Mobilization and the Collapse of the Soviet State* (Cambridge: Cambridge University Press, 2002).

44. ZANU-PF would later form from ZANU. Many senior ZANU-PF officials were early ZANU leaders. Terence Ranger, "The Death of Chaminuka: Spirit Mediums, Nationalism and the Guerilla War in Zimbabwe," *African Affairs* 81, no. 324 (1982): 367; Jocelyn Alexander, JoAnn McGregor, and Terence Ranger, *Violence and Memory: One Hundred Years in the "Dark Forests" of Matabeleland* (Oxford: James Currey, 2000), 174; Norma Kriger, *Zimbabwe's Guerrilla War: Peasant Voices* (Cambridge: Cambridge University Press, 1992); David Lan, *Guns and Rain: Guerrillas and Spirit Mediums in Zimbabwe* (Oxford: James Currey, 1985).

45. Daniel Compagnon, *A Predictable Tragedy: Robert Mugabe and the Collapse of Zimbabwe* (Philadelphia: University of Pennsylvania Press, 2011), 14–15.

46. Alexander, *Unsettled Land*, 106.

47. Catholic Commission for Justice and Peace in Zimbabwe, "Report on the 1980s Disturbances in Matabeleland and the Midlands" (Bulawayo: Catholic Commission for Justice and Peace in Zimbabwe, 1997); Catholic Commission for Justice and Peace in Zimbabwe, *Gukurahundi in Zimbabwe: A Report on the Disturbances in Matabeleland and the Midlands, 1980–1988* (London: Hurst, 2007), 8.

48. Zimbabwe Human Rights NGO Forum, "Order out of Chaos, or Chaos out of Order? A Preliminary Report on Operation 'Murambatsvina'" (Harare: Zimbabwe Human Rights NGO Forum, 2005); "Aftermath of a Disastrous Venture: A Follow-up Report on 'Operation Murambatsvina'" (Harare: Zimbabwe Human Rights NGO Forum, 2005); Amnesty International, "Zimbabwe: Six Years on Victims of Operation Murambatsvina Still Struggling to Survive" (Amnesty International, 2011).

49. E.g., Zimbabwe Human Rights NGO Forum, "Monthly Violence Reports"; Daniel Fairbanks, rancher, interview, January 27, 2007.

50. Zimbabwe Human Rights NGO Forum, "Who Was Responsible? Alleged Perpetrators and Their Crimes during the 2000 Parliamentary Election Period" (Harare: Zimbabwe Human Rights NGO Forum, 2001), 2; Justice

for Agriculture and General Agriculture and Plantation Workers Union of Zimbabwe, "Reckless Tragedy: Irreversible?," Research and Advocacy Unit (RAU), http://www.kubatana.net/html/archive/landr/081212jag.asp?sector=LANDR&year=0&range_start=1.

51.  Solidarity Peace Trust, "National Youth Service Training: 'Shaping Youths in a Truly Zimbabwean Manner'" (Port Shepstone, South Africa: Solidarity Peace Trust, 2003), 38.

52.  See Blair Rutherford, who is an authority on the subject of farm workers in Zimbabwe. His work forms the cornerstone of academic research on the subject, while Sam Moyo and Walter Chambati have also made key contributions: Evert Waeterloos and Blair Rutherford, "Land Reform in Zimbabwe: Challenges and Opportunities for Poverty Reduction among Commercial Farm Workers," *World Development* 32, no. 3 (2003); Blair Rutherford, "Belonging to the Farm(er): Farm Workers, Farmers, and the Shifting Politics of Citizenship," in Hammar, Raftopoulos, and Jensen, *Zimbabwe's Unfinished Business*; "'Settlers' and Zimbabwe: Politics, Memory, and the Anthropology of Commercial Farms during a Time of Crisis," *Identities: Global Studies in Culture and Power* 11 (2004); "Shifting the Debate on Land Reform, Poverty and Inequality in Zimbabwe, an Engagement with Zimbabwe's Land Reform: Myths and Realities," *Journal of Contemporary African Studies* 30, no. 1 (2012); *Working on the Margins: Black Workers, White Farmers in Postcolonial Zimbabwe* (Harare: Weaver Press; London: Zed Books, 2001); "Commercial Farm Workers and the Politics of (Dis)Placement in Zimbabwe: Colonialism, Liberation and Democracy," *Journal of Agrarian Change* 1, no. 4 (2001). See also Sam Moyo, Blair Rutherford, and Dede Amanor-Wilks, "Land Reform and Changing Social Relations for Farm Workers in Zimbabwe," *Review of African Political Economy* 27, no. 84 (2000); Walter Chambati, "Restructuring of Agrarian Labour Relations after Fast Track Land Reform in Zimbabwe," *Journal of Peasant Studies* 38, no. 5 (2011).

53.  UNDP, "Comprehensive Economic Recovery in Zimbabwe," 157–58; Amnesty International, "Time for Accountability," 18; Zimbabwe Human Rights NGO Forum and Justice for Agriculture, "Adding Insult to Injury," 26–27.

54.  Chambati, "Restructuring," 1053.

55.  Sam Moyo et al., "Fast Track Land Reform Baseline Survey in Zimbabwe: Trends and Tendencies, 2005/06" (Harare: AIAS Monograph, 2009), 22.

56.  See appendix A for more information on the survey. One anonymous farmer survey respondent gave a brief description of how farm invaders tried to murder him: "Attempted garrotte on motor bike." A different farm survey respondent stated: "Settlers assaulted us constantly and family members too. [They] tried to kill one of my sons." Another respondent stated: "Tied up and beaten with my parents. [They] tried to electrocute my father and held hostage."

57.  E.g., Zimbabwe Human Rights NGO Forum, "Monthly Violence Reports"; Zimbabwe Human Rights NGO Forum, "Who Was Responsible?"; Zimbabwe Human Rights NGO Forum, "Politically Motivated Violence."

58.  Sadomba, "Zimbabwe's Land Revolution," 92–93.

59. Ibid., 93.
60. Robert Gabriel Mugabe, *Inside the Third Chimurenga* (Harare: Department of Information and Publicity, Office of the President and Cabinet, 2001), 73.
61. Ben Cousins and Ian Scoones, "Contested Paradigms of 'Viability' in Redistributive Land Reform: Perspectives from Southern Africa," *Journal of Peasant Studies* 37, no. 1 (2010): 35.
62. Alexander, *Unsettled Land*; Lan, *Guns and Rain*; Terence Ranger, *Peasant Consciousness and Guerrilla War in Zimbabwe: A Comparative Study* (London: James Currey, 1985); Norma Kriger, *Guerrilla Veterans in Post-war Zimbabwe* (Cambridge: Cambridge University Press, 2003).
63. Alexander and McGregor, "Elections, Land," 510.
64. Moyo, "Land and Natural Resource Redistribution"; JoAnn McGregor, "Politics of Disruption: War Veterans and the Local State in Zimbabwe," *African Affairs* 101 (2002).
65. Christian Mucheke, legal officer in the President's Office, interview, May 17, 2009.
66. *New York Times*, "Rare Poll Suggests Zimbabwe Is Weary of Its Longtime Leader," http://www.nytimes.com/2000/03/12/world/rare-poll-suggests-zimbabwe-is-weary-of-its-longtime-leader.html; R. W. Johnson, "State Terror Sweeps Zimbabwe," Helen Suzman Foundation, http://www.hsf.org.za/resource-centre/focus/issues-11–20/issue-18-second-quarter-2000/state-terror-sweeps-zimbabwe.
67. Compagnon, *A Predictable Tragedy*, 174.
68. Ibid.
69. Edison Bubye, police officer, Zimbabwe Republic Police, interview, July 24, 2008.
70. Qtd. in Miles Tendi, "Patriotic History and Public Intellectuals Critical of Power," *Journal of Southern African Studies* 34, no. 2 (2008): 387.
71. Thompson Mupfure, veteran of the Liberation War and senior politician, interview, January 24 and 25, 2007.
72. Josiah Tungamirai, "Recruitment to ZANLA: Building up a War Machine," in *Soldiers in Zimbabwe's Liberation War*, ed. Ngwabi Bhebe and Terence Ranger (London: James Currey, 1995), 37.
73. Hastings Lundi, senior Central Intelligence Organisation agent, interview, April 9, 2009.
74. E.g., Miles Tendi, *Making History in Mugabe's Zimbabwe* (Oxford: Peter Lang, 2010), 73–107; Mugabe, *Inside the Third Chimurenga*.
75. E.g., Mugabe, *Inside the Third Chimurenga*.
76. CIA, "World Factbook," CIA, https://www.cia.gov.
77. A measure of the average number of years a person can live in full health.
78. World Health Organization, "Healthy Life Expectancy (Hale) at Birth (Years)," http://www.who.int/whosis/indicators/2007HALE0/en/; World Health Organization, "World Health Statistics," http://www.who.int/gho/publications/world_health_statistics/EN_WHS10_Full.pdf; World Health Organization, "Zimbabwe Statistics," http://www.who.int/countries/zwe/en/.

79. Human Rights Now, "Poor Healthcare Endangering Mothers in Zimbabwe," Amnesty International, http://blog.amnestyusa.org/escr/poor-healthcare-endangering-mothers-in-zimbabwe/; Andrew Meldrum, "Zimbabwe's Health-Care System Struggles On," *The Lancet* 371, no. 9618 (2008).
80. Robertson, "Zimbabwe's Hyperinflation"; *The Economist*, "Bags of Bricks"
81. Hanke, "R.I.P. Zimbabwe Dollar."
82. Vitaliy Kramarenko, Lars Engstrom, Genevieve Verdier, Gilda Fernandez, S. Erik Oppers, Richard Hughes, Jimmy McHugh, and Warren Coats, "Zimbabwe: Challenges and Policy Options after Hyperinflation" (International Monetary Fund, 2010).
83. South Africa is not included in this figure because its relatively large economy makes it difficult to compare data with neighboring states. Its performance profile is consistent with Botswana, Zambia, Mozambique, and Namibia.
84. UNDP, "The Real Wealth of Nations: Pathways to Human Development" (New York: United Nations Development Programme, 2010).
85. Hanlon, Manjengwa, and Smart, *Zimbabwe Takes Back Its Land*.
86. Scoones et al., *Zimbabwe's Land Reform*.
87. Scoones et al.'s research was supported by Agritex, the government agricultural extension organization. This official government sanctioning of their research almost certainly resulted in preferential research access.
88. Moyo, "Three Decades," 496.
89. Hanlon, Manjengwa, and Smart, *Zimbabwe Takes Back Its Land*.
90. Moyo, "Three Decades," 496.
91. Ian Scoones, Nelson Marongwe, Blasio Mavedzenge, Felix Murimbarimba, Jacob Mahenehene, and Sukume Chrispen, "Zimbabwe's Land Reform: Challenging the Myths," *Journal of Peasant Studies* 38, no. 5 (2011): 968–69.
92. For example, 94% of farmer survey respondents had left their farms by 2005, and 98.2% had experienced an act of coercion by 2005.

CHAPTER 2

1. E.g., Mugabe, *Inside the Third Chimurenga*; Tom Lodge, Denis Kadima, and David Pottie, eds., *Zimbabwe: 2000 General Elections*, compendium of Elections in Southern Africa (2002) (Electoral Institute for Sustainable Democracy in Africa, 2002).
2. Norma Kriger, "ZANU(PF) Strategies in General Elections, 1980–2000: Discourse and Coercion," *African Affairs* 104, no. 414 (2005).
3. Moyo, "Land and Natural Resource Redistribution," 204.
4. E.g., Daniel Inkankezi, senior official in military intelligence, Zimbabwe National Army, interview, April 11, 2009.
5. John Nkomo served as vice president of Zimbabwe from 2009 to 2013, and I was given access to his personal records from the Lancaster House conference of 1979. These afforded a detailed insight into ZANU's negotiations and the constraints faced by the nationalist, Rhodesian, and British representatives.
6. Africa All Party Parliamentary Group, "Land in Zimbabwe: Past Mistakes, Future Prospects" (London: AAPPG, 2009), 19.

7.  Ibid., 24.
8.  Ibid., 25.
9.  Ibid., 28.
10. Ibid., 25.
11. Peter Msasa, military intelligence agent, Zimbabwe National Army, interview, October 23, 2008.
12. Inkankezi, senior official in military intelligence, Zimbabwe National Army. E.g., Jocelyn Alexander, *Unsettled Land: State-Making and the Politics of Land in Zimbabwe, 1893–2003;* "The Unsettled Land: The Politics of Land Redistribution in Matabeleland, 1980–1990," *Journal of Southern African Studies* 17, no. 4 (1991); "State, Peasantry and Resettlement in Zimbabwe," *Review of African Political Economy* 21, no. 61 (1994); Alexander and McGregor, "Elections, Land and the Politics of Opposition in Matabeleland"; Palmer, "Land Reform in Zimbabwe, 1980–1990."
13. E.g., Mugabe, *Inside the Third Chimurenga.*
14. E.g., Ibid., 40, 87.
15. Norma Kriger, "Zimbabwe: Political Constructions of War Veterans," *Review of African Political Economy* 30, no. 96 (2003): 326.
16. Kriger, "From Patriotic Memories," 1161–64.
17. Ibid., 1166.
18. Ibid., 1154.
19. Brian Raftopoulos, "Zimbabwe: Race and Nationalism in a Post-colonial State," in *Inventions and Boundaries: Historical and Anthropological Approaches to the Study of Ethnicity and Nationalism,* ed. P. Kaarsholm and J. Hultin (Roskilde, Denmark: International Development Studies, Roskilde University, 1994).
20. Kriger, "Zimbabwe: Political Constructions"; Kriger, "From Patriotic Memories."
21. Knox Chitiyo, "Land Violence and Compensation," *Track Two* 9, no. 1 (2000); Wilfred Mhanda, "The Role of War Veterans in Zimbabwe's Political and Economic Processes," Solidarity Peace Trust, http://www.solidarity-peacetrust.org/1063/the-role-of-war-veterans/.
22. Bubye, police officer, Zimbabwe Republic Police.
23. Ronald Jongwe, member of the Zimbabwe National Army, interview, October 21, 2008.
24. Ibid.
25. Bubye, police officer, Zimbabwe Republic Police.
26. Kriger, "From Patriotic Memories"; Bubye, police officer, Zimbabwe Republic Police.
27. Lundi, senior Central Intelligence Organisation agent.
28. Jongwe, member of the Zimbabwe National Army.
29. Zvakanyorwa Wilbert Sadomba, *War Veterans in Zimbabwe's Revolution* (Woodbridge, UK: James Currey, 2011).
30. Mucheke, legal officer in the President's Office.
31. Sam Moyo and Paris Yeros, "The Radicalised State: Zimbabwe's Interrupted Revolution," *Review of African Political Economy* 34, no. 111 (2007): 111.

32. Ibid., 111–12.
33. Moyo, "Land and Agrarian Question," 15–16; Stephen Chan, *Robert Mugabe: A Life of Power and Violence* (London: I. B. Taurus, 2003), 149; Moyo, "Land Occupation Movement," 314.
34. Kriger, "From Patriotic Memories," 1166–67.
35. Moyo, "Land Occupation Movement," 314.
36. Chan, *Robert Mugabe*, 149.
37. Sadomba, "Decade of Zimbabwe's Land Revolution," 86.
38. Inkankezi, senior official in military intelligence, Zimbabwe National Army.
39. Tendi, *Making History in Mugabe's Zimbabwe*.
40. Bubye, police officer, Zimbabwe Republic Police.
41. ICG cites higher figures, but it is unclear how it arrived at them. See International Crisis Group, "Blood and Soil: Land, Politics and Conflict Prevention in Zimbabwe and South Africa" (Brussels: ICG, 2004).
42. Kriger, "From Patriotic Memories," 1162.
43. Sadomba, "Decade of Zimbabwe's Land Revolution," 82.
44. Amanda Hammar and Brian Raftopoulos, "Zimbabwe's Unfinished Business: Rethinking Land, State and Nation," in *Zimbabwe's Unfinished Business*, ed. Amanda Hammar, Brian Raftopoulos, and Stig Jensen (Harare: Weaver Press, 2003), 7.
45. Ken Flower, *Serving Secretly* (London: John Murray, 1987), 248.
46. Selby, "Commercial Farmers," 255.
47. Admos Chimhowu, "Moving Forward in Zimbabwe: Reducing Poverty and Promoting Growth," University of Manchester, Brooks World Poverty Institute, http://www.bwpi.manchester.ac.uk/research/ResearchAreaProjects/Zimbabwe/Moving_forward_in_Zimbabwe_whole_report.pdf.
48. International Monetary Fund, "World Economic Outlook Database: Zimbabwe."
49. Kinsey, "Land Reform, Growth and Equity," 174.
50. Moyo, "Land and Agrarian Question," 18.
51. United Nations, "Report of the Panel of Experts on the Illegal Exploitation of Natural Resources and Other Forms of Wealth of the Democratic Republic of the Congo," http://www.un.org/News/dh/latest/drcongo.htm.
52. Norma Kriger, "Liberation from Constitutional Constraints: Land Reform in Zimbabwe," *SAIS Review* 27, no. 2 (2007): 70.
53. Justin Pearce, "Mugabe's Costly Congo Venture," http://news.bbc.co.uk/1/hi/world/africa/611898.stm; BBC, "World: Africa Zimbabwe Army in Congo Diamond Deal," BBC News, http://news.bbc.co.uk/1/hi/world/africa/455882.stm; International Institute for Strategic Studies, "Zimbabwe's Congolese Imbroglio," *Strategic Comments* 5, no. 2 (1999); UN, "Report of the Panel of Experts on the Illegal Exploitation of Natural Resources and Other Forms of Wealth of the Democratic Republic of the Congo"; Zimbabwe Human Rights NGO Forum, "Organised Violence and Torture in Zimbabwe in 1999" (Harare: Zimbabwe Human Rights NGO Forum, 1999).
54. Petros Mzingwane, war veteran and "new" farmer, interview, March 4, 2007.
55. Ibid.

56.  Denton Masumu, political affairs officer in the Liberation War, interview, February 9, 2007.

57.  Lundi, senior Central Intelligence Organisation agent; Chenjerai Mapufuli, farm mechanic, interview, September 14, 2006; Tendayi Garamapudzi, farm foreman, interview, September 15, 2006.

58.  Bubye, police officer, Zimbabwe Republic Police.

59.  Alex Siwaze, veteran of the Liberation War, interview, January 26, 2007.

60.  There was also no consensus on the land issue among war veterans or universal opposition to the MDC. There is no doubt that many former combatants sought land, but many did not. Indeed, numerous war veterans ardently supported the MDC. This is demonstrated in part by a faction of war veterans that split from the main war veterans' organization in May 2000, the Zimbabwe National Liberation War Veterans Association (ZNLWVA). These dissidents formed the Zimbabwe Liberators' Platform for Peace and Development (ZLPPD) in order to dissociate themselves from the violent land invasions that had begun a few months earlier.

61.  Andrew Morfu, horticulture manager, interview, September 16, 2006.

62.  Richardson Banongwe, livestock foreman, interview, August 7, 2006.

63.  Mupfure, veteran of the Liberation War and senior politician.

64.  Moyo, "Land Occupation Movement," 316.

65.  Ketani Makabusi, farm manager, interview, March 5, 2007.

66.  Ibid.

67.  Agnes Sengwe, member of the Zimbabwe National Army, interview, March 23, 2009.

68.  Bubye, police officer, Zimbabwe Republic Police.

69.  Samuel Limpopo, police officer, Zimbabwe Republic Police, interview, October 17, 2008.

70.  For more discussion of squatting see Alexander, "Squatters," and Moyo, "Land and Natural Resource Redistribution," 207.

71.  Marongwe, "Farm Occupations and Occupiers," 165, 75.

72.  Amanda Hammar, "'The Day of Burning': Eviction and Reinvention in the Margins of Northwest Zimbabwe," *Journal of Agrarian Change* 1, no. 4 (2001).

73.  Lundi, senior Central Intelligence Organisation agent.

74.  Ibid.

75.  Bubye, police officer, Zimbabwe Republic Police.

76.  Compagnon, *A Predictable Tragedy*, 174.

77.  E.g., Mugabe, *Inside the Third Chimurenga*, 95.

78.  Lundi, senior Central Intelligence Organisation agent.

79.  Ibid.

80.  Alexander and McGregor, "Elections, Land," 510.

81.  McGregor, "Politics of Disruption," 10.

82.  Moyo, "Land and Natural Resource Redistribution."

83.  Alexander and McGregor, "Elections, Land," 512.

84.  Lundi, senior Central Intelligence Organisation agent.

85. Support for Lundi's claims comes from an article in the *Herald* (government-owned newspaper) that read in part: "In order to safeguard the interests of their kith and kin in the country, the British and Scandinavian countries rallied behind the formation of the opposition MDC." Qtd. in Ian Phimister and Brian Raftopoulos, "Mugabe, Mbeki and the Politics of Anti-imperialism," *Review of African Political Economy* 31, no. 101 (2004).
86. Moyo, "Land and Agrarian Question," 17.
87. Moyo, "Land and Natural Resource Redistribution," 202–3.
88. Jabulani Sibanda, ZANU-PF provincial chairman, war veteran, leader of war veterans' association, "new" farmer, interview, January 26, 2007.
89. E.g., Mugabe, *Inside the Third Chimurenga*, 71.
90. Alexander and McGregor, "Elections, Land," 511.
91. E.g., Moyo, "Land and Agrarian Question," 14.
92. Qtd. in Alexander and McGregor, "Elections, Land," 511. ZANU-PF rhetoric about the British became hostile toward the end of the 1990s, mainly because of disputes with Britain over the funding of land redistribution programs. However, the Zimbabwean government had enjoyed a higher level of cooperation and support from the British in the past than political rhetoric during the land seizure era would lead one to assume. Edward Chidembo, a senior police officer interviewed for this book, pointed out that the British Military Advisory Team (BMAT) had helped train the Zimbabwe army and British police had helped train the Zimbabwe Republic Police. Chidembo asked, "If he hated the British so much why would the police be trained be, given technical support to improve the police force and the army if he hated the West or the whites so much?" Chidembo's answer was that the situation was simply too politically expedient for ZANU-PF to ignore.
93. Lundi, senior Central Intelligence Organisation agent.
94. Mugabe, *Inside the Third Chimurenga*, 79.
95. Sibanda, ZANU-PF provincial chairman, war veteran, leader of war veterans' association, "new" farmer.
96. Moyo, "Land Occupation Movement," 316; "Land and Agrarian Question," 19.
97. Moyo, "Land and Natural Resource Redistribution," 202.
98. Jongwe, member of the Zimbabwe National Army.
99. Mucheke, legal officer in the President's Office; Mupfure, veteran of the Liberation War and senior politician; Inkankezi, senior official in military intelligence, Zimbabwe National Army; Lundi, senior Central Intelligence Organisation agent; Matthew Coolidge, rancher, interview, February 1, 2007; Charles Morton, rancher, interview, January 18, 2007; George Harding, farmer, interview, August 29, 2006; Martin Sutherland, rancher, interview, September 20, 2006; Penny Madison, farmer's spouse, interview, July 17, 2006; Ronald Madison, farmer, interview, July 17, 2006; James Adams, farmer, interview, July 14, 2006.
100. Harding, farmer.
101. Tendi, *Making History in Mugabe's Zimbabwe*, 121.
102. Sibanda, ZANU-PF provincial chairman, war veteran, leader of war veterans' association, "new" farmer.

103.  Inkankezi, senior official in military intelligence, Zimbabwe National Army.
104.  Worker perspectives were particularly valuable given their position between loyalty to farmers for the benefits of employment, and loyalty to farm invaders for the benefits promised by land and asset redistribution.
105.  Thomas Rackomechi, farm foreman, interview, July 23, 2006.
106.  James Mwengi, farm foreman, interview, July 23, 2006.
107.  E.g., Moyo, "Land and Natural Resource Redistribution," 202.
108.  Rackomechi, farm foreman.
109.  John Nkomo, Minister for Lands, Land Reform and Resettlement, ZANU-PF national chairman, Speaker of parliament; former minister of special affairs in the President's Office, former Minister of Home Affairs, Lancaster House signatory, war veteran, interview, February 7, 2007.
110.  Lundi, senior Central Intelligence Organisation agent.
111.  Ibid.
112.  Nkomo, Minister for Lands, Land Reform and Resettlement, ZANU-PF national chairman; Speaker of parliament, former minister of special affairs in the President's Office, former Minister of Home Affairs, Lancaster House signatory, war veteran.
113.  E.g., Thomas Barkley, farmer, interview, September 13, 2006.
114.  Felix Umchabezi, veteran of the Liberation War and ZAPU publicity officer, interview, January 26, 2007.
115.  Inkankezi, senior official in military intelligence, Zimbabwe National Army.
116.  Ibid.
117.  Lundi, senior Central Intelligence Organisation agent.
118.  Ibid.
119.  Mucheke, legal officer in the President's Office.
120.  Lundi, senior Central Intelligence Organisation agent.
121.  Rutherford, "'Settlers' and Zimbabwe," 556.
122.  E.g., William Shore, farmer, interview, August 10, 2006; Thomas Barker, farmer, interview, July 27, 2006.
123.  Tendi, *Making History in Mugabe's Zimbabwe*, 121.
124.  Makabusi, farm manager.
125.  Rackomechi, farm foreman.
126.  It is unlikely that strong bias is reflected in these data because the survey made clear to respondents that their participation was anonymous. Moreover, nearly all participants were no longer living on their farms, and many no longer lived in Zimbabwe, suggesting that there would be no major reason for many respondents to provide an incorrect response to questions about political party affiliation.
127.  Survey respondents were automatically anonymized so no actual respondent names are associated with survey data in this book. Some respondents provided their names voluntarily; these instances are identified. "Private support" is defined as nonpublic support including voting, financial, or emotional support. "Public support" is defined as attendance not intended

to remain private such as participating in political rallies, public displays of financial support, encouraging workers to vote for the MDC, or seeking office as an MDC official. For instance, farmer William Thackeray said that some farmers had messages such as "Vote MDC," "Turn it down," and "We Want Him Out" on their vehicles. William Thackeray, farmer, interview, July 21, 2006.

128. E.g., some respondents said they provided transport equally for workers to attend both MDC and ZANU-PF rallies.
129. Lundi, senior Central Intelligence Organisation agent.
130. Ibid.
131. Minister of justice, legal and parliamentary affairs, 1989–2000 (he is also a wealthy businessman); Lundi, senior Central Intelligence Organisation agent.
132. Lundi, senior Central Intelligence Organisation agent.
133. Ibid.
134. Ibid.
135. Ibid.
136. Cliffe et al., "Overview of Fast Track Land Reform," 913.
137. Sadomba, "Decade of Zimbabwe's Land Revolution," 85.
138. Edward Chidembo, senior police officer, Zimbabwe Republic Police, interview, October 26, 2008; Msasa, military intelligence agent, Zimbabwe National Army.
139. Mzingwane, war veteran and "new" farmer.
140. Amnesty International, "Time for Accountability," 4.
141. Nic Cheeseman and Blessing-Miles Tendi, "Power-Sharing in Comparative Perspective: The Dynamics of 'Unity Government' in Kenya and Zimbabwe," *Journal of Modern African Studies* 48, no. 2 (2010): 210.
142. Inkankezi, senior official in military intelligence, Zimbabwe National Army.
143. Msasa, military intelligence agent, Zimbabwe National Army.
144. Nicholas Panhane, war veteran and provincial leader for ZANU-PF, interview, February 7, 2007.
145. Inkankezi, senior official in military intelligence, Zimbabwe National Army.
146. Chan, *Robert Mugabe*, 151.
147. Lundi, senior Central Intelligence Organisation agent.
148. Ibid.
149. Limpopo, police officer, Zimbabwe Republic Police.
150. Sebungwe, senior army officer, Zimbabwe National Army.
151. Ibid.
152. Ibid.
153. The protections for heads of state were apparently imperfect in Mugabe's view. A confidential US embassy diplomatic cable revealed a statement attributed to Jonathan Moyo, minister of information: "Moyo noted that MUGABE genuinely fears 'HANGING' if he leaves office and [Moyo] suggested international guarantees for his safety could help persuade MUGABE to go." See US Embassy in Harare, "Jonathan Moyo on Mugabe Succession, U.S. Policy," WikiLeaks, https://cablegatesearch.wikileaks.org/search.php.

154.    "Former Army Commander Reportedly Approaches MDC Secretly with Amnesty Deal Proposal," WikiLeaks, https://cablegatesearch.wikileaks.org/search.php.

155.    "MDC to Offer Amnesty to Key Military Figures," WikiLeaks, http://wikileaks.org/cable/2000/04/00HARARE1970.html.

156.    "Former Army Commander Reportedly Approaches MDC Secretly with Amnesty Deal Proposal."

157.    Ibid.

158.    Mupfure, veteran of the Liberation War and senior politician.

159.    Tendi, "Sundayview."

160.    Lundi, senior Central Intelligence Organisation agent.

161.    Brian Raftopoulos, "Briefing: Zimbabwe's 2002 Presidential Election," *African Affairs* 101 (2002): 414.

162.    Sadomba, "Decade of Zimbabwe's Land Revolution."

163.    Msasa (military intelligence agent, interviewed in Harare, October 23, 2008) described the influence this way: "The farmers would provide everything [for workers] like food, salaries, housing, schools, clinic, and which Mugabe can't do that. So they [farmers] were so powerful." An anonymous farm survey respondent stated, "I was anti Mugabe and ZANU-PF and had a very stable labour force (many were born on the farm). The word that filtered back was that ZANU considered that anyone who was good to their labour was the enemy as these workers had no complaints against the system due to the fact they had good permanent employment with good facilities, housing, schools, etc."

164.    Makabusi, farm manager.

165.    Tichafa Ncema, manager, interview, September 15, 2006.

166.    Richard Chipembere, farm foreman, interview, August 31, 2006.

167.    Cliffe et al., "Overview of Fast Track Land Reform," 914.

168.    Rutherford, "'Settlers' and Zimbabwe," 555–56.

169.    Lundi, senior Central Intelligence Organisation agent.

170.    Msasa, military intelligence agent, Zimbabwe National Army.

171.    Panhane, war veteran and provincial leader for ZANU-PF.

172.    Ibid.

173.    Anne Hellum and Bill Derman, "Land Reform and Human Rights in Contemporary Zimbabwe: Balancing Individual and Social Justice through an Integrated Human Rights Framework," *World Development* 32, no. 10 (2004).

174.    Mugabe, *Inside the Third Chimurenga*, 71.

175.    Mupfure, veteran of the Liberation War and senior politician.

176.    Sadomba, "Decade of Zimbabwe's Land Revolution," 88.

177.    Msasa, military intelligence agent, Zimbabwe National Army.

178.    Kriger, "From Patriotic Memories," 1166.

179.    Mupfure, veteran of the Liberation War and senior politician.

180.    US Embassy in Harare, "Former Army Commander Reportedly Approaches MDC Secretly with Amnesty Deal Proposal."

181.    Mupfure, veteran of the Liberation War and senior politician.

182.　Tendi, *Making History in Mugabe's Zimbabwe.*
183.　E.g., Alexander and McGregor, "Elections, Land," 510; Moyo, "Land and Natural Resource Redistribution"; McGregor, "Politics of Disruption," 10.
184.　Cheeseman and Tendi, "Power-Sharing in Comparative Perspective"; e.g., Mugabe, *Inside the Third Chimurenga*; Tendi, *Making History in Mugabe's Zimbabwe.*

## CHAPTER 3

1.　International Crisis Group, "Blood and Soil," 75.
2.　Moyo, "Land and Natural Resource Redistribution," 207; Selby, "Commercial Farmers and the State," 7.
3.　Dumiso Dabengwa, Minister of Home Affairs, interview, February 9, 2007.
4.　Chidembo, senior police officer, Zimbabwe Republic Police.
5.　Lundi, senior Central Intelligence Organisation agent.
6.　Inkankezi, senior official in military intelligence, Zimbabwe National Army; Msasa, military intelligence agent, Zimbabwe National Army.
7.　Inkankezi, senior official in military intelligence, Zimbabwe National Army.
8.　Masumu, political affairs officer in the Liberation War.
9.　Lundi, senior Central Intelligence Organisation agent.
10.　Inkankezi, senior official in military intelligence, Zimbabwe National Army.
11.　Lundi, senior Central Intelligence Organisation agent.
12.　Ibid.
13.　Mugabe, *Inside the Third Chimurenga.*
14.　Msasa, military intelligence agent, Zimbabwe National Army.
15.　Sengwe, member of the Zimbabwe National Army.
16.　Mucheke, legal officer in the President's Office.
17.　Lundi, senior Central Intelligence Organisation agent.
18.　Msasa, military intelligence agent, Zimbabwe National Army.
19.　Bubye, police officer, Zimbabwe Republic Police.
20.　Mucheke, legal officer in the President's Office; Msasa, military intelligence agent, Zimbabwe National Army.
21.　Msasa, military intelligence agent, Zimbabwe National Army.
22.　Ibid.
23.　Jackson Sanyati, Member in Charge for an eastern district, Zimbabwe Republic Police, interview, October 5, 2008; Bubye, police officer, Zimbabwe Republic Police; Limpopo, police officer, Zimbabwe Republic Police; Chidembo, senior police officer, Zimbabwe Republic Police.
24.　Mucheke, legal officer in the President's Office.
25.　Bubye, police officer, Zimbabwe Republic Police.
26.　Mucheke, legal officer in the President's Office.
27.　International Crisis Group, "Blood and Soil," 75; Alexander and McGregor, "Elections, Land," 511; e.g., Gerry Garner, farmer, interview, February 26 and March 2, 2007; Jongwe, member of the Zimbabwe National Army.
28.　Msasa, military intelligence agent, Zimbabwe National Army.
29.　Mucheke, legal officer in the President's Office.
30.　Ibid.

31. Mupfure, veteran of the Liberation War and senior politician.

32. Thompson Mupfure also explained how these individuals were incentivized to participate: "These would have been people probably who already had committed crime elsewhere at some other time and they are being given the opportunity to pay back because, 'We did not throw you into prison, and so this is payback time and so you must follow instructions. Go and kill so-and-so. Go and beat up so-and-so. Go and loot.' And they were very much willing to do and so forth" (Ibid.).

33. Mucheke, legal officer in the President's Office.

34. Inkankezi, senior official in military intelligence, Zimbabwe National Army.

35. Joyce Mukwa, farm clerk, interview, September 18, 2006. This point is supported by Martin Wilson: "You could tell by the standard of the huts that they weren't planned to be permanent structures" (Martin Wilson, farmer, interview, August 3, 2006).

36. Mapufuli, farm mechanic.

37. Morfu, horticulture manager.

38. Philip Mahobohobo, dairy manager, interview, August 18, 2006.

39. Mucheke, legal officer in the President's Office.

40. Alexander, *Unsettled Land*, 186; Lundi, senior Central Intelligence Organisation agent; Dabengwa, Minister of Home Affairs.

41. Mupfure, veteran of the Liberation War and senior politician.

42. Dabengwa, Minister of Home Affairs.

43. International Crisis Group, "Blood and Soil," 76.

44. Dabengwa, Minister of Home Affairs. Hunzvi's apparent effort to prevent the demonstrations becoming violent should not be confused with altruism or respect for the rule of law. Hunzvi was using his ability to rouse the war veterans to pressure ZANU-PF into making concessions both to war veterans and to himself.

45. Dabengwa, Minister of Home Affairs.

46. Ibid.

47. Felix Umchabezi, veteran of the Liberation War, corroborates Dabengwa's claim that Dabengwa sought to bring an end to escalating unrest on farms but was contradicted by Mugabe: "The then Minister of Home Affairs, Mr. Dabengwa said, 'No, no, no stop this. This is nonsensical.' And again, when Mugabe came back, he said, 'No, let's continue.' So it really was not something the cabinet deliberated, discussed, and you know, weighed the advantages and disadvantages of it, no" (Felix Umchabezi, veteran of the Liberation War, interview, January 26, 2007).

48. Dabengwa, Minister of Home Affairs.

49. Ibid.

50. Grant Ferrett, "In Search of Fuel," BBC, http://news.bbc.co.uk/1/hi/programmes/from_our_own_correspondent/690291.stm.

51. Dabengwa, Minister of Home Affairs.

52. Ibid.

53. Moyo, "Land and Natural Resource Redistribution," 207.

54. Mzingwane, war veteran and "new" farmer.

55. Matondi, "Understanding Fast Track Land Reforms," 6.
56. Ibid.
57. Lundi, senior Central Intelligence Organisation agent.
58. Mupfure, veteran of the Liberation War and senior politician.
59. Siwaze, veteran of the Liberation War.
60. "Gazetting" functioned as a public notice in the newspaper that the farm was designated by the government for resettlement.
61. Lundi, senior Central Intelligence Organisation agent.
62. Ibid.
63. Ibid.
64. Ibid.
65. Ibid.
66. Ibid.; Msasa, military intelligence agent, Zimbabwe National Army.
67. Mapufuli, farm mechanic.
68. Garamapudzi, farm foreman.
69. E.g., Mugabe, *Inside the Third Chimurenga*, 141.
70. Kriger, "From Patriotic Memories," 1163–64.
71. Msasa, military intelligence agent, Zimbabwe National Army.
72. Sanyati, Member in Charge for an eastern district, Zimbabwe Republic Police.
73. Msasa, military intelligence agent, Zimbabwe National Army.
74. Sebungwe, senior army officer, Zimbabwe National Army.
75. Bubye, police officer, Zimbabwe Republic Police.
76. Sanyati, Member in Charge for an eastern district, Zimbabwe Republic Police.
77. Bubye, police officer, Zimbabwe Republic Police.
78. US Embassy in Harare, "Wolpe/Mugabe Tete-a-Tete," WikiLeaks, https://cablegatesearch.wikileaks.org/search.php.
79. Sanyati, Member in Charge for an eastern district, Zimbabwe Republic Police.
80. Adams, farmer.
81. Brian Wheeler, rancher, interview, September 18, 2006.
82. Morfu, horticulture manager.
83. Telmore Nyakasanga, farm foreman, interview, September 13, 2006.
84. Sanyati, Member in Charge for an eastern district, Zimbabwe Republic Police.
85. Lundi, senior Central Intelligence Organisation agent.
86. Dabengwa, Minister of Home Affairs.
87. International Crisis Group, "Blood and Soil," 77–78.
88. Moyo and Yeros, "The Radicalised State," 114.
89. Inkankezi, senior official in military intelligence, Zimbabwe National Army.
90. Phillan Zamchiya, "A Synopsis of Land and Agrarian Change in Chipinge District, Zimbabwe," *Journal of Peasant Studies* 38, no. 5 (2011): 1103.
91. Chidembo, senior police officer, Zimbabwe Republic Police.
92. Timothy Ngavi, accountant for the Grain Marketing Board, interview, January 25, 2009. During my interview with Peter Msasa, a military intelligence

agent, he showed me his mobile phone, where he was receiving messages about seed being sold on the black market. Seed was being sold in quantities as large as 520 tons and down to 10 bags in what he described as a thriving and active black market.

93. Alexander, *Unsettled Land*, 188.
94. Human Rights Watch, "Fast Track Land Reform in Zimbabwe" (UNHCR, 2002); International Crisis Group, "Blood and Soil."
95. Cliffe et al., "Overview of Fast Track Land Reform," 912.
96. Charles M. B. Utete, "Report of the Presidential Land Review Committee on the Implementation of the Fast Track Land Reform Programme, 2000–2002 ('Utete Report')" (Harare: Presidential Land Review Committee, 2003), 6.
97. Zimbabwe Human Rights NGO Forum, "Enforcing the Rule of Law in Zimbabwe" (Harare: Zimbabwe Human Rights NGO Forum, 2001), 22.
98. International Crisis Group, "Blood and Soil," 76–77.
99. Alexander, *Unsettled Land*, 189.
100. Mupfure, veteran of the Liberation War and senior politician.
101. Bubye, police officer, Zimbabwe Republic Police.
102. Inkankezi, senior official in military intelligence, Zimbabwe National Army.
103. Lundi, senior Central Intelligence Organisation agent.
104. Ibid.
105. Matondi, "Understanding Fast Track Land Reforms," 13.
106. Ibid., 14.
107. Mupfure, veteran of the Liberation War and senior politician.
108. Moyo, "Land and Natural Resource Redistribution"; "Land Occupation Movement"; "Land and Agrarian Question"; Hanlon, Manjengwa, and Smart, *Zimbabwe Takes Back Its Land*.

CHAPTER 4

1. Lan, *Guns and Rain*, 124.
2. Qtd. in Ibid.
3. Ranger, *Peasant Consciousness*, 177.
4. Terence Ranger, "Zimbabwe and the Long Search for Independence," in *History of Central Africa: The Contemporary Years*, ed. David Birmingham and Phyllis M. Martin (London: Longman, 1998), 215.
5. Sebungwe, senior army officer, Zimbabwe National Army.
6. Kriger, *Zimbabwe's Guerrilla War*, 155.
7. Ibid., 156.
8. Welshman Mabhena, veteran of the Liberation War, politburo member, governor of Matabeleland North, former senior ZANU-PF official, interview, January 22, 2007.
9. Alexander, McGregor, and Ranger, *Violence and Memory*, 174.
10. Lan, *Guns and Rain*, 129–30; Kriger, *Zimbabwe's Guerrilla War*, 102–4.
11. Ranger, "The Death of Chaminuka," 367.
12. Charles M. Chavunduka and Daniel W. Bromley, "Considering the Multiple Purposes of Land in Zimbabwe's Economic Recovery," *Land Use Policy* 30 (2012): 673.

13. Msasa, military intelligence agent, Zimbabwe National Army.
14. Chidembo, senior police officer, Zimbabwe Republic Police.
15. Morfu, horticulture manager; Nyakasanga, farm foreman.
16. Beton Mopane, farm mechanic, interview, September 8, 2006.
17. Morfu, horticulture manager.
18. Lundi, senior Central Intelligence Organisation agent.
19. Mupfure, veteran of the Liberation War and senior politician.
20. Siwaze, veteran of the Liberation War.
21. Makabusi, farm manager.
22. Elizabeth Shore, farmer's spouse, interview, July 13, 2006.
23. Bubye, police officer, Zimbabwe Republic Police.
24. Mopane, farm mechanic.
25. Ibid.
26. Garner, farmer.
27. Makabusi, farm manager.
28. Alexander, "'Squatters,' Veterans and the State," 101; Raftopoulos, "The State in Crisis," 231; Alexander, *Unsettled Land*, 185; Inkankezi, senior official in military intelligence, Zimbabwe National Army.
29. Sadomba, "Decade of Zimbabwe's Land Revolution," 88.
30. Inkankezi, senior official in military intelligence, Zimbabwe National Army.
31. Arthur Breckinridge, farmer security coordinator, interview, July 31, 2006.
32. E.g., Trudy Grant, farmer's spouse, interview, August 15, 2006.
33. Bubye, police officer, Zimbabwe Republic Police.
34. Makabusi, farm manager.
35. Ibid.
36. Ibid.
37. Ibid.
38. Wheeler, rancher.
39. Makabusi, farm manager.
40. Ibid.
41. Mupfure, veteran of the Liberation War and senior politician.
42. Lundi, senior Central Intelligence Organisation agent; Andrew McKinley, farmer and activist, interview, August 23, 2006; Debbie McKinley, farmer's spouse and activist, interview, August 23, 2006.
43. Garner, farmer.
44. Jongwe, member of the Zimbabwe National Army.
45. Mupfure, veteran of the Liberation War and senior politician.
46. The farmer survey provides an insight into the rewards given to youths, but farmers could not always know exactly how farm invaders were rewarded.
47. Msasa, military intelligence agent, Zimbabwe National Army.
48. Lundi, senior Central Intelligence Organisation agent; Msasa, military intelligence agent, Zimbabwe National Army.
49. Msasa, military intelligence agent, Zimbabwe National Army.
50. Ibid.
51. Inkankezi, senior official in military intelligence, Zimbabwe National Army.

52. Imminence Ngiwa, foreman and tractor driver, interview, September 17, 2006; Mahobohobo, dairy manager.
53. Mwengi, farm foreman; Garner, farmer.
54. Chesterton Hove, manager, interview, September 21, 2006; Nyakasanga, farm foreman.
55. Inkankezi, senior official in military intelligence, Zimbabwe National Army.
56. Msasa, military intelligence agent, Zimbabwe National Army.
57. Youths from communal areas were also hired.
58. Mahobohobo, dairy manager.
59. Mucheke, legal officer in the President's Office.
60. Morfu, horticulture manager.
61. Wilson, farmer.
62. Patterson Rukodzi, senior instructor at a youth militia training camp, interview, February 21, 2007.
63. Makabusi, farm manager.
64. Sutherland, rancher.
65. Wheeler, rancher.
66. Joachim van Vaaden, rancher, interview, August 4, 2006.
67. Eric Fillmore, farmer, interview, July 31, 2006.
68. Aaron Buchanan, farmer, interview, July 18, 2006; Breckinridge, farmer security coordinator.
69. Madison, farmer; farmer's spouse.
70. Rob Dawes, farmer, interview, August 6, 2006.
71. Cynthia Dawes, farmer's spouse, interview, August 6, 2006.
72. Wheeler, rancher.
73. Bubye, police officer, Zimbabwe Republic Police.
74. Mucheke, legal officer in the President's Office.
75. Tafadzwa Tegwani, magistrate, interview, March 11, 2007.
76. George Lyons, rancher, interview, January 28, 2007; Joan Lyons, rancher's spouse, interview, January 28, 2007.
77. Tegwani, magistrate.
78. Kevin Elbridge, farmer, interview, January 11, 2007.
79. Makabusi, farm manager.
80. E.g., Morton, rancher; Henry Monroe, rancher, interview, January 23, 2007; Edwin Kennedy, rancher, interview, January 18, 2007; John Hayes, farmer, interview, September 8, 2006; Benjamin Colfax, farmer, interview, August 29, 2006; Lyons, rancher; Garner, farmer; Bubye, police officer, Zimbabwe Republic Police; Msasa, military intelligence agent, Zimbabwe National Army; Mupfure, veteran of the Liberation War and senior politician. Anonymous farmer interview respondents provided additional examples: "Legal system was a waste of time. They just tore it all up—court rulings." "When we showed legal documents we had won in court, etc. the level of intimidation increased!"
81. Zamchiya, "Synopsis of Land and Agrarian Change," 1111.
82. Hellum and Derman, "Land Reform and Human Rights," 1789–90.

83.   Mugabe, *Inside the Third Chimurenga*, 110.
84.   Kriger, "Liberation from Constitutional Constraints," 71.
85.   Mugabe, *Inside the Third Chimurenga*, 96.
86.   E.g., Moyo, "Land and Natural Resource Redistribution"; Rachel L. Swarns, "Zimbabwe Talks Tough but Steps Softly in Battle over Land," *New York Times*, April 11, 2000.
87.   Mucheke, legal officer in the President's Office.
88.   Jongwe, member of the Zimbabwe National Army.
89.   Rackomechi, farm foreman.
90.   Mucheke, legal officer in the President's Office.
91.   E.g., McKinley, farmer and activist; farmer's spouse and activist.
92.   Martin Grover, farmer, interview, August 6, 2006.
93.   Mwengi, farm foreman.
94.   E.g., Cheeseman and Tendi, "Power-Sharing in Comparative Perspective."
95.   Knox Chitiyo, "Making the Case for Security Sector Reform in Zimbabwe" (RUSI, 2009), 4.
96.   Zamchiya, "Synopsis of Land and Agrarian Change," 1101.
97.   Herbert Nchenchi, game hunt manager, interview, February 11, 2007.
98.   Nyakasanga, farm foreman.
99.   US Department of State, "Zimbabwe Human Rights Practices, 1994" (Washington, DC: US Department of State, 1995).
100.  Fairbanks, rancher.
101.  Chidembo, senior police officer, Zimbabwe Republic Police.
102.  Bubye, police officer, Zimbabwe Republic Police.
103.  Ibid.
104.  Chidembo, senior police officer, Zimbabwe Republic Police.
105.  Sanyati, Member in Charge for an eastern district, Zimbabwe Republic Police.
106.  Bubye, police officer, Zimbabwe Republic Police.
107.  Chidembo, senior police officer, Zimbabwe Republic Police.
108.  Sanyati, Member in Charge for an eastern district, Zimbabwe Republic Police.
109.  Chidembo, senior police officer, Zimbabwe Republic Police.
110.  Sanyati, Member in Charge for an eastern district, Zimbabwe Republic Police.
111.  Inkankezi, senior official in military intelligence, Zimbabwe National Army.
112.  Jongwe, member of the Zimbabwe National Army.
113.  Sengwe, member of the Zimbabwe National Army.
114.  Ibid.
115.  Tyson Manyame, member of the Zimbabwe National Army, interview, May 17, 2015.
116.  Jongwe, member of the Zimbabwe National Army.
117.  Sebungwe, senior army officer, Zimbabwe National Army.
118.  Msasa, military intelligence agent, Zimbabwe National Army. Zimbabwe African People's Union (ZAPU) was the competing nationalist group in the Liberation War, led by Joshua Nkomo. ZAPU, which over time comprised

largely ethnic Ndebeles, was seen as a rival to Mugabe's Shona-dominated ZANU party. Mugabe targeted ZAPU supporters and ethnic Ndebeles during the *Gukurahundi* massacres in the early 1980s.

CHAPTER 5

1. Central Statistical Office, "Census 2002: Zimbabwe Preliminary Report" (Harare: CSO, 2002), 1; CIA, "World Factbook 2002: Zimbabwe," http://www.faqs.org/docs/factbook/print/zi.html.
2. Robertson, General Zimbabwe Statistics.
3. A. P. Reeler, "Role of Militia Groups in Maintaining Zanu Pf's Political Power," http://www.kubatana.net/docs/hr/reeler_militia_mar_030,331.pdf; Alexander, *Unsettled Land*, 186, 88; Adrienne LeBas, "Polarization as Craft: Party Formation and State Violence in Zimbabwe," *Comparative Politics* 38, no. 4 (2006): 428.
4. LeBas, "Polarization as Craft," 428.
5. Alexander, *Unsettled Land*, 186, 88.
6. Central Statistical Office, "Census 2002."
7. Sebungwe, senior army officer, Zimbabwe National Army.
8. Institute for Security Studies, "Trends and Markers: Recent Data, Statistics and Indicators," http://www.issafrica.org/.
9. Lundi, senior Central Intelligence Organisation agent.
10. In support of Lundi's statement, a confidential US government diplomatic cable referencing the 2002 presidential election also called into question the official election results provided by Mudede. See US Embassy in Harare, "Zimbabwe: How Mugabe Stole the Election," WikiLeaks, https://cablegate-search.wikileaks.org/search.php.
11. Tegwani, magistrate; Sengwe, member of the Zimbabwe National Army; Jongwe, member of the Zimbabwe National Army; Siwaze, veteran of the Liberation War.
12. Nancy Hoover, farmer, interview, August 19, 2006.
13. Sisi Khampepe and Dikgang Moseneke, "Report on the 2002 Presidential Elections of Zimbabwe" (2002).
14. Zimbabwe Human Rights NGO Forum, "Political Violence Report: Consolidated Report for 1–15 March 2002" (Harare: Zimbabwe Human Rights NGO Forum, 2002), 21–22, 25;"Of Stuffed Ballots and Empty Stomachs: Reviewing Zimbabwe's 2005 Parliamentary Election and Post- election Period" (Harare: Zimbabwe Human Rights NGO Forum, 2005);"How to Rig an Election': Evidence of a Systematic Campaign to Prevent a Free and Fair Poll" (Harare: Zimbabwe Human Rights NGO Forum, 2001).
15. Raftopoulos, "Briefing: Zimbabwe's 2002 Presidential Election."
16. US Embassy in Harare, "Zimbabwe: How Mugabe Stole the Election."
17. US government diplomatic cables also detail how the election fraud occurred. In some cases polling agents were chased away and the ballot boxes were seized by the government, whereas in other cases it is likely that CIO agents were posing as polling agents (Ibid.). In urban areas, the number of polling stations was reduced by half, resulting in queues of over a kilometer

and waits of up to 30 hours: "Mugabe Declared Winner of Zimbabwe Presidential [Title Incomplete]," WikiLeaks, https://cablegatesearch.wikileaks.org/search.php.

18.  US Embassy in Harare, "Mugabe Declared Winner of Zimbabwe Presidential [Title Incomplete]."

19.  Zimbabwe Human Rights NGO Forum, "Who Is Responsible? A Preliminary Analysis of Pre-election Violence in Zimbabwe," 10.

20.  Author's survey; Utete, "Report of the Presidential Land Review Committee." There were an estimated 5,446 commercial farms in Zimbabwe, according to CFU data, of which 3,338 were located in Mashonaland. This figure is higher than the generally accepted figure of 4,300 farmers because some farmers held more than one farm title (for CFU data see Rory Pilossof, *Unbearable Whiteness of Being: Farmers' Voices from Zimbabwe* [Harare: Weaver Press, 2012]). Figures on permanent farm workers are based on the survey of farmers.

21.  Sebungwe, senior army officer, Zimbabwe National Army.

22.  Zimbabwe Human Rights NGO Forum, "Who Is Responsible," 11.

23.  US Embassy in Harare, "Despite Stiff Competition, Potential for [Title Incomplete]," WikiLeaks, https://cablegatesearch.wikileaks.org/search.php.

24.  Sebungwe, senior army officer, Zimbabwe National Army.

25.  Rukodzi, senior instructor at a youth militia training camp.

26.  Amnesty International, "Toll of Impunity."

27.  Ibid.

28.  Ibid.

29.  Mupfure, veteran of the Liberation War and senior politician.

30.  Rukodzi, senior instructor at a youth militia training camp.

31.  Limpopo, police officer, Zimbabwe Republic Police.

32.  Amnesty International, "Toll of Impunity."

33.  Farmer survey respondents were anonymous.

34.  LeBas, "Polarization as Craft," 429.

35.  McKinley, farmer's spouse and activist.

36.  Msasa, military intelligence agent, Zimbabwe National Army.

37.  Zimbabwe Human Rights NGO Forum, "Who Is Responsible," 10.

38.  Mucheke, legal officer in the President's Office.

39.  Cindy Anderson, farmer's spouse, interview, October 24, 2008; High Court of Zimbabwe, "The State versus Munetsi Kadzinga" (2006).

40.  Limpopo, police officer, Zimbabwe Republic Police.

41.  Mucheke, legal officer in the President's Office.

42.  Msasa, military intelligence agent, Zimbabwe National Army.

43.  Mucheke, legal officer in the President's Office.

44.  Ibid.

45.  Ibid.

46.  Sebungwe, senior army officer, Zimbabwe National Army.

47.  Ibid. Sebungwe elaborated on the methods used by this group: "I don't know how they do it and where they were trained to do that, but even a new Mercedes Benz, if you just give them 10 minutes to tamper around with that car

it will suddenly burst a tire [while being driven] or both [tires]. Even if you take it to quality control people of the tires, they will tell you this tire is perfect, it's new, but you will suddenly have it bursting." However, such methods were usually reserved for senior individuals whose murder was not so easily undertaken and needed the "cover" of an accident to maintain plausible deniability.

48.  Sebungwe, senior army officer, Zimbabwe National Army.

49.  The following extended account of a farmer murder comes from an interview with Cindy Anderson, the spouse of Charles Anderson, who was murdered in Mashonaland Central on June 2, 2002. In this account Cindy Anderson describes in detail how she and her family, including her children, had returned to their homestead to find that a hole had been cut in the homestead security fence. While Charles Anderson went around the back of the house to investigate, Cindy Anderson told her children to lock themselves in the farm truck for protection. Cindy Anderson stated: "Then I heard shots very soon after my husband went round the back and I just screamed for him, and then the next minute this tall thin black man with a hood over his [head]—it was like a makeshift hood—it was just like an old flour sack or something with holes cut in it, over his head, and he came round the front. He had a gun over his shoulder." The shots killed Charles Anderson. Cindy Anderson emphasized that despite a weapon being fired, this agent "wasn't agitated or walking quickly, he was just taking his time." Anderson continued: "I went towards the back to try and see where my husband was and then one of them came from the back, the one that actually had shot my husband, he came from the back with an AK and he started screaming at me." Cindy Anderson stated, "I just kept staring at him in the face, you know. I wanted to make sure that I would never forget his face, and he just screaming at me to stop looking at his face, otherwise he'd shoot me." The agent told Cindy Anderson to lie down. At this time her children were still in the vehicle: "This guy was standing over me screaming 'I'm going to shoot you, I'm going to shoot you.' And then the other guy went down and got the boys from the car . . . and brought them up and was, you know, prodding them with the gun." The hooded individual and one of the other agents commandeered Anderson's vehicle and drove off, appearing to forget the third agent, who chased after them on foot. Two of these agents were later apprehended by police, but the hooded agent was never found. Munetsi Kadzinga and Benedict Makumbe were both accused of the murder, while the third individual whose face was covered with a hood has never been identified. Munetsi Kadzinga had a criminal history, and Cindy Anderson was told that he was an "escaped prisoner." He was captured and put on trial, while Makumbe allegedly fled the country and has not been tried. In Kadzinga's trial it was found that the AK-47 used in the commission of the crime came from ZANU-PF minister John Nkomo's driver: "[Makumbe] also said that the minister and other 'superiors' had assigned Makumbe and the accused to threaten and frighten away the white farmers in the Chiweshe area [Mashonaland Central]" (High Court of Zimbabwe, "The State versus

Munetsi Kadzinga"). It is significant that the weapon used to murder Anderson was an AK-47, as such weapons are rarely owned by civilians in Zimbabwe, and are almost always the property of the state security services. However, while it is improbable, but not impossible, to accept that the driver of a
senior government minister could be robbed of an AK-47 assault rifle, little
appears to be made in the court documents of how extremely unusual it is
for this to have occurred or for a civilian to be in possession of such a
weapon. Moreover, the claim by the defense that the accused were following
instructions from senior officials was dismissed by the court: "The accused's
version that he was coerced into this enterprise by Makumbe, who was
acting on so-called superior instructions, is exceedingly difficult to accept"
("The State versus Munetsi Kadzinga"). In addition, responsibility for the
planning and actual murder is placed on Kadzinga, while the court assigned
less blame to Makumbe. Cindy Anderson noted that even though the trial
was against the murder of her husband, "it was actually very difficult for
anyone to find out when the trial was being held, and it was actually, from
what I gathered, quite dangerous for them to be even querying about the
trial." Kadzinga was eventually found guilty of murder while committing an
armed robbery—which dovetails with his alleged history. As previously
noted, Makumbe is still at large, while the third, hooded individual has
never been identified. If the account by state security agents is to be believed,
and there is no evidence not to believe it, then it is this third individual who
was likely the CIO agent monitoring the commission of the killing.

50.   Van Vaaden, rancher.
51.   Lundi, senior Central Intelligence Organisation agent.
52.   Lundi elaborated on the factions in the state security service, noting that
      there were factions for the three most powerful people in Zimbabwe: Presi-
      dent Robert Mugabe, General Solomon Mujuru, and Minister Emmerson
      Mnangagwa. Lundi explained that branches of the police, army, and secret
      service were all aligned to these factions. Speaking about the secret service,
      Lundi stated: "You find the major protagonists in ZANU-PF, they have got
      quite a loyal following in the CIO. So the CIO is kind of a moribund—it's a
      mix and match of people who follow different—who have got sympathies
      and loyalties to different people in ZANU-PF. So I might be aligned to
      Mujuru, and the other guy is aligned to Mnangagwa, the other guy is aligned
      to Mugabe. So in a sense there is also a tussle within the CIO itself, people
      fighting to uphold the supremacy of their good friend, as it were"
      (Ibid.).While normally individuals in these factions worked professionally,
      they also served the needs of the faction leaders. For example, Lundi related
      how he had personal experience witnessing members of General Solomon
      Mujuru's faction using military aircraft from the Air Force of Zimbabwe for
      the business interests of General Mujuru. Lundi stated that during Zimba-
      bwe's military participation in the Second Congo War (Democratic Repub-
      lic of the Congo) that began in 1998, members of Mujuru's faction used the
      air force aircraft to transport shovels—which were in extremely short supply
      in DR Congo at the time—for the use in mines where Mujuru held interests.

Lundi noted that while the flight to DR Congo from Zimbabwe carried shovels, the returning flight carried "bags of money" that belonged to Mujuru. There were also times when rivalries emerged between factions. Christian Mucheke, legal officer in the President's Office, stated that these rivalries occurred during disputes over which faction would seize valuable farms with large quantities of agri-property. He emphasized that at times they could become violent with agents from factions seeking to assassinate each other.

53. Limpopo, police officer, Zimbabwe Republic Police.
54. Ibid.
55. Bubye, police officer, Zimbabwe Republic Police.
56. Mupfure, veteran of the Liberation War and senior politician.
57. Limpopo, police officer, Zimbabwe Republic Police.
58. Mupfure, veteran of the Liberation War and senior politician.
59. Mzingwane, war veteran and "new" farmer.
60. Chidembo, senior police officer, Zimbabwe Republic Police.
61. Tegwani, magistrate.
62. Bubye, police officer, Zimbabwe Republic Police.
63. Dawes, farmer. Rob Dawes's discovery that the bartender was a CIO informer was made when workers told him about the bartender's activities, and was supported by the fact that the bartender received a portion of one of the neighboring farms when the farmer was evicted.
64. Bubye, police officer, Zimbabwe Republic Police.
65. Mukwa, farm clerk.
66. Nchenchi, game hunt manager.
67. Msasa, military intelligence agent, Zimbabwe National Army.
68. Ibid.
69. Hove, manager.
70. Mukwa, farm clerk.
71. Ngiwa, foreman and tractor driver.
72. Mupfure, veteran of the Liberation War and senior politician.
73. Mucheke, legal officer in the President's Office.
74. Morfu, horticulture manager.
75. Thompson Mbezi, livestock foreman, interview, January 28, 2007.
76. Hove, manager.
77. Limpopo, police officer, Zimbabwe Republic Police.
78. Sebungwe, senior army officer, Zimbabwe National Army.
79. Mucheke, legal officer in the President's Office.
80. Ngiwa, foreman and tractor driver.
81. Mapufuli, farm mechanic.
82. Makabusi, farm manager.
83. Mucheke, legal officer in the President's Office.
84. Mahobohobo, dairy manager.
85. Rutherford, *Working on the Margins*; Waeterloos and Rutherford, "Land Reform in Zimbabwe"; Rutherford, "'Settlers' and Zimbabwe," 548.
86. Msasa, military intelligence agent, Zimbabwe National Army.

87.  Chambati, "Restructuring of Agrarian Labour Relations," 1051.
88.  Shore, farmer's spouse; Mwengi, farm foreman; Rackomechi, farm foreman.
89.  Rutherford, "'Settlers' and Zimbabwe," 549.
90.  Moyo, "Three Decades of Agrarian Reform," 497.
91.  Waeterloos and Rutherford, "Land Reform in Zimbabwe," 541.
92.  Godfrey Magaramombe, "Rural Poverty: Commercial Farm Workers and Land Reform in Zimbabwe," presented to SARPN conference "Land Reform and Poverty Alleviation in Southern Africa," Pretoria, South Africa, 2001, 1.
93.  Mucheke, legal officer in the President's Office.
94.  Magaramombe, "Rural Poverty," 1.
95.  Chambati, "Restructuring of Agrarian Labour Relations," 1051.
96.  Utete, "Report of the Presidential Land Review Committee," 5–6, 43, 49.
97.  Moyo, "Three Decades of Agrarian Reform," 508.
98.  Brian Raftopoulos, "The Crisis in Zimbabwe, 1998–2008," in *Becoming Zimbabwe: A History from the Pre-colonial Period to 2008*, ed. B. Raftopoulos and A. Mlambo (Harare: Weaver Press, 2009), 672.
99.  Chavunduka and Bromley, "Considering the Multiple Purposes of Land," 672.
100. Zimbabwe Human Rights NGO Forum, "Who Was Responsible."
101. Msasa, military intelligence agent, Zimbabwe National Army.
102. Mucheke, legal officer in the President's Office.
103. Umchabezi, veteran of the Liberation War and ZAPU publicity officer.
104. Kriger, *Zimbabwe's Guerrilla War*, 156.
105. Mabhena, veteran of the Liberation War, politburo member, governor of Matabeleland North, former senior ZANU-PF official.
106. Lan, *Guns and Rain*, 129–30; Kriger, *Zimbabwe's Guerrilla War*, 102–4; Mabhena, veteran of the Liberation War, politburo member, governor of Matabeleland North, former senior ZANU-PF official; Ranger, "The Death of Chaminuka," 367.
107. Nyakasanga, farm foreman.
108. Makabusi, farm manager.
109. Sebungwe, senior army officer, Zimbabwe National Army.
110. Msasa, military intelligence agent, Zimbabwe National Army.
111. Mwengi, farm foreman.
112. Mucheke, legal officer in the President's Office.
113. Msasa, military intelligence agent, Zimbabwe National Army.
114. Chipembere, farm foreman.
115. Msasa, military intelligence agent, Zimbabwe National Army.
116. Garamapudzi, farm foreman.
117. Msasa, military intelligence agent, Zimbabwe National Army.
118. Garamapudzi, farm foreman.
119. Fairbanks, rancher.
120. Morfu, horticulture manager.
121. Nyakasanga, farm foreman.
122. Colfax, farmer.
123. Mbezi, livestock foreman.

124. E.g., Zimbabwe Human Rights NGO Forum, "Monthly Violence Reports"; e.g., Amnesty International, "Toll of Impunity"; "Amnesty International Report 2002—Zimbabwe," Amnesty International, http://www.unhcr.org/refworld/docid/3cf4bc048.html.
125. Mukwa, farm clerk.
126. Hove, manager.
127. Lyons, rancher. Farmers often had detailed knowledge of violence against workers because in many cases they provided either direct medical assistance or transport to local clinics for professional medical care.
128. Garamapudzi, farm foreman.
129. Ncema, farm manager.
130. Garamapudzi, farm foreman.
131. Mahobohobo, dairy manager.
132. Ngiwa, foreman and tractor driver.
133. Rackomechi, farm foreman.
134. Garner, farmer.
135. E.g., Zimbabwe Human Rights NGO Forum, "Torture by State Agents in Zimbabwe: January 2001 to August 2002," 47–48; "Only Bruises on the Soles of Their Feet! Torture and Falanga in Zimbabwe"; Justice for Agriculture Zimbabwe and General Agricultural and Plantation Workers Union of Zimbabwe, "Destruction of Zimbabwe's Backbone Industry in Pursuit of Political Power" (Harare: JAG and the GAPWUZ, 2008), 20–23.
136. Mapufuli, farm mechanic.
137. Sanyati, Member in Charge for an eastern district, Zimbabwe Republic Police.
138. McKinley, farmer's spouse and activist.
139. George Sherman, farmer, interview, August 2, 2006.
140. Sebungwe, senior army officer, Zimbabwe National Army.
141. Lundi, senior Central Intelligence Organisation agent.
142. Lundi stated that the original facility had been built during the Rhodesian era and still had government literature in it from the Rhodesian government. He said that it had been added to by the Zimbabwe government over the years with guidance from the Chinese, Russians, and freelance former Mossad agents.
143. Mucheke, legal officer in the President's Office.
144. Hove, manager.
145. Mwengi, farm foreman.
146. Mupfure, veteran of the Liberation War and senior politician.
147. Chris Cleveland, farmer, interview, August 3, 2006; Catherine Cleveland, farmer's spouse, interview, August 3, 2006; Mupfure, veteran of the Liberation War and senior politician.
148. Garner, farmer.
149. Lyons, rancher.
150. Cleveland, farmer; farmer's spouse.
151. Hove, manager.
152. McKinley, farmer's spouse and activist.

153. Van Vaaden, rancher.
154. Commercial Farmers Union, "Retrenchment of Agricultural Workers in Zimbabwe," Commercial Farmers Union, http://www.cfuzim.org/~cfuzimb/images/si62002advice.pdf.
155. Dawes, farmer.
156. Gerald Burr, farmer, interview, August 11, 2006; Fillmore, farmer.
157. Commercial Farmers Union, "Retrenchment of Agricultural Workers in Zimbabwe."

## CHAPTER 6

1. E.g., Mugabe, *Inside the Third Chimurenga*, 40–43; Utete, "Report of the Presidential Land Review Committee," 10–14.
2. Utete, "Report of the Presidential Land Review Committee," 19.
3. George Kay, *Rhodesia: A Human Geography* (London: University of London Press, 1970), 18.
4. R. Anderson, *An Agricultural Survey of Southern Rhodesia. Part II: Agro-Economic Survey* (Salisbury [S. Rhodesia]: Printed by the Government Printer, 1961), 36.
5. If a farmer owned more than one farm, he would usually have a primary farm, normally where the homestead was located.
6. Shore, farmer.
7. Information from telephone conversation with salesman in the United Kingdom, May 2009.
8. James Shore, farmer, interview, July 27, 2006.
9. Information from telephone conversation with sales agent in the United Kingdom, May 2009.
10. A UK John Deere salesman stated in May 2009 that prices that year were about 27% higher than in 2005. Moreover, there are numerous configurations for such equipment that raise costs, and it is likely that prices in southern Africa would be lower anyway because of a presumed European and North American premium.
11. Wilson, farmer.
12. Lundi, senior Central Intelligence Organisation agent.
13. Jongwe, member of the Zimbabwe National Army.
14. Garamapudzi, farm foreman.
15. A detailed research methods discussion (see appendix A) shows that this survey sample is roughly representative of Zimbabwe farmers. Thus, the higher representation in Mashonaland demonstrated in the survey is approximately representative of the national distribution.
16. "Violence" includes assault, murder, attempted murder, rape, and torture; "Intimidation" includes abduction / unlawful arrest, verbal threat, *jambanja*, and property damage / theft.
17. Pseudo-war veterans are an exception in this table and should be considered differently from other farm invaders in table 6.8, because they almost always played a support role in seizing farms and agri-property.
18. Moyo, "Three Decades of Agrarian Reform," 505.

19. Utete, "Report of the Presidential Land Review Committee."
20. Msasa, military intelligence agent, Zimbabwe National Army.
21. Mzingwane, war veteran and "new" farmer.
22. David Coltart, senator and Minister for Education, interview, January 22 and 25, 2007.
23. Fairbanks, rancher.
24. Moyo, "Three Decades of Agrarian Reform," 503.
25. Chidembo, senior police officer, Zimbabwe Republic Police.
26. Hayes, farmer.
27. Limpopo, police officer, Zimbabwe Republic Police.
28. Some "new" farmers were called "weekend farmers" because they only came to their newly seized farm at the end of the week, often for social rather than agricultural reasons. Chidembo, senior police officer, Zimbabwe Republic Police.
29. Madison, farmer; farmer's spouse.
30. Sebungwe, senior army officer, Zimbabwe National Army.
31. Mukwa, farm clerk.
32. Sengwe, member of the Zimbabwe National Army.
33. Nyakasanga, farm foreman.
34. Inkankezi, senior official in military intelligence, Zimbabwe National Army.
35. Elbridge, farmer.
36. Garamapudzi, farm foreman.
37. Morfu, horticulture manager.
38. Ibid.
39. Mupfure, veteran of the Liberation War and senior politician.
40. The assertion that Mashonaland was particularly targeted is not meant to imply that other regions did not have fertile farming of valuable assets. Masvingo, Manicaland, and Midlands had much fertile land, and Matabeleland had well-stocked ranching.
41. Cliffe et al., "Overview of Fast Track Land Reform," 913.
42. Arnold Bembezi, farmer, interview, March 20, 2007.
43. Ncema, manager.
44. Sengwe, member of the Zimbabwe National Army.
45. Moyo, "Three Decades of Agrarian Reform," 501.
46. Neil Wright, representative from the Commercial Farmers Union, email to author, November 20, 2014.
47. Ibid. In practice very few farmers received compensation. Those who did almost always received just a portion that had been vastly reduced in value because of skyrocketing inflation.
48. Wright, representative from the Commercial Farmers Union.
49. Ibid.
50. Moyo, "Three Decades of Agrarian Reform," 501.
51. Shore, farmer's spouse.
52. Shore, farmer.
53. Makabusi, farm manager.
54. Barkley, farmer.

55. Makabusi, farm manager.
56. Jane Garfield, farmer's spouse, interview, August 28, 2006; Rupert Garfield, farmer, interview, August 28, 2006.
57. Sherman, farmer.
58. Ibid.
59. Chidembo, senior police officer, Zimbabwe Republic Police; Jongwe, member of the Zimbabwe National Army; Senator Negomo, Chiweshe Chief, interview, March 12, 2007.
60. Chidembo, senior police officer, Zimbabwe Republic Police.
61. Interview respondent Timothy Ngavi, who worked for a state-owned enterprise called the Grain Marketing Board, discussed his own "tour" to seek land.
62. E.g., Monroe, rancher.
63. Lundi, senior Central Intelligence Organisation agent.
64. Ibid.
65. Ibid.
66. Cleveland, farmer; farmer's spouse.
67. Ngiwa, foreman and tractor driver.
68. Limpopo, police officer, Zimbabwe Republic Police.
69. United Nations Development Programme, "Comprehensive Economic Recovery in Zimbabwe."
70. Ibid., 155.
71. Ibid.
72. Ibid., 156.
73. Ibid., 159, 62.
74. Food and Agriculture Organization / World Food Programme, "Food and Agriculture Organization / World Food Programme Crop and Food Supply Assessment Mission to Zimbabwe," http://www.fao.org/docrep/010/ai469e/ai469e00.htm.
75. Utete, "Report of the Presidential Land Review Committee," 5.
76. Ibid., 20. A1 farms were small-scale holdings that came in village or self-contained types. A2 were medium and large-scale commercial farms.
77. United Nations Development Programme, "Comprehensive Economic Recovery in Zimbabwe," 183–84.
78. Utete, "Report of the Presidential Land Review Committee," 5.
79. United Nations Development Programme, "Comprehensive Economic Recovery in Zimbabwe," 161.
80. Ibid., 183–84.
81. Zamchiya, "Synopsis of Land and Agrarian Change."
82. Garamapudzi, farm foreman.
83. E.g., Zimbabwe Human Rights NGO Forum, "Report on Political Violence in Bulawayo, Harare, Manicaland, Mashonaland West, Masvingo, Matabeleland North, Matabeleland South and Midlands" (Harare: Zimbabwe Human Rights NGO Forum, 2000); "Who Was Responsible? Alleged Perpetrators and Their Crimes during the 2000 Parliamentary Election Period"; "Monthly Violence Reports."

84. Phillan Zamchiya, "The Role of Politics and State Practices in Shaping Rural Differentiation: A Study of Resettled Small-Scale Farmers in South-Eastern Zimbabwe," *Journal of Southern African Studies* 39, no. 4 (2013): e.g., 940–53.

85. In 2006 I met two commercial farmers in a Mashonaland province who were the only remaining white commercial farmers in their district. In a private discussion one farmer espoused dislike for the ruling party but was quickly corrected by the other farmer who reminded him that their professed allegiance to ZANU-PF was the only reason they remained on their land. This underscores the benefits of professing party allegiance.

86. Terminology used in research on Zimbabwe is often marked by challenges in defining terms. Sam Moyo as well as Scoones et al. use the term "elite," but it is often unclear what "elite" they are referring to. I prefer the term "senior officials" to refer to a relatively select group of well-connected, relatively wealthy and influential individuals, usually holding more senior political and military positions but which also included business people. "Professionals" refer to the group that is also relatively well connected and wealthy, but to a lesser extent than senior officials.

87. Rukuni and Jensen, "Land, Growth and Governance."

88. Sadomba, "Decade of Zimbabwe's Land Revolution," 97.

89. Msasa, military intelligence agent, Zimbabwe National Army.

90. Ibid.

91. Chidembo, senior police officer, Zimbabwe Republic Police.

92. Mzingwane, war veteran and "new" farmer.

93. Lundi, senior Central Intelligence Organisation agent.

94. Sengwe, member of the Zimbabwe National Army.

95. Inkankezi, senior official in military intelligence, Zimbabwe National Army.

96. Chidembo, senior police officer, Zimbabwe Republic Police.

97. For many farmer survey respondents, more than one farm invader undertook initial incidents, so the total exceeds 100%.

98. "Member of CIO from the President's Office." "Colonel Colin Moyo; Brigadier Lifa." "Head of CIO Manicaland—Innocent Chibaya." "Major Mhandu claimed he was a training officer in Tanzania." "Chief Inspector." "General Vitalis Zvinawashe." "Army Captain and Majors and other ranks; CIO senior figures; police senior figures." "Member of CIO and President's office were embedded in the original group [who] came the first night." "General Solomon Mujuru; Comrade Zhou (ex-colonel 5th Brigade and Mujuru's 'batman' and ruthless enforcer)." "The top army [officials]; CIO and police personnel were allocated land on the farm." "Believe [it was a] member of CIO/CID with 20 vets / pseudo vets escorted by neighbour." "Group Captain [in the] Airforce; Head of CIO for [the] district." "Assistant Commissioner of Police, Shepard Gwesera; Local police Member in Charge Mr Mabunda." "CIO head of youth in the district." "Inspector of police; Colonel I/C 5th Brigade; Air Force commander." "Major Maponga—army." "CIO Lifa; CIO Mutongwana." "Air Force Wing Commanders." "Inspector of Beatrice police station." "Obert Mpofu, Governor Mat[abeleland] North, Inspector of police (Inyathi), Colonel I/C 5th Brigade (Gweru), Air Force Commander (Gweru),

War vet commander (Nkayi)." "The governor of Mat[abeleland] North, Obert Mpofu, and other leading members of the prisons department looted the farm."

99. Breckinridge, farmer security coordinator; Joan Breckinridge, spouse of farmer security coordinator, interview, July 31, 2006.
100. Sherman, farmer.
101. Wheeler, rancher.
102. Msasa, military intelligence agent, Zimbabwe National Army.
103. David Smith, "Mugabe and Allies Own 40% of Land Seized from White Farmers—Inquiry," *Guardian*, http://www.guardian.co.uk/world/2010/nov/30/zimbabwe-mugabe-white-farmers.
104. Lundi, senior Central Intelligence Organisation agent; Peta Thornycroft and Sebastien Berger, "Robert Mugabe Has Built up 10,000-Acre Farm of Seized Land," *Telegraph*, http://www.telegraph.co.uk/news/worldnews/africaandindianocean/zimbabwe/6231765/Robert-Mugabe-has-built-up-10,000-acre-farm-of-seized-land.html; Smith, "Mugabe and Allies Own 40% of Land."
105. Fillmore, farmer; John Hendricks, farmer, interview, August 2, 2006; Grant, farmer's spouse; Garfield, farmer's spouse; farmer.
106. Makabusi, farm manager.
107. Zamchiya, "Synopsis of Land and Agrarian Change."
108. Ian Scoones et al., "Zimbabwe's Land Reform," 976–80.
109. Ibid., 980–81.
110. Ibid., 976–77.
111. Ibid., 976.
112. Moyo, "Three Decades of Agrarian Reform," 496.
113. Dawes, farmer; Lyons, rancher.
114. Ian Scoones et al., "Zimbabwe's Land Reform," 980.
115. Ibid., 979.
116. Ibid., 978–80.
117. Ibid., 976.
118. Zamchiya, "Synopsis of Land and Agrarian Change," e.g., 1101.
119. Scooneset al., "Zimbabwe's Land Reform," 978–80.
120. Ibid., 976–80.
121. Ibid., 976.
122. Ibid.
123. Sengwe, member of the Zimbabwe National Army. "Offer letters" were permits issued to land claimants, part of the process of officially being allocated land, but they gave no formal title to the land. The official allocation of land to beneficiaries, especially for the A2 scheme, involved indicating on maps or on the actual land the plots to be allocated and the provision of an offer letter supported this allocation. Most A1 beneficiaries were shown what land was to be allocated to them, and some received offer letters (Moyo, "Three Decades of Agrarian Reform," 509.). The provision of offer letters from various government officials was, in practice, often disorderly and highly prone to corrupt practices (Lundi, senior Central Intelligence Organisation agent; Msasa, military intelligence agent, Zimbabwe National Army).

124.  Sengwe, member of the Zimbabwe National Army.
125.  Garfield, farmer.
126.  Zamchiya, "Role of Politics," 944.
127.  Lundi, senior Central Intelligence Organisation agent.
128.  Ngavi, accountant for the Grain Marketing Board.
129.  Cliffe et al., "Overview of Fast Track Land Reform," 915.
130.  Sam Moyo, "Land Concentration and Accumulation after Redistributive Reform in Postsettler Zimbabwe," *Review of African Political Economy* 38, no. 128 (2011): 260.
131.  Lundi, senior Central Intelligence Organisation agent.
132.  Cleveland, farmer; farmer's spouse.
133.  Mucheke, legal officer in the President's Office.
134.  Lundi, senior Central Intelligence Organisation agent.
135.  Msasa, military intelligence agent, Zimbabwe National Army.
136.  Lundi, senior Central Intelligence Organisation agent.
137.  Zamchiya, "Synopsis of Land and Agrarian Change"; "Role of Politics."
138.  Zamchiya, "Synopsis of Land and Agrarian Change," 1101.
139.  Siwaze, veteran of the Liberation War.
140.  Msasa, military intelligence agent, Zimbabwe National Army.
141.  Tendi, "Patriotic History."
142.  Craig J. Richardson, "How the Loss of Property Rights Caused Zimbabwe's Collapse" (Cato Institute, 2005), 2; Compagnon, *A Predictable Tragedy*.

CHAPTER 7
1.  Inkankezi, senior official in military intelligence, Zimbabwe National Army.
2.  Ibid.
3.  Lundi, senior Central Intelligence Organisation agent.
4.  Mupfure, veteran of the Liberation War and senior politician.
5.  Mzingwane, war veteran and "new" farmer.
6.  Inkankezi, senior official in military intelligence, Zimbabwe National Army.
7.  Siwaze, veteran of the Liberation War.
8.  Inkankezi, senior official in military intelligence, Zimbabwe National Army.
9.  Ibid.
10.  Garner, farmer.
11.  Inkankezi, senior official in military intelligence, Zimbabwe National Army.
12.  Ngiwa, foreman and tractor driver.
13.  Inkankezi, senior official in military intelligence, Zimbabwe National Army.
14.  Mopane, farm mechanic.
15.  Mupfure, veteran of the Liberation War and senior politician; Inkankezi, senior official in military intelligence, Zimbabwe National Army; Lundi, senior Central Intelligence Organisation agent; Siwaze, veteran of the Liberation War; Msasa, military intelligence agent, Zimbabwe National Army; Bubye, police officer, Zimbabwe Republic Police; Garner, farmer; Hendricks, farmer; Fillmore, farmer.
16.  Mucheke, legal officer in the President's Office.
17.  Inkankezi, senior official in military intelligence, Zimbabwe National Army.

18. Fillmore, farmer.
19. Mahobohobo, dairy manager.
20. Lundi, senior Central Intelligence Organisation agent.
21. David Karimanzira, governor of Harare.
22. Lundi, senior Central Intelligence Organisation agent.
23. Mucheke, legal officer in the President's Office.
24. Ibid.
25. Ibid.
26. Seized farm equipment was sometimes used in communal areas or sold to invaders who had taken over farms. When possible, equipment was sold in neighboring Zambia and Mozambique, where prices were higher.
27. James Shore, farmer, interview, May 23, 2011.
28. Burr, farmer.
29. Makabusi, farm manager.
30. Previously the ZANU-PF governor of Matabeleland North and minister of mines at times of print.
31. Siwaze, veteran of the Liberation War.
32. Ibid.
33. Selby, "Commercial Farmers and the State."
34. Lundi, senior Central Intelligence Organisation agent.
35. Msasa, military intelligence agent, Zimbabwe National Army.
36. Garfield, farmer's spouse.
37. Sebungwe, senior army officer, Zimbabwe National Army.
38. Mopane, farm mechanic.
39. Nyakasanga, farm foreman.
40. Moyo, "Three Decades of Agrarian Reform," 496.
41. Bubye, police officer, Zimbabwe Republic Police.
42. Msasa, military intelligence agent, Zimbabwe National Army.
43. McKinley, farmer's spouse and activist.
44. Barkley, farmer.
45. Moyo, "Three Decades of Agrarian Reform," 496.
46. Scoones et al., *Zimbabwe's Land Reform*.
47. Adams, farmer.
48. Farmers' concerns about the breakdown of their community were frequently cited in farmer interviews.
49. Shore, farmer's spouse.
50. International Crisis Group, "Blood and Soil," 107.
51. Adams, farmer.
52. Lundi, senior Central Intelligence Organisation agent.
53. Ibid.
54. IMF, "World Economic Outlook Database: Zimbabwe"; CIA, "World Fact-book 2002: Zimbabwe."
55. Utete, "Report of the Presidential Land Review Committee," 25.
56. Not all of it was technically available, as some farmers moved equipment off the farms. However, the point remains that very large supplies of agri-property could be seized.

57.  Tara McIndoe Calder, "Letter to Author about the Land Seizure Era," email, May 25, 2010; Robertson, General Zimbabwe Statistics.
58.  Inkankezi, senior official in military intelligence, Zimbabwe National Army.
59.  To give a sense of the value of agri-property, a new midsize New Holland tractor cost US$42,000. Assuming that the tractor was older and the market for tractors was depressed, the tractor would hypothetically be worth US$20,000.
60.  Shore, farmer.
61.  Inkankezi, senior official in military intelligence, Zimbabwe National Army.
62.  Shore, farmer's spouse.
63.  Adams, farmer.
64.  Nyakasanga, farm foreman.
65.  Mupfure, veteran of the Liberation War and Senior Politician.
66.  Ibid.

## CHAPTER 8

1.  Selby, "Commercial Farmers and the State"; Justice for Agriculture Zimbabwe and the General Agricultural and Plantation Workers Union of Zimbabwe, "Destruction of Zimbabwe's Backbone Industry."
2.  Mwengi, farm foreman.
3.  Mzingwane, war veteran and "new" farmer.
4.  Shore, farmer; Wilson, farmer; van Vaaden, rancher.
5.  McKinley, farmer and activist; farmer's spouse and activist.
6.  Farm invaders began to threaten farmers with jail if they took assets because farm invaders claimed the assets belonged to the state—a thinly veiled personal claim to them.
7.  Barkley, farmer.
8.  Mukwa, farm clerk.
9.  Kathy Grover, farmer's spouse, interview, August 6, 2006; Grover, farmer.
10.  Hoover, farmer.
11.  Chipembere, farm foreman.
12.  Pius Ncube, Roman Catholic archbishop and human rights activist, interview, January 23, 2007.
13.  Wilson, farmer.
14.  Lyons, rancher; rancher's spouse.
15.  Hayes, farmer.
16.  Shore, farmer's spouse.
17.  Mukwa, farm clerk.
18.  Nchenchi, game hunt manager. Msasa and Mucheke explained that killing a farmer was a very big step, and it is clear from interviews with them that it could not happen without clear authorization "from the top" (Msasa, military intelligence agent, Zimbabwe National Army; Mucheke, legal officer in the President's Office).
19.  Mahobohobo, dairy manager.
20.  Nyakasanga, farm foreman.
21.  Nchenchi, game hunt manager.

22. Sanyati, Member in Charge for an eastern district, Zimbabwe Republic Police.
23. Umchabezi, veteran of the Liberation War and ZAPU publicity officer.
24. Chipembere, farm foreman.
25. Umchabezi, veteran of the Liberation War and ZAPU publicity officer.
26. Mbezi, livestock foreman.
27. Makabusi, farm manager.
28. Mbezi, livestock foreman.
29. Garamapudzi, farm foreman.
30. Zacharia Nyembwi, head of compound and foreman, interview, January 28, 2007.
31. Mapufuli, farm mechanic.
32. Ibid.
33. Mbezi, livestock foreman.
34. Mucheke, legal officer in the President's Office.
35. McKinley, farmer's spouse and activist.
36. Monroe, rancher.
37. Ibid.
38. Mapufuli, farm mechanic.
39. Mahobohobo, dairy manager.
40. Mukwa, farm clerk.
41. Mopane, farm mechanic.
42. Shore, farmer; Hendricks, farmer; Elbridge, farmer; Kennedy, rancher; McKinley, farmer and activist; John Taylor, farmer, interview, August 23, 2006; James Knox, farmer, interview, September 15, 2006; Coolidge, rancher; Wheeler, rancher; Morton, rancher.
43. Tim Sherman, farmer, interview, August 2, 2006.
44. Justice for Agriculture Zimbabwe and the General Agricultural and Plantation Workers Union of Zimbabwe, "Destruction of Zimbabwe's Backbone Industry," 37.
45. Barkley, farmer; Robert G. Evans, "Center Pivot Irrigation" (2001), 3.
46. Barkley, farmer.
47. Elbridge, farmer.
48. Sherman, farmer.
49. Justice for Agriculture Zimbabwe and the General Agricultural and Plantation Workers Union of Zimbabwe, "Destruction of Zimbabwe's Backbone Industry," 43, 44.
50. Mucheke, legal officer in the President's Office.
51. Al Jensen, farmer, interview, September 21, 2006.
52. Ngavi, accountant for the Grain Marketing Board.
53. Shore, farmer's spouse.
54. Jensen, farmer.
55. Ngavi, accountant for the Grain Marketing Board.
56. The GMB was not only highly political and thus favoring farm invaders' interests, but given the extent of corruption, it was also unable to find money to pay farmers.

57. Amnesty International, "Toll of Impunity."

58. Zimbabwe Government, "Rural Land Occupiers (Protection from Eviction) Act" (2001); Human Rights Watch, "Fast Track Land Reform in Zimbabwe."

59. Amnesty International, "Toll of Impunity." Excluding rape, murder, and fraud.

60. Caitlin Shay, "Fast Track to Collapse: How Zimbabwe's Fast-Track Land Reform Program Violates International Human Rights Protections to Property, Due Process, and Compensation," *American University International Law Review* 27, no. 1 (2012).

61. United Nations Development Programme, "Comprehensive Economic Recovery in Zimbabwe," 70.

62. International Crisis Group, "Blood and Soil," 106.

63. Garamapudzi, farm foreman. Garamapudzi stated that after his colleagues achieved the eviction of their farmer employer, they found themselves destitute and asked him to try to get their "boss" to return and resume farming so they could regain employment.

64. E.g., Dawes, farmer; Wilson, farmer; Hayes, farmer.

65. Barker, farmer; Barkley, farmer.

66. Shore, farmer's spouse.

67. Fillmore, farmer.

68. CIA, "World Factbook 2002: Zimbabwe."

69. Makabusi, farm manager.

70. Fillmore, farmer.

71. Shore, farmer.

72. Ibid.

73. Fillmore, farmer.

74. Sherman, farmer.

75. Nchenchi, game hunt manager.

76. Monroe, rancher.

77. Mwengi, farm foreman.

78. Mukwa, farm clerk.

79. Sherman, farmer.

80. Eric Mifflin, missionary in a farming community, interview, August 5, 2006.

81. Garfield, farmer's spouse.

82. Selby, "Commercial Farmers and the State," 303.

83. Sebungwe, senior army officer, Zimbabwe National Army.

84. Cleveland, farmer.

85. Some farmers were so closely associated with their farms that local people referred to the farmer by the farm name rather than the farmer's name.

86. Elbridge, farmer.

87. Ibid.

88. Shore, farmer.

89. Lyons, rancher.

90. Anderson, farmer's spouse.

91. Morton, rancher.

92. Barkley, farmer.

93. Garfield, farmer.
94. Fairbanks, rancher.
95. Shore, farmer.
96. Fairbanks, rancher.
97. Makabusi, farm manager.
98. Barkley, farmer.
99. International Crisis Group, "Blood and Soil," 106.
100. IRIN, "Zimbabwe: Govt Moves to Enforce Eviction Orders," http://www. irinnews.org/report/33562/zimbabwe-govt-moves-to-enforce-eviction-orders; Rachel L. Swarns, "Zimbabwe Starts Arresting White Farmers Defying Eviction," *New York Times*, August 17, 2002, http://www.nytimes. com/2002/08/17/world/zimbabwe-starts-arresting-white-farmers-defying-eviction.html.
101. Burr, farmer; Dawes, farmer; Barker, farmer; Madison, farmer's spouse; farmer; Sherman, farmer; Grover, farmer's spouse; Hayes, farmer.
102. Shore, farmer.
103. The month of August applies particularly to tobacco, but also to other crops even though they were planted slightly later in the cropping season. Maize, for instance, was usually planted in November, but land preparation took place much earlier in the year and required expenditures for fuel, equipment maintenance, and labor costs, allowing the central point about the August "deadline" to remain.
104. Justice for Agriculture Zimbabwe and the General Agricultural and Plantation Workers Union of Zimbabwe, "Destruction of Zimbabwe's Backbone Industry"; Zimbabwe Human Rights NGO Forum, "Monthly Violence Reports."

CHAPTER 9

1. B. Kinsey, "Comparative Economic Performance of Zimbabwe's Re-settlement Models," in *Delivering Land and Securing Rural Livelihoods: Post-independence Land Reform and Resettlement in Zimbabwe*, ed. M. Roth and F. Gonese (Harare: University of Zimbabwe; Madison: University of Wisconsin, 2003).
2. World Bank, "General Zimbabwe Data," http://data.worldbank.org/country/zimbabwe?display=graph.
3. Based on constant local currency; "Zimbabwe Statistics."
4. World Bank, "General Zimbabwe Data."
5. Tony Hawkins, "Zimbabwe—Land Reform. How Successful?" http://www. cfuzim.org/index.php/land-facts/3700-zimbabwe-land-reform-how-successful.
6. Robertson, "Zimbabwe's Hyperinflation"; *Economist*, "Bags of Bricks."
7. United Nations Development Programme, "Comprehensive Economic Recovery in Zimbabwe," 157–58.
8. Ngavi, accountant for the Grain Marketing Board; *Zimbabwe Situation*, "Zanu PF Chefs Risk Losing Land," http://www.zimbabwesituation.com/news/ zimsit_g_zanu-pf-bigwigs-risk-losing-land-the-zimbabwe-independent/.

9. Food and Agriculture Organization/World Food Programme, "Food and Agriculture Organization / World Food Programme Crop and Food Supply Assessment Mission to Zimbabwe."

10. Utete, "Report of the Presidential Land Review Committee," 5.

11. Godfrey Mudimu, "Zimbabwe Food Security Issues Paper," Forum for Food Security in Southern Africa, http://www.odi.org/sites/odi.org.uk/files/odi-assets/publications-opinion-files/5613.pdf.

12. International Federation of Red Cross and Red Crescent, "100,000 Cases," 5.

13. IRIN, "Zimbabwe: Three-Quarters of the People Need Food Aid," http://www.irinnews.org/report/82649/zimbabwe-three-quarters-of-the-people-need-food-aid.

14. International Federation of Red Cross and Red Crescent, "Zimbabwe: Food Insecurity," in *Emergency Appeal* (International Federation of Red Cross and Red Crescent Societies, 2012).

15. "Trading Sexual Favours for Food and School Fees in Zimbabwe," International Federation of Red Cross and Red Crescent Societies, https://www.ifrc.org/en/news-and-media/news-stories/africa/zimbabwe/trading-sexual-favours-for-food-and-school-fees-in-zimbabwe-65351/.

16. United Nations Development Programme, "Comprehensive Economic Recovery in Zimbabwe," 157–58; Amnesty International, "Time for Accountability," 18; Zimbabwe Human Rights NGO Forum and Justice for Agriculture Trust in Zimbabwe, "Adding Insult to Injury," 26–27.

17. Scoones et al., *Zimbabwe's Land Reform*; "Zimbabwe's Land Reform."

18. *Zimbabwe Situation*, "Zanu PF Chefs Risk Losing Land"; Regerai Tututuku, "Evicted Villagers Demand Land Report," *Zimbabwean*, http://www.thezimbabwean.co/news/zimbabwe-news/70407/evicted-villagers-demand-land-report.html; Nelson Sibanda, "Resettled Farmers to Lose Land," *Zimbabwe Situation*, http://www.zimbabwesituation.com/news/zimsit-m-resettled-farmers-to-lose-land/; Zimeye, "Bloodbath in Shamva as Goche's Farm Faces Invasion," http://www.zimeye.com/breaking-news-bloodbath-in-shamva-as-goches-farm-faces-invasion/.

19. Zamchiya, "Role of Politics."

20. Ngavi, accountant for the Grain Marketing Board.

21. Ngavi indicated the control over the GMB eventually shifted to the army as part of "Operation Maguta," which saw the army deployed in an effort to increase food production. Production figures have not supported the government's claims about the success of this project.

22. Shore, farmer.

23. Zamchiya, "Role of Politics," 945–46.

24. Ngavi, accountant for the Grain Marketing Board.

25. Zamchiya, "Role of Politics."

26. Dawes, farmer.

27. Scoones et al., *Zimbabwe's Land Reform*; "Zimbabwe's Land Reform."

28. Moyo, "Three Decades of Agrarian Reform."

29. Scoones et al., *Zimbabwe's Land Reform*; "Zimbabwe's Land Reform"; Hanlon, Manjengwa, and Smart, *Zimbabwe Takes Back Its Land*.

30. Regerai Tukutuku, "White Farmers Knew What to Do Says Muzenda," *Zimbabwe Situation*, 2014.
31. Ibid.
32. Hanlon, Manjengwa, and Smart, *Zimbabwe Takes Back Its Land*.
33. E.g., Moyo, "Three Decades of Agrarian Reform," 519; Scoones et al., *Zimbabwe's Land Reform*.
34. Moyo, "Three Decades of Agrarian Reform," 494.
35. E.g., Shore, farmer.

## Conclusion

1. Alexander, *Unsettled Land*; Tendi, *Making History in Mugabe's Zimbabwe*; Compagnon, *A Predictable Tragedy*.
2. E.g., Moyo, "Land and Natural Resource Redistribution"; "Land and Agrarian Question"; "Land Occupation Movement."
3. E.g., Alexander and McGregor, "Elections, Land," 510; Moyo, "Land and Natural Resource Redistribution"; McGregor, "Politics of Disruption," 10; e.g., Mugabe, *Inside the Third Chimurenga*.
4. Scoones et al., *Zimbabwe's Land Reform*; "Zimbabwe's Land Reform."
5. Scoones et al., *Zimbabwe's Land Reform*.
6. Ibid., 238–39.
7. Interview with Daniel Inkankezi, senior military intelligence agent, Harare, April 11, 2009; interview with Hastings Lundi, senior CIO agent, Harare, April 9, 2009.
8. Qtd. in Tendi, *Making History in Mugabe's Zimbabwe*, 170, 244.
9. Mupfure, veteran of the Liberation War and senior politician.
10. Chidembo, senior police officer, Zimbabwe Republic Police.
11. E.g., Oxford Analytica, "Zimbabwe's 'Look East' Disappoints," *Forbes*, http://www.forbes.com/2007/12/27/zimbabwe-harare-mugabe-cx-1228oxford.html; Andrew Malone, "Mugabe's Darkest Secret: An £800bn Blood Diamond Mine He's Running with China's Red Army," *Daily Mail*, http://www.dailymail.co.uk/news/worldnews/article-1313123/Robert-Mugabes-darkest-secret-An-800bn-blood-diamond-run-Chinas-Red-Army.html; Al Jazeera, "US: China Lacks 'Morals' in Africa," http://english.aljazeera.net/news/africa/2010/12/201012981346664660.html.
12. Chidembo, senior police officer, Zimbabwe Republic Police.
13. Mupfure, veteran of the Liberation War and senior politician.
14. Msasa, military intelligence agent, Zimbabwe National Army.
15. E.g., *Economist*, "Hurry Up," http://www.economist.com/node/15022632.
16. World Bank, "Agriculture for Development," in *World Development Report* (Washington, DC: World Bank, 2007).
17. Klaus Deininger, "Land Policies for Growth and Poverty Reduction" (Washington, DC: World Bank, 2003).

## Appendix A

1. See www.hrforumzim.org.
2. Refworld, "U.S. Department of State Country Report on Human Rights Practices 2002—Zimbabwe," UNHCR, http://www.refworld.org/docid/3e918c2f10.html.
3. Data were unavailable for January and July to December 2000.
4. This book uses the figure of 4,300 farmers because it is a widely cited and generally accepted figure. See the introduction of this book for additional information on the number of farmers operating in 2000.

# References

Africa All Party Parliamentary Group. "Land in Zimbabwe: Past Mistakes, Future Prospects." London: AAPPG, 2009.

Alexander, Jocelyn. "Squatters,' Veterans and the State in Zimbabwe." In *Zimbabwe's Unfinished Business*, edited by Amanda Hammar, Brian Raftopoulos, and Stig Jensen, 83–117. Harare: Weaver Press, 2003.

Alexander, Jocelyn. "State, Peasantry and Resettlement in Zimbabwe." *Review of African Political Economy* 21, no. 61 (1994): 325–45.

Alexander, Jocelyn. *Unsettled Land: State-Making and the Politics of Land in Zimbabwe, 1893-2003*, Oxford: James Currey, 2006.

Alexander, Jocelyn. "The Unsettled Land: The Politics of Land Redistribution in Matabeleland, 1980–1990." *Journal of Southern African Studies* 17, no. 4 (1991): 581–610.

Alexander, Jocelyn, and JoAnn McGregor. "Elections, Land and the Politics of Opposition in Matabeleland." *Journal of Agrarian Change* 1, no. 4 (2001): 510–33.

Alexander, Jocelyn, JoAnn McGregor, and Terence Ranger. *Violence and Memory: One Hundred Years in the "Dark Forests" of Matabeleland*. Oxford: James Currey, 2000.

Al Jazeera. "US: China Lacks 'Morals' in Africa." December 9, 2010. http://english. aljazeera.net/news/africa/2010/12/201012981346664660.html.

Amnesty International. "Amnesty International Report 2002—Zimbabwe." May 28, 2002. http://www.unhcr.org/refworld/docid/3cf4bc048.html.

Amnesty International. "Time for Accountability." London: Amnesty International, 2008.

Amnesty International. "Toll of Impunity." 2002. https://www.amnesty.org/en/documents/afr46/034/2002/en/.

Amnesty International. "Zimbabwe: Six Years on Victims of Operation Murambatsvina Still Struggling to Survive." 2011.

Anderson, R. *An Agricultural Survey of Southern Rhodesia. Part II: Agro-Economic Survey*. Salisbury (S. Rhodesia): Printed by the Government Printer, 1961.

Baldauf, Scott. "Mugabe Using Police to Crush Opposition, MDC Says." *Christian Science Monitor*, August 20, 2009. http://www.csmonitor.com/World/Africa/2009/0820/p06s08-woaf.html.

BBC. "Meagre Harvest in Zimbabwe." BBC News, February 13, 2002. http://news.bbc.co.uk/1/hi/business/1818263.stm.

BBC. "World: Africa Zimbabwe Army in Congo Diamond Deal." BBC News, September 23, 1999. http://news.bbc.co.uk/1/hi/world/africa/455882.stm.

Beissinger, Mark R. *Nationalist Mobilization and the Collapse of the Soviet State.* Cambridge: Cambridge University Press, 2002.

Brass, Paul R. *Theft of an Idol.* Princeton, NJ: Princeton University Press, 1997.

Catholic Commission for Justice and Peace in Zimbabwe (CCJP). *Gukurahundi in Zimbabwe: A Report on the Disturbances in Matabeleland and the Midlands, 1980–1988.* 2007 ed. London: Hurst, 2007.

CCJP. "Report on the 1980s Disturbances in Matabeleland and the Midlands." Bulawayo: Catholic Commission for Justice and Peace in Zimbabwe, 1997.

Central Statistical Office. "Census 2002: Zimbabwe Preliminary Report." Harare: CSO, 2002.

Chambati, Walter. "Restructuring of Agrarian Labour Relations after Fast Track Land Reform in Zimbabwe." *Journal of Peasant Studies* 38, no. 5 (2011): 1047–68.

Chan, Stephen. *Robert Mugabe: A Life of Power and Violence.* London: I. B. Taurus, 2003.

Chavunduka, Charles M., and Daniel W. Bromley. "Considering the Multiple Purposes of Land in Zimbabwe's Economic Recovery." *Land Use Policy* 30 (2012): 670–676.

Cheeseman, Nic, and Blessing-Miles Tendi. "Power-Sharing in Comparative Perspective: The Dynamics of 'Unity Government' in Kenya and Zimbabwe." *Journal of Modern African Studies* 48, no. 2 (2010): 203–29.

Chimhowu, Admos. "Moving Forward in Zimbabwe: Reducing Poverty and Promoting Growth." University of Manchester, Brooks World Poverty Institute. http://documents.manchester.ac.uk/display.aspx?DocID=18896.

Chitiyo, Knox. "Land Violence and Compensation." *Track Two* 9, no. 1 (2000).

Chitiyo, Knox. "Making the Case for Security Sector Reform in Zimbabwe." RUSI, 2009.

CIA. "World Factbook." https://www.cia.gov.

CIA. "World Factbook 2002: Zimbabwe." http://www.faqs.org/docs/factbook/print/zi.html.

Cliffe, Lionel, Jocelyn Alexander, Ben Cousins, and Rudo Gaidzanwa. "An Overview of Fast Track Land Reform in Zimbabwe: Editorial Introduction." *Journal of Peasant Studies* 38, no. 5 (2011): 907–38.

Commercial Farmers Union. "Retrenchment of Agricultural Workers in Zimbabwe." http://www.cfuzim.org/~cfuzimb/images/si62002advice.pdf.

Compagnon, Daniel. *A Predictable Tragedy: Robert Mugabe and the Collapse of Zimbabwe.* Philadelphia: University of Pennsylvania Press, 2011.

Cousins, Ben, and Ian Scoones. "Contested Paradigms of 'Viability' in Redistributive Land Reform: Perspectives from Southern Africa." *Journal of Peasant Studies* 37, no. 1 (2010): 31–66.

Deininger, Klaus. "Land Policies for Growth and Poverty Reduction." Washington, DC: World Bank, 2003.

*Economist.* "Bags of Bricks." http://www.economist.com/node/7843601. August 24, 2006.

*Economist.* "Hurry Up." December 3, 2009. http://www.economist.com/node/15022632.

Electoral Institute for Sustainable Democracy in Africa (EISA). "Zimbabwe Referendum 2000: Results." http://www.eisa.org.za/WEP/zimresults2000r.htm.

EISA. "Zimbabwe: 2000 House of Assembly Provincial Results." 2000. http://www.content.eisa.org.za/old-page/zimbabwe-2000-house-assembly-provincial-results.

Evans, Robert G. "Center Pivot Irrigation." 2001.

Ferrett, Grant. "In Search of Fuel." BBC, March 25, 2000. http://news.bbc.co.uk/1/hi/programmes/from_our_own_correspondent/690291.stm.

Flower, Ken. *Serving Secretly.* London: John Murray, 1987.

Food and Agriculture Organization of the United Nations. "Future Energy Requirements for Africa's Agriculture." http://www.fao.org/docrep/V9766E/v9766e05.htm#4.6.%20zimbabwe.

Food and Agriculture Organization/World Food Program. "Food and Agriculture Organization / World Food Programme Crop and Food Supply Assessment Mission to Zimbabwe." June 18, 2008. http://www.fao.org/docrep/010/ai469e/ai469e00.htm.

Hagar, Sarah. "Poor Healthcare Endangering Mothers in Zimbabwe." Amnesty International, *Human Rights Now* blog, March 9, 2011. http://blog.amnestyusa.org/escr/poor-healthcare-endangering-mothers-in-zimbabwe/.

Hammar, Amanda. "'The Day of Burning': Eviction and Reinvention in the Margins of Northwest Zimbabwe." *Journal of Agrarian Change* 1, no. 4 (2001): 550–74.

Hammar, Amanda. "A Measure of Just Demand? A Response to Mamdani." Association of Concerned African Scholars. http://concernedafricascholars.org/docs/acasbulletin82–88hammar.pdf.

Hammar, Amanda, and Brian Raftopoulos. "Zimbabwe's Unfinished Business: Rethinking Land, State and Nation." In *Zimbabwe's Unfinished Business*, edited by Amanda Hammar, Brian Raftopoulos, and Stig Jensen. Harare: Weaver Press, 2003.

Hanke, Steve H. "R.I.P. Zimbabwe Dollar." CATO Institute. http://www.cato.org/zimbabwe.

Hanlon, Joseph, Jeanette Manjengwa, and Teresa Smart. *Zimbabwe Takes Back Its Land.* Sterling, VA: Kumarian Press, 2013.

Hawkins, Tony. "Zimbabwe—Land Reform. How Successful?" http://www.cfuzim.org/index.php/land-facts/3700-zimbabwe-land-reform-how-successful.

Hellum, Anne, and Bill Derman. "Land Reform and Human Rights in Contemporary Zimbabwe: Balancing Individual and Social Justice through an Integrated Human Rights Framework." *World Development* 32, no. 10 (2004): 1785–805.

HMSO. "Southern Rhodesia: Report of the Constitutional Conference, Lancaster House, London, September–December 1979." London: Lancaster House, December 21, 1979.

Holsti, Kalevi J. *The State, War, and the State of War.* Cambridge: Cambridge University Press, 1996.

Human Rights Watch. "Fast Track Land Reform in Zimbabwe." United Nations High Command for Refugees, 2002.

International Crisis Group. "Blood and Soil: Land, Politics and Conflict Prevention in Zimbabwe and South Africa." Brussels: ICG, 2004.

International Federation of Red Cross and Red Crescent (IFRC). "100,000 Cases: The Spectre of Cholera Remains in Zimbabwe." 2009.

IFRC. "Trading Sexual Favours for Food and School Fees in Zimbabwe." https://www.ifrc.org/en/news-and-media/news-stories/africa/zimbabwe/trading-sexual-favours-for-food-and-school-fees-in-zimbabwe-65351/.

IFRC. "Zimbabwe: Food Insecurity." In *Emergency Appeal*. IFRC, 2012.

International Institute for Strategic Studies. "Zimbabwe's Congolese Imbroglio." *Strategic Comments* 5, no. 2 (1999): 1–2.

International Monetary Fund (IMF). "World Economic Outlook Database." http://www.imf.org.

IMF. "World Economic Outlook Database: Zimbabwe." April 2008. http://www.imf.org/external/pubs/ft/weo/2008/01/weodata/index.aspx.

Institute for Security Studies. "Trends and Markers: Recent Data, Statistics and Indicators." http://www.issafrica.org/.

IRIN. "Zimbabwe: Govt Moves to Enforce Eviction Orders." August 15, 2002. http://www.irinnews.org/report/33562/zimbabwe-govt-moves-to-enforce-eviction-orders.

IRIN. "Zimbabwe: Three-Quarters of the People Need Food Aid." January 29, 2009. http://www.irinnews.org/report/82649/zimbabwe-three-quarters-of-the-people-need-food-aid.

Johnson, R. W. "State Terror Sweeps Zimbabwe." Helen Suzman Foundation. 2000. http://www.hsf.org.za/resource-centre/focus/issues-11–20/issue-18-second-quarter-2000/state-terror-sweeps-zimbabwe.

Justice for Agriculture Zimbabwe and the General Agricultural and Plantation Workers Union of Zimbabwe. "Destruction of Zimbabwe's Backbone Industry in Pursuit of Political Power." Harare: JAZ and the GAPWUZ, 2008.

Justice for Agriculture Zimbabwe and the General Agricultural and Plantation Workers Union of Zimbabwe. "Reckless Tragedy: Irreversible?" Research and Advocacy Unit (RAU), December 12, 2008. http://www.kubatana.net/html/archive/landr/081212jag.asp?sector=LANDR&year=0&range_start=1.

Kaldor, Mary. *New and Old Wars*. 2nd ed. Cambridge: Polity Press, 2006.

Kalyvas, Stathis N. *The Logic of Violence in Civil War*. New York: Cambridge University Press, 2006.

Kay, George. *Rhodesia: A Human Geography*. London: University of London Press, 1970.

Khampepe, Sisi, and Dikgang Moseneke. "Report on the 2002 Presidential Elections of Zimbabwe." 2002.

Kinsey, Bill H. "Comparative Economic Performance of Zimbabwe's Re-settlement Models." In *Delivering Land and Securing Rural Livelihoods: Post-independence Land Reform and Resettlement in Zimbabwe*, edited by M. Roth and F. Gonese. Harare: University of Zimbabwe; Madison: University of Wisconsin, 2003.

Kinsey, Bill H. "Land Reform, Growth and Equity: Emerging Evidence from Zimbabwe's Resettlement Programme." *Journal of Southern African Studies* 25, no. 2 (June 1999): 173–96.

Kramarenko, Vitaliy, Lars Engstrom, Genevieve Verdier, Gilda Fernandez, S. Erik Oppers, Richard Hughes, Jimmy McHugh, and Warren Coats. "Zimbabwe: Challenges and Policy Options after Hyperinflation." International Monetary Fund, 2010.

Kriger, Norma. "From Patriotic Memories to 'Patriotic History' in Zimbabwe, 1990–2005." *Third World Quarterly* 27, no. 6 (2006): 1151–69.

Kriger, Norma. *Guerrilla Veterans in Post-war Zimbabwe*. Cambridge: Cambridge University Press, 2003.

Kriger, Norma. "Liberation from Constitutional Constraints: Land Reform in Zimbabwe." *SAIS Review* 27, no. 2 (2007): 63–76.

Kriger, Norma. "ZANU(PF) Strategies in General Elections, 1980–2000: Discourse and Coercion." *African Affairs* 104, no. 414 (2005): 1–34.

Kriger, Norma. *Zimbabwe's Guerrilla War: Peasant Voices*. Cambridge: Cambridge University Press, 1992.

Kriger, Norma. "Zimbabwe: Political Constructions of War Veterans." *Review of African Political Economy* 30, no. 96 (2003): 323–28.

Lan, David. *Guns and Rain: Guerrillas and Spirit Mediums in Zimbabwe*. Oxford: James Currey, 1985.

LeBas, Adrienne. "Polarization as Craft: Party Formation and State Violence in Zimbabwe." *Comparative Politics* 38, no. 4 (2006): 419–38.

Lodge, Tom, Denis Kadima, and David Pottie, eds. *Zimbabwe: 2000 General Elections*. Compendium of Elections in Southern Africa: EISA, 2002.

Magaramombe, Godfrey. "Rural Poverty: Commercial Farm Workers and Land Reform in Zimbabwe." Presented to the SARPN conference "Land Reform and Poverty Alleviation in Southern Africa." Pretoria, South Africa, 2001.

Malone, Andrew. "Mugabe's Darkest Secret: An £800bn Blood Diamond Mine He's Running with China's Red Army." *Daily Mail*, September 17, 2010. http://www.dailymail.co.uk/news/worldnews/article-1313123/Robert-Mugabes-darkest-secret-An-800bn-blood-diamond-run-Chinas-Red-Army.html.

Mamdani, Mahmood. "Lessons of Zimbabwe." *London Review of Books* 30, no. 23 (2008): 17–21.

Marongwe, Nelson. "Farm Occupations and Occupiers in the New Politics of Land in Zimbabwe." In *Zimbabwe's Unfinished Business*, edited by Amanda Hammar, Brian Raftopoulos, and Stig Jensen, 155–90. Harare: Weaver Press, 2003.

Matondi, Prosper B. "Understanding Fast Track Land Reforms in Zimbabwe." In *Zimbabwe's Fast-Track Land Reform*, 1–17. London: Zed Books, 2012.

McAdam, Doug, Sidney Tarrow, and Charles Tilly, eds. *Dynamics of Contention*. Cambridge: Cambridge University Press, 2001.

McGregor, JoAnn. "Politics of Disruption: War Veterans and the Local State in Zimbabwe." *African Affairs* 101 (2002): 9–37.

Meldrum, Andrew. "Zimbabwe's Health-Care System Struggles On." *Lancet* 371, no. 9618 (2008): 1059–1060.

Mhanda, Wilfred. "The Role of War Veterans in Zimbabwe's Political and Economic Processes." Solidarity Peace Trust, April 7, 2011. http://www.solidaritypeacetrust.org/1063/the-role-of-war-veterans/.

Moyo, Sam. "The Land and Agrarian Question in Zimbabwe." Presented to the conference "The Agrarian Constraint and Poverty Reduction: Macroeconomic Lessons for Africa." Addis Ababa, 2004.

Moyo, Sam. "Land and Natural Resource Redistribution in Zimbabwe: Access,
Equity and Conflict." *African and Asian Studies* 4, nos. 1–2 (2005): 187–223.

Moyo, Sam. "Land Concentration and Accumulation after Redistributive Reform
in Postsettler Zimbabwe." *Review of African Political Economy* 38, no. 128 (2011):
257–76.

Moyo, Sam. "The Land Occupation Movement and Democratisation in Zimbabwe:
Contradictions of Neoliberalism." *Millennium: Journal of International Studies*
30 (2001).

Moyo, Sam. "Three Decades of Agrarian Reform in Zimbabwe." *Journal of Peasant
Studies* 38, no. 3 (2011): 493–531.

Moyo, Sam, Walter Chambati, Tendai Murisa, Dumisani Siziba, Charity Dangwa,
Kingstone Mujeyi, and Ndabezinhle Nyoni. "Fast Track Land Reform Baseline
Survey in Zimbabwe: Trends and Tendencies, 2005/06." Harare: AIAS Mono-
graph, 2009.

Moyo, Sam, Blair Rutherford, and Dede Amanor-Wilks. "Land Reform & Changing Social Relations for Farm Workers in Zimbabwe." *Review of African Political
Economy* 27, no. 84 (June 2000): 181–202.

Moyo, Sam, and Paris Yeros. "Land Occupations and Land Reform in Zimbabwe:
Towards the National Democratic Revolution." In *Reclaiming the Land: The Re-
surgence of Rural Movements in Africa, Asia and Latin America*, edited by Sam
Moyo and Paris Yeros, 165–205. London: Zed Books, 2005.

Moyo, Sam, and Paris Yeros. "The Radicalised State: Zimbabwe's Interrupted Revolution." *Review of African Political Economy* 34, no. 111 (2007): 103–21.

Mudimu, Godfrey. "Zimbabwe Food Security Issues Paper." Forum for Food Security in Southern Africa. http://www.odi.org/sites/odi.org.uk/files/odi-assets/
publications-opinion-files/5613.pdf.

Mugabe, Robert Gabriel. *Inside the Third Chimurenga*. Harare: Department of Information and Publicity, Office of the President and Cabinet, 2001.

New York Times. "Rare Poll Suggests Zimbabwe Is Weary of Its Longtime Leader."
*New York Times*, March 12, 2000. http://www.nytimes.com/2000/03/12/world/
rare-poll-suggests-zimbabwe-is-weary-of-its-longtime-leader.html.

Oxford Analytica. "Zimbabwe's 'Look East' Disappoints." *Forbes*, December
28, 2007. http://www.forbes.com/2007/12/27/zimbabwe-harare-mugabe-cx-1228
oxford.html.

Palmer, Robin. "Land Reform in Zimbabwe, 1980–1990." *African Affairs* 89, no. 355
(1990): 163–81.

Pearce, Justin. "Mugabe's Costly Congo Venture." BBC, July 25, 2000. http://news.
bbc.co.uk/1/hi/world/africa/611898.stm.

Petersen, Roger D. *Understanding Ethnic Violence*. Cambridge: Cambridge University Press, 2002.

Phimister, Ian, and Brian Raftopoulos. "Mugabe, Mbeki and the Politics of
Anti-imperialism." *Review of African Political Economy* 31, no. 101 (2004):
385–400.

Pilossof, Rory. "Possibilities and Constraints of Market-Led Land Reforms in Southern Africa: An Analysis of Transfers of Commercial Farmland in Postcolonial Zimbabwe, 1980–2000." *Journal of Agrarian Change* (2014): n.p.

Pilossof, Rory. *The Unbearable Whiteness of Being: Farmers' Voices from Zimbabwe.* Harare: Weaver Press, 2012.

Raftopoulos, Brian. "Briefing: Zimbabwe's 2002 Presidential Election." *African Affairs* 101(2002): 413–26.

Raftopoulos, Brian. "The Crisis in Zimbabwe, 1998–2008." In *Becoming Zimbabwe: A History from the Pre-colonial Period to 2008*, edited by B. Raftopoulos and A. Mlambo. Harare: Weaver Press, 2009.

Raftopoulos, Brian. "The State in Crisis: Authoritarian Nationalism, Selective Citizenship and Distortions of Democracy in Zimbabwe." In *Zimbabwe's Unfinished Business*, edited by Amanda Hammar, Brian Raftopoulos, and Stig Jensen, 217–242. Harare: Weaver Press, 2003.

Raftopoulos, Brian. "Zimbabwe: Race and Nationalism in a Post-colonial State." In *Inventions and Boundaries: Historical and Anthropological Approaches to the Study of Ethnicity and Nationalism*, edited by P. Kaarsholm and J. Hultin. Roskilde, 75–102. Denmark: International Development Studies, Roskilde University, 1994.

Ranger, Terence. "The Death of Chaminuka: Spirit Mediums, Nationalism and the Guerilla War in Zimbabwe." *African Affairs* 81, no. 324 (1982): 349–69.

Ranger, Terence. *Peasant Consciousness and Guerrilla War in Zimbabwe: A Comparative Study.* London: James Currey, 1985.

Ranger, Terence. "Zimbabwe and the Long Search for Independence." In *History of Central Africa: The Contemporary Years*, edited by David Birmingham and Phyllis M. Martin, 203–29. London: Longman, 1998.

Reeler, A. P. "Role of Militia Groups in Maintaining Zanu Pf's Political Power." March 2003. http://www.kubatana.net/docs/hr/reeler_militia_mar_030331.pdf.

Refworld. "U.S. Department of State Country Report on Human Rights Practices 2002—Zimbabwe." United Nations High Commissioner for Refugees, March 31, 2003. http://www.refworld.org/docid/3e918c2f10.html.

Richardson, Craig J. "How the Loss of Property Rights Caused Zimbabwe's Collapse." Cato Institute, 2005.

Robertson, John. "Zimbabwe's Hyperinflation." *Harvard International Review*, July 17, 2009. http://hir.harvard.edu/zimbabwe-s-hyperinflation.

Rukuni, Mandivamba, and Stig Jensen. "Land, Growth and Governance: Tenure Reform and Visions of Progress in Zimbabwe." In *Zimbabwe's Unfinished Business*, edited by Amanda Hammar, Brian Raftopoulos, and Stig Jensen, 243–262. Harare: Weaver Press, 2003.

Rutherford, Blair. "Belonging to the Farm(Er): Farm Workers, Farmers, and the Shifting Politics of Citizenship." In *Zimbabwe's Unfinished Business*, edited by Amanda Hammar, Brian Raftopoulos, and Stig Jensen, 191–216. Harare: Weaver Press, 2003.

Rutherford, Blair. "Commercial Farm Workers and the Politics of (Dis)Placement in Zimbabwe: Colonialism, Liberation and Democracy." *Journal of Agrarian Change* 1, no. 4 (2001): 626–51.

Rutherford, Blair. "'Settlers' and Zimbabwe: Politics, Memory, and the Anthropology of Commercial Farms during a Time of Crisis." *Identities: Global Studies in Culture and Power* 11 (2004): 543–62.

Rutherford, Blair. "Shifting the Debate on Land Reform, Poverty and Inequality in Zimbabwe, an Engagement with Zimbabwe's Land Reform: Myths and Realities." *Journal of Contemporary African Studies* 30, no. 1 (2012): 147–57.

Rutherford, Blair. *Working on the Margins: Black Workers, White Farmers in Postcolonial Zimbabwe*. Harare: Weaver Press; London: Zed Books, 2001.

Sadomba, Zvakanyorwa Wilbert. "A Decade of Zimbabwe's Land Revolution: The Politics of the War Veteran Vanguard." In *Land and Agrarian Reform in Zimbabwe*, edited by Sam Moyo and Walter Chambati, 79–121: Dakar: Codesria, 2013.

Sadomba, Zvakanyorwa Wilbert. *War Veterans in Zimbabwe's Revolution*. Woodbridge, UK: James Currey, 2011.

Scoones, Ian, Nelson Marongwe, Blasio Mavedzenge, Jacob Mahenehene, Felix Murimbarimba, and Chrispen Sukume. *Zimbabwe's Land Reform: Myths and Realities*. Woodbridge, UK: James Currey, 2010.

Scoones, Ian, Nelson Marongwe, Blasio Mavedzenge, Felix Murimbarimba, Jacob Mahenehene, and Sukume Chrispen. "Zimbabwe's Land Reform: Challenging the Myths." *Journal of Peasant Studies* 38, no. 5 (2011): 967–93.

Selby, Angus. "Commercial Farmers and the State: Interest Group Politics and Land Reform in Zimbabwe." University of Oxford, 2006.

Shay, Caitlin. "Fast Track to Collapse: How Zimbabwe's Fast-Track Land Reform Program Violates International Human Rights Protections to Property, Due Process, and Compensation." *American University International Law Review* 27, no. 1 (2012).

Short, Clare. "Letter to Minister Kangai." *Guardian*. http://politics.guardian.co.uk/foi/images/0,9069,1015120,00.html.

Sibanda, Nelson. "Resettled Farmers to Lose Land." *Zimbabwe Situation*, October 23, 2014. http://www.zimbabwesituation.com/news/zimsit-m-resettled-farmers-to-lose-land/.

Smith, David. "Mugabe and Allies Own 40% of Land Seized from White Farmers—Inquiry." *Guardian*, November 30, 2010. http://www.guardian.co.uk/world/2010/nov/30/zimbabwe-mugabe-white-farmers.

Solidarity Peace Trust. "National Youth Service Training: 'Shaping Youths in a Truly Zimbabwean Manner.'" Port Shepstone, South Africa: Solidarity Peace Trust, 2003.

Swarns, Rachel L. "Zimbabwe Starts Arresting White Farmers Defying Eviction." *New York Times*, August 17, 2002. http://www.nytimes.com/2002/08/17/world/zimbabwe-starts-arresting-white-farmers-defying-eviction.html.

Swarns, Rachel L. "Zimbabwe Talks Tough but Steps Softly in Battle over Land." *New York Times*, April 11, 2000.

Tendi, Miles. *Making History in Mugabe's Zimbabwe*. Oxford: Peter Lang, 2010.

Tendi, Miles. "Patriotic History and Public Intellectuals Critical of Power." *Journal of Southern African Studies* 34, no. 2 (2008): 379–96.

Tendi, Miles. "Sundayview: What If 'Yes' Vote Had Won in 2000 Referendum?" *Standard*. http://www.thestandard.co.zw/opinion/27903-sundayview-what-if-yes-vote-had-won-in-2000-referendum.html.

Thornycroft, Peta, and Sebastien Berger. "Robert Mugabe Has Built up 10,000-Acre Farm of Seized Land." *Telegraph*, September 25, 2009. http://www.telegraph.co.uk/news/worldnews/africaandindianocean/zimbabwe/6231765/Robert-Mugabe-has-built-up-10000-acre-farm-of-seized-land.html.

Tilly, Charles. *Politics of Collective Violence*. Cambridge: Cambridge University Press, 2003.

Tukutuku, Regerai. "White Farmers Knew What to Do Says Muzenda." *Zimbabwe Situation*, 2014. http://www.zimbabwesituation.com/news/zimsit_w_white-farmers-knew-what-to-do-says-muzenda-the-zimbabwean/

Tungamirai, Josiah. "Recruitment to ZANLA: Building up a War Machine." In *Soldiers in Zimbabwe's Liberation War*, edited by Ngwabi Bhebe and T. Ranger. London: James Currey, 1995.

Tututuku, Regerai. "Evicted Villagers Demand Land Report." *Zimbabwean*. http://www.thezimbabwean.co/news/zimbabwe-news/70407/evicted-villagers-demand-land-report.html.

United Nations. "Report of the Panel of Experts on the Illegal Exploitation of Natural Resources and Other Forms of Wealth of the Democratic Republic of the Congo." http://www.un.org/News/dh/latest/drcongo.htm.

United Nations Development Programme (UNDP). "Comprehensive Economic Recovery in Zimbabwe." 2008.

UNDP. "The Real Wealth of Nations: Pathways to Human Development." New York: United Nations Development Programme, 2010.

US Department of State. "Zimbabwe Human Rights Practices, 1994." Washington, DC: US Department of State, 1995.

US Embassy in Harare. "Despite Stiff Competition, Potential for [Title Incomplete]." WikiLeaks. https://cablegatesearch.wikileaks.org/search.php.

US Embassy in Harare. "Former Army Commander Reportedly Approaches MDC Secretly with Amnesty Deal Proposal." WikiLeaks. https://cablegatesearch.wikileaks.org/search.php.

US Embassy in Harare. "Despite Stiff Competition Potential for [Title Incomplete]." WikiLeaks. https://cablegatesearch.wikileaks.org/search.php.

US Embassy in Harare. "Jonathan Moyo on Mugabe Succession, U.S. Policy." WikiLeaks. https://cablegatesearch.wikileaks.org/search.php.

US Embassy in Harare. "MDC to Offer Amnesty to Key Military Figures." WikiLeaks. http://wikileaks.org/cable/2000/04/00HARARE1970.html.

US Embassy in Harare. "Mugabe Declared Winner of Zimbabwe Presidential [Title Incomplete]." WikiLeaks. https://cablegatesearch.wikileaks.org/search.php.

US Embassy in Harare. "Wolpe/Mugabe Tete-a-Tete." WikiLeaks. https://cablegatesearch.wikileaks.org/search.php.

US Embassy in Harare. "Zimbabwe: How Mugabe Stole the Election." WikiLeaks. https://cablegatesearch.wikileaks.org/search.php.

Utete, Charles M. B. "Report of the Presidential Land Review Committee on the Implementation of the Fast Track Land Reform Programme, 2000–2002 ('Utete Report')." Harare: Presidential Land Review Committee, 2003.

Waeterloos, Evert, and Blair Rutherford. "Land Reform in Zimbabwe: Challenges and Opportunities for Poverty Reduction among Commercial Farm Workers." *World Development* 32, no. 3 (2003): 537–53.

Weiner, Dan, Sam Moyo, Barry Munslow, and Phil O'Keefe. "Land Use and Agricultural Productivity in Zimbabwe." *Journal of Modern African Studies* 23, no. 02 (1985): 251–85.

Wines, Michael. "Corruption and Despair Choke Zimbabwe." *New York Times*, October 19, 2003. http://www.nytimes.com/2003/10/19/world/corruption-and-despair-choke-zimbabwe.html?scp=11&sq=zimbabwe&st=nyt.

World Bank. "Agriculture for Development." In *World Development Report*. Washington DC: World Bank, 2007.

World Bank. "General Zimbabwe Data." http://data.worldbank.org/country/zimbabwe?display=graph.

World Bank. "Sub-Saharan Africa Country Statistics." http://databank.worldbank.org/data/views/reports/tableview.aspx?isshared=true.

World Bank. "Zimbabwe Crop Production Index." http://data.worldbank.org/indicator/AG.PRD.CROP.XD/countries/1W-ZW-ZA?display=graph.

World Bank. "Zimbabwe Statistics." http://data.worldbank.org/country/zimbabwe.

World Health Organization (WHO). "Healthy Life Expectancy (Hale) at Birth (Years)." http://www.who.int/whosis/indicators/2007HALE0/en/.

WHO. "World Health Statistics." 2010. http://www.who.int/gho/publications/world_health_statistics/EN_WHS10_Full.pdf.

WHO. "Zimbabwe Statistics." http://www.who.int/countries/zwe/en/.

Zamchiya, Phillan. "The Role of Politics and State Practices in Shaping Rural Differentiation: A Study of Resettled Small-Scale Farmers in South-Eastern Zimbabwe." *Journal of Southern African Studies* 39, no. 4 (2013): 937–53.

Zamchiya, Phillan. "A Synopsis of Land and Agrarian Change in Chipinge District, Zimbabwe." *Journal of Peasant Studies* 38, no. 5 (2011): 1093–122.

Zimbabwe Government. "Rural Land Occupiers (Protection from Eviction) Act." 2001.

Zimbabwe Human Rights NGO Forum. "Aftermath of a Disastrous Venture: A Follow-up Report on 'Operation Murambatsvina.'" Harare: Zimbabwe Human Rights NGO Forum, 2005.

Zimbabwe Human Rights NGO Forum. "Enforcing the Rule of Law in Zimbabwe." Harare: Zimbabwe Human Rights NGO Forum, 2001.

Zimbabwe Human Rights NGO Forum. "'How to Rig an Election': Evidence of a Systematic Campaign to Prevent a Free and Fair Poll." Harare: Zimbabwe Human Rights NGO Forum, 2001.

Zimbabwe Human Rights NGO Forum. "Monthly Violence Reports." In *Monthly Violence Reports*. Harare: Zimbabwe Human Rights NGO Forum, 2001–2008.

Zimbabwe Human Rights NGO Forum. "Of Stuffed Ballots and Empty Stomachs: Reviewing Zimbabwe's 2005 Parliamentary Election and Post-election Period." Harare: Zimbabwe Human Rights NGO Forum, 2005.

Zimbabwe Human Rights NGO Forum. "Only Bruises on the Soles of Their Feet! Torture and Falanga in Zimbabwe." Harare: Zimbabwe Human Rights NGO Forum, 2009.

Zimbabwe Human Rights NGO Forum. "Order out of Chaos, or Chaos out of Order? A Preliminary Report on Operation 'Murambatsvina.'" Harare: Zimbabwe Human Rights NGO Forum, 2005.

Zimbabwe Human Rights NGO Forum. "Organised Violence and Torture in Zimbabwe in 1999." Harare: Zimbabwe Human Rights NGO Forum, 1999.

Zimbabwe Human Rights NGO Forum. "Political Violence Report, May 2006." Harare: Zimbabwe Human Rights NGO Forum, 2006.

Zimbabwe Human Rights NGO Forum. "Political Violence Report: Consolidated Report for 1–15 March 2002." Harare: Zimbabwe Human Rights NGO Forum, 2002.

Zimbabwe Human Rights NGO Forum. "Politically Motivated Violence in Zimbabwe 2000–2001." Harare: Zimbabwe Human Rights NGO Forum, 2001.

Zimbabwe Human Rights NGO Forum. "Report on Political Violence in Bulawayo, Harare, Manicaland, Mashonaland West, Masvingo, Matabeleland North, Matabeleland South and Midlands." Harare: Zimbabwe Human Rights NGO Forum, 2000.

Zimbabwe Human Rights NGO Forum. "Torture by State Agents in Zimbabwe: January 2001 to August 2002." Harare: Zimbabwe Human Rights NGO Forum, 2003.

Zimbabwe Human Rights NGO Forum. "Who Is Responsible? A Preliminary Analysis of Pre-election Violence in Zimbabwe." Harare: Zimbabwe Human Rights NGO Forum, 2000.

Zimbabwe Human Rights NGO Forum. "Who Was Responsible? Alleged Perpetrators and Their Crimes during the 2000 Parliamentary Election Period." Harare: Zimbabwe Human Rights NGO Forum, 2001.

Zimbabwe Human Rights NGO Forum and Justice for Agriculture Trust in Zimbabwe. "Adding Insult to Injury." Harare: Zimbabwe Human Rights NGO Forum and the Justice for Agriculture Trust in Zimbabwe, 2007.

*Zimbabwe Situation.* "Zanu PF Chefs Risk Losing Land." June 20, 2014. http://www.zimbabwesituation.com/news/zimsit_g_zanu-pf-bigwigs-risk-losing-land-the-zimbabwe-independent/.

Zimeye. "Bloodbath in Shamva as Goche's Farm Faces Invasion." November 25, 2014. http://www.zimeye.com/breaking-news-bloodbath-in-shamva-as-goches-farm-faces-invasion/.

# Index

CPSIA information can be obtained
at www.ICGtesting.com
Printed in the USA
BVOW06s0842280118

506371BV00002B/7/P